Agile Software Architecture

Agile Software Architecture
Aligning Agile Processes and Software Architectures

Edited by

Muhammad Ali Babar

Alan W. Brown

Ivan Mistrik

AMSTERDAM • BOSTON • HEIDELBERG • LONDON
NEW YORK • OXFORD • PARIS • SAN DIEGO
SAN FRANCISCO • SINGAPORE • SYDNEY • TOKYO

Morgan Kaufmann is an imprint of Elsevier

Acquiring Editor: *Todd Green*
Editorial Project Manager: *Lindsay Lawrence*
Project Manager: *Punithavathy Govindaradjane*
Designer: *Maria Inês Cruz*

Morgan Kaufmann is an imprint of Elsevier
225 Wyman Street, Waltham, MA 02451, USA

Library of Congress Cataloging-in-Publication Data
Agile software architecture : aligning agile processes and software architectures / edited by Muhammad Ali Babar, Alan W. Brown, Ivan Mistrik.
     pages cm
  Includes bibliographical references and index.
  ISBN 978-0-12-407772-0 (pbk.)
1.   Agile software development. 2.   Software architecture. I.   Ali Babar, Muhammad. II.   Brown, Alan W., 1962- III.   Mistrik, Ivan.
  QA76.76.D47A3844 2013
  005.1'2–dc23
                                                                                                2013040761

British Library Cataloguing-in-Publication Data
A catalogue record for this book is available from the British Library

ISBN: 978-0-12-407772-0

This book has been manufactured using Print On Demand technology. Each copy is produced to order and is limited to black ink. The online version of this book will show color figures where appropriate.

For information on all MK publications visit our website at *www.mkp.com*

Contents

PART 2   MANAGING SOFTWARE ARCHITECTURE IN AGILE PROJECTS

CHAPTER 6   Supporting Variability Through Agility to Achieve Adaptable Architectures

PART 4   INDUSTRIAL VIEWPOINTS ON AGILE ARCHITECTING

Acknowledgments

The editors would like to acknowledge the significant effort Kai Koskimies made during different phases of this book's editing phases. Judith Stafford also helped in framing the initial proposal for this book. We also sincerely thank many authors who contributed their works to this book. The international team of anonymous reviewers gave detailed feedback on early versions of chapters and helped us to improve both the presentation and accessibility of the work. Ali Babar worked on this project while based at Lancaster University UK and IT University of Copenhagen, Denmark. Finally, we would like to thank the Elsevier management and editorial teams, in particular to Todd Green and Lindsay Lawrence, for the opportunity to produce this unique collection of articles covering the wide range of areas related to aligning agile processes and software architectures.

About the Editors

MUHAMMED ALI BABAR

Dr. M. Ali Babar is a Professor of Software Engineering (Chair) at the School of Computer Science, the University of Adelaide, Australia. He also holds an Associate Professorship at IT University of Copenhagen, Denmark. Prior to this, he was a Reader in Software Engineering at Lancaster University UK. Previously, he worked as a researcher and project leader in different research centers in Ireland and Australia. He has authored/co-authored more than 140 peer-reviewed research papers in journals, conferences, and workshops. He has co-edited a book, *Software Architecture Knowledge Management: Theory and Practice*. Prof. Ali Babar has been a guest editor of several special issues/sections of *IEEE Software, JSS, ESEJ, SoSyM, IST*, and *REJ*. Apart from being on the program committees of several international conferences such as WICSA/ECSA, ESEM, SPLC, ICGSE, and ICSSP for several years, Prof. Ali Babar was the founding general chair of the Nordic-Baltic Symposium on Cloud Computing and Internet Technologies (NordiCloud) 2012. He has also been co-(chair) of the program committees of several conferences such as NordiCloud 2013, WICSA/ECSA 2012, ECSA2010, PROFES2010, and ICGSE2011. He is a member of steering committees of WICSA, ECSA, NordiCloud and ICGSE. He has presented tutorials in the areas of cloud computing, software architecture and empirical approaches at various international conferences. Prior to joining R&D field, he worked as a software engineer and an IT consultant for several years in Australia. He obtained a PhD in computer science and engineering from University of New South Wales, Australia.

ALAN W. BROWN

Alan W. Brown is Professor of Entrepreneurship and Innovation in the Surrey Business School, University of Surrey, UK. where he leads activities in the area of corporate entrepreneurship and open innovation models. In addition to teaching activities, he focuses on innovation in a number of practical research areas with regard to global enterprise software delivery, agile software supply chains, and the investigation of "open commercial" software delivery models. He has formerly held a wide range of roles in industry, including Distinguished Engineer and CTO at IBM Rational, VP of Research at Sterling Software, Research Manager at Texas Instruments Software, and Head of Business Development in a Silicon Valley startup. In these roles Alan has worked with teams around the world on software engineering strategy, process improvement, and the transition to agile delivery approaches. He has published over 50 papers and written four books. He holds a Ph.D. in Computing Science from the University of Newcastle upon Tyne, UK.

IVAN MISTRIK

Ivan Mistrik is a computer scientist who is interested in system and software engineering (SE/SWE) and in system and software architecture (SA/SWA); in particular, he is interested in life cycle system/software engineering, requirements engineering, relating software requirements and architectures, knowledge management in software development, rationale-based software development, aligning enterprise/system/software architectures, and collaborative system/software engineering. He has more than forty years' experience in the field of computer systems engineering as an information systems developer, R&D leader, SE/SA research analyst, educator in computer sciences, and ICT management consultant. In the past 40 years, he has worked primarily at various R&D institutions and has consulted on a variety of large international projects sponsored by ESA, EU, NASA, NATO, and UN. He has also taught university-level computer sciences courses in software engineering, software architecture, distributed information systems, and human-computer interaction. He is the author or co-author of more than 80 articles and papers that have been published in international journals and books and presented at international conferences and workshops; most recently, he wrote the chapter "Capture of Software Requirements and Rationale through Collaborative Software Development" in the book *Requirements Engineering for Sociotechnical Systems*, the paper "Knowledge Management in the Global Software Engineering Environment," and the paper "Architectural Knowledge Management in Global Software Development." He has also written over 90 technical reports and presented over 70 scientific/technical talks. He has served on many program committees and panels of reputable international conferences and organized a number of scientific workshops, most recently two workshops on Knowledge Engineering in Global Software Development at the International Conference on Global Software Engineering 2009 and 2010. He has been a guest editor of *IEE Proceedings Software: A Special Issue on Relating Software Requirements and Architectures*, published by IEE in 2005. He has also been lead editor of the book *Rationale Management in Software Engineering*, published in 2006; the book *Collaborative Software Engineering*, published in 2010; and the book *Relating Software Requirements and Architectures*, published in 2011. He has also co-authored the book *Rationale-Based Software Engineering*, published in May 2008. He is a lead editor of the *Expert Systems Special Issue on Knowledge Engineering in Global Software Development* to be published in 2012, and he has organized the IEEE International Workshop on the Future of Software Engineering for/in the Cloud (FoSEC) that was held in conjunction with IEEE Cloud 2011. He was a guest editor of the *Journal of Systems and Software Special Issue on the Future of Software Engineering for/in the Cloud* in 2013 and a lead editor of the book on *Aligning Enterprise, System, and Software Architectures* to be published in 2012.

List of Contributors

Sarah Al-Azzani
University of Birmingham, Birmingham, UK

Ahmad Al-Natour
University of Birmingham, Birmingham, UK

Paris Avgeriou
University of Groningen, Groningen, The Netherlands

Muhammad Ali Babar
The University of Adelaide, Adelaide, SA, Australia

Rami Bahsoon
University of Birmingham, Birmingham, UK

Kawtar Benghazi
Universidad de Granada, Granada, Spain

Jan Bosch
Chalmers University of Technology, Gothenburg, Sweden

Georg Buchgeher
Software Competence Center Hagenberg (SCCH), Hagenberg, Austria

Lawrence Chung
University of Texas at Dallas, Richardson, TX, USA

James O. Coplien
Gertrud & Cope, Espergærde, Denmark

Jane Cleland-Huang
DePaul University, Chicago, IL, USA

Adam Czauderna
DePaul University, Chicago, IL, USA

Jessica Díaz
Universidad Politécnica de Madrid (Technical U. of Madrid), Madrid, Spain

Peter Eeles
IBM, London, UK

Veli-Pekka Eloranta
Tampere University of Technology, Tampere, Finland

Uwe Friedrichsen
Codecentric AG, Solingen, Germany

Matthias Galster
University of Canterbury, Christchurch, New Zealand

Juan Garbajosa
Universidad Politécnica de Madrid (Technical U. of Madrid), Madrid, Spain

Stephen Harcombe
Northwich, Cheshire, UK

Richard Hopkins
IBM, Cleveland, UK

Ben Isotta-Riches
Aviva, Norwich, UK

Kai Koskimies
Tampere University of Technology, Tampere, Finland

José Luis Garrido
Universidad de Granada, Granada, Spain

Mehdi Mirakhorli
DePaul University, Chicago, IL, USA

Manuel Noguera
Universidad de Granada, Granada, Spain

Jennifer Pérez
Universidad Politécnica de Madrid (Technical U. of Madrid), Madrid, Spain

Janet Randell
Aviva, Norwich, UK

Trygve Reenskaug
University of Oslo, Oslo, Norway

Antonio Rico
Universidad de Granada, Granada, Spain

Jan Salvador van der Ven
Factlink, Groningen, The Netherlands

Michael Stal
Siemens AG, Corporate Research & Technology, Munich, Germany

Rainer Weinreich
Johannes Kepler University Linz, Linz, Austria

Agustín Yagüe
Universidad Politécnica de Madrid (Technical U. of Madrid), Madrid, Spain

Foreword by John Grundy
Architecture vs Agile: competition or cooperation?

Until recently, conventional wisdom has held that software architecture design and agile development methods are somehow "incompatible," or at least they generally work at cross-purposes [1]. Software architecture design has usually been seen by many in the agile community as a prime example of the major agile anti-pattern of "big design up front." On the other hand, agile methods have been seen by many of those focusing on the discipline of software architecture as lacking sufficient fore-thought, rigor, and far too dependent on "emergent" architectures (a suitable one of which may never actually emerge). In my view, there is both a degree of truth and a substantial amount of falsehood in these somewhat extreme viewpoints. Hence, the time seems ripe for a book exploring leading research and practice in an emerging field of "agile software architecture," and charting a path for incorporating the best of both worlds in our engineering of complex software systems.

In this foreword, I briefly sketch the background of each approach and the anti-agile, anti-software architecture viewpoints of both camps, as they seem to have become known. I deliberately do this in a provocative and all-or-nothing way, mainly to set the scene for the variety of very sensible, balanced approaches contained in this book. I hope to seed in the reader's mind both the traditional motivation of each approach and how these viewpoints of two either-or, mutually exclusive approaches to complex software systems engineering came about. I do hope that it is apparent that I myself believe in the real benefits of both approaches and that they are certainly in no way incompatible; agile software architecting—or architecting for agile, if you prefer that viewpoint—is both a viable concept and arguably the way to approach the current practice of software engineering.

SOFTWARE ARCHITECTURE—THE "TRADITIONAL" VIEW

The concept of "software architecture"—both from a theoretical viewpoint as a means of capturing key software system structural characteristics [2] and practical techniques to develop and describe [3, 4]—emerged in the early to mid-1980s in response to the growing complexity and diversity of software systems. Practitioners and researchers knew implicitly that the concept of a "software architecture" existed in all but the most trivial systems. Software architecture incorporated elements including, but not limited to, human machine interfaces, databases, servers, networks, machines, a variety of element interconnections, many diverse element properties, and a variety of further structural and behavioral subdivisions (thread management, proxies, synchronization, concurrency, real-time support, replication, redundancy, security enforcement, etc.). Describing and reasoning about these elements of a system became increasingly important in order to engineer effective solutions, with special purpose "architecture description languages" and a wide variety of architecture modeling profiles for the Unified Modeling Language (UML). Software architecting includes defining an architecture from various perspectives and levels of abstraction, reasoning about the architecture's various properties, ensuring the architecture is realizable by a suitable implementation which will meet system requirements, and evolving and integrating complex architectures.

A number of reusable "architecture patterns" [3] have emerged, some addressing quite detailed concerns (e.g., concurrency management in complex systems), with others addressing much larger-scale organizational concerns (e.g., multitier architectures). This allowed a body of knowledge around software architecture to emerge, allowing practitioners to leverage best-practice solutions for common problems and researchers to study both the qualities of systems in use and to look for improvements in software architectures and architecture engineering processes.

The position of "software architecting" in the software development lifecycle was (and still is) somewhat more challenging to define. Architecture describes the solution space of a system and therefore traditionally is thought of as an early part of the design phase [3, 4]. Much work has gone into developing processes to support architecting complex systems, modeling architectures, and refining and linking architectural elements into detailed designs and implementations. Typically, one would identify and capture requirements, both functional and nonfunctional, and then attempt to define a software architecture that meets these requirements.

However, as all practitioners know, this is far easier said than done for many real-world systems. Different architectural solutions themselves come with many constraints—which requirements can be met and how they can be met, particularly nonfunctional requirements, are important questions. Over-constrained requirements may easily describe a system that has no suitable architectural realization. Many software applications are in fact "systems of systems" with substantive parts of the application already existent and incorporating complex, existent software architecture that must be incorporated. In addition, architectural decisions heavily influence requirements, and coevolution of requirements and architecture is becoming a common approach [5]. Hence, software architectural development as a top-down process is under considerable question.

AGILE METHODS—THE "TRADITIONAL" VIEW

The focus in the 1980s and 90s on extensive up-front design of complex systems, development of complex modeling tools and processes, and focus on large investment in architectural definition (among other software artifacts) were seen by many to have some severe disadvantages [6]. Some of the major ones identified included over-investment in design and wasted investment in over-engineering solutions, inability to incorporate poorly defined and/or rapidly changing requirements, inability to change architectures and implementations if they proved unsuitable, and lack of a human focus (both customer and practitioner) in development processes and methods. In response, a variety of "agile methods" were developed and became highly popular in the early to mid- 2000s. One of my favorites and one that I think exemplifies the type is Kent Beck's eXtreme Programming (XP) [7].

XP is one of many agile methods that attempt to address these problems all the way from underlying philosophy to pragmatic deployed techniques. Teams comprise both customers and software practitioners. Generalist roles are favored over specialization. Frequent iterations deliver usable software to customers, ensuring rapid feedback and continuous value delivery. Requirements are sourced from focused user stories, and a backlog and planning game prioritizes requirements, tolerating rapid evolution and maximizing value of development effort. Test-driven development ensures requirements are made tangible and precise via executable tests. In each iteration, enough work is done to pass these tests but no more, avoiding over-engineering. Supporting practices, including 40-hour weeks, pair programming, and customer-on-site avoid developer burnout, support risk mitigation and shared ownership, and facilitate human-centric knowledge transfer.

A number of agile approaches to the development of a "software architecture" exist, though most treat architecture as an "emergent" characteristic of systems. Rather than the harshly criticized "big design up front" architecting approaches of other methodologies, spikes and refactoring are used to test potential solutions and continuously refine architectural elements in a more bottom-up way. Architectural spikes in particular give a mechanism for identifying architectural deficiencies and experimenting with practical solutions. Refactoring, whether small-scale or larger-scale, is incorporated into iterations to counter "bad smells,"—which include architectural-related problems including performance, reliability, maintainability, portability, and understandability. These are almost always tackled on a need-to basis, rather than explicitly as an up-front, forward-looking investment (though they of course may bring such advantages).

SOFTWARE ARCHITECTURE—STRENGTHS AND WEAKNESSES WITH REGARD TO AGILITY

Up-front software architecting of complex systems has a number of key advantages [8]. Very complex systems typically have very complex architectures, many components of which may be "fixed" as they come from third party systems incorporated into the new whole. Understanding and validating a challenging set of requirements may necessitate modeling and reasoning with a variety of architectural solutions, many of which may be infeasible due to highly constrained requirements. Some requirements may need to be traded off against others to even make the overall system feasible. It has been found in many situations to be much better to do this in advance of a large code base and complex architectural solution to try and refactor [8]. It is much easier to scope resourcing and costing of systems when a software architecture that documents key components exists upfront. This includes costing nonsoftware components (networks, hardware), as well as necessary third party software licenses, configuration, and maintenance.

A major criticism of upfront architecting is the potential for over-engineering and thus over-investment in capacity that may never be used. In fact, a similar criticism could be leveled in that it all too often results in an under-scoped architecture and thus under-investing in required infrastructure, one of the major drivers in the move to elastic and pay-as-you-go cloud computing [9]. Another major criticism is the inability to adapt to potentially large requirements changes as customers reprioritize their requirements as they gain experience with parts of the delivered system [6]. Upfront design implies at least some broad requirements—functional and nonfunctional—that are consistent across the project lifespan. The relationship between requirements and software architecture has indeed become one of mutual influence and evolution [5].

AGILE—STRENGTHS AND WEAKNESSES WITH REGARD TO SOFTWARE ARCHITECTURE

A big plus of agile methods is their inherent tolerance—and, in fact, encouragement—of highly iterative, changeable requirements, focusing on delivering working, valuable software for customers. Almost all impediments to requirements change are removed; in fact, many agile project-planning methods explicitly encourage reconsideration of requirements and priorities at each iteration review—the mostly widely known and practiced being SCRUM [10]. Architectural characteristics of the system can be explored using spikes and parts found wanting refactored appropriately. Minimizing architectural changes by focusing on test-driven development—incorporating appropriate tests for performance, scaling, and reliability—goes a long way to avoiding redundant, poorly fitting, and costly over-engineered solutions.

While every system has a software architecture, whether designed-in or emergent, experience has shown that achieving a suitably complex software architecture for large-scale systems is challenging with agile methods. The divide-and-conquer approach used by most agile methods works reasonably well for small and some medium-sized systems with simple architectures. It is much more problematic for large-scale system architectures and for systems incorporating existent (and possibly evolving!) software architectures [8]. Test-driven development can be very challenging when software really needs to exist in order to be able to define and formulate appropriate tests for nonfunctional requirements. Spikes and refactoring support small-system agile architecting but struggle to scale to large-scale or even medium-scale architecture evolution. Some projects even find iteration sequences become one whole refactoring exercise after another, in order to try and massively reengineer a system whose emergent architecture has become untenable.

BRINGING THE TWO TOGETHER—AGILE ARCHITECTING OR ARCHITECTING FOR AGILE?

Is there a middle ground? Can agile techniques sensibly incorporate appropriate levels of software architecture exploration, definition, and reasoning, before extensive code bases using an inappropriate architecture are developed? Can software architecture definition become more "agile," deferring some or even most work until requirements are clarified as develop unfolds? Do some systems best benefit from some form of big design up front architecting but can then adopt more agile approaches using this architecture? On the face of it, some of these seem counter-intuitive and certainly go against the concepts of most agile methods and software architecture design methods.

However, I think there is much to be gained by leveraging strengths from each approach to mitigate the discovered weaknesses in the other. Incorporating software architecture modeling, analysis, and validation in "architectural spikes" does not seem at all unreasonable. This may include fleshing out user stories that help to surface a variety of nonfunctional requirements. It may include developing a variety of tests to validate that these requirements are met. If a system incorporates substantive existing system architecture, exploring interaction with interfaces and whether the composite system meets requirements by appropriate test-driven development seems like eminently sensible early-phase, high-priority work. Incorporating software architecture-related stories as priority measures in planning games and SCRUM-based project management also seems compatible with both underlying conceptual models and practical techniques. Emerging toolsets for architecture engineering, particularly focusing on analyzing nonfunctional properties, would seem to well support and fit agile practices.

Incorporating agile principles into software architecting processes and techniques also does not seem an impossible task, whether or not the rest of a project uses agile methods. Iterative refinement of an architecture—including some form of user stories surfacing architectural requirements, defining tests based on these requirements, rapid prototyping to exercise these tests, and pair-based architecture modeling and analysis—could all draw from the demonstrated advantages of agile approaches. A similar discussion emerges when trying to identify how to leverage design patterns and agile methods, user-centered design and agile methods, and model-driven engineering and agile methods [1, 11, 12]. In each area, a number of research and practice projects are exploring how the benefits of agile methods might be brought to these more "traditional" approaches to software engineering, and how agile approaches might incorporate well-known benefits of patterns, User Centered Design (UCD), and Model Driven Engineering (MDE).

LOOKING AHEAD

Incorporating at least some rigorous software architecting techniques and tools into agile approaches appears—to me, at least—to be necessary for successfully engineering many nontrivial systems. Systems made up of architectures from diverse solutions with very stringent requirements, particularly challenging, nonfunctional ones, really need careful look-before-you-leap solutions. This is particularly so when parts of the new system or components under development may adversely impact existing systems (e.g., introduce security holes, privacy breaches, or adversely impact performance, reliability, or robustness). Applying a variety of agile techniques—and the philosophy of agile—to software architecting also seems highly worthwhile. Ultimately, the purpose of software development is to deliver high-quality, on-time, and on-budget software to customers, allowing for some sensible future enhancements. A blend of agile focus on delivery, human-centric support for customers and developers, incorporating dynamic requirements, and—where possible—avoiding over-documenting and over-engineering exercises, all seem to be of benefit to software architecture practice.

This book goes a long way toward realizing these trends of agile architecting and architecting for agile. Chapters include a focus on refactoring architectures, tailoring SCRUM to support more agile architecture practices, supporting an approach of continuous architecture analysis, and conducting architecture design within an agile process. Complementary chapters include analysis of the emergent architecture concept, driving agile practices by using architecture requirements and practices, and mitigating architecture problems found in many conventional agile practices.

Three interesting works address other topical areas of software engineering: engineering highly adaptive systems, cloud applications, and security engineering. Each of these areas has received increasing attention from the research and practice communities. In my view, all could benefit from the balanced application of software architecture engineering and agile practices described in these chapters.

I do hope that you enjoy this book as much as I enjoyed reading over the contributions. Happy agile software architecting!

John Grundy
Swinburne University of Technology,
Hawthorn, Victoria, Australia

References

[1] Nord RL, Tomayko JE. Software architecture-centric methods and agile development. IEEE Software 2006;23(2):47–53.
[2] Garlan D, Shaw M. Software architecture: perspectives on an emerging discipline. Angus & Robertson; 1996.
[3] Bass L, Clements P, Kazman R. Software architecture in practice. Angus & Robertson; 2003.

[4] Kruchten P. The 4 + 1 view model of architecture. IEEE Software 1995;12(6):42–50.

[5] Avgeriou P, Grundy J, Hall JG, Lago P, Mistrík I. Relating software requirements and architectures. Springer; 2011.

[6] Beck K, Beedle M, Bennekum van A, Cockburn A, Cunningham W, Fowler M, et al. Manifesto for agile software development, http://agilemanifesto.org/; 2001.

[7] Beck K. Embracing change with extreme programming. Computer 1999;32(10):70–7.

[8] Abrahamsson P, Babar MA, Kruchten P. Agility and architecture – can they co-exist? IEEE Software 2010;27(2):16–22.

[9] Grundy J, Kaefer G, Keong J, Liu A. Software engineering for the cloud. IEEE Software 2012;29(2):26–9.

[10] Schwaber K. Agile project management with SCRUM. O'Reily; 2009.

[11] Dybå T, Dingsøyr T. Empirical studies of agile software development: A systematic review. Inform Software Tech 2008;50(9–10):833–59.

[12] McInerney P, Maurer F. UCD in agile projects: dream team or odd couple? Interactions 2005;12(6):19–23.

Foreword by Rick Kazman

Since their first appearance over a decade ago, the various flavors of agile methods and processes have received increasing attention and adoption by the worldwide software community. So it is natural that, with this increased attention, software engineers are concerned about how agile methods fit with other engineering practices.

New software processes do not just emerge out of thin air; they evolve in response to a palpable need. In this case, the software development world was responding to a need for projects to be more responsive to their stakeholders, to be quicker to develop functionality that users care about, to show more and earlier progress in a project's lifecycle, and to be less burdened by documenting aspects of a project that would inevitably change.

Is any of this inimical to the use of architecture? I believe that the answer to this question is a clear "no." In fact, the question for a software project is not "should I do agile or architecture?" but rather questions such as "How much architecture should I do up front versus how much should I defer until the project's requirements have solidified somewhat?", "When and how should I refactor?", "How much of the architecture should I formally document, and when?", and "Should I review my architecture—and, if so, when?". I believe that there are good answers to all of these questions, and that agile methods and architecture are not just well-suited to live together but in fact critical companions for many software projects.

We often think of the early software development methods that emerged in the 1970s—such as the waterfall method—as being plan-driven and inflexible. But this inflexibility is not for nothing. Having a strong up-front plan provides for considerable predictability (as long as the requirements don't change too much) and makes it easier to coordinate large numbers of teams. Can you imagine a large construction or aerospace project without heavy up-front planning?

Agile methods and practitioners, on the other hand, often scorn planning, instead preferring teamwork, frequent face-to-face communication, flexibility, and adaptation. This enhances invention and creativity. The next Pixar hit movie will not be created by an up-front planning process—it is the result of a seemingly infinite number of tweaks and redos.

Agile processes were initially employed on small- to medium-sized projects with short time frames and enjoyed considerable early success. In the early years, agile processes were not often used for larger projects, particularly those employing distributed development. But these applications of agile methodologies are becoming increasingly common. What are we to make of this evolution? Or, to put it another way, is the agile mindset right for every project?

In my opinion, successful projects clearly need a successful blend of the two approaches. For the vast majority of nontrivial projects this is not and never should be an either/or choice. Too much up-front planning and commitment can stifle creativity and the ability to adapt to changing requirements. Too much agility can be chaos. No one would want to fly in an aircraft with flight control software that had *not* been rigorously planned and thoroughly analyzed. Similarly, no one would want to spend 18 months planning an e-commerce web site for their latest cell phone model, or video game, or women's shoe style (all of which are guaranteed to be badly out of fashion in 18 months).

There are two activities that can add time to the project schedule: (1) Up-front design work on the architecture and up-front risk identification, planning, and resolution work, and (2) Rework due to fixing defects and addressing modification requests. Intuitively, these two activities trade off against each other.

What we all want is the sweet spot—what George Fairbanks calls "just enough architecture." This is not just a matter of doing the right amount of architecture work, but also doing it at the right time. Agile projects tend to want to evolve the architecture, as needed, in real time, whereas large software projects have traditionally favored considerable up-front analysis and planning.

And it doesn't stop at the architecture. Surely we also want "just enough" architecture documentation. So, when creating documentation, we must not simply document for the purpose of documentation. We must write with the reader in mind: If the reader doesn't need it, don't write it. But always remember that the reader may be a maintainer or other newcomer not yet on the project!

What about architecture evaluation? Does this belong in an agile project? I think so. Meeting stakeholders' important concerns is a cornerstone of agile philosophies. An architecture evaluation is a way of increasing the probability that this will actually occur. And an architecture evaluation need not be "heavyweight." These can be easily scaled down and made an organic part of development—no different than testing or code walkthroughs—that support the goals of an agile project.

So what should an architect do when creating the architecture for a large-scale agile project? Here are my thoughts:

- If you are building a large, complex system with relatively stable and well-understood requirements and/or distributed development, doing a large amount of architecture work up-front will likely pay off. On larger projects with unstable requirements, start by quickly designing a candidate architecture even if it leaves out many details.
- Be prepared to change and elaborate this architecture as circumstances dictate, as you perform your spikes and experiments, and as functional and quality attribute requirements emerge and solidify.
- On smaller projects with uncertain requirements, at least try to get agreement on the major patterns to be employed. Don't spend too much time on architecture design, documentation, or analysis up front.

Rick Kazman
University of Hawaii and SEI/CMU,
Honolulu, Hawaii, USA

Preface

Today's software-driven businesses feel increasing pressure to respond ever more quickly to their customer and broader stakeholder needs. Not only is the drive for increased business flexibility resulting in new kinds of products being brought to market, it's also accelerating evolution of existing solutions and services. Handling such rapid-paced change is a critical factor in enterprise software delivery, driven by market fluctuations, new technologies, announcements of competitive offerings, enactment of new laws, and more. But change cannot mean chaos. In software-driven businesses, all activities—and change activities in particular—must be governed by a plethora of formal and informal procedures, practices, processes, and regulations. These governance mechanisms provide an essential function in managing and controlling how software is delivered into production.

Traditionally, the pressure on enterprise software delivery organizations has been to balance their delivery capabilities across four key dimensions:

- *Productivity* of individuals and teams, typically measured in terms of lines of code or function points delivered over unit time.
- *Time-to-market* for projects to complete and deliver a meaningful result to the business. This can be measured in average time for project completion, project over-runs, or turnaround time from request for a new capability to its delivery in a product.
- *Process maturity* in the consistency, uniformity and standardization of practices. Measurements can be based on adherence to common process norms or on maturity approaches, such as capability maturity model levels.
- *Quality* in shipped code, errors handled, and turnaround of requests. Measures are typically combinations of defect density rates and errors fixed per unit time.

However, with the increasing pressure to respond more quickly, finding an appropriate balance across these enterprise software delivery success factors is increasingly difficult. For example, efforts to enhance productivity by introducing large off-shore teams have frequently resulted in a negative impact on the quality of delivered solutions. Likewise, increasing process maturity by introducing common process governance practices has typically extended time-to-market and reduced flexibility.

These challenges are moving organizations toward rapidly embracing agile software delivery techniques. Since the publication of the *Manifesto for Agile Software Development* over a decade ago, there has been widespread adoption of techniques that embody the key tenets of the "agile manifesto" to the point that a number of surveys offer evidence that agile practices are the dominant approaches in many of today's software delivery organizations. However, these approaches are not without their critics. Notably, agile delivery of software faces increasing pressure as the context for software delivery moves from smaller colocated teams toward larger team structures involving a complex software supply chain of organizations in multiple locations. In these situations, the lighter-weight practices encouraged by agile software delivery approaches come face-to-face with the more extensive control structures inherent in any large-scale software delivery effort. How can flexibility and speed of delivery be maintained when organizational inertia and complex team dynamics threaten to overwhelm the essential nature of an agile approach?

For many people, the focus of this question revolves around the central theme of software and systems architecture. It is this architectural aspect that provides coherence to the delivered system. An architectural style guides the system's organization, the selection of key elements and their interfaces, and the system's behavior through collaboration among those elements. A software architecture encompasses the significant decisions about the organization of the software system, the selection of structural elements and interfaces by which the system is composed, and determines their behavior through collaboration among these elements and their composition into progressively larger subsystems. Hence, the software architecture provides the skeleton of a system around which all other aspects of a system revolve. Consequently, decisions concerning a system's software architecture play a critical role in enhancing or inhibiting its overall flexibility, determine the ease by which certain changes to the system can be made, and guide many organizational aspects of how a system is developed and delivered.

Over the past decade, many different opinions and viewpoints have been expressed on the term "agile software architecture." However, no clear consensus has yet emerged. Fundamental questions remain open to debate: how much effort is devoted to architecture-specific tasks in an agile project, is the architecture of an agile software system designed up front or does it emerge as a consequence of ongoing development activities, who participates in architectural design activities, are specific architectural styles more appropriate to agile software delivery methods, how are architecturally-significant changes to a system handled appropriately in agile software delivery methods, and so on.

This book provides a collection of perspectives that represent one of the first detailed discussions on the theme of agile software architecture. Through these viewpoints, we gain significant insight into the challenges of agile software architecture from experienced software architects, distinguished academics, and leading industry commentators.

The book is organized into four major sections.

- Part I: *Fundamentals of Agile Architecting* explores several of the most basic issues surrounding the task of agile software delivery and the role of architectural design and decision-making.
- Part II: *Managing Software Architecture in Agile Projects* considers how core architectural ideas impact other areas of software delivery, such as knowledge management and continuous system delivery.
- Part III: *Agile Architecting in Specific Domains* offers deeper insight into how agile software architecture issues affect specific solution domains.

- Part IV: *Industrial Viewpoints on Agile Architecting* takes a practical delivery perspective on agile software delivery to provide insights from software engineers and the lessons learned from the systems they have been responsible for delivering.

As we summarize below, each of the chapters of this book provides you with interesting and important insights into a key aspect of agile software architecture. However, more importantly, the comprehensive nature of this book provides us with the opportunity to take stock of how the emergence of agile software delivery practices change our understanding of the critical task of architecting enterprise-scale software systems.

PART I: FUNDAMENTALS OF AGILE ARCHITECTING

Over the past few years, an increasingly large number of researchers and practitioners have been emphasizing the need to integrate agile and software architecture-centric approaches to enable software development professionals to benefit from the potential advantages of using agile approaches without ignoring the important role of architecture-related issues in software development projects—a trend that can be called "*agile* architecting." This section includes four chapters that are aimed at emphasizing the importance of integrating agile and architectural approaches, as well as providing a set of practices and principles that can be leveraged to support agile architecting. As such, the key objectives of the chapters included in this section are the following:

- To provide a good understanding of the role and importance of software architecture within software development teams using agile approaches, and
- To describe and illustrate a few practices for supporting agile architecting in large-scale industrial software development.

In Chapter 2, Coplien and Reenskaug provide a detailed comparison of the evolution of thinking about architecture in the building construction and the software worlds. Such comparison is important and relevant for gaining an understanding of the importance and role of integrating architecture-focused and agile approaches due to similarities in constructing buildings and software in areas such as design patterns. The authors argue that most of the progress in architectural thinking in both fields is the result of learning in the field of design and in collective human endeavor. They present and discuss a paradigm called DCI (data, context, and interaction) that places the human experiences of design and use of programs equally at center stage. According to the authors, DCI follows a vision of having computers and people mutually supportive in Christopher Alexander's sense of great design. They explain different aspects of the DCI, its philosophical basis, and practical relevance to software and systems delivery.

In Chapter 3, Stal emphasizes the importance of systematic refactoring of software architecture to prevent architectural erosion. The author argues that like any other changes in a software intensive system, architectural modifications are also quite common. According to the author, a systematic architectural refactoring enables a software architect to prevent architectural erosion by evaluating the existing software design before adding new artifacts or changing existing ones. That means software architects proactively identify architectural problems and immediately resolve them to ensure architectural sustainability. The author has presented an agile architectural refactoring approach that consists of problem identification, application of appropriate refactoring techniques, and testing of the resulting architecture. According to the author, the architecture refactoring is often combined with code refactoring activities for the best value-add. Additionally, the refactoring patterns can offer a toolset to software engineers.

In Chapter 4, Cleland-Huang, Czauderna, and Mirakhorli present an approach aimed at addressing the challenges associated with eliciting and analyzing Architecturally Significant Requirements (ASRs) during the early phases of a project. Compared with existing heavy-weight approaches (e.g., win-win and i*) to elicit and analyze ASRs, they present a lightweight approach based on the use of personas of different stakeholders of a system. They introduce the notion of architecturally-savvy persona (ASP) for eliciting and analysing stakeholders' quality concerns and to drive and validate the architectural design. The authors present several personas from different domains and explain how personas can be used for discovering, analyzing, and managing architecturally significant requirements, and designing and evaluating architectural solutions. Through illustrated examples, the authors also show how ASPs can be used to discover quality attributes, steer architectural design, and support traceability.

In Chapter 5, van der Ven and Bosch address the important topic of improving the architecture design decisions-making process when using agile development methods. The authors present a framework of three axes that can be used to project the architectural decision process, which they evaluate in five industrial case studies. The findings from the case studies provide evidence to support the utility and usefulness of the presented Triple-A Framework for helping locate the places where the architecture process can be improved as the agility of a project changes.

PART II: MANAGING SOFTWARE ARCHITECTURE IN AGILE PROJECTS

Traditionally, various kinds of activities have been associated with the software development process and seen as important areas of software engineering. These activities include the main phases of a waterfall process, such as requirements analysis, design, coding, testing, integration, deployment, and maintenance. In addition, there are more focused subactivities that either crosscut these main phases or are part of them. An example of the former is variability handling; an example of the latter is software architecture analysis.

The need for all these activities has been recognized during several decades of industrial software development, and there is no reason to doubt their rationale. Whatever the process model is, the concerns that are behind these activities must somehow be taken care of. The agile movement does not say that these concerns are groundless, but rather that the activities are not sequential in nature, and that for the most part these concerns can be satisfied without heavy management, relying more on the capabilities of teams and individuals. In particular, we believe that the agile movement is now mature enough to more explicitly consider how various kinds of focused subactivities can be manifested in an agile setting, without deviating from the agile path. The chapters in this part argue that by doing this, it is possible to strengthen agile projects from the viewpoint of a particular concern that can otherwise be easily overlooked.

A particularly interesting crosscutting concern is variability—that is, the ability of a software system to be adapted for a specific context. This is a central quality property of almost any software system, essential not only for maintenance and reuse but also for development time flexibility. The most systematic approaches for handling variability have been developed in the context of product lines. On the other hand, the core of agility is to embrace change. In a way, both product lines and agile methods strive for malleable software: the former tries to plan and specify the required variability beforehand and build variation points to support it, while the latter emphasizes practices that allow responding to changing requirements during development. Obviously, agile methods benefit from software solutions that support flexible changes in the system, and on the other hand the heavy-weightiness of traditional product-line engineering could be relieved by agile approaches.

In Chapter 6, Galster and Avgeriou discuss the challenges and benefits of combining variability handling and agility, and propose an approach for agile-inspired variability handling. In contrast to pure agile, their approach involves certain upfront planning, namely the identification and expression of the desired variability—the so-called variability profile—and an initial sketch of the software architecture with variation points. Initial variability profiles and architectural sketches with variation points can be regarded as the minimal amount of planning required for lightweight variability handling during the development process. These artifacts are revised iteratively in the process when new variability requirements emerge. The approach is demonstrated using a realistic running example.

Another concern which is generally overlooked in agile contexts is ensuring the quality of software architecture. Software architecture is typically not identified as a first-class artifact with explicit presentation in agile approaches. Accordingly, a central concern in agile is not the quality of software architecture, but rather the overall quality of the produced system as experienced by the customer. Still, architectural analysis offers obvious benefits independently of the process paradigm. Software architecture is a first expression of the system to be produced, and in principle it allows the identification of problems and risks before spending resources to implement something that is not admissible. Unfortunately, most of the architectural analysis techniques have been developed with a traditional waterfall mindset, assuming comprehensive architectural descriptions and the availability of considerable time and resources. Furthermore, architectural analysis has been traditionally regarded as a one-shot activity, carried out when the architecture has been designed. This has made it hard to integrate architectural analysis as a part of agile development.

In Chapter 7, Buchgeher and Weinreich point out that in agile approaches, software architecture is incomplete and continuously evolving. Thus, any architecture analysis method applied in the agile context should be incremental, allowing continuous analysis activity that can be carried out with reasonable resources and time. An obvious approach for less resource-demanding architecture analysis is automation: if a substantial part of the work can be automated with a simple tool, the analysis can be performed in agile development without unreasonable deviation from the agile principles. This could be compared to tool-assisted testing of the implementation. On the other hand, the scope of automated architecture analysis is necessarily limited: this is a tradeoff between coverage and efficiency.

Buchgeher and Weinreich discuss the benefits and problems of different architecture analysis approaches in agile software development, and conclude that a potential technique in this context would be so-called dependency analysis. This is an analysis technique which aims to extract static dependencies from the source code and compare the actually implemented architecture with the intended one, using the dependencies as an indication of architecture-level relationships. They further present a tool-assisted approach, LISA (Language for Integrated Software Architecture), to support this kind of continuous architecture analysis in an agile project context. This approach has been studied in several projects, including a sizable industrial one.

Another general crosscutting concern of software development is the management of various kinds of knowledge produced and consumed during the development process. Regarding software architecture, the term architecture knowledge management (AKM) has been coined to refer to all the activities related to the creation, managing, and using representations of software architecture and its rationale. Traditionally, these kinds of activities are downplayed in agile development in favor of face-to-face communication. However, there can be many reasons that make more systematic approaches to AKM necessary in real life, regardless of the process paradigm. For example, in large multisite projects architectural knowledge needs to be transferred between hundreds of stakeholders and globally distributed sites, and for systems with a lifespan of decades, the architectural knowledge has to be transferred over many generations of architects.

In Chapter 8, Eloranta and Koskimies suggest that it would be possible to achieve a lightweight approach to AKM suitable for agile development by combining the use of an architectural knowledge repository with a decision-based architecture evaluation technique. This kind of evaluation technique analyzes the architecture decision by decision, in a bottom-up manner, rather than taking a top-down, holistic view of the architecture. Thus, decisions can be analyzed as soon as they are made in agile development, without a need for an offline, heavyweight architectural evaluation. Since a decision-based analysis makes the architectural decisions and their rationale explicit, a significant portion of architectural knowledge emerges and can be recorded in a repository as a side effect of the analysis. Using existing techniques for generating specialized documents from the repository, an agile project can be augmented with virtually effortless architectural documentation services. The authors further study in detail how the proposed approach could be applied in the context of the observed architectural practices in industry.

The core activity related to software architecture is of course the actual design of the architecture. Many agile approaches are deliberately vague about this activity. Early agilists even argued that architecture need not be explicitly designed, but just emerges during the development. While this might be true in some cases, today it is generally understood that software architecture and its design play a significant role in agile development—especially in large-scale projects. However, the incremental and iterative nature of agile development poses a major challenge for software architecture design: how to build software architecture in a systematic manner piecewise, in parallel with the implementation.

In Chapter 9, Pérez, Diaz, Garbajosa, and Yagüe address this question by introducing the concept of a working architecture. This is an architecture that evolves together with the implemented product. A central element of a working architecture is a malleable, incomplete, so-called plastic partial component. A new working architecture can be expressed in each agile iteration cycle using such components. Eventually, the components become complete, constituting the final architecture associated with the delivered product. The approach supports changes in the requirements by maintaining traceability links between features and their realization in the working architecture. Given a change in the features, the involved parts of the working architecture can be automatically detected using such links. The proposed techniques are integrated with Scrum, and tried out in a large case study project.

PART III: AGILE ARCHITECTING IN SPECIFIC DOMAINS

Agile architecting in specific domains share many commonalities and many of their concerns overlap, but they also have marked differences in focus and approach. Each solves problems for different stakeholders, uses different technologies, and employs different practices. The specialization on their respective solutions has made it difficult to transfer methods and knowledge across a broad range of topics. One way to align these topics is to shift the focus from solution to problem domains. As the system evolves, verifying its security posture is indispensable for building deployable software systems. Traditional security testing lacks flexibility in (1) providing early feedback to the architect on the resilience of the software to predict security threats so that changes are made before the system is built, (2) responding to changes in user and behavior requirements that could impact the security of software, and (3) offering real design fixes that do not merely hide the symptoms of the problem (e.g., patching). There is a need for an architecture-level test for security grounded on incremental and continuous refinements to support agile principles.

Part III contains two chapters looking at agile architecting in specific domains. The chapters in this section present practical approaches and cases. Chapter 10 focuses on architecture-centric testing for security from an agile perspective and Chapter 11 describes supporting agile software development and deployment in the cloud using a multitenancy multitarget architecture (MT^2A).

In Chapter 10, Al-Azzani, Bahsoon, and Natour suggest using architecture as an artifact for initiating the testing process for security, through subsequent and iterative refinements. They extend the use of implied scenario detection technique to reveal undesirable behavior caused by ambiguities in users' requirements and to analyze its security implications. The approach demonstrates how architecture-centric evaluation and analysis can assist in developing secure agile systems. They apply the approach to a case study to evaluate the security of identity management architectures. They reflect on the effectiveness of the approach in detecting vulnerable behaviors, and the cost-effectiveness in refining the architecture before vulnerabilities are built into the system.

Chapter 11 emphasizes the need for a systematic approach for supporting agile software development and deployment in the cloud. Rico, Noguera, Garrido, Benghazi, and Chung propose a MT^2A for managing the cloud adoption process. Multitenancy (MT) architectures (MTAs) allow for multiple customers (i.e., tenants) to be consolidated into the same operational system, reducing the overhead via amortization over multiple customers. Lately, MTAs are drawing increasing attention, since MT is regarded as an essential attribute of cloud computing. For MTAs to be adopted in practice, however, agility becomes critical; there should be a fast change to the system so as to accommodate potential tenants in as short a period of time as possible. In this chapter, they introduce a MT^2A. MT^2As are an evolution to traditional MTAs that reduce the various overhead by providing multiple services instead of a single service. In MT^2As, there are new components added to its corresponding MTAs for managing the (now possibly) multiservice. MT^2As enhance the agility of MTAs, not only in deployment but also in development, by enabling the reuse of common components of the architecture. In this chapter, they also present an implementation of the architecture through an MT2 system called Globalgest.

PART IV: INDUSTRIAL VIEWPOINTS ON AGILE ARCHITECTING

For many people involved in creating, maintaining, or evolving software-intensive systems, the reality of any approach is the extent to which it helps with the day-to-day challenges of building complex software efficiently to support the business's needs. Hence, any discussion on agile software architecture would be incomplete without considering the practical realities that face software engineers when they deliver new capabilities into production. Here, the drive for speed and adaptability offered by an agile approach must be aligned with the broader project delivery needs to supply the capabilities required by the stakeholders to a deadline and at a cost that makes business sense to the managing organizations. This equation is yet more difficult to resolve where such projects are large in scale, take place over many months or years, and involve hundreds of people from perhaps dozens of different organizations.

Part IV contains four chapters that explore some of the practical considerations in agile software architecture from the viewpoint of practicing software architects.

Chapter 12 considers the challenges facing agile software development practices in the context of large-scale complex systems delivery situations. Hopkins and Harcombe explore what happens when rapid delivery cycles and flexible decision-making come up against large-scale systems engineering concerns typical of enterprise solutions—hundreds of people, long project lifetimes, extensive requirements planning, and a constant ebb and flow of changing priorities. A particular interest of this chapter is efficiency in large-scale software delivery, and the need to manage distributed teams in the most effective manner possible. Through a series of examples, Hopkins and Harcombe discuss critical success factors for agile software delivery, and the critical role that architectural planning and design can play in ensuring that as the project scale increases, the value of an agile approach is amplified rather than being overwhelmed.

In Chapter 13, Eeles considers the importance of supporting evolution and change to a software-intensive system, and the practical implications of creating a "change-ready" system. From his perspective, a focus on how a system changes throughout its lifetime shapes the critical choices an architect makes during design and construction of that system. Important elements of this viewpoint are highlighted by tracing the history of software development practices from waterfall phases through iterative design to agile techniques. A particular focus of the chapter is the innovation that is essential in both the delivered system, and in the environment of tools and practices that produces that system. Based on his work on several industrial projects, Eeles makes a series of important observations to guide architects in delivering solutions that are more adaptable to changing needs.

In Chapter 14, Friedrichsen addresses a question central to many discussions surrounding agile approaches to architecting software: In agile projects, is the architecture of the system designed up-front, or does it emerge over time as the result of the agile software development process? For Friedrichsen, the idea of emergent architecture is the result of constant refactoring of a system based on a well-defined set of architectural principles. The chapter considers the importance of such an emergent style of architecture, its key properties, and the kinds of situations in which this emergent approach has particular value. One of the main conclusions is that, in practice, a hybrid form combining both explicit and emergent architectural techniques is feasible and useful.

Finally, Chapter 15 describes the journey toward more agile software development practices that took place in one IT team as it took on the task of evolving a complex software platform at a large insurance company in the United Kingdom. Isotta-Riches and Randell discuss their motivations for adopting a more agile software development approach, and the challenges they faced making the changes they needed to their practices, processes, and skills. The importance of focusing on new architectural thinking in the teams was soon considered to be central to this journey, and the chapter highlights how this need surfaced, what they did to explore its implications, and how they dealt with the challenges raised. As often occurs in practice, the result was a compromise between the purity of an agile approach as found in textbooks, and the need to address the practical business reality driving the project's timeframe, capabilities, and costs. The chapter offers sobering lessons for all those involved with creating not only elegant solutions to problems, but also systems that pay their way.

Muhammad Ali Babar
Alan W. Brown
Ivan Mistrik

Making Software Architecture and Agile Approaches Work Together: Foundations and Approaches

1

Muhammad Ali Babar

The University of Adelaide, Adelaide, SA, Australia

CHAPTER CONTENTS

1.1 INTRODUCTION

The Agile software development (ASD) paradigm has been widely adopted by hundreds of large and small companies in an effort to reduce costs and increase their ability to handle changes in dynamic market conditions. Based on the principles of the Agile Manifesto,[a] Agile practitioners have proposed several methods and approaches, such as Scrum [1], feature-driven development [2], extreme programming [3], and test-driven development. We refer to all of them as ASD methods in this chapter. While there is no doubt that there has been manifold increase in the adoption of ASD methods by all sorts of companies, there has always been a growing skepticism about the reliability, effectiveness, and efficiency of those ASD methods that do not pay sufficient attention to the important roles of SA-related principles, practices, and artifacts [4–6]. It has been widely recognized that SA can be an effective tool to cut development and evolution cost and time and to increase the conceptual integrity and quality of a system [7]. However, the followers of ASD methods view architecture-centric approaches as part of the plan-driven development paradigm [4]. According to them, upfront design and evaluation of SA as high ceremony activities are likely to consume a lot of time and effort without providing a system's customers with valuable deliverables (i.e., code for features). The proponents of SA believe that sound architectural practices cannot be followed using agile approaches.

It can be asserted that this situation has arisen from two extreme views of ASD methods and SA-centric methods. The supporters of architecture-centric approaches appear to be less convinced that any software-intensive system of a significant size can be successfully built and evolved without paying sufficient attention to architectural issues, especially in domains such as automotive, telecommunication, finance, and medical devices. The advocates of ASD methods appear to apply *You aren't gonna need it* thinking to architecture-centric activities (e.g., design, evaluation, documentation). According to them, refactoring can help fix most of a software-intensive system's structural problems. It has been claimed that refactoring is worthwhile as long as the high-level design is good enough to limit the need for large-scale refactoring [6,8,9]. And many experiences show that large-scale refactoring often results in significant defects, which are very costly to address later in the development lifecycle.

Most of the descriptions of ASD methods pay very little attention to common architectural design activities [10], such as architectural analysis, architectural synthesis, architectural evaluation, and the artifact types [10] associated with these activities. Most of the ASD methods tend to assume that architectural design is high-level design without explicit structuring forces, such as quality attributes. Thapparambil [11] asserts that *Refactoring is the primary method to develop architecture in the Agile world*. The primary incremental design practice of the second edition of the XP book [3] claims that architecture can emerge in daily design. The emergent design means that architecture relies on looking for potentially poor architectural solutions in the implemented code and making a better architecture when needed through refactory. According to this approach, architecture emerges from code rather than some upfront structure.

It is beginning to be recognized that both disciplines (i.e., ASD methods and architecture-centric approaches) have important and complementary roles in

---

[a]http://agilemanifesto.org/

software development and evolutionary activities. While ASD methods promise to enable companies to achieve efficiency, quality, and flexibility for accommodating changes, it is critically important to follow solid architectural practices for large-scale software development projects. There is also a growing recognition of the importance of paying more attention to architectural aspects in agile approaches [4–6,12].

This situation has stimulated several efforts aimed at identifying the mechanics and prerequisites of integrating appropriate architecture-centric principles and practices in ASD methods [4,8]. One of the main objectives of these efforts is to help practitioners to understand the contextual factors and reasons for paying attention—or not—to the role and importance of a system's SA when implementing ASD methods [8,13]. Researchers and practitioners have also identified the technical and organizational challenges involved in integrating Agile approaches in traditional software development methods [14,15]. However, while anecdotal evidence reveals that there are large organizations in the midst of agile transformation, and that the architectural issues are being addressed, there has been no significant effort to synthesize and present a reliable body of knowledge about the architecture-centric challenges faced by ASD projects and potential solutions to those challenges.

This book provides a unique and comprehensive body of knowledge about the challenges and opportunities for making agile and architectural approaches coexist when developing safety, business, security, or mission-critical, software-intensive systems and services. The body of knowledge presented in this book is expected to help companies and practitioners build their architectural capabilities in the context of ASD methods or enable architectural-centric companies to make their approaches and practices agile and lean. That means companies will be able to adopt ASD methods without compromising on the architectural aspects of their software-intensive systems. The theories and practical examples in this book will enable companies of all sizes and contexts to gain the expertise, knowledge, and technological know-how to combine the strengths and benefits of architectural and ASD methods to achieve their goals. Quality, productivity, and profitability can be increased by improving the efficiency and effectiveness of companies' software development processes.

In the following sections and subsections, we briefly describe some of the well-known architecture-centric concepts and approaches and their origins and applicability contexts. It can be asserted that the SA-related concepts and principles described in this chapter can be tailored and integrated into ASD methods. Then we provide a brief description of two of the most popular ASD methods. And eventually, we discuss a few ways to integrate architecture-centric approaches in ASD methods.

1.2 SOFTWARE ARCHITECTURE

Software architecture is an important sub-discipline of software engineering. While SA's important role in achieving the quality goals of a software-intensive system gained popularity during the 1990s, the idea of ensuring software quality through high-level design decisions emerged in the 1970s. Parnas showed how modularization and information hiding could be used as a means of improving a system's flexibility and comprehensibility [16]. Soon after, Stevens et al. presented the idea of module coupling and cohesion as a characteristic of quality software design [17]. However, software engineers did not realize the importance of the relationship between non-functional requirements (NFRs) and SA design until the early 1990s. The practice of using design patterns and architectural styles for producing quality designs in short periods of time provided impetus for new interest in addressing quality issues at the architecture level [18–20].

Software architecture may mean different things for different people. It is difficult to claim that there is a widely accepted definition of SA in the software industry [21]. One of the first definitions of SA was provided by Perry and Wolf in their widely cited paper [22]. They define SA as follows:

$$SA = \{Elements, Form, Rationale\}$$

According to this definition SA is a combination of (1) a set of architectural elements (i.e., processing, data, and connecting), (2) the form of these elements as principles guiding the relationship between the elements and their properties, and (3) the rationale for choosing elements and their form in certain way. This definition provided a basis for initial research in the area of SA. The recent trend of describing SA as a set of design decisions and the rationale underpinning those design decisions has highlighted the importance of rationale in making and describing design decisions [23].

Bass, Clements, and Kazman [24] have defined SA in this way: *The software architecture of a system is the set of structures needed to reason about the system, which comprise software elements, relations among them, and properties of both.*

Structures in SA represent the partitioning and interaction decisions made to divide the responsibilities of satisfying requirements among a set of components and defining components' relationships with each other. A structural partitioning is guided by the specific requirements and constraints of an application. One of the main considerations during the partitioning decisions is to create a loosely coupled architecture from a set of highly cohesive components to minimize dependencies between components. By controlling unnecessary dependencies, the effect of changes in different component is localized [7]. The structural partitioning should be driven by both functional requirements and NFRs. Architectural structures of large-scale, software intensive systems are considered critical to the satisfaction of many NFRs. Each architectural structure can help architects reason about a system's different quality attributes. Architectural structures are documented using various architectural views [7].

1.2.1 Software architecture process and architecture lifecycle

It is also important to have a good understanding of the SA design process and the so-called lifecycle of SA. It is usually assumed that architecture design is a creative activity without a well-defined process. It can be considered a correct assumption for a large many systems' architecture design. However, in a serious attempt to design and evaluate SA for a large-scale, complex system, it is important that there is a disciplined process that can support the creativity with a more controlled and reflective approach. Moreover, like any other artifact, SA also has a lifecycle that goes through different phases and activities. Each phase of the architecture lifecycle has its own prerequisites for use and applicability.

Several process models and methods have been devised and promoted for supporting the SA process. Some of the well-known ones are the attribute-driven design (ADD) method [7], business architecture process and organization [25], the Rationale Unified Process's 4+1 Views [26], Siemens' 4 Views [27], and architectural separation of concerns [28]. In order to rationalize the options available to software project managers and architects, the developers of five well-known architecture design methods decided to develop a new general model of SA design by merging their respective SA design methods [29]. The original general model of architecture design consisted of three activities. This general model was extended by Tang and colleagues [30] to cover architectural materialization and evolution activities. For this chapter, we have slightly modified the names of the activities in the model. Each of the activities in the general model of architecture design has been briefly described below (see Figure 1.1):

1. Analyze problem domain: This activity consists of several sub-activities and tasks. This activity aims at defining the problems to be solved. Some of the main activities can be examining the architectural requirements (or even eliciting and clarifying architectural requirements), going through the stakeholders' concerns and context to separate and prioritize the architecturally significant requirements (ASRs) from those that are not architecturally significant.
2. Design and describe architectural decisions: This activity aims at making key architectural design decisions based on the ASRs. An architect may consider several available design options before selecting the ones that appear to be the most appropriate and optimal. An architect is also responsible for documenting the designed architecture using appropriate documentation notations and templates.
3. Architectural evaluation: This activity intends to ensure that the architectural solutions chosen during the previous process are the right ones. Hence, the proposed architectural solutions are evaluated against the ASRs.

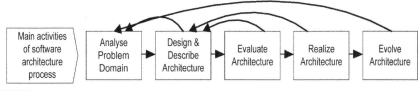

FIGURE 1.1

A model of software architecture process.

Based on [31].

4. Realize architecture: This is a phase wherein a designed architecture is
deconstructed into a detailed design and implemented. During this phase,
software developers make several dozen decisions which need to be aligned with
the high-level architecture design decisions. That means software developers
need to ensure that their decisions are in conformance with the architecture
designed by an architect.

5. Maintenance of architecture: This involves making architectural changes as the
architecture evolves because of enhancement and maintenance requirements,
which place several new demands on the architecture underpinning a system. From
the knowledge management perspective, prior design decisions are reassessed for
the potential impact of the required changes and new decisions are made to
accommodate the required changes without damaging the architectural integrity.

It should be noted that the abovementioned activities do not follow a sequential
process like the waterfall model. Rather, these activities are undertaken in a quite
iterative/evolutionary manner and tasks related to one particular activity can be
performed and/or revisited while performing any other activity. In the following
sub-sections, we briefly discuss different methods and techniques that are designed
to support the SA process described in this section.

1.2.2 Architecturally significant requirements

Software requirements are mainly divided into functional requirements and NFRs.
Functional requirements correspond to desired features of a system; while NFRs specify the required properties of a system. There are various terms used for NFRs, such as
quality attributes, constraints, goals, and non-behavioral requirements [32]. Recently, it
is being recognized that all these terms can be used for ASRs, but ASRs may include
functional requirements as well. For this chapter, we specifically use the term architecturally significant requirements (ASR) [33]. Chen and colleagues have recently defined
ASRs as *those requirements that have a measurable impact on a software system's
architecture* [33]. Some obvious examples of ASRs are reliability, modifiability, performance, and usability. ASRs are usually subjective, relative, and interacting [32,33].
They are subjective, because they can be viewed, interpreted, and analyzed differently
by different people and in different contexts. ASRs are also relative, because the importance of each ASR is often determined relative to other ASRs in a given context. ASRs
are considered to interact in the sense that attempting to achieve a particular ASR may
in turn positively or negatively affect other ASRs. ASRs are often specified by a system's main stakeholders, such as end users, developers, managers, and maintainers.
The ASRs are used to guide the SA design and analysis processes [7].

ASRs are less understood and managed than functional requirements [7,33–35].
This situation of ASRs not gaining sufficient attention upfront is quite common irrespective of the software development paradigm being used, whether Agile or non-
Agile. Chung et al. claim that quality requirements (or ASRs as we call them) are
generally stated informally during requirements analysis, are often contradictory,

can be difficult to enforce during software development, and are not easy to validate when the software system is ready for delivery [32]. It is asserted that one of the main reasons for this state is the number and definitions of quality attributes that can be considered for a system. There are as many as 161 quality attributes listed in [32], which are not claimed to be an exhaustive list. Moreover, the existence of numerous classifications of quality attributes is another hurdle to fully comprehending the meaning of quality attributes. Moreover, there is no universal definition of so-called quality attributes (such as performance, availability, modifiability, and usability) that usually form the core of any set of ASRs. However, a precise specification of ASRs is important for facilitating rigorous analysis. In order to address this situation, SA researchers have proposed several approaches, such as scenarios for characterizing quality attributes [7,36], framework-based approach to characterizing ASRs [33], and architecturally savvy personas [37]. All three of these approaches are not only complementary to each other when it comes to eliciting and specifying ASRs for architecture design and evaluation but can also be easily integrated in ASD methods for treating the ASRs' as first-class entities.

The approach based on architecturally savvy personas has been described in Chapter 4 of this book. Chen and colleagues have provided an evidence-based framework for systematically characterizing ASRs [33]. The framework is expected to cater to different stakeholders' needs for eliciting, specifying, and understanding ASRs for designing and evaluating architectural design decisions. Scenarios have been used for a long time in several areas of different disciplines (military and business strategy, decision making,). Scenarios are expected to be an effective means of specifying quality attributes for SA processes because they are normally very concrete, enabling the user to easily and precisely understand their detailed effect [38]. A scenario is a textual, system-independent specification of a quality attribute [7]. A well-structured scenario must clearly state an ASR in terms of stimulus and response. It is important that a scenario have clearly identifiable response measures to successfully analyze SAs. Bass et al. [7] provided a framework (shown in Table 1.1) to structure scenarios.

Table 1.1 Six Elements Scenario Generation Framework [7]

Elements	Brief Description
Stimulus	A condition that needs to be considered when it arrives at a system
Response	The activity undertaken after the arrival of the stimulus
Source of stimulus	An entity (human, system, or any actuator) that generates the stimulus
Environment	A system's condition when a stimulus occurs, e.g., overloaded, running, etc.
Stimulated artifact	Some artifact that is stimulated; may be the whole system or a part of it
Response measure	The response to the stimulus should be measurable in some fashion so that the requirement can be tested

The scenario generation framework shown in Table 1.1 is considered quite effective for eliciting and structuring scenarios gathered from stakeholders. It is argued that this framework provides a relatively rigorous and systematic approach to capture and document quality-sensitive scenarios, which can be used to select an appropriate reasoning framework for analyzing SA. Scenarios can be abstract or concrete. Abstract scenarios are used to aid in the bottom-up elicitation of scenarios. The abstract scenarios are system independent and focused on ASRs. Concrete scenario is a textual specification of an ASR for a particular system.

1.2.3 Software architecture design methods

The software architecture community has developed several methods and techniques to support the architecture design process. One of the key differentiating aspects of the design methods developed by the SA researchers and practitioners is that they elevate ASRs from being almost totally ignored to being an important consideration during SA design. Each of architecture-centric design methods has its strengths and weaknesses. One way of leveraging their strengths and overcoming weak points is to select different approaches and techniques from different methods and apply them based on contextual requirements.

Bosch [39] proposed a method that explicitly considers ASRs during the design process. Hofmeister and colleagues proposed a framework—global analysis—to identify, accommodate, and describe ASRs early into the design phase [27]. However, these methods have their critics for considering functional requirements ahead of ASRs. The work of Chung et al. provides a framework to systematically deal with NFRs during the design process [32]. The NFR framework helps formally reason about the relationship between a design decision and supported or inhibited quality attributes. However, it does not provide support to explicitly perform trade-off analysis between competing design decisions. Researchers from the Software Engineering Institute (SEI) have developed several methods to support architecture design—for example, ADD [7] and attribute-based architecture styles [40]. Al-Naeem et al. [41] have proposed an architectural decision-making support framework for designing an architecture that is composed of design decisions already evaluated with respect to desired quality attributes and organizational constraints.

From this brief analysis of the well-known architecture-centric design methods, it is clear that an architecture design method should not only help identify suitable design solutions with respect to ASRs but must also include an activity to determine if the proposed architecture design has the potential to fulfill the required ASRs. Most of the existing design methods attempt to leverage knowledge-based approaches in terms of applying design patterns and architectural styles. However, most of the existing architecture-centric methods are considered heavyweight and ceremonial. Hence, they need to be appropriately tailored and contextualized for ASD environments. Several research efforts are geared toward providing guidance on how to tailor architecture design and evaluation methods for agile methods [42,43].

1.2.4 **Documenting software architecture**

It is well recognized that architecture is a vehicle for communication among stakeholders. Hence, it should be described unambiguously and in sufficient details, which can provide relevant information to each type of stakeholder [44]. Architectural documentation is also a vital artifact for several key activities, such as architecture decisions analysis, work breakdown, and post-deployment maintenance [7]. Architecture documentation may consume a large amount of resources that need to be justifiably allocated. That is why architecture documentation is not commonly practiced in general and in agile and lean worlds in particular. An important issue in architecture documentation is to choose a suitable means of architecture description that can serve the main goals (e.g., communication, analysis, implementation, and maintenance) of documenting SAs.

The boxes and lines notation is probably the most commonly used technique for explaining or documenting architectural decisions [21]. However, without having sufficient contextual information, such architectural description can be interpreted in several ways. Moreover, the boxes and lines notation does not capture several other types of information (such as interfaces and behavioral aspects). Hence, this notation is not considered expressive enough to communicate architectural decisions in a manner that serves the abovementioned main objectives of architecture documentation.

Recently, there has been an increasing emphasis on documenting SAs using different views suitable to different stakeholders [45]. An architectural view is a representation of a system from a related set of concerns, which are important to different stakeholders. Hence, each view addresses the concerns of one or more of a system's stakeholders. The term "view" is used to express a system's architecture with respect to a particular viewpoint. According to the IEEE standards for describing SA [45], architectural description is organized into various views. One of the most popular views-based approaches is called "4+1" views [26]. The 4+1 view model intends to describe an SA using five concurrent views. Each of them addresses a specific set of concerns.

- Logical view denotes the partitions of the functional requirements onto the logical entities in an architecture. This view illustrates a design's object model in an object-oriented design approach.
- Process view is used to represent some types of ASRs, such as concurrency and performance. This view can be described at several levels of abstraction, each of which addresses an individual issue.
- Development view illustrates the organization of the actual software modules in the software development environment. This view also represents internal properties, such as reusability, ease of development, testability, and commonality. It is usually made up of subsystems, which are organized in a hierarchy of layers. This view also supports allocation of requirements and work division, cost assessment, planning, progress monitoring, and reasoning about reuse, portability and security.

- Physical view represents the mapping of the architectural elements captured in the logical, process, and development views onto networks of computers. This view takes into consideration the NFRs (e.g., availability, reliability (fault tolerance), performance (throughput), and scalability).
- Scenarios are used to demonstrate that the elements of other views can work together seamlessly. This fifth view is made up of a small subset of important scenarios and has two main objectives: design driver, and validation/illustration.

Clements and colleagues have proposed another approach, called Views and Beyond (V&B) [44], to documenting SA using views. Like the IEEE Std 1471, their approach is based on the philosophy that instead of prescribing a fixed set of views like Kruchten, SA should be documented using whatever views are useful for a system being designed. The V&B approach's main contribution is to map concrete architectural styles to views and providing templates to capture relevant information. Apart from architecture documentation approaches, the SA community has proposed several ADLs (such as Rapide [46] and Unicon [47]), which are considered formal approaches to describing SA. There have been two comparative studies of the Architectural Description Languages (ADLs) reported in [48,49]. Unified Modeling Language (UML) [50] has become a *de facto* standard notation for documenting a software for any kinds of software development environment, agile or non-agile. Before a major upgrade in the UML 2.0, the UML had nine diagrams: class diagram, object diagram, use case diagram, sequence diagram, collaboration diagram, state chart diagram, activity diagram, component diagram, and deployment diagram. The UML 2.0 has addressed a major weakness of UML by providing new diagrams for describing the structure and behavior of a system.

1.2.5 Software architecture evaluation

Software architecture evaluation is an important activity in the software architecting process. The fundamental goal of architecture evaluation is to assess the potential of a proposed/chosen architecture to deliver a system capable of fulfilling required quality requirements and to identify any potential risks [51,52]. Researchers and practitioners have proposed a large number of architecture evaluation methods for which a classification and comparison framework has also been proposed [53]. Most widely used architecture evaluation methods are scenario-based. These methods are called scenario-based because scenarios are used to characterize the quality attributes required of a system. It is believed that scenario-based analysis is suitable for development-time quality attributes (such as maintainability and usability) rather than for run-time quality attributes (such as performance and scalability), which can be assessed using quantitative techniques such as simulation or mathematical models [39]. Among the well-known, scenario-based architecture evaluation methods are the SA analysis method (SAAM) [54], the architecture tradeoff analysis method (ATAM) [55], the architecture level maintainability analysis (ALMA) [56], and the performance assessment of SA (PASA) [57].

SAAM is the earliest method proposed to analyze architecture using scenarios. The analysis of multiple candidate architectures requires applying SAAM to each of the proposed architectures and then comparing the results. This can be very costly in terms of time and effort if the number of architectures to be compared is large. SAAM has been further extended into a number of methods, such as SAAM for complex scenarios [58], extending SAAM by integration in the domain-centric and reuse-based development process [59], and SAAM for evolution and reusability [60]. ATAM grew out of SAAM. The key advantages of ATAM are explicit ways of understanding how an architecture supports multiple competing quality attributes and of performing trade-off analysis. ATAM uses both qualitative techniques, such as scenarios, and quantitative techniques for measuring the qualities of the architecture.

Benstsson and Bosch proposed several methods (such as SBAR [61], ALPSM [62], and ALMA) [56]. All these methods use one or a combination of various analysis techniques (i.e., scenarios, simulation, mathematical modeling, or experience-based reasoning [39]). All of these methods use scenarios to characterize quality attributes. The desired scenarios are mapped onto architectural components to assess the architecture's capability to support those scenarios or identify the changes required to handle those scenarios. PASA is an architecture analysis method that combines scenarios and quantitative techniques [57]. PASA uses scenarios to determine a system's performance objectives and applies principles and techniques from software performance engineering (SPE) to determine whether an architecture is capable of supporting the performance scenarios. PASA includes performance-sensitive architectural styles and anti-patterns as analysis tools and formalizes the architecture analysis activity of the performance engineering process reported in [63].

1.3 AGILE SOFTWARE DEVELOPMENT AND ARCHITECTURE

Agile software development methods promise to support continuous feedback and accommodate changes in software requirements throughout the software development life cycle, support close collaboration between customers and developers, and enable early and frequent delivery of software features required for a system [4]. The ASD methods are based on the Agile Manifesto that was published by a group of software developers and consultants in 2001. According to the Agile Manifesto:

We are uncovering better ways of developing software by doing it and helping others do it. Through this work we have come to value:

- *Individuals and interactions* over process and tools,
- *Working software* over comprehensive documents,
- *Customer collaboration* over contract negotiation,
- *Responding to change* over following a plan.

That is, while there is value in the items on the right, we value the items on the left more

This manifesto describes the core values underpinning the agile community's views about different aspects of software development processes, people, practices, and artifacts. According to this manifesto, the ASD methods are designed and implemented in ways that are aligned with the core ASD values, such as individuals and interactions over process and tools, working software over comprehensive documentation, customer collaboration over contract negotiation, and responding to change over following a plan [13]. Agile Alliance has also enlisted a number of common principles for agile processes, including customer satisfaction through early and continuous software delivery, co-located active customer participation, ability to handle change even late in the software development lifecycle, simplicity of software development processes, short feedback loops, mutual trust, and common code ownership [14].

Some of the well-known ASD methods are extreme programming (XP) [3], Crystal Clear [64] and Scrum [1]. There are a large number of books and research papers for describing the details of each of the well-known and widely practiced ASD methods. We can refer a reader of this chapter to two good sources [65,66] for introductory information about different ASD methods such as Scrum, feature driven development, dynamic software development method, adaptive software development, extreme programming, and crystal methodologies. Since there are a large variety of ASD and practices, it seems appropriate that we keep our views and discussions focused on integrating architectural approaches into a few well-known and widely adopted ASD methods. Hence, this chapter will briefly touch on two of the well-known ASD methods—Scrum, an agile project management method, and XP. By limiting the number of agile methods for discussion with respect to architectural principles and practices, we expect to provide a precise but more coherent and deep discussion of how to make ASD methods and architecture-centric practices work in harmony to leverage the advantages of both disciplines for developing high-quality and cost-effective software iteratively and incrementally without unnecessary project delays and risks.

1.3.1 Scrum

Scrum has emerged as one of the leading (if not the leading) ASD method that has been designed to manage software development projects. Scrum is a term used in the game of rugby where it means "getting an out-of-play ball back into the game" through team efforts [67]. In software development, Scrum is an iterative and incremental project management approach that provides a simple *inspect and adapt* framework rather than specific techniques. Scrum-based projects deliver software in increments called *sprints* (usually 3-4 week iterations, or even 2 weeks in some instances). Each sprint starts with planning, during which user stories are taken from backlogs based on priorities, and ends with a sprint review. The planning activity is expected to last for a few hours (e.g., 4 hours) and not too long. The sprint review meeting can also last around 4 hours. All the key stakeholders are expected to participate in the sprint planning and the sprint review meetings at the beginning and completion of each sprint.

A Scrum team holds a short meeting (e.g., maximum 15 mininutes) at the beginning of each day. This meeting is called the "daily Scrum meeting," and is aimed at enabling each team member to addresses only three questions: "What did I do yesterday, what will I do today, and what are the showstoppers in my work?" Each Scrum project is expected to have at least three artifacts: product backlogs, sprint backlogs, and burn-down charts. The software architecture community has also borrowed the term "backlogs" and proposed that the architecting process should keep an architectural backlog when architecture is being designed and evaluated iteratively. The Scrum backlogs consist of requirements that need to be implemented during the current or future sprint cycles. An iterative and incremental approach to architecting also incorporates the concept of architectural backlogs [10]. A third artifact is the daily burn-down chart that is aimed at providing a status report in terms of the cumulative work yet to be done.

1.3.2 Extreme programming

Extreme programming is another popular agile approach that was developed based on commonsense principles and practices taken to extreme levels. Like other ASD methods, XP also advocates short iteration and frequent releases of working code with the aim of increasing productivity but still accommodating requirements changes. XP was designed for collocated teams of eight to ten developers working with object-oriented programming language. The approach quickly became popular, among software developers who were not satisfied with the traditional software development approaches like waterfall. Following are some of the key XP practices.

- *Planning game*: A close interaction between customers and developers is encouraged for estimating and prioritizing requirements for the next release. The requirements are captured as users' stories on story cards. The programmers are expected to plan and deliver only the user stories agreed upon with customers.
- *Small releases*: An initial version of a system is released for operation after a few iterations. New features are delivered in subsequent releases on a daily or weekly basis.
- *Metaphor*: The development team and customers develop a set of metaphors for modeling the system to be developed.
- *Simple design*: XP encourages developers to keep the design of a system as simple as possible. According to Beck *say everything once and only once.*
- *Tests*: The test-first principle means developers write acceptance tests for their code before they write the code itself. Customers write functional tests for each iteration, and at the end of each iteration, all tests are expected to run successfully.
- *Refactoring*: The design of a system evolved by transforming existing design of the system in a way that all the test cases run successfully.
- *Pair programming*: The production code is written by two developers sitting next to each other on a computer.

- *Continuous integration*: All new code is integrated into the system as frequently as possible. All functional tests must still pass after integration or the new code is discarded.
- *Collective ownership*: All developers working on a system jointly own the code. That means any developer can make changes anywhere in the code at any time it is felt necessary.
- *On-site customer*: A customer sits with the development team all the time. The onsite customer answers questions, performs acceptance tests, and ensures progress on the development.
- *Fourty-hour weeks*: If someone from the development team has to work overtime in two consecutive weeks, it is a sign of a big problem. The requirements should be selected for each iteration in a way that developers do not need to put in overtime.
- *Open workspace*: Developers have a common workspace set up with small cubicles around the periphery and a common development machine in the center for pair programmers.
- *Just rules*: A team's members subscribe to a set of rules. The rules can be changed at any time as long as there is a consensus about how to assess the effects of the change.

1.4 MAKING ARCHITECTURAL AND AGILE APPROACHES WORK

It has been stated throughout this chapter that there is a growing recognition of the importance of paying more attention to architectural aspects in Agile approaches [4–6,14]. Hence, there are an increasing number of efforts aimed at identifying the technical and organizational challenges involved in integrating agile approaches in traditional software development methods [14,15]. These efforts have resulted in several proposals for combining the strengths of the core elements of agile and architecture-centric approaches. For example, Refs. [68,69] combine the strengths of the core elements of the risk-driven, architecture-centric rational unified process (RUP) and the XP [3] process. The combinations were enabled by the fact that RUP and XP share the cornerstones of iterative, incremental, and evolutionary development [70]. Nord and Tomayko [4] propose an integration of specific SEI architecture-centric methods into the XP framework [71]. Many others have emphasized the importance of finding a middle ground between two extreme views of architecture-centric and agile approaches [9,13,12]. Beck has also emphasized the importance of paying sufficient attention to quality attributes and the need of scaling XP based on the context. For example, he states the following in the second edition of his book, *XP Explained: Embracing Change*:

> A system isn't certifiably secure unless it has been built with a set of security principles in mind and has been audited by a security expert. While compatible with XP, these practices have to be incorporated into the team's daily work.

With awareness and appropriate adaptations, XP does scale. Some problems can be simplified to be easily handled by a small XP team. For others, XP must be augmented. The basic value and principles apply at all scales. The practices can be modified to suit your situation.

It can be argued that one of the important prerequisites for bridging the gap between agile and architectural approaches is to build and disseminate an evidence-based body of knowledge about the points of conflict and conciliation between agile and architectural principles, practices, and their proponents' views. Such a body of knowledge should also include the challenges that software development teams face when they attempt to follow architecturally savvy principles in an agile development shop and the problems and risks that may have appeared in agile projects that did not incorporate architecture-centric principles and practices. We have taken an empirical approach to gain and disseminate an understanding of the challenges of and solutions for combining agile and architecture-centric approaches [42,72,73]. We have reached several conclusions about combining agile and architectural approaches, and some of those findings have been summarized in this chapter to provide a reader with an appropriate context from which to read and benefit from the rest of the chapters in this book. Table 1.2 represents our understanding of placing some of the well-known agile practices along with architectural practices to show that many of the agile practices have equivalent principles or practices in architecture disciplines, and these can easily be tailored and applied in agile settings.

One key observation from our ongoing research on agile and architecture has been reported in [73]. According to that observation, there is an increased emphasis on the vital role of and responsibilities of software architects in successfully combining agile and architecture methodologies. Software architects are expected to act as facilitators in whole software development projects and as the representatives of a system's overall quality attributes. From our other research [72], we have identified some of the key types of tasks an architect in an agile environment is expected to perform in order to successfully combine architecturally savvy principles and practices (outlined in previous sections) and ASD methods.

- An architect should have a good understanding of agile approaches.
- An architect should know how to sell a key design decision to product owners in conflicting situations.
- A project architect should know the overall architecture, required features, and implementation status.
- An architect should document and communicate the architecture to all the stakeholders.
- An architect should be willing to wear multiple architectural hats—solution architect, software architect, and implementation architect—or should be able convince his/her organization to have different architectural roles established depending on the nature of a project.
- An architect should spearhead an effort to institutionalize the role of architects as facilitators and service providers in projects.

Table 1.2 Placing Agile and Architectural Practices with Each Other

Some of the ASD Practices	Frequency of Use
Sprint	Iterative nature of general model of software architecture (SA) design with backlogs of architectural concerns to be addressed
Sprint planning	Prioritizing architecturally significant requirements for each iteration
Sprint review	Architectural review
Daily meetings	Sharing architecture rationale and knowledge in architecture group meetings
Onsite customer	Involvement of key stakeholder in as many phases of architecting lifecycle as possible
Continuous integration	Architecture-level integration and interoperability—quality attribute approaches
Refactoring	Architecture-level refactoring using patterns and architectural styles
Metaphor	SA design and architecturally savvy personas
Simple design	Pattern-based design to keep the design simple and well known
Collective code ownership	Buy-in of stakeholders on key architectural design decisions
Coding standards	Architectural templates and standards to support common goals and standards
Test-driven development	Architecture-based testing

It is important to keep in mind that software architects usually design architecture, but it is developers who materialize the designed architecture. Hence, software developers should be equally responsible for treating SA as a first-class entity that provides the blueprint of the whole system. That is why we have argued that the role of software developers is equally important in successfully combining agile and architecture approaches; a development team must decide how to use various architectural artifacts and documents. However, there is little knowledge about how ASD teams perceive and use SA. This knowledge should be considered important because if an ASD team considers SA relevant to their tasks, there would not be much effort required to convince them to apply the architectural principles and practices that can be relevant to their project and context.

Falessi et al. [74] reported that agile developers had positive views of SA because Agile developers used architectural artifacts for communication among team members, provided input on subsequent design decisions, documented design assumptions, and evaluated design alternatives, to name a few. Falessi and colleagues' findings were consistent to what we had found from the study reported in [72]. Other recently proposed solutions for combining architecture-centric and agile approaches include the Responsibility-Driven Architecture (RDA) approach presented by Blair and his colleague [75]. Their approach exploits the concepts of real option theory using a spreadsheet-based simple tool. Faber presented an approach to help architecture and software development teams focus on NFRs that are usually ignored in most ASD methods [76]. According to his approach, an architect takes ownership and responsibility for representing NFRs at all stages of the software development lifecycle. Madison [77] has described the architect as a linchpin who can tie up agile and architecture approaches, and he strongly advocates the use of agile for getting to a good architecture by suitably combining architectural functions (such as communication, quality attributes, and design patterns) and architectural skills at four points (i.e., upfront planning, storyboarding, sprint, and working software).

Several solutions for combining agile and architecture methods are detailed in this book. The first part of this book, Fundamentals of Agile Architecting, has several chapters that report approaches and techniques for combining some architectural issues and approaches with ASD methods. The problems addressed in that part include architecture level refactoring, design decision making in agile methods, and leveraging personas to elicit, specify, and validate ASRs. For example, Michael Stal has shown how to refactor at the architecture level by exploiting knowledge about architectural styles and patterns and ASRs. Stal states that a systematic architectural refactoring can help prevent architectural erosion by evaluating the existing software design before adding new artifacts or changing existing ones. Van der Ven and Bosch have proposed an approach to improving architecture design decision making in agile settings. The findings from their case study provide practical insights for agile architecture design decision making. Cleland-Huang and her colleagues present a persona-based approach to eliciting and addressing ASRs. They provide several concrete examples to show how to use ASPs for deriving architecture design and evaluation.

The second part of this book, Managing Architecture in Agile Projects, includes chapters that provide methods, approaches, and tools for addressing important problems, such as variability management, knowledge management, and architecture evaluation, in projects using ASD methods. Several of the architectural principles and practices presented in the first part of this chapter have been leveraged in the approaches presented in the second part of the book for support of agile architecting (e.g., variability management in agile projects, architectural knowledge management in Scrum projects, and incremental architecture evaluation).

The third part of this book, Agile Architecting in Specific Domains, includes solutions that combine agility and architecture for new and emerging technological solutions, such as cloud computing. Testing cloud-based applications and designing and deploying multi-tenancy applications are significantly complicated and onerous activities and there is relatively little knowledge about how to effectively and efficiently perform them in an agile and lean manner. These chapters propose agile ways to design and analyze multi-tenancy applications and to test them by leveraging architecture-centric principles and artifacts. The presented approaches are good examples of agile architecting.

Having read and understood the theoretical principles and approaches that should underpin agile architecting and having seen their applications for different systems in various domains, A reader of this book will likely enjoy reading some real-world examples of agile architecting to learn from industrial efforts in this area. The fourth part of this book includes four chapters that have been written based on several industrial projects that make architecture and agile work together in their respective environments. For example, Hopkins and Harcombe discuss the factors that need to be considered when planning the delivery of large-scale agile projects; architecture planning is a centerpiece of advice that they provide to combine agile approaches and architecture for large-scale software development projects. Eeles's work focuses on sharing experiences of designing and evolving "change-ready" systems by leveraging agile and architectural principles. Friedrichsen brings up the role of well-defined architectural principles for supporting continuous refactoring as a means of emergent software design championed by agile followers. The last set of industrial insights comes from the tale of evolving a complex software platform combining agile practices and architectural principles. The industrial chapter provides useful information and insights about drawing a compromise between the purity of agile approaches and practical business concerns that need significant attention paid to architectural role and integrating.

It is argued that there is an important and urgent need to understand the importance, opportunities, and challenges involved in making architecture-centric and agile approaches for developing software intensive systems and services work together. One of our key goals is to build an evidence-based body of knowledge by identifying and understanding the main points of clashes when combining agile and architecture and how those clashes can be turned into advantages based on a project's needs and context. This book offers several views and approaches aimed at helping companies and individuals learn and apply appropriate methods, strategies, and tools to make architecture and agile approaches work together for agile architecting. We hope readers (both researchers and practitioners) not only find the approaches presented in this book useful and applicable but also share their experiences of combining agile and architecture by publishing the failure and success stories in order to contribute to the growing body of knowledge on this topic that is hugely important to the software development community.

Acknowledgments

Some of the most significant contributions to my understanding and writings on this topic were made by Professor Philippe Kruchten and Professor Pekka Abrahamsson through sharing their writings, ideas, and experiences. Some of the ideas presented in this chapter came through my collaboration with Minna Pikkarainen and Toumas Ihme of VTT, Finland. This chapter also benefited from the knowledge that I gained from the articles submitted to our call to a special issue of IEEE Software back in 2009/2010. Kieran Conboy also helped in collecting the data. Some content is based on my research in the FLEXI ITEA2 project. I also acknowledge the generosity of my co-editors of this book for allowing me to author this chapter.

References

[1] Schwaber K. Agile project management with scrum. Washington, USA: Microsoft Press; 2004.

[2] Palmer SR, Felsing JM. A practical guide to feature-driven development. USA: Prentice Hall; 2002.

[3] Beck K. Extreme programming explained: embrace change. Reading, MA: Addison Wesley Longman, Inc.; 2000.

[4] Nord RL, Tomayko JE. Software architecture-centric methods and agile development. IEEE Softw 2006;23:47–53.

[5] Parsons R. Architecture and agile methodologies—how to get along. In: WICSA; 2008.

[6] Ihme T, Abrahamsson P. Agile architecting: the use of architectural patterns in mobile java applications. Int J Agile Manufacturing 2005;8:1–16.

[7] Bass L, Clements P, Kazman R. Software architecture in practice. 2nd ed. Boston, MA: Addison-Wesley; 2003.

[8] Kruchten P. Situated agility. In: 9th International conference on agile processes and eXtreme programming in software engineering, Limerick, Ireland; 2008.

[9] Boehm B. Get ready for agile methods, with care. IEEE Computer 2002;35:64–9.

[10] Hofmeister C, Kruchten P, Nord RL, Obbink H, Ran A, America P. A general model of software architecture design derived from five industrial approaches. J Sys Softw 2007;80:106–26.

[11] Thapparambil P. Agile architecture: pattern or oxymoron? Agile Times 2005;6:43–8.

[12] Ali Babar M, Abrahamsson P. Architecture-centric methods and agile approaches. In: Proceedings of the 9th international conference on agile processes and eXtreme programming in software engineering Limerick, Ireland; 2008. p. 242–3.

[13] Kruchten P. Voyage in the agile memeplex. ACM queue 2007; July/August:38–44.

[14] Lycett M, Macredie RD, Patel C, Paul RJ. Migrating agile methods to standardized development practice. IEEE Comput 2003;36:79–85.

[15] Boehm B, Taylor R. Management challenges to implementing agile processes in traditional development organizations. IEEE Softw 2005;22:30–9.

[16] Parnas DL. On the criteria to be used in decomposing systems into modules. Commun ACM 1972;15:1053–8.

[17] Stevens WP, Myers GJ, Constantine LL. Structured design. IBM Sys J 1974;13:115–39.

[18] Gamma E, Helm R, Johnson R, Vlissides J. Design patterns-elements of reusable object-oriented software. Reading, MA: Addison-Wesley; 1995.

[19] Garlan D, Shaw M. An introduction to software architecture. Pennsylvania: SEI, Carnegie Mellon University; 1994.

[20] Kazman R, Barbacci M, Klein M, Carriere SJ. Experience with performing architecture tradoff analysis. In: Proceedings of the 21th international conference on software engineering. New York, USA: ACM Press; 1999. p. 54–63.

[21] Gorton I. Essential software architecture. Heidelberg: Springer; 2006.

[22] Perry DE, Wolf AL. Foundations for the study of software architecture. ACM SIGSOFT 1992;17:40–52.

[23] Ali Babar M, Dingsoyr T, Lago P, Van Vliet H. Software architecture knowledge management: theory and practice. Heidelberg: Springer-Verlag; 2009.

[24] Bass L, Clements P, Kazman R. Software architecture in practice. 3rd ed. Massachusetts: Addison-Wesley; 2013.

[25] America P, Rommes E, Obbink H. Multi-view variation modeling for scenario analysis. In: Proceedings of fifth international workshop on product family engineering. Siena, Italy: Springer-Verlag; 2003.

[26] Kruchten P. Architectural blueprints—the "4+1" view model of software architecture. IEEE Softw 1995;12:42–50.

[27] Hofmeister C, Nord RL, Soni D. Applied software architecture. Reading, MA: Addison-Wesley; 2000.

[28] Ran A. ARES conceptual framework for software architecture. In: Jazayeri M, Ran A, Linden FVD, editors. Software architecture for product families: principles and practice. Boston, MA: Addison-Wesley; 2000.

[29] Hofmeister C, Kruchten P, Nord RL, Obbink H, Ran A, America P. A general model of software architecture design derived from five industrial approaches. J Sys Softw 2006;80:106–26.

[30] Tang A, Avgeriou P, Jansen A, Capilla R, Babar MA. A comparative study of architecture knowledge management tools. J Sys Softw 2010;83:352–70.

[31] Tang A, Avgeriou P, Jansen A, Capilla R, Babar MA. A comparative study of architecture knowledge management tools. J Sys Softw 2010;83(3):352–70.

[32] Chung L, Nixon BA, Yu E, Mylopoulos J. Non-functional requirements in software engineering. Boston: Kluwer Academic Publishing; 1999.

[33] Chen L, Babar MA, Nuseibeh B. Characterizing architecturally significant requirements. IEEE Softw 2013;30:38–45.

[34] Bass L, Klein M, Bachmann F. Quality attribute design primitives and the attribute driven design method. In: The 4th international workshop on software product-family engineering; 2002.

[35] Bruin HD, Vliet HV. Quality-driven software architecture composition. J Sys Softw 2003;66:269–84.

[36] Barbacci M, Klein MH, Longstaff TA, Weinstock CB. Quality attributes. Pennsylvania: Software Engineering Institute, Carnegie Mellon University; 1995.

[37] Cleland-Huang J, Czauderna A, Keenan E. A persona-based approach for exploring architecturally significant requirements in agile projects. In: 19th International working conference requirements engineering: foundation for software quality (REFSQ). Essen, Germany: Springer; 2013.

[38] Lassing N, Rijsenbrij D, Vliet HV. How well can we predict changes at architecture design time? J Sys Softw 2003;65:141–53.

[39] Bosch J. Design and use of software architectures: adopting and evolving a product-line approach. Boston, MA: Addison-Wesley; 2000.

[40] Klein M, Kazman R. Attribute-based architectural styles, Tech Report CMU/SEI-99-TR-022. Software Engineering Institute, Carnegie Mellon University; 1999.

[41] Al-Naeem T, Gorton I, Ali Babar M, Rabhi F, Benatallah B. A quality-driven systematic approach for architecting distributed software applications. In: Proceedings of the 27th international conference on software engineering, ICSE, St. Louis, USA; 2005. p. 244–53.

[42] Babar MA. An exploratory study of architectural practices and challenges in using agile software development approaches. In: Joint working IEEE/IFIP conference on software architecture 2009 and european conference on software architecture (WICSA/ECSA). Cambridge, UK: IEEE Computer Society; 2009.

[43] Babar MA, Ihme T, Pikkarainen M. An industrial case of exploiting product line architectures in agile software development. In: 13th international conference on software product lines (SPLC) San Francisco, California, USA; 2009.

[44] Clements P, Bachmann F, Bass L, Garlan D, Ivers j, Little R, et al. Documenting software architectures: views and beyond. USA: Addison-Wesley; 2002.

[45] IEEE. IEEE recommended practices for architecture description of software-intensive systems. In: IEEE Std 1471-2000; 2000.

[46] Luckham DC, Kenney JJ, Augustin LM, Vera J, Bryan D, Mann W. Specification and analysis of software architecture using Rapide. IEEE Trans Softw Eng 1995;21:336–55.

[47] Shaw M, DeLine R, Klein D, Ross T, Young D, Zelesnik G. Abstractions for software architecture and tools to support them. IEEE Trans Softw Eng 1995;21:314–35.

[48] Clements PC. A survey of architecture description languages. In: Proceedings of the 8th international workshop on software specification and design. Germany; 1996.

[49] Medvidovic N, Taylor RN. A classification and comparison framework for software architecture description languages. IEEE Trans Softw Eng 2000;26:70–93.

[50] Fowler M. UML distilled: A Brief Guide to the Standard Object Modelling Language. 3rd ed. Boston, MA: Addison-Wesley; 2004.

[51] Lassing N, Rijsenbrij D, Hv Vliet. The goal of software architecture analysis: confidence building or risk assessment. In: Proceedings of first BeNeLux conference on software, architecture; 1999.

[52] Maranzano JF, Rozsypal SA, Zimmerman GH, Warnken GW, Wirth PE, Weiss DM. Architecture reviews: practice and experience. IEEE Softw 2005;22:34–43.

[53] Babar MA, Zhu L, Jeffery D. A framework for classifying and comparing software architecture evaluation methods. In: Australian software engineering conference (ASWEC). Melbourne, Australian; 2004.

[54] Kazman R, Bass L, Abowd G, Webb M. SAAM: a method for analyzing the properties of software architectures. In: Proceedings of the 16th international conference on software, engineering; 1994. p. 81–90.

[55] Clements P, Kazman R, Klein M. Evaluating software architectures: methods and case studies. Boston, MA: Addison-Wesley; 2002.

[56] Bengtsson P, Lassing N, Bosch J, van Vliet H. Architecture-level modifiability analysis (ALMA). J Sys Softw 2004;69:129–47.

[57] Williams LG, Smith CU. PASA: an architectural approach to fixing software performance problems. In: Proceedings of the international conference of the Computer Measurement Group, Reno, USA; 2002.

[58] Lassing N, Rijsenbrij D, Hv Vliet. On software architecture analysis of flexibility, complexity of changes: size isn't everything. In: Second nordic software architecture workshop (NOSA '99); 1999.

[59] Molter G. Integrating SAAM in domain-centric and reuse-based development processes. In: Second nordic workshop software architecture (NOSA '99); 1999.

[60] Lung C, Bot S, Kalaichelvan K, Kazman R. An approach to software architecture analysis for evolution and reusability. In: CASCON '97, Toronto, Canada; 1997.

[61] Bengtsson PO, Bosch J. Scenario-based architecture reengineering. In: Fifth international conference on software reuse (ICSR5), Victoria, Canada; 1998.

[62] Bengtsson PO, Bosch J. Architecture level prediction of software maintenance. In: Third European conference on software maintenance and reengineering, Amsterdam, Netherlands; 1999.

[63] Smith CU, Williams LG. Performance solutions: a practical guide to creating responsive, scalable software. Boston, MA: Addison-Wesley; 2002.

[64] Cockburn A. Crystal clear: a human-powered methodology for small teams. Boston, USA: Addison-Wesley; 2004.

[65] Abrahamsson P, Salo O, Ronkainen J, Warsta J. Agile software development methods: review and analysis. Oulu, Finland: VTT Publications 478; 2002.

[66] Cohen D, Lindvall M, Costa P. An introduction to agile methods. Adv Comput 2004;61:1–66.

[67] Schwaber K, Beedle M. Agile software development with scrum. Upper Saddle River, NJ: Prentice-Hall; 2002.

[68] Ambler SW. Agile modeling: effective practices for eXreme programming and the unified process. New York: John Wiley & Sons; 2002.

[69] IBM. RUP for extreme programming (xp) plug-ins. IBM; 2004.

[70] Larman C. Agile and iterative development: a manager's guide. Boston, MA: Addison Wesley Professional; 2003.

[71] Beck K, Andres C. Extreme programming explained: embrace change. 2nd ed. Reading, MA.: Addison Wesley Longman; 2004.

[72] Ali Babar M, Iheme T, Pikkarainen M. An industrial case of exploiting product line architectures in agile software development. In: Proceedings of the 13th international software product line conference (SPLC), San Francisco, USA; 2009.

[73] Abrahamsson P, Babar MA, Kruchten P. Agility and architecture: can they coexist? IEEE Softw 2010;27:16–22.

[74] Falessi D, Cantone G, Sarcià SA, Calavaro G, Subiaco P, D'Amore C. Peaceful coexistence: agile developer perspectives on software architecture. IEEE Softw 2010;27:23–5.

[75] Blair S, Watt R, Cull T. Responsibility-driven architecture. IEEE Softw 2010;27:26–32.

[76] Faber R. Architects as service providers. IEEE Softw 2010;27:33–40.

[77] Madison J. Agile architecture interactions. IEEE Softw 2010;27:41–8.

Fundamentals of Agile Architecting

The DCI Paradigm: Taking Object Orientation into the Architecture World

James O. Coplien[*] and Trygve Reenskaug[†]

[*]*Gertrud & Cope, Espergærde, Denmark*
[†]*University of Oslo, Oslo, Norway*

CHAPTER CONTENTS

2.1 INTRODUCTION

Software architecture started as Fred Brooks's vision of a good metaphor for how we do software, in particular for the early work of the programming-in-the-large forms of design. Somewhere along the line the metaphor took on a life of its own and lost many of its original roots. The metaphor became a place for noncoders to hang their hats, and architecture too often appears in the development process only as the source of artifacts that are thrown over the wall.

In this chapter, we look at the history of software architecture with a focus on recent history characterized by object-oriented design. Object-oriented design broadly characterizes many historic and contemporary methods that go by many names. All of them share the notion of encapsulation of state and behavior in a run-time unit with a unique identity, and all of them separate the client of an object from the object itself by deferring the binding of the name of an object operation until its invocation. But, more fundamentally, they return to the basics of architecture foreseen by Vitruvius embodying a balance of critical thought and practical application [1]:

...[A]rchitects who have aimed at acquiring manual skill without scholarship have never been able to reach a position of authority to correspond to their pains, while those who relied only upon theories and scholarship were obviously hunting the shadow, not the substance. But those who have a thorough knowledge of both, like men armed at all points, have the sooner attained their object and carried authority with them.

Or, as Richard Gabriel notes [2, p. 231]:

... Vitruvius, the classic Roman architect, characterized architecture as the joining of Commodity, Firmness, and Delight ... In software engineering—if there really be such a thing—we have worked thoroughly on Firmness, some during the last 10 years on Commodity, and none on Delight. To the world of computer science, there can be no such thing as Delight because beauty and anything from the arts or the so-called soft part of human activity has nothing to do with science—it is mere contingency.

Perhaps it's noteworthy that, with market cap as a measure of success, the best of the best in contemporary computing for the mass consumer have the hallmark of being driven by customer delight.

This chapter refocuses the discussion of software architecture on its historical roots, in part by invoking the work of architects whose work has influenced the recent history of software architecture—in particular, Christopher Alexander and other postmodernists. This is not just for the sake of nostalgia, but also to drive beyond the superficial trappings of contemporary methods to the fundamentals that make us human. Most contemporary software architecture efforts remain mired in the modern school, although they clumsily strive to apply agile vocabulary and principles. This leads to frequent breakdowns in the metaphor. Architecture is used equally often to politically co-opt tangential areas, such as knowledge management and project management reinterpreted in a modernist framework, or to provide a vehicle for one organization to exercise political control over another. On the other hand, the agile position on architecture articulated here not only borrows directly from the postmodern school but can also be reconciled with its principles of balanced, practical human focus on life activity over structure for its own sake.

This chapter places the relatively new DCI (Data, Context, and Interaction) paradigm on a firm architectural footing. DCI can be viewed as a culmination of many design goals over the years. In particular, this chapter illustrates how DCI addresses the fundamental issues that have arisen when drawing human users into code design. Such problems have manifested themselves as misfits in the worldview of object orientation in the modern school, and we show how we address them with the DCI paradigm.

2.1.1 Agile apologia

It should, but sadly cannot, go without saying that these perspectives on design support what today is broadly called "agile" in software. At the highest level, DCI is a celebration of the human in computing in the sense that the original goals of object orientation (OO) also put the end user at center stage. A postmodern perspective is firmly ensconced in "[i]ndividuals and interactions over processes and tools" [3]; this facet shows through in DCI's emphasis of interactive software and human mental models. DCI is a boon to code intentionality at the system level, which many hold to be the *vade mecum* of software architecture, in obvious support of "working software over comprehensive documentation" [3]. Embracing human mental models and including architecture in the user interface, developed through the socialization of domain models and use cases, recalls "customer collaboration over contract negotiation" [3]. And a careful separation of the dominant shear layers of software development—domain data and business use cases—is high-order evidence of "responding to change over following a plan" [3].

2.1.2 Architecture and DCI

It is possible to present DCI as a programming technique that emphasizes object models and interactions between objects rather than classes. At a higher level, however, DCI is more properly considered as a paradigm for system construction that entails fundamentally different mental models than its predecessors. Just as the architecture of the built world progresses through paradigm shifts, such as the school of the *beaux-arts* giving way to art nouveau and art deco in turn, so DCI introduces a new paradigm of software design at the level of software system architecture.

2.2 THE VISION: WHAT IS ARCHITECTURE?

Architecture is a longstanding metaphor for software design and construction and particularly for programming-in-the-large. Software engineering has largely embraced this metaphor in many forms, ranging from the use of the software title *architect* to the metaphors offered by the pattern discipline.

Architecture is the form of any system created through conscious design, and it thus has strong human elements both in its process and its product. The term *form* implies a deep mental model of the essence of some structure. A structure has form; a given form awaits implementation in structure. For example, an image comes into your mind when we invoke the word *chair*. For most people it's not a wholly concrete image: it may not even have a color until the question causes you to assign it one. We might suggest that we meant to have you think of a five-legged chair and, although you are likely to have envisioned only four legs, you likely will not protest that such a structure violates the *form* of *chair*.

A software architecture may characterize many different systems with potentially different features implemented in different programming languages. We are likely to say that two different consumer banking systems have the same architecture even though they offer accounts with many different parameters. Form is the deep essence of what is common between these systems, just as Victorian architecture is the essence of common elements across innumerable houses. Victorian architecture, client-server architecture, and model-view-controller (MVC) architecture are about form. That they drive structure doesn't mean that they can't be conceptualized independent of structure. In fact, the presence of structure obfuscates form with distracting detail and nonessential elements. Architecture drives to the essence of a system.

The term *architecture* broadly touches a host of concerns in the built world, which perhaps can best be summarized in the terms popularized by the late Roman architect Vitruvius: *utilitas*, *firmitas*, and *venustas*. As captured by these terms, much of the classic architectural vision speaks of quality of human life. While the link of architecture to fashion and even to esthetics is controversial [4], commodity and utility (*utilitas*) are fundamental; so is beauty. Architecture is not without an engineering component that encompasses materials and techniques of construction, as good construction must be durable (*firmitas*) and arguably timeless [5]. Last, but certainly not least, architecture should inspire a human sense of delight (*venustas*). We can distill "delight" as comfort, beauty, or awe.

Because form is a result of design, and not of analysis, architecture lives squarely in the space of design. Architecture itself is therefore not principally about knowledge management, although knowledge management activities such as domain analysis and pattern mining often serve as powerful preludes to architecture. It is exactly this confusion in software, however, that often distances architecture efforts from the code and breeds skepticism among coders. Nowhere has this split become more pronounced than in the transition of software to agile software development, which is largely a movement among designers and coders.

2.2.1 Why do we do architecture?

It might be useful to revisit some of the key goals of architecture. As mentioned above, Vitruvius reduced the purpose of architecture to *utilitas* (commodity or utility), *firmitas* (firmness), and *venustas* (delight). These goals echo strongly in software, which has adopted them with its own emphases. More broadly, architecture is, and always has been, about *form*. Except among specialists, the English word *form* is often confounded with structure, and software folks in particular often incorrectly infer that a system's architecture is the *structure* of its artifacts.

The proper architectural usage of the term *form* has historically been more precise. It is important to differentiate form from structure: Form is the essence of structure. We can talk in detail about the form of gothic cathedrals even without having a gothic cathedral at hand. Form is the conceptualization of structure in terms of the relationship among parts and between the parts and their environment. Many given structures can implement a given form, just as there are many (different) gothic cathedrals, all of which implement the forms of gothic cathedrals.

2.2.2 Into software

These fundamental notions of the built world found parallels in the 1960s world of software construction. The architecture metaphor for software development, and particularly for programming-in-the-large, originated with Fred Brooks in the 1960s.

Brooks himself was a bit skeptical of his own brainchild but, after discussions with Jerry Weinberg, became convinced of its metaphoric value for the software world [6].

Software has strongly embraced this metaphor, both for its casual parallels to programming-in-the-large on one hand and for some of its specific techniques on the other. Software engineering tends to emphasize the former, with the strongest parallels relating to the concerns around the coarse or large structure of software and how it relates to the prominent architectural features in the framing of an edifice in the built world. The pattern discipline [5] is an example of the latter, whose philosophies of local adaptation and piecemeal growth became an alternative to big-up-front-design in the 1990s and flourished in the guise of the agile movement in the ensuing decade.

The architecture metaphor flourishes in software engineering literature today. The engineering and architectural metaphors arose only a few years apart. It should come as no surprise that the architectural metaphor stands out most strongly in the software engineering community, which views software as an extension of the engineering metaphor. Software engineering would expand rapidly as a metaphor in the late 1960s because of its popularization by Peter Naur in conjunction with the nascent software engineering community and its first conference in 1968 [7]. As with all metaphors, this one isn't perfect, but it tends to be more strongly flawed than most other metaphors, including that for architecture [8].

Today, the architectural principles of the built world continue to be mirrored in its software namesake in varying degrees. One can most often find the principles of *firmitas* in software engineering's exercising of the analogous English language terms *stability* and, more indirectly, *maintainability*. Software engineering's exploration of *utilitas* is isolated largely to the area of requirements management and formalism, touching the final built product largely through automated requirements translation rather than any act of design. *Venustas* in software languishes in the branches of both software architecture and software engineering, making only an occasional appearance in the human–computer interaction (HCI) and user experience (UX) fields, which have their own communities that are again often distanced from implementation or any human concern. In fact, the industry definition of software engineering itself is rather devoid of any human properties such as *venustas* or even *utilitas*: "The application of a systematic, disciplined, quantifiable approach to the development, operation, and maintenance of software" [8].

Architecture thrives in a more humane way in the pattern community, outside software engineering, where beauty is still valued. However, the pattern community has paid little heed to utility; it is still largely a community of architecture for the coders, whose carpenter-like perspective is often indifferent to and sometimes antagonistic to end-user *venustas*. There are noteworthy counterexamples, of course, particularly in the HCI community (e.g., [9]), which struggles to bear the standard of *venustas* for the industry.

2.2.3 Why software architecture?

If building architecture is about *utilitas*, *firmitas*, and *venustas*, what is software architecture about? Here, the parallel between the architecture of the built world and software architecture works in good measure.

Most software architecture literature emphasizes *firmitas* in the guise of *maintainability*. Software first must work when it is delivered, and then keep working as requirements change. Even building architects emphasize the role of good architecture in supporting evolution through changing requirements, as Brandt describes in his classic *How Buildings Learn* [10]. Good architecture also offers building blocks, vocabulary, and world models necessary for worthy software.

Some software architecture schools (and the pattern discipline in particular) emphasize the notion of *venustas*: the beauty of software. Most software literature emphasizes the beauty of the code. We are exhorted to write clean codes [11] or, taking the architectural metaphor more literally, habitable codes [2]. But there is another aspect to *venustas* that too often goes unheeded in software, and particularly among the software engineering crowd: the *venustas* of the interface. Good interfaces are attractive and usable. This deep kind of beauty goes beyond what just graphic designers do, but touches deep mental models in the end user.

This perspective on *venustas* leads us directly into *utilitas*. Does architecture relate to usability? In fact, the program structure and the end-user structure have much to do with each other in an object-oriented system: that is much of the essence of Kay's Dynabook vision and of the MVC vision. It's about matching machines to people in much the same way that architecture matches a house to its inhabitants. This fact is lost on most contemporary programmers. The interface is the product; the code is just the stuff that has to go along to make it work [12, p. 5].

2.2.4 Architecture and the agile agenda

An agile approach is as much a *sine qua non* of contemporary development as architecture might have been in the 1980s. After the birth pangs of Agile dismissed the value of up-front architecture, or at least marginalized it, the industry is coming around to a more moderate position that accommodates a tenuous co-existence between them. DCI is one of the leading comprehensive approaches that span this territory, as well as spanning the range of concerns from domain analysis down to coding concerns, and everything in between.

In this chapter, as we examine the relationships between agile, architecture, and DCI, the question certainly arises about what boundaries to draw around *agile*. Agile development as a titled movement is young, dating back to the Agile Manifesto in 2001 [3]. Nonetheless, like all manifestos, it standardized what at the time was broadly established practice [13]. A look at history and publications suggests that its popularity can be traced back to a turning in the industry that started gaining momentum in the early 1990s. The 1990s became the decade of doubt, during which many sacred cows fell or were at least wounded. Architecture was unfortunately one of the casualties, but it has newfound legs and is regaining credibility as the industry discovers that emergence alone doesn't create good designs in time frames that the market expects.

The original agile agenda took an anti-architecture turn in reaction to the top-down, overly prescriptive architecture techniques of the 1980s. (*Those* in turn were a reaction to the perceived lack of software discipline in the 1960s and 1970s.)

Instead of looking to architecture (form), this new generation would look to *processes*, in the sense of autopoietic (self-maintaining) systems. The hope was that architecture would become emergent, thereby skirting the delay and cost of big up-front architecture efforts. The Agile Manifesto [3] attempted to capture this perspective through its focus on people, communications, pragmatism, market connection, and flexibility over stipulated processes and technologies. Agile would echo and amplify the pattern community's early leanings away from modernism toward postmodernism.

2.2.5 DCI as an integrative view of the architecture metaphor

One can view DCI as a way of integrating the positive contributions of diverse communities such as HCI, software engineering, software architecture, and programming language. DCI strives to embrace the end UX, the need for low-cost software comprehension and extension, while still maintaining stable software artifacts with long service lives and providing a practical and elegant expression of its practice in accessible programming language technology. DCI didn't come about as an engineered solution to a wish list of such needs, but as a worldview rooted in the broad concerns of the relationship between computers and their users.

What does that worldview look like? It's about thinking of the computer as an extension of self that is, as Raskin says, "responsive to human needs and considerate of human frailty" [12, p. 6] and that serves human value. This means being attentive to the mental models both of end users and of programmers. End users care most about what the system *does* while expecting the system to support their mental model. Programmers are also concerned about what the system *is*. In the same sense that the architecture of a village, or a resort, or an individual house is an extension of self—an ecosystem of forms that provide a framework for symbiosis between its inhabitants—so should the computer be an extension of its human subjects. This comes down to simple concepts like clear interaction metaphors, parallelism between programming constructs and the mental constructs of the end users, and clearly understandable program code. Most of these concepts relate to form, and that puts us squarely in the center of architectural dialog.

2.3 FORM AND FUNCTION IN ARCHITECTURAL HISTORY

It's instructive to locate DCI's place in the march of programming history, extrapolating its trajectory from past practices that will be familiar to most readers here. We find striking similarities in the progression of ideas in the arts and in the architecture of the built world, particularly as regards the age-old discussion of form versus function, as well as the place of control versus harmonization, and of technology versus human concern.

The built world and software would jointly consider these questions in the Design Movement—a loose collection of workshops, essays, and books in the 1970s and

1980s [14,15]. Peter Naur of computing fame was among them, and the building architect Christopher Alexander—whose name would later become synonymous with patterns—was a major contributor to this body of literature. The debates and innovations of this era provide an interesting backdrop against which to discuss the DCI paradigm.

The modernist school of design could be said to dominate most of software history, and certainly its foundational years. Software gained its footing in a 1960s culture that firmly believed in the triumph of technology, including bold visions of artificial intelligence (that seem to resurge every few years with much less accompanying progress) and robots to automate our daily chores. In concert with this shiny, robotic world we find very little *venustas* in software. And while the times shaped our vision of software, it's noteworthy that software also shaped the times. Consider this man-bites-dog 1965 quote from Archer [16]:

> *The most fundamental challenge to conventional ideas on design, however, has been the growing advocacy of systematic methods of problem solving, borrowed from computer techniques and management theory, for the assessment of design problems and the development of design solutions.*

Software focused on construction, perhaps because it could: notions of coupling and cohesion, apart from their roots in organizational concerns, were easy to understand and to reduce to a number. With the echoes of 1960s modernism resonating from a recent past, the programming community gravitated naturally to these numbers that conveyed a sheen of science. It was all about *technical* goodness. Christopher Alexander would take note of this trap in the software world as late as the mid-1990s [17]:

> *Please forgive me; I'm going to be very direct and blunt for a horrible second. It could be thought that the technical way in which you currently look at programming is almost as if you were willing to be "guns for hire." In other words, you are the technicians. You know how to make the programs work. "Tell us what to do, Daddy, and we'll do it."*

This worldview is so strong in software that it is taken for granted. It's important at some point to emphasize that the software world adopted the architectural metaphor selectively, and this would be a good time to raise this issue. Of deeper importance here is that much of its use of metaphors is uninformed. A good example is the cacophony of attempts to automate pattern detection in programs, with a concomitant flurry of publications. None of them cite Alexander's own earlier forays into this territory, their failure, and the fundamentals beneath the failure [18].

Another longstanding foible of the software community lies in the confusion of form with structure. Early architects turned to platforms and modules first, and protocols and interfaces only second, in their realization of the architectural vision. Architecture has always been closely coupled to the idea of reuse, and reuse almost always played out at the level of masses of software. Though the underlying economic motivations of this position were lost on few, there seemed to be few alternatives. Libraries and platforms flourished. This approach would be tempered somewhat with the rise of frameworks—partially filled-out architectures—only in the 1990s, some 30 years after the rise of the architectural metaphor in software.

Form suffered more subtle slights at the hands of software practice. Form, in architecture, starts either in the eye of the beholder or, as Alexander would have it, in deep processes that transcend even human existence. This notion dominates the conscience of the architectural profession in its use of the term. Software more commonly adapts a more vulgar use of the term rooted in engineering and technique. In the world of class-oriented programming, snippets of system behavior don't exist outside the form of classes. Even in prototype-based approaches (such as that espoused by *self* [19]) behavior follows structure (of instances) rather than form. *Venustas* suffers directly, and *utilitas* in a less direct way.

2.3.1 Historic movements and ideologies

There are strong parallels between *L'École des Beaux-Arts* and the primordial hacker culture of programming in 1960s-era MIT. The metaphor continues on the side of the built world into the mass-produced art of the Great Exhibition in the Crystal Palace in London in 1851, and the Arts and Crafts movement; in the advent of Software Engineering at the Garmisch conference in 1968 and the rapid rise of reuse and structured design; and in the Arts and Crafts movement in England in 1861 and the rise of "anthropomorphic" techniques of object orientation in the 1980s. Objects were, in many ways, the *art nouveau* of the programming world.

Even as architecture would evolve through *art nouveau* and *art deco* into the modernism of the twentieth century, so object orientation would become a diminishingly human-centric concept in an increasingly technology-based community. The same kind of linguistic focus one finds in James Joyce's literature could be found in the language wars of 1980s computer science. The technological focus of modernism maps to the case tool craze of the 1980s. And the increasing focus on twentieth-century objectivism found a natural home in the 1980s' programming notion of objects: manifestations of concrete, real-world things.

Software architecture took a strange turn in the 1990s as the object-oriented programming community discovered patterns. The concept of patterns was refined in the built world by architect Christopher Alexander, a postmodernist who detests card-carrying postmodernists. In Alexander's definition, patterns are incrementally built elements of form necessary to the wholeness of, or a kind of quality that defies delineation of, some built whole. Each one transforms the whole from a less-whole state to a more-whole state. These patterns link together in a grammar that contextualizes each one and that imposes constraints on their ordering of application.

Software practitioners adopted the pattern metaphor to describe what they knew were essential forms of custom construction in specific domains. Because they are customized to a domain or particular problem, they aren't the general fodder of academic literature. The pattern community in fact consciously distanced itself from academic sponsorship and discarded academic mores of originality in favor of the broad practices of communities in the wild [20].

These foundations of patterns constituted a left turn because, first, they were more of a conscious departure from the *status quo* than a complementary framework to it. Good patterns didn't describe how to do object-oriented programming—that is, they did not take ordinary object-oriented staples such as encapsulation, polymorphism, and inheritance as their building blocks. Rather, they tended to describe how to create code when pure object ideals or directly applied language constructs failed. Patterns became a way to describe how to survive software development when saddled with the dire constraints of object orientation, and they gave legitimacy to constructs that consciously violated sacred principles, such as identity (most Gang of Four (GOF) patterns [21] break it), cohesion (most GOF patterns achieve their goal by distributing computation into additionally created objects), subtyping through inheritance (patterns such as Façade allow simulation of inheritance with cancelation), and so forth.

Beyond this technical redirection we find even deeper ideals. Patterns grew up outside the community of software architecture and largely outside the field of software engineering; you find pattern literature in those fields only late in the maturity of the community. Rather than adhering to the largely technical agenda of those communities, patterns were explicitly about people. Patterns clearly blossomed in part because the early days of object orientation had laid the foundation for a human agenda of programming through approaches such as anthropomorphic design, and through the link that MVC created between objects and the human clients of computation. Elaboration of any true human agenda within object orientation itself was largely muted in the 1980s by the louder voices of programming language (modernism and James Joyce again) and automation (Computer-Aided Software Engineering (CASE) tools).

2.3.2 Enter postmodernism

Computing today is enmeshed in a long-running slog of transition into postmodernism: the triumph of ideas over objects [15, p. 8]. These same terms that are used in the arts apply equally as well to software, and will figure in our dissection of DCI. In software, the pattern discipline of the 1990s published the first tomes of progress in this area. Like its counterpart in the built world and in movements such as *art deco*, the postmodern software world is focused on software for the masses, on compositional strategies over individual parts, and a focus on change rather than static beauty: "... to live in a perpetual present and in a perpetual change that obliterates tradition" [22]. We find these notions in the rise of intentional programming, generative programming, multi-paradigm design, and aspect-oriented programming (AOP).

2.3.3 Architecture finds an object foothold

As generations of programmers are born into settings that are increasingly removed from Fred Brooks' environs, year after year, so the mores of the software engineer's version of architecture diverge increasingly from the roots of architecture in the built world.

Grady Booch arguably stood as the original doyen of object-oriented software architecture. It was largely through his extensive work and leadership that the object community came to embrace the architectural metaphor. Booch will best be remembered for his contribution to system modeling and to his cloud-icon notation, affectionately referred to as "Booch diagrams." Along with Jacobsson's use case contributions [23], it would later modulate the largely Object Modeling Technique (OMT)-based semantics of the Unified Modeling Language (UML).

Most practitioners from the past two decades of the last century will remember class diagrams as the primary useful component of UML, certainly as regards architecture. Jacobsson's use cases, in the meantime, were relegated an important position alongside of, but not central to, architectural concerns. Architecture became synonymous with *structure*; behavior was something else. Architecture and class diagrams were for architects; use cases and message sequence charts were for analysts. And it was the job of the programmers—software's ersatz carpenters—to reconcile these two perspectives. There were, of course, noteworthy exceptions. UML 2.0 would compensate for UML 1.0's paucity in this area, but did so at the expense of visual verbosity. Service-Oriented Architecture (SOA) defined services, but at a level that was usually far removed from the code; it is probably a better metaphor for urban planning than for the architecture of a house.

Thus the object community stumbled into a dichotomy between form and function. Computer practitioners were perhaps predisposed to such a dichotomy anyhow: the previous generations had seen a split of records versus functions; I-space versus D-space; database versus process; entity-relationship versus data flow.

The architects of the built world were no strangers to this dichotomy of form and function, either. Design has often been a question of *utilitas* versus form.

2.3.4 Software engineering and architecture today

The same term in software more often relates to engineering practices than to the broader concerns of architecture. While architecture of the built world is indeed concerned about both the form of the whole (and, to a degree, of its parts) and about the engineering concerns of construction, software engineering tends to emphasize the structural, methodical, and mechanical concerns. The software architectural landscape is littered with formalisms that speak more to construction than aesthetics. Even when invoking the pattern metaphor, most software patterns are more about engineering concerns than about any explicit nod to *firmitas*, *utilitas*, or *venustas*. Alexander's original notion of generativity (indirect emergence of form) became confused with a notion of cleverness or obscurity, and patterns took more of a form of "aha" puzzles and their solutions than with human comfort or quality of life.

2.3.5 Measures of the vision

Software adopted architecture with the hope (justifiable perhaps only through revisionist thinking) that it would help teams create software structures that could be reasoned about in respective isolation. These units were informally called *modules*, and their degree of independence, *modularity*. Constantine proposed measures of good modularity based on the internal connectivity of a module (cohesion) and lack of connectivity between modules (de-coupling). Conway proposed that good modularity leads to team autonomy [24], and given that small, autonomous teams were more productive than monolithic groups, architecture would aid productivity.

More informally, architecture was seen as a discipline for the good of discipline. There is a tendency to believe that good architecture leads to systems that perform better and are more secure, but such claims relate less to any given architectural principle than to the timing of big-picture deliberations in the design cycle and to the proper engagement of suitable stakeholders. Architecture was an artifact that encouraged a front-loading of key activities that become awkward if pushed until too late.

In fact, the object paradigm was unwittingly created with noble architectural ends: support the creation of built artifacts that could adapt to and better support the quality of human life. Little of this rationale appears to owe to the architectural metaphor or any roots in design theory, but the two roads would cross many times after meandering independently for many years.

2.4 WHAT IS OBJECT ORIENTATION? ACHIEVING THE VISION

Computers were invented largely as mental aids. In inventing object-orientation, Alan Kay envisioned objects as a recursion on the concept of a computer. His metaphor of objects was that of a large network of interacting objects, each one of which was designed in-the-small to perform its own task well. From the perspective of the system architect, one can view such objects as bricks whose individual contributions to architectural semantics are low. Elements of human value would appear at larger scales as emergent properties arising from the interaction of these large numbers of individual objects with integrity.

2.4.1 The Kay model

As inferred above, Kay's vision can be interpreted from an architectural perspective, or system level, as a metaphor for self-maintaining ecosystems. A system's structure is a consequence of its local adaptations over time. The human's place in this system is as the translator of real-world nuggets into the language of the computer, at the level of its organs or, perhaps more instructively, of its cells. In the purest form of this system, the end user was removed from the burden of overall system design. Starting with a platform like Smalltalk, an end user could ideally express a few increments of interest where the computer could augment the end user's needs, and could make the system do their bidding by the incremental addition of a few objects.

It's crucial to note that the Kay model is highly distributed: It is in essence a network paradigm of computation. The overlap of this model with parallelism and concurrency is complex and difficult to delineate, and the industry is not yet at a point of integrating these perspectives, though there have been numerous research attempts to do so.

We can say that the Kay model expects order to arise as an emergent result from the construction and interaction of individual objects of integrity. This early aspect of object-oriented programming, amplified by the pattern discipline's love affair with emergence, can certainly be identified as one of the roots of the agile ideology.

In what too easily can be considered a side note, Kay was acutely aware of the fundamental dynamic aspects of human mental models. Returning to the original Dynabook paper [25], we find:

> *Two of Piaget's fundamental notions are attractive from a computer scientist's point of view.*
>
> *The first is that knowledge, particularly in the young child, is retained as a series of* operational models, *each of which is somewhat ad hoc and need not be logically consistent with the others. (They are essentially algorithms and strategies rather than logical axioms, predicates, and theorems.)*

2.4.2 Mental system models

Doug Englebart had earlier developed even deeper foundations for what later was to become object-oriented programming. Rather than thinking of the computer as an externalized tool or component, his vision incorporated the computer as an extension of human capabilities. Englebart speaks of augmenting the human intellect (though his work doesn't focus on the internal structuring of programs).

Behind Englebart's vision stand human mental models and a hope to extend those models into the computer. It became an early goal of object-oriented programming to capture those models. Kay writes [25]:

> *We feel that a child is a "verb" rather than a "noun," an actor rather than an object; he* is not *a scaled-up pigeon or rat; he is trying to acquire a model of his surrounding environment in order to deal with it; his theories are "practical" notions of how to get from idea A to idea B rather than "consistent" branches of formal logic, etc. We would like to hook into his current modes of thought in order to influence him rather than just trying to replace his model with one of our own.*

More prominently, MVC and Kay's brainchild Smalltalk would use objects to capture these mental models in the running program, in the "mind" of the machine.

2.4.3 Model-view-controller

MVC embraced Englebart's vision of computers as extensions of the human mind, and translated that vision into an object-oriented world in which an interactive human interface played a central role. This interactivity was central to Englebart's notion of mental augmentation.

The central architectural paradigm, then, was to maintain synchronization between the end-user worldview and its representation as computer data. As with most design paradigms, the major organizing principle was partitioning. MVC's main partitioning structure is its *views*, each one of which corresponds to some *tool* by which the end user interacts with the computer. At a lower level, each tool comprised a dynamically assembled network of objects. Thus, the architecture had a large dynamic component of changing object connections and changing views. For any given view, there was a relatively stable configuration of objects that could be characterized by the same pattern: the relationships between its *models*, the *view* itself, and the *controller*. The *models* are the computer representation of the end-user mental model of some object, and in fact are what programmers usually think of in association with the term *object*. The *view* arranges the presentation of those objects to the end user, usually in a visual form. The *controller* is responsible for creating and coordinating views and, together with the views, handles operations such as selection.

It is important to understand that MVC was not conceived as a library-on-the-side to add interactivity to a working program, but rather as the nervous system of the silicon part of the human–computer system. More broadly, MVC as an architectural paradigm includes the end user as well, and we now use the name MVC-U—where U stands for the end user—to emphasize this aspect of its design.

2.4.4 Patterns

The software pattern discipline took major departures from the Alexandrian vision of architecture, and these departures are no more apparent anywhere than in object-oriented practice. The *Design Patterns* book [21] was selective in its application of Alexandrian ideals. On one hand the GOF recognized that software has crosscutting constructs that aren't visible in the code, but are nonetheless part of the design vision of the programmer. This notion of scaling beyond individual objects to relationships takes us firmly into the realm of architecture.

Patterns were arguably one of the strongest foundations of the agile agenda. The ideas of piecemeal growth and local adaptation that are fundamental to pattern-based developments would be taken up almost verbatim by the pattern community. Agilists would embrace Alexander's valuation of human concerns over method less than a decade later.

2.4.5 Use cases

Human users usually approach a system with a concrete use case in mind. When you go up to an ATM, you bring your withdraw-money script or transfer-money script with you in your head. You have to learn it from scratch only the first time; the MVC approach helps your right brain train your left brain as you gain repeated experience with the script, or use case. The use case eventually becomes part of your left-brain mental model: this is long-term learning. This model has strong links to the right brain and its conceptualization of the "things" of the user world.

These use cases are only *complicated* (short of being *complex* or *chaotic*) in the Snowden taxonomy [26], which suggests that the emergence-based model of object system behavior is overkill while paradoxically being impoverished in intentionality. Class-oriented code is hard to write and harder to maintain. The programmer cannot reason about how the end-user conceptualizes system functionality, which ends in a modeling stalemate between the end user and the programmer [27]. An example of a consequence of this mismatch is the frustration one experiences with a popular word processor when trying to insert a graphic in the middle of a paragraph: the mental models for the programmer and end user are clearly different.

Contrary to the Kay paradigm, the use case paradigm is a centralized view of computation. Use cases aren't really part of the "object canon." (Jacobsson's use cases indeed have an object model, but it is a meta-model that structures related scenarios rather than the mental models within scenarios.)

UML was an attempt to bring use cases together with the more data-centric facilities of the Booch method [28], drawing largely on Rumbaugh's OMT notation. The result is neither a paradigm nor a computational model, but a language for communicating such models or paradigms.

Use cases have a reputation of being anti-agile because they were widely abused in the 1980s. However, they are curiously suitable to incrementally structuring requirements in agile, and overcome many of the risks of the more popular concept of user stories [29].

2.4.6 **Many views of objects and the boundaries of MVC**

The MVC vision in many ways tried to reconcile the network paradigm of Kay with the use case paradigm. It embraced the communication paradigm that one can extrapolate from Kay's vision: that is, that at its foundation, a system is a collection of many cooperating objects. On the other hand, MVC focused on the link between the objects and human mental models in concert with Englebart's vision of computers (and objects by extension) as human mental adjuncts. The vision goes back to thing-model-view-controller in 1978 [30], which evolved into MVC. By drawing the human being into the world of interacting objects, MVC investigates the nature of interactions between objects—interactions that have their roots in the end-user mental model.

While Kay expressed his vision in terms of networks of communicating objects, he relegated the intelligence of design—of programming—to the level of the individual objects themselves, trusting the structure of their interworking to self-organization. This perspective is much in line with Alexander's vision of emergent structure. This perspective tacitly supported the idea that objects could be designed from the inside looking out instead of precipitating from a wider perspective of their place in system behavior. Unfortunately, this viewpoint became institutionalized in the class: a way of designing individual objects from their identity as individuals rather than their roles in contextualized system operations.

MVC has only scratched the surface of Kay's communication paradigm. MVC captured the way that people view the "things" in the computer's representation of their world. In the programmer's world, this is the program-in-the-large or, grossly, the form of the system data. The part of MVC that helps people understand the whole of the data forms necessary to a given set of related tasks speaks largely to the right brain. The brain takes in the screen information as a whole without specifically analyzing each part or its functionality. At any given time we have a static worldview and a static architecture, poised to transition into a successor static worldview after some event (usually from the user) drove the computer through useful business processing. This processing was opaquely relegated to the model part of MVC, and it was easy to map MVC models onto Kay's autonomous objects.

Once the user has established this connection with the computer—which typically takes 10 seconds [31]—the end user now sets about achieving a business goal. That goal often entails multiple interactions between the user and the system following a script in the user's mind. This script is a *gestalt*, though it can be chunked along the boundaries between the end users' classifications of the "things" in their world according to use. When in this operational mode, we conceive of real-world things according to their use in the moment; in a rain shower, a newspaper becomes a hat; for a motorcyclist, a garbage bag becomes rain gear. The left brain is dominant in carrying out these interactions towards the business goal: a focused, analytical use of the program-in-the-small.

This worldview isn't so easy to map into Kay's model because the end-user details of object behavior do cut across objects but are stable in the long term. There was nothing in object architecture that provided a reasonable home for a (static) architectural representation of these dynamics. By contrast, the procedural world of Fortran, Pascal, and C gave a home to these models at the expense of the right brain.

MVC didn't attack this right-brained aspect of user mental models. Other tool metaphors arose for these activities, most of them falling outside the architectural metaphor, and few of them led to concrete engineering practices. One powerful idea that combined both these worlds was Laurel's vision of the HCI through the metaphor of theater, where the objects in a system become reminiscent of actors in a play and the user becomes a member of the audience [27]. But the most popularized model of the interactions between people and computers came in Ivar Jacobsson's use cases [23].

Sadly, both the Fortran/Pascal model and the use case model viewed what-the-system-is and what-the-system-does as separate concerns. That naturally led to the creation of separate artifacts in design and programming. Multiparadigm design [32] advised us to use procedures for algorithmic-shaped constructs and classes for the more static elements of design; this led to terrible patterns of coupling between the two worlds.

The idealistic Kay vision suggests that individual, small methods on small objects would naturally interact to do the right thing. A good metaphor is to compare these objects with people in a room who are asked to divide themselves into four groups of approximately equal size. It seems to work even without any central control. Snowden characterizes such systems as *complex systems* [4]. In summary, the original object vision didn't go far enough to capture the essence of the real world it was meant to model.

2.5 SHORTCOMINGS OF THE MODELS

Software's dance with architecture was initially exploratory and playful, but the years have hardened it either into law or habit. Many of the paradigms of the early years became institutionalized in programming languages, methodologies, and standards. In retrospect, experimentation with the metaphor stopped too early, and today it's difficult to gain acceptance for any notion of "architecture" that lies outside the hardened standards. Many of our previous attempts to describe DCI on an architectural level have fallen on deaf ears because the self-titled architects can't recognize it as falling within their sphere of influence or exercise of power, and so they too easily dismiss it.

Architects speak of *shear layers* in built artifacts. Different parts of a house evolve more rapidly than others; a house needs a new roof every few years but rarely needs a new exterior wall. Good architecture provides good interfaces that separate the shear layers of its implementation: a necessity for evolution and maintenance. Class-oriented programming puts both data evolution and method evolution in the same shear layer: the class. Data tend to remain fairly stable over time, while methods change regularly to support new services and system operations. The tension in these rates of change stresses the design.

DCI is an attempt to overcome these elements of structural inertia by returning to first principles and the deep elements of object foundations. Its premises seem to be born out in early experimentation and application. The rest of this chapter will focus on the dialog between the pre-DCI world and *status quo* to help readers hone their understanding of the state of the art in object-oriented programming.

2.5.1 The network paradigm

Kay's original formulation missed the what-the-system-does component of design. It worked fine for simple programs where each unit of business functionality can be encapsulated in an object, but it left no place to reason about system behavior across objects. Further, Kay and Ingalls rolled out this vision in a language called Smalltalk, which was widely adopted as a way to implement designs based on class thinking and class models rather than object models.

The class model places the programmer inside of the object, cognizant of its internal workings and constructions, but insulated from the interactions between its own objects and other objects in the system. This is a strange man-bites-dog reversal of the normal sense of encapsulation. The same class boundary that protects the internals of a design from concerns outside the interface, so that the programmer can reason about them locally, also insulates the programmer from the crucial design concern of interactions between objects. Each class ignores other classes' design concerns—and since there is nothing but classes in a class-oriented language, there is no locus of understanding relationships between classes.

Programming languages institutionalized this paradigm through encapsulation techniques. Programming environments provide little aid for reasoning about any structure beyond the class. One can argue that good environments express inheritance relationships between classes; however, inheritance is only a syntactic convenience that leaves the computational model untouched. Further, it is a temporary compile-time artifact that lies between human mental models in analysis and object instances at run time. It doesn't change the semantics of any object-oriented program if we flatten all base classes into a single derived class composition.

Design methods also institutionalized this worldview. One of the best known is responsibility-driven design, popularized through CRC (Classes, Responsibilities, and Collaborators) cards. While responsibility-driven design has the strong advantage of starting with scenarios or other use cases, the resulting artifacts ossify the behavior elements into static relationships between classes, as the name "CRC" exhibits. In fact, end users don't conceptualize system behavior in terms of classes (which are total classifications of form) but instead in terms of roles (which are partial classifications of form). Experience proved this to be a problematic approach. Rebecca Wirfs-Brock has since wanted to rename them to "RRC Cards" (Roles, Responsibilities, and Collaborators). She has instead kept the original acronym but has replaced "Class" with "Candidate"—like a *role* [33].

Good code conveys designer intent; great code captures end user intent. The ability of code to express intent is called *intentionality*. The embedding of the network paradigm, the class paradigm, and other early architectural metaphors for objects has caused intentionality of system behavior to dissolve. DCI restores this intentionality to architecture by explicitly capturing use cases in a contextualized form.

2.5.2 Model-view-controller

MVC missed the what-the-system-does component of design. It worked well for simple designs. MVC is better thought of as a virtual machine than as the architecture built on top of it. It encouraged the atomic interaction style of HCI innate in the Kay worldview: a paradigm that viewed each object as being able to handle the user request atomically without much consideration for *sequences* of tasks between objects and the end user. MVC has been institutionalized with varying degrees of fidelity into many environments, such as Apple's Cocoa framework.

MVC's interests are largely orthogonal to DCI; the two are complementary. Historically, MVC emphasized data over interaction. While most programmers followed this paradigm and took it not only as the primary metaphor but the exclusive metaphor for their system design, it is not exclusive of the use case focus afforded by DCI.

2.5.3 Patterns

Though the GOF patterns claim Alexander's vision as their heritage, they are so remote from Alexander's vision of architecture as to be barely recognizable as patterns. Alexander's forms bore a clear tie to the patterns of events that they supported;

there is little of this in the GOF patterns. Alexander's patterns were rooted squarely in the business domain and solved end-user problems; GOF patterns have no mapping to or from the users of the system. Alexander's patterns were fractal in scale; the GOF patterns live largely in the programming-in-the-small world.

Last, while most GOF patterns live in a class world rather than an object world, they hardly represent any uniform paradigm grounded either in objects or in classes. The overview of FAÇADE invokes the word *object* only once; *class* appears seven times [21, p. 185]. ITERATOR, however, mentions *class* six times and *object* nine times [21, pp. 257–258].

Because of their Alexandrian heritage, many OO practitioners came to believe that GOF patterns provided software architecture foundations. Software architecture practice embraced patterns, and that usually meant GOF patterns. This perspective reinforces the Kay programming-in-the-small model to this day.

2.5.4 Use cases

In the end, a program offers a service. Object-oriented design has poor intentionality for a use-case world model. Most object systems express and organize concepts closer to the program data model than to its process or behavior model. The data part of software architecture is certainly a crucial perspective, but it's only half the story. What's worse is that the data view fails to express most of the client value of a software product. We sell use cases, not classes, and not even objects: end users don't usually conceptualize system behavior in terms of classes.

From an architectural perspective, this leads the designer—who works at the source-code level—out of touch with the dynamics of the whole. The hope held by the network model is that emergence will win out.

From a broader perspective, it's noteworthy that OO became the technology of choice for reusable libraries of containers, user interface components, and other APIs where the programmer can reason within a single class about the consequences of a business operation. While objects took off in these infrastructure areas, they rarely thrived in applications with complex workflows.

DCI embraces the power of the emergence as in Alexandrian patterns but adds a focus on the *intent* of the design. A collection of well-constructed objects will no more generate meaningful system behavior on their own than a collection of building materials will generate a structure suitable for human activity (Figure 2.1). As such, DCI can be seen as a paradigm that builds on Kay's original vision of socially responsible objects working together to generate collective system behavior, but which extends that model to explicitly articulate intended behavior. This inclusion of intent leads us into the arena of system behavior, *its* form, and the articulation of this form.

One might ask: *whose* intent? The literature of contemporary software architecture is littered with allusions to the architect's intent. DCI holds the end user volition over that of the architect. This is more in line with the agile agendas of "individuals and interactions over processes and tools," and the agendas of customer collaboration, working software, and changes in the customer space [3].

FIGURE 2.1

Design emergence. www.cartoonstock.com

2.5.5 The object canon

Some object fundamentals are basic enough to transcend the schools of object orientation: encapsulation, polymorphism, and friends. Each of these design techniques brings its own problems: information hiding is good, but hidden things are hard to find; polymorphism is a form of hyper-galactic GOTO. DCI strives to address many of these problems.

2.5.5.1 Object-oriented programming isn't about classes

Few programmers program objects or design objects. The class is most often the unit of design. This is absurd from an architectural perspective. Architecture traditionally has been about creating the artifice delivered to the end user. Carpenters use scaffolding and tools to achieve the architect's vision, and a great architect will be in there with the carpenters swinging a hammer. Most contemporary architectural thinking, however, seems to leave behind any thoughtful relationship between form and function but focuses instead on the tools. This may well be because great architectural talent arises from domain knowledge, and it's difficult to treat architecture as a generic discipline within the (generic) discipline of programming. In the end, architecture has arisen as a generic discipline of tools rather than the result of a quest for beauty and utility.

The preponderance of class-thinking in software engineering likely arose from two sources: programming language technology, and interactive computing. Programming languages introduced types as a convenience that helped the compiler generate efficient code, and types were later adopted as a way to communicate a module's intent to its user. Class relationships such as subtyping, commonly implemented using inheritance, provided an attractive mechanism to link programmer modeling to the compiler-type system. This led to programming-by-increment using subclassing, as well as arguments for code reuse based on inheritance, that caught the imagination of software engineering. This was UML heaven.

Interactive computing inverted the traditional batch computational model. There is no human presence in a batch program, so the sequencing of function executions depends only on the data. Latency was not a core concern. Design becomes an issue of sequencing function invocations. In an interactive program, the human presence injects events into the program that result in unpredictable sequences of function invocations, and a quick response is imperative. Function sequencing is unpredictable, and the data model dominates. Classes were viewed largely as "smart data" and became the loci of design, with most of the functionality subordinate to the data model. Early object orientation thrived on the noun–verb model of computation, where the "verb" component was usually a simple, atomic operation that could be localized to a class. Use cases were too easily forgotten in deference to the computational model arising from point-and-click.

2.5.5.2 Class thinking isn't limited to class systems

The problem of single-object-think is aggravated by class orientation but is not unique to class-oriented thinkers. Most object methods are curiously reminiscent of a Kantian object world where individual objects act alone and programmers live inside of objects looking out: there is rarely any sense of collective behavior in object-oriented systems, and there is rarely any degree of behavioral (self-)organization. We are told that objects are smart data, but a closer inspection of both data and system behavior shows something profoundly amiss with that characterization.

2.5.5.3 Lack of locality of intentionality

Adele Goldberg used to say, "In object-oriented programming, it always happens Somewhere Else." Part of this owes to the innate thesis of object orientation itself: that intelligence is collective rather than localized. This shows up in three ways: polymorphism, deep object hierarchies, and deep class hierarchies.

Most object-oriented thinkers will link Adele's quote to polymorphism, which is a kind of hyper-galactic shift in execution context that occurs with each method invocation. Polymorphism hampers our ability to understand code statically: we can follow the sequencing of method invocations only at run time. It's perhaps no accident that there has been an increased focus on testing and techniques like test-driven development with the advent of object-oriented programming: If you can't analyze, test.

Second, object hierarchies tend to be deep. More precisely, objects usually lack a hierarchical structure but possess more of the structure of the network paradigm of computation. To an architect who bases a system on units that interact via interprocess communication, object orientation has the feeling of message passing and of asynchrony. Objects in fact embraced the message metaphor explicitly; that it might infer asynchrony or parallelism is perhaps unfortunate. That detail notwithstanding, object orientation still has the feel of a pass-the-ball style of computation. This is a serious obstacle to program comprehension and intentionality because the program counter passes many abstraction layers on its way to accomplishing its goal.

Object orientation is designed so we are not supposed to know where the program counter will end up on a method call: object encapsulation and method selection insulate us from that coupling. We gain syntactic decoupling; we lose system-level comprehension. The supposed semantic decoupling of objects participating in a use case is largely an illusion, because in the end, each method executes in the business context both of the preceding and ensuing execution. It is difficult to reason soberly about a method in isolation, with respect to business goals.

Third (and closely related to the second) is that class hierarchies are also deep. Let's borrow an example from our good friends in academia who seem wont to employ zoo animals and shapes in their pedagogical examples. Here is the `round-RectPrototype` method of `Rectangle`, from Squeak:

```
roundRectPrototype
    ∧ self authoringPrototype useRoundedCorners
            color: ((Color
                r: 1.0
                g: 0.3
                b: 0.6)
                alpha: 0.5);
            borderWidth: 1;
            setNameTo: 'RoundRect'
```

How many classes do you need to understand to fully understand this code? Most programmers will answer that we need just to understand `Rectangle`. In fact, objects of the `Rectangle` class include seven other `Rectangle` methods, but also reflect a flattening of a hierarchy including `Morph` (with 47 methods) and `Object` (with 30 methods). The illusion exists at compile time that I need to understand only this method or perhaps only this class. Programming languages hide the rest.

Much of program design, and programming language design, is in fact about separation of concerns. The lines that separate concerns can be thought of as reasoning boundaries whose goal is to delineate domains of comprehension. It's fine if such boundaries encapsulate the code relevant to a given "endeavor of understanding." But for non-trivial *system* behavior, class inheritance layering and object layering of object-orientation cut across the fundamental unit of business delivery: the use case. Further, the additional class boundaries along the inheritance hierarchy add accidental complexity from the perspective of reasoning about system operations. And polymorphism de-contextualizes method selectors enough to make it impossible to reason about the behavior of any contiguous chunk of static source code one writes in a given language and programming environment.

2.5.5.4 Summary of the shortcomings
All of these shortcomings can be summarized as variants on one theme:

> *Traditional object orientation organizes concepts at the extremes either of a rather free-form network structure or of a single, punitive hierarchy of forms.*

The DCI paradigm strives to express a network model rather than a hierarchy, but provides disciplines for intentionality of form rather than leaving it to emergence.

2.5.5.5 Epicycles: early visions of relief

Researchers over the years have recognized this problem and have discussed it in various guises, and a number of attempts have appeared to address it. Most of these solutions somehow relate to removing the limitations of thinking in a single Cartesian hierarchy by introducing richer forms of expression, all with the goal of higher code intentionality.

Howard Cannon's Flavors system [34] was an attempt to move beyond a strict classification that forced every object to be of one class at a time, to one that permitted the class itself to be a composition of multiple class-like things. Multiple dispatch [4] was an attempt to stop classifying methods in terms of their method selector and the single type of a single object, but instead to classify each method as potentially belonging partly to several classes at once. The *self* language [19] tried to destroy the very notion of classification as found in a traditional class, and to return to the object foundations that drew objects from the end-user mental model. Dependency injection [35] strove to blend the functionality of two objects into one. Multi-paradigm design [32,36] refused to view the world according to a single classification scheme, making it possible to carve up different parts of the system in different ways.

The goal of AOP is similar to that of mix-ins, except its crosscutting units are more invasive at a finer level of granularity. Aspects are reminiscent of multi-paradigm design in that they allow a degree of separation of function and structure, but aspects' functional structure is much richer. It is more like having multiple knives carving up the same part of the system at the same time, whereas multi-paradigm design ensured that the knives didn't cross. Further, AOP again is about thinking in classes rather than thinking in objects: it is a very static way to attach a kit of adjustments to a program at compile time, even though it uses reflection to achieve its end.

While most of AOP is about a decorative rearranging of code, and while that rearrangement arguably makes it more difficult to reason about aspectualized code, it in fact does provide a slightly enhanced computational model because of its emphasis on reflection. The original AOP vision is in fact rooted in reflection and a desire to apply the kinds of reflection available in Lisp to non-Lisp languages like Java. Still, more than 15 years after its conception, one of AOP's inventors points out that it has failed to live up to even one of the three propositions justifying its potential value [37].

Most of these architectural "advances" can be viewed metaphorically as ornamentation of a base architecture rather than new paradigms in their own right. Rather than fixing the fundamental flaws in the vision of the paradigm, they tended to "patch" the paradigm with respect to singular concerns of coupling, cohesion, or evolution.

These discourses wouldn't be the only time in history that epicycle-like structures would arise to rescue object orientation. Flavors in fact can be viewed as a precursor to the DECORATOR pattern; multiple dispatch and dependency injection, to the VISITOR pattern; multi-paradigm design, perhaps as a weak form of the STRATEGY pattern. None of these approaches underscored the original principles of object orientation;

rather, they offered localized repairs to the damage caused by applying the principles of class-based programming.

There are two notable techniques that challenged the hierarchical structures of class-based systems: a return to pure objects, and reflection.

The Actor paradigm [38] is typical of a pure object worldview. Its semantics are expressed in terms of interactions between objects that provide services, and it is a very good approximation to the network model. The *self* language challenged the notion of classes themselves. The *self* language, of course, can be viewed as an unabashed return to the fully network-based metaphor of computation in a way that applied it so uniformly as to minimize the problems of a class-based system. It's hard (but not impossible) to find hierarchy in the *self* world.

In the real world, many social interactions are in fact emergent while others (like the course of a train along its track) are designed in advance. Sometimes a design problem arises that is difficult to regularize in any architectural form. The software design-level parallels to this adaptation are reflection and introspection. This is the realm of meta-object protocols (MOPs). MOPs have failed to gain traction over the years for a number of reasons. They require a mindset change that cannot be rooted in static, syntactic program analysis alone; few programming languages have risen to the occasion to express it; and methods that lead to the right reflection structures are elusive.

2.6 DCI AS A NEW PARADIGM

DCI is a new paradigm of software architecture that emphasizes human mental models and improved system comprehension over class-oriented programming. Why is DCI a new paradigm? Many of its rules and tools are reminiscent of the most fundamental practices of class orientation: encapsulation, cohesion, objects with identity and state that represent local areas of domain concern, and so forth.

Part of what makes DCI a new paradigm is that it provides a new, expressive way to view some of the same semantics that lie latent in the network computational model. Real-world objects in fact don't interact randomly or with total blindness to their environment, but form communities and chains of responsibility. DCI makes these structures visible in ways that class-oriented design techniques do not.

Many of the resolutions to the single-hierarchy problem mentioned in Section 2.5.5.5 did not fundamentally change the taxonomy of form, and only AOP changed the computational model. DCI is less about decorating or augmenting existing form than about carving a new form out of space itself: the form of function.

DCI is also progressive in how it uses carefully constrained reflection to provide the flexibility necessary to express the kinds of re-associations between objects that arise in dynamic human mental models.

2.6.1 A DCI overview

We here give a brief overview of DCI from an architectural perspective. Such an overview cannot be complete in the space allotted. For more detailed information on DCI, see [39] or [40].

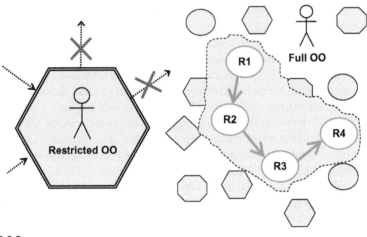

FIGURE 2.2

Comparison of Restricted OO and DCI worldviews.

In the previous section, we discussed the shortcomings of the class-oriented computational models. The shortcomings were related to the free-form network structure of objects and to a punitive hierarchy of forms. DCI employs intentional network structures and restricted classes to overcome these shortcomings.

Figure 2.2 serves as a background for the discussion. The shapes symbolize a universe of run-time objects. The system can be studied either from the inside of a particular object or from outside the objects in the space between them.

2.6.1.1 Full OO

In full OO, we see the outsides of the objects and the messages that flow between them. Each object appears as a service. Its inner construction is hidden by its encapsulation and does not concern us.

A DCI network has a bound form. It is intentional and is designed to achieve a certain use case. A particular execution involves a sequence of objects where each is responsible for fulfilling its part of the use case. Different executions of the same use case may involve different objects, but the network topology will remain the same. The nodes in the network are the *roles* that objects play, and the edges between them are the communication paths. The roles are wrapped in a DCI *context*; there is one such context for each use case. In Figure 2.2, the roles are marked R1, R2, and so on. There is an ephemeral bond between the role and the object behind it.

Communication is now a first-class citizen of computer programming.

2.6.1.2 Restricted OO

We are here placed on the inside of an object. We can see everything that is defined by the object's class with its superclasses. The class comprises both data and methods—state and behavior. The class won't appear in the code at run time; the intellectual concept called the class is absent. What exists is run-time objects. As we sit inside our class coding, it is difficult to reason about other classes. We already know this from the Kay model, or network model, of OO computation. We can envision those objects but we can't know much about them. In fact, object orientation explicitly prevents us from knowing anything about any other object in our program because interactions between objects are polymorphic. Seeing an invocation of method *bar* on object *foo* doesn't help us find *bar*. There is an explicit abstraction layer between objects that prevents us from reasoning about them in concert. For this reason, we restrict our classes from sending messages to objects in the environment. Such messages are blocked with red crosses in Figure 2.2. We call this style of programming Restricted OO because instances appear as self-contained services that are isolated from their environment.

While a restricted class says everything about the inside of an object and nothing about the objects surrounding it, a DCI context says everything about a network of communicating objects and nothing about their inner construction.

2.6.1.3 Data, Context, and Interaction

DCI is an acronym standing for *Data*, *Context*, and *Interaction*.

With DCI, we move all methods that relate to object interaction out of the classes, attach them to the roles in the appropriate contexts, and call them role methods. What remains are the *data* classes. They are Restricted OO because all interactions with the environment have been moved out. The roles are wrapped in a DCI *context* and their role methods collectively specify the *interaction* between objects that achieves a use case.

In a role method, we see an invocation of method *bar* on role *foo*. We know the method since it is attached to the role *foo*, and there is no polymorphism in a DCI context. We can, therefore, reason about the chain of methods that realize a use case.

There are three fundamental advantages of DCI. First, the complexity of the class is significantly reduced because it is Restricted OO and no longer contains any interaction code. Second, role methods now appear adjacent to the methods in their collaborator roles, thus keeping the code for the overall interaction algorithm in one place where we can inspect it and reason about it. Third, the context is adaptive and self-organizing because it binds the roles to objects afresh for each use-case invocation.

Bank accounts serve as a frequent DCI example, with classes for different kinds of accounts. We want to support a system operation to transfer money between those accounts. As designers, we envision ourselves in the run-time system and ask what objects we need and what responsibilities they must support to be able to transfer the money. One possible mental model has three roles: *Source Account*, *Destination Account*, and *Transfer Amount*. The role methods makes the *Source Account* decrement its balance by the *Transfer Amount*, after which it asks the *Destination Account* to increase its balance by the same amount.

Role names like *Source Account*, *Destination Account*, and *Transfer Amount* come directly from the end user mental model. You can easily reconstruct them by asking anyone around you to give a succinct, general description of how to transfer funds between their accounts, and listen carefully to what they say. They will refer to the objects involved in the transaction. More precisely, they invoke the names of those objects according to their roles in the money-transfer transaction. These are the new design entities, the roles, which form the locus of business logic.

The context encapsulates the roles, their logic, and the interactions between them. After all, roles make sense only in a context: these roles make sense only in the context of money transfer. We might call the class `MoneyTransferContext`.

Now we have a system of source code where the data, defined by the restricted classes, is separated from the business sequencing, defined by the context. We separate the shear layers of what-the-system-is and what-the-system-does for independent maintenance. System behavior and locally focused class methods evolve at different rates. In traditional architectures, they are linked in a single administrative unit that either can cause the stable parts to inadvertently become dependent on rapidly changing requirements, or make rapidly evolving code overly dependent on code with high inertia.

We need to return once more to run time. DCI depends on a powerful run-time environment that dynamically associates objects with the roles they play in a given use case. A program instantiates the appropriate context object at the moment it is asked to enact a use case. Each context in turn associates each role with an object that plays that role for the duration of the use case.

This association between roles and objects makes each object appear to support all of the corresponding role methods as part of its interface. While the DCI computational model doesn't stipulate how the run-time system should do this, it can be thought of as extending each object's method dispatch table with the methods for the roles it plays. This can be done by directly manipulating the dispatch table in single-hierarchy languages (e.g., Python or Smalltalk), and can be done with traits in languages that have a stronger dual-hierarchy tradition (Scala, Ruby, and C++). More advanced implementations affect a just-in-time binding between a role method and its object at the point of invocation.

2.6.2 Relating DCI to the original OO vision
2.6.2.1 How DCI achieves the vision of Restricted OO
DCI draws heavily on the domain modeling that one finds in both Lean Architecture [39] and in the original MVC framework [40]. MVC's first foundation is integrated domain services. The data classes in the DCI paradigm correspond almost exactly with the model classes of MVC.

Furthermore, DCI's primary computational model is based on objects rather than classes. One understands program behavior in terms of the logic in its roles; those roles are just behavior-annotated names for the objects involved in the use case. This is reminiscent of the network model of computation inherent in the original object vision.

2.6.2.2 How DCI overcomes the shortcomings of class-oriented programming

By capturing the system view of state and behavior, DCI and its grounding in mental models go beyond the more nerd-centric vision of late-1980s object orientation to the visions of mental augmentation and human-centeredness.

Though both DCI and the original object vision take networks as their model of computation, DCI reveals the network structure with more intentionality. Think of a train system as an analogy. Trains and train stations are objects. We can think of train behavior in terms of its arrival at a station: stopping, letting off passengers, closing the doors, and starting off again. We can think about stations in terms of receiving and sending off passengers. DCI captures the regular patterns of trains visiting successive stations by expressing the sequence of station stops. DCI makes the tracks between stations explicit. That helps us understand local operations (such as boarding or disembarking) in terms of the overall business purpose, which is to transport people between the station where they board and that at which they depart.

2.6.3 DCI and the agile agenda

The agile agenda discarded many trappings of modernism: the triumph of technology over nature, the notion of form being subservient to function (instead of function having its own form), the notion of automation (automatically generated code) in deference to human craftsmanship, and many more.

DCI is very much in line with these architectural shifts in agile. DCI is much more about mental models than about technology—more about the end user's intent than the architect's intent. Good software, like a good house, suits those who inhabit it. On the technology side, the focus is on thinking and the creation of good separation of form. While some technological underpinnings are of course necessary to support the DCI model of computation, this issue has not risen to the level of language debate or of a battle of technological prowess.

DCI leads the programmer and the user of the code (sometimes the same person) into a dialog that helps capture mental models in the code. DCI offers a home for the end user mental model directly in the code in contexts and domain classes. That obviates the need for an additional level of documentation, removing a level of handoff and translation between the end user and the programmer.

DCI audits favorably against the Agile Manifesto [3]. The agenda of "individuals and interactions over processes and tools" is evident in giving the human-computer interface full first-class status in use cases. This "individual" may be the end user whose use cases relate to the business, or the programmer whose use cases are likely classic algorithms. Instead of depending on intermediate documentation to express the requirements, we go quickly to the code where we express the mental model directly; that means that we're more likely to get working software than in the more myopic class-centered design. We focus on customer collaboration—both between the team and the client at the level of use cases, and between the product and the client at the level of the mental models. We lubricate change by separating the shear layers of data and function.

2.7 DCI AND ARCHITECTURE

DCI is in fact a radical break with the contemporary software architecture canon. Most software architecture metaphors are based on the source code or static (often class) structure. One darling of contemporary design is class hierarchy—a form that is absent at run time. Most contemporary expositions of run-time architecture are metaphors or computational models rather than models of form; actors [38] and reflection come to mind. The DCI paradigm explicitly captures run-time models in the architecture—the form of function.

We can view DCI as an architectural school firmly ensconced in the postmodern worldview. It breaks with the modernistic notion that the technology (e.g., coupling and cohesion) is primary and instead adopts a more utilitarian, human posture. It is less about language (most modern programming languages can express DCI designs) or implementation technology (there are many stylistic variants of DCI) than about the computational model shared across the mind of the end user and the mind of the machine.

Today's class-oriented architect can't easily envision the form of the running artifact because the associations between objects at run time are somehow too dynamic. DCI constrains the run-time connections to a form prescribed by the context, giving the architect the power to conceptualize and shape the run-time system (Figure 2.3).

Most important, DCI provides a home for the form of function. A context encapsulates the interaction of a set of roles. Each role describes how its corresponding object interacts with other roles to carry out a system operation. The network of interactions between roles (the *I* in DCI) is the form of that function.

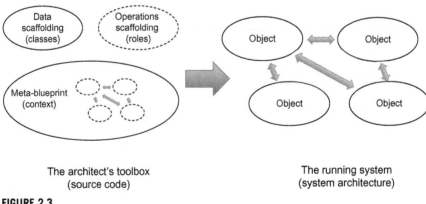

FIGURE 2.3

Designing a DCI application.

2.7.1 **DCI and the postmodern view**

DCI is an approach to system architecture that is characterized by several postmodern notions:

- Value ideas over objects, including the expression of the forms of both data and function;
- Favoring compositional strategies over individual parts;
- A broad-based, human-centric agenda; and
- Focus on change.

DCI has been embedded in a design approach called Lean Architecture [39] that has other aspects of the postmodern school, most notably the importance of process.

2.7.1.1 Ideas over objects

Architects of the built world have long been fascinated with form and function. The phrase "form follows function" is a vernacular English language idiom that stood as a truism for ages. Contemporary architects are wont to critique this posture and offer alternatives such as: "Form follows failure" [41], which evokes the need for change and dynamics in converging on a suitable architecture (Section 2.7.1.4).

Returning to object orientation's roots in a worldview of emergent behavior, we can view the form (think architecture) of a program as the result of accumulated learning over generations of program evolution. The accumulated knowledge is broadly called domain knowledge. Program form, then, has much of its roots in human conceptualizations of work. In the vein of postmodernism, DCI is about ideas over objects—more about the human side of systems than the system materials. These ideas take the shape of algorithms, use cases, or the patterns of arrangement of material beyond individual building blocks. DCI's role interactions help us reason about these ideas.

2.7.1.2 Compositional strategies over individual parts

The modernist school emphasized the primacy of structure. In the built world we find buildings like the Pompidou Centre in Paris that let the structure "all hang out." Class-based programming forces functional designers to become structural designers by thrusting them within a class framework. It is difficult to work at the level of pure form (e.g., abstract base classes) because there is no architectural home for functional concerns at the system level—only at the level of the data.

DCI is instead about compositional strategies: how to capture function and form and to reintegrate them under a computational model at run time. That model also integrates objects into a contextualization of their collective behavior. Programmers can now reason about system behavior because all code for any given use case is collocated in a single class. Execution hand-offs across objects (represented by roles) are statically bound rather than polymorphic.

2.7.1.3 A human-centric agenda

Team Autonomy: DCI data classes correspond to the domain organizational structure, and contexts correspond to system-level deliverables. Recalling Conway's Law [24], this structuring supports team autonomy. Class-oriented architectures split use-case code across the classes that form the major administrative units of object-oriented programming. In DCI, the code for a given use case is in the roles encapsulated by the single context class for that use case.

End-User Focus: DCI moves programming closer to the end users by embracing their mental models. It moves programming beyond the realm of a select few (called programmers) into the realm of the many (called end users). It places programming in an ecosystem of system behavior rather than a separate area of its own. This recalls postmodernism's shift from art for the elite to art for the masses.

2.7.1.4 Focus on change

Change is about the kind of human-centered context and relationships, larger than objects, of the DCI paradigm. Consider this postmodern insight [42]:

> *Complex systems are shaped by all the people who use them, and in this new era of collaborative innovation, designers are having to evolve from being the individual authors of objects, or buildings, to being the facilitators of change among large groups of people.*
>
> *Sensitivity to context, to relationships, and to consequences are key aspects of the transition from mindless development to design mindfulness.*

DCI realizes the pattern ideals of piecemeal growth and local adaptation to the extent that developers can add new use cases as stand-alone code modules independent of the domain structure.

DCI is not only about "design mindfulness," but more so about systems thinking. Being able to reason about use cases makes it possible to reason about system state and behavior instead of just object state and behavior. We can now reason about evolution at the system operation level in the context of supporting knowledge about market and end user-needs. This is architectural thinking; class-based programming is limited to organizing kinds of software building materials in class hierarchies.

The evolution of the form takes place at the level of social awareness or progress at the level of the ideas. This *idea* focus (discussed above in Section 2.3.2) is the first-order focus of change: Necessity is the mother of invention. Structure emerges from function during design. The functions of human endeavor arise from the supporting forms in the environment. DCI supports this function-centered focus in design as well as a structure-focused awareness in program use.

2.7.2 Patterns and DCI

Though patterns were broadly adopted for their power in describing geometric form (classes and objects), they in fact have strong roots in temporal geometry. Alexander prefaces his discussion of emergent structure with geometric patterns, but the geometric patterns are prefaced with a discussion of patterns of events. Indeed, Alexander sees deeply into a time–space relationship that makes it difficult to separate the two [5, pp. 65–66]:

> *It is the people around us, and the most common ways we have of meeting them, of being with them, it is, in short, the ways of being which exist in our world, that makes it possible for us to be alive.*
>
> *We know, then, that what matters in a building or a town is not its outward shape, its physical geometry alone, but the events that happen there.*
>
> . . .
>
> *A building or town is given its character, essentially, by those events which keep on happening there most often.*

This aspect of patterns is missing from almost all software practice. DCI is one of the first software architecture approaches to embrace and build on this aspect of Alexander's work.

DCI also echoes the Alexandrian agenda in its end-user focus. Alexander put house design in the hands of those who inhabit them. A house must relate to their mental model, to which end the architect must step aside [43, p. 38]:

> *On the other hand, people need a chance to identify with the part of the environment in which they live and work; they want some sense of ownership, some sense of territory. The most vital question about the various places in any community is always this: Do the people who use them own them psychologically? Do they feel that they can do with them as they wish; do they feel that the place is theirs; are they free to make the place their own?*

The architect should focus on fine craftsmanship and beauty that harmonizes the human perspective with context of use in a fundamental way that transcends culture. DCI is such an architectural framework, and it defers the cultural (domain) questions to the mental models of the occupiers of the code: the end users and the programmers. Classic software architects are likely to find this agile perspective disempowering.

It is possible to view DCI as a unification of two orthogonal architectures: the data architecture ensconced in classes (Restricted OO), and the behavior architecture ensconced in roles (the Full OO part). This view is particularly suitable to those who take a software construction perspective on architecture instead of thinking ahead to the run-time delivered system. A more subtle and deeper view of DCI notes that it in fact combines these two forms into one at run time, albeit dynamically in a way that is impossible to wholly capture in closed form. Yet the main rhythms and shapes of both the dynamics and statics can be expressed respectively in the roles and classes of DCI source code.

This view is very close to Japanese models of the relationship of space to time and the way that space provides potential for some happening in time (e.g., 間 or "ma", sometimes translated "space–time"). Such Japanese roots are at the core of Alexander's worldview. Alexander himself reveals this perspective in his writing [5, p. x]:

> *These patterns of events are always interlocked with certain geometric patterns in the space.*

and [5, p. 70]:

> *The activity and its physical space are one. There is no separating them.*

2.7.3 DCI and the network computation view

Perhaps one of the most telling distinctions of DCI is the place it relegates to the human in the design process. If we think of the network model of computation in the extreme, design and intelligence are local; system behavior is emergent.

Designers often put this network view on a par with patterns. Alexander's works feed this speculation with references to emergence and to techniques such as automatic writing. However, a closer inspection of Alexander makes the human component of his design world obvious. He speaks more often about the power of community in sustaining a pattern language than he does about the role of the architect.

In some sense, the network computation view was based on well-intentioned individuals, with the metaphor relating to localized design ownership and collective execution. But this model lacked Alexander's notion of patterns—both in time and in space. Patterns, unlike Alexander's more fundamental Theory of Centres [44], are a human and social phenomenon.

DCI provides a vision of the role of human intellect, will, and design above the network model of computation. Humans design the contexts (social interpretations of collected behaviors) and the interaction of their roles to reflect the recurring "patterns of events" between objects.

We can revisit reflection in this context. The network model of computation is rooted in emergent behavior. True emergence requires flexibility in software architecture that outstrips most architectural techniques, because it becomes difficult to tease out the underlying patterns. You might drive to work via a different route every day based on individual reflection that changes the path of interactions between your car and the intersections it passes.

DCI supports a weak form of reflection whereby contexts can reason about the binding of role behavior to objects at run time. This reflection supports a form of emergence in which modules come and go dynamically according to system use. Every use case *enactment* creates a dynamic module (a context object) as a configuration of interacting objects.

2.7.4 Firmitas, utilitas, and venustas

DCI contributes to stability in its data architecture in the same way as Restricted OO. Most such approaches will still use classes for the data architecture. But these classes are now freed from the rapid changes in behavior driven by new business requirements. The architecture becomes more stable, and *firmitas* is served.

An important part of *utilitas* isn't in the software itself but in the relationship between the software and the end user. DCI gives the end-user mental model of behavior a home in the code. That lessens the risk of a translation error as can occur when splitting a use case across the widely separated domain classes implicated in a system operation. The architectural focus turns from rudimentary technical merits to first-class *utilitas*.

In the end, DCI is about integrating human experience with computer support. Rather than separate man and machine through layers of translation and design, DCI strives for the vision of integrating the machine seamlessly into end user expectations. When used to manage the suitable selection of the computer as a tool of human mental augmentation, DCI can reduce work effort, rework, and the frustrating surprises that make computer life hell. DCI makes the program understandable so the coder can feel at home. It's about making the code habitable, in the direction of *venustas*.

2.8 CONCLUSION

DCI advances software into the human components of the architectural metaphor more deeply than class-oriented programming and other preceding paradigms. Further, DCI explicitly supports the agile agenda at the same level of the architectural values that serve a broader human agenda, with support for:

- end users and programmers as human beings with rich mental models;
- readable code to more easily achieve working software;
- creating a home for the customer engagements of domain analysis and use cases; and
- clean evolution along the dominant domains of change in software.

DCI is typical of the broader promises of a postmodern approach to architecture and problem-solving. Elements of DCI reflect a broader change in the design climate in software and the broader technical world, and the broader integration of computing systems that go far beyond the business applications of yesteryear to today's social networking infrastructure. Networks of interacting objects reflect the increasing consciousness about networks of interacting human beings through computer systems today and foresee the needs of architectural forms that can express these complex forms. Articulations of such understanding, such as DCI, will enable the leaps of functionality that this new world order will demand of their computing systems.

The interesting aspect of this new world order is that, unlike many software architecture approaches in this book, it is much less about technology than about human mental models of their world. As the great architecture efforts of classic civilizations have always strived to support the social functioning of the cultures in which they arise, so DCI and its related postmodern techniques can lay groundwork with the potential to raise the quality of life in all endeavors connected with computing. In a world where over 20% of people are connected to the Internet, with rapid growth, it goes without saying that a large fraction of human endeavor is at stake.

References

[1] Pollio V. Vitruvius: the ten books of architecture. New York: Dover; 1960. Translated by Morris Hickey Morgan.

[2] Gabriel R. Patterns of software: tales from the software community. New York: Oxford University Press; 1996, p. 9–16.

[3] Beck K, Beedle M, van Bennekum A, Cockburn A, Cunningham W, Fowler M, et al. The agile manifesto, http://www.agilemanifesto.org; 2001 [accessed 13.07.2013].

[4] Rybczinski W. Home: a short history of an idea. New York: Penguin; 1987.

[5] Alexander C. The timeless way of building. New York: Oxford University Press; 1979.

[6] Weinberg G. Personal interview with Jerry Weinberg; 31 May 1999.

[7] Naur P, Randell B, editors. Proceedings of the NATO conference on software engineering. NATO Science Committee; 1968.

[8] Coplien J. It's not engineering, Jim. IEEE Careers web log, http://www.computer.org/portal/web/buildyourcareer/Agile-Careers/-/blogs/it-s-not-engineering-jim; 2012 [accessed 5.12.2012].

[9] Tidwell J. In: Designing interfaces. 2nd ed. Sebastopol, CA: O'Reilly Media; 2012.

[10] Brandt S. How buildings learn: what happens to them after they're built. London: W&N; 1997.

[11] Martin RC. Clean code. Upper Saddle River, NJ: Prentice-Hall; 2008.

[12] Raskin J. The humane interface. Reading, MA: Addison-Wesley; 2000.

[13] Coplien J. Agile: 10 years on. InfoQ series on the 10th anniversary of the Agile Manifesto, http://www.infoq.com/articles/agile-10-years-on; 2011 [13.07.2013].

[14] Cross N. Developments in design methodology. New York: John Wiley and Sons; 1984.

[15] Thackara J. Design after modernism. London: Thames and Hudson; 1988.

[16] Archer LB. Systematic method for designers. In: Cross N, editor. Developments in design methodology. Chichester: John Wiley and Sons; 1984.

[17] Alexander C. The origins of pattern theory: the future of the theory, and the generation of a living world. IEEE Software 1999;16(5):71–82.

[18] Coplien J. Coding patterns. C++ Report 1996;8(9):18–25.

[19] Ungar D, Randy S. Self: the power of simplicity, http://labs.oracle.com/self/papers/self-power.html; 1987.

[20] Coplien J. The culture of patterns. In: Lazarevic B, editor. Computer Science and Information Systems Journal 1, 2, Belgrade, Serbia and Montenegro; November 15, 2004. p. 1–26.

[21] Gamma E, Helm R, Johnson R, Vlissides J. Design patterns of reusable object-oriented software. Reading, MA: Addison-Wesley; 2005.

[22] Jameson F. Postmodernism and consumer society. In: Foster H, editor. The anti-aesthetic. Port Townsend, WA: Bay Press; 1983.

[23] Jacobson I. Object-oriented software engineering: a use case driven approach. Reading, MA: Addison-Wesley; 1992.

[24] Conway M. How do committees invent? Datamation 1968;14(4):28–31.

[25] Kay A. A personal computer for children of all ages, http://history-computer.com/Library/Kay72.pdf; 1972 [accessed 15.06.2012].

[26] Snowden DJ, Boone WE. A leader's framework for decision making. Harv Bus Rev 2007;85:69–76.

[27] Laurel B. Computers as theatre. Reading, MA: Addison-Wesley; 1993.

[28] Booch G. Software engineering with Ada. Redwood City, CA: Benjamin-Cummings; 1987.

[29] Cockburn A. Why I still use use cases, http://alistair.cockburn.us/Why + I + still + use + use + cases; 2008 [accessed 2.06.2012].

[30] Reenskaug T. Thing-model-view-controller, http://heim.ifi.uio.no/trygver/1979/mvc-1/1979–05-MVC.pdf; 1978.

[31] Card SK, Moran TP, Newell A. The psychology of human–computer interaction. Hillsdale, NJ: Lawrence Erlbaum; 1983, p. 390.

[32] Coplien J. Multi-paradigm design in C++, http://793481125792299531-a-gertrudandcope-com-s-sites.googlegroups.com/a/gertrudandcope.com/info/Publications/Mpd/Thesis.pdf; 2000.

[33] Wirfs-Brock R. Personal E-mail of 14 October 2009.

[34] Cannon H. Flavors: a non-hierarchical approach to object-oriented programming, http://www.softwarepreservation.org/projects/LISP/MIT/nnnfla1-20040122.pdf; 1979.

[35] Jenkov J. Dependency injection, http://tutorials.jenkov.com/dependency-injection/index.html, n.d.

[36] Budd T. Multi-paradigm design in Leda. Reading, MA: Addison-Wesley; 1994.

[37] Lopes C. Speech at AOSD 2012, 29 March 2012.

[38] Hewitt C. Actor model of computation, http://arxiv.org/abs/1008.1459; 2010.

[39] Bjørnvig G, Coplien J. Lean architecture for agile software production. Chichester: Wiley; 2010.

[40] Reenskaug T. The common sense of object-oriented programming, http://folk.uio.no/trygver/2009/commonsense.pdf; 2009 [accessed 8.06.2012].

[41] Petroski H. Form follows failure. Technol Mag 1992;8(2).

[42] Thackara J. In the bubble: designing in a complex world; n.d. p. 7.

[43] Alexander C. The Oregon experiment. New York: Oxford University Press; 1978.

[44] Alexander C. In: The nature of order. The luminous ground, vol. 1. New York: Oxford University Press; 2004.

Further Reading

[1] IEEE Standard Glossary of Software Engineering Terminology, IEEE Computer Society, 1990.

[2] Archer LB. Whatever became of design methodology? In: Cross N, editor. Developments in design methodology. Chichester: John Wiley and Sons; 1984.

[3] Evans E. Domain-driven design. Reading, MA: Addison-Wesley; 2003.

[4] Fowler M. Dependency injection, http://martinfowler.com/articles/injection.html; 2004.

[5] Kay A. The early history of Smalltalk, http://gagne.homedns.org/tgagne/contrib/EarlyHistoryST.html; 2007.

[6] Kiczales G, Hilsdale E, Hugunin J, Kersten M, Palm J, Griswold WG. An overview of Aspect J. In: Proceedings of ECOOP; 2001.

[7] Neighbors JM. Software construction using components. Technical report 160, Department of Information and Computer Science, University of California, Irvine, 1980.

[8] Reenskaug T. Model-view-controller: its past and its present, http://heim.ifi.uio.no/trygver/2003/javazone-jaoo/MVC_pattern.pdf; 2003 [accessed 9.06.2012].

[9] Reenskaug T. Working with objects: the OORAM software engineering method. Englewood Cliffs, NJ: Prentice-Hall; 1996.

[10] Steele GL. Common list: the language. Bedford, MA: Digital Press; 1990 [chapter 28].

Refactoring Software Architectures

3

Michael Stal

Siemens AG, Corporate Research & Technology, Munich, Germany

CHAPTER CONTENTS

3.1 INTRODUCTION

On one hand, uncontrolled growth of a software system leads to architectural issues that are difficult and expensive to eliminate. On the other hand, change is the rule and not the exception in software engineering, or, as the philosopher Heraclitus (535-475 BC) once put it, *"panta rhei."* Changes come in different flavors, such as redefining or adding requirements, changing infrastructure and technology, or causing changes by bugs and wrong decisions. But no matter where these changes originate, they need special attention from software architects. If software architects always focus on adding new features, they will continuously extend and increase the existing system design until eventually it becomes unmanageable and unable to be maintained. Some of the architecture extensions may even prove to be inadequate. Whenever wrong decisions are carved in stone, it will become expensive, difficult, or almost impossible to avoid the consequences of these wrong decisions.

Hence, to avoid design erosion, software architects need to embrace change by systematically alternating design activities with iterative architecture assessment and refactoring. Refactoring is a method of improving structure without changing the external behavior of a system. Introducing a systematic refactoring approach and refactoring patterns helps software engineers leverage proven solutions when dealing with recurring refactoring necessities. Thus, they can avoid design erosion.

3.2 DEALING WITH DESIGN FLAWS

For the development of a telecommunications system, software architects initially defined a sound architectural baseline (see Figure 3.1). Time pressure and additional requirements forced software engineers to continuously modify and adapt the architecture. Unfortunately, they didn't follow a systematic approach for this purpose, instead using ad hoc patches and backpacks to evolve the system. After a while, the resulting software architecture became overly complex and inexpressive and suffered from decreased modifiability. Moreover, additional indirection layers led to performance penalties.

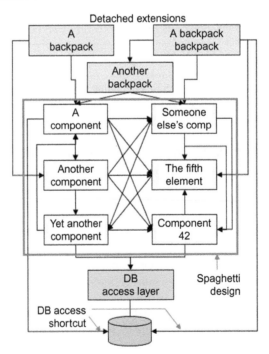

FIGURE 3.1

Design erosion is caused by unsystematic architecture evolution and lack of architecture improvement activities.

How could software engineers avoid such design erosion? First, any software architecture should not be built using a "Big Bang" approach, but rather in small iterations where each iteration maps one requirement or a small set of requirements to concrete architectural decisions. Using a piecemeal growth approach helps control risks through early detection of architecture issues. Second, instead of carving architecture decisions in stone, architects should reassess their design in all iterations, identify potential design issues, and resolve them by refactoring. This approach helps cure the problem instead of dealing with symptoms. Moreover, it prevents expensive reengineering activities after system delivery.

3.3 EVOLUTION AND STYLES OF REFACTORING—CODE REFACTORING

Martin Fowler defined code refactoring to be the process of changing a computer program's source code without modifying its external functional behavior [1]. For example, the *extract method* supports extracting commonly repeated code fragments, moving them to their own methods instead. This improves both maintainability and modifiability (see Figure 3.2).

The example illustrates that code refactoring helps reduce complexity without changing the external behavior. Code refactoring should be applied whenever developers add new functionality, fix bugs, or improve their code according to design or code reviews.

```
void printFormatted(string text) {
    System.out.println("Copyright (c) 2008, Siemens AG");
    System.out.println("Author: Michael Stal");
    printRest(text);
}
```

```
void printFormatted(string text) {
    printHeader();
    printRest(text);
}
printHeader() {
    System.out.println("Copyright (c) 2008, Siemens AG");
    System.out.println("Author: Michael Stal");
}
```

FIGURE 3.2

The *extract method* extracts code fragments to own methods.

But how can engineers recognize that they should improve the structure of an implementation? For this purpose, various hints exist (also known as code smells) that indicate the potential necessity of code refactoring, for example in instances of:

- code that is duplicated,
- methods that span dozens of lines, or,
- frequent use of switch statements.

Whenever developers encounter such bad smells, they should improve and stabilize the existing solution. In the ideal case, proven solutions already exist for the refactoring problem at hand.

3.4 EVOLUTION AND STYLES OF REFACTORING— REFACTORING TO PATTERNS

Joshua Kerievsky evolved this idea one step further by introducing refactoring to patterns [2]. Its general idea is to substitute "proprietary" solutions with design patterns. The argument is that if there is a design pattern for a particular problem, it is very likely that the pattern can offer a better solution than any home-grown design.

Instead of hardwiring links to observers of event notifications, the *Observer* design pattern [3] introduces flexible and dynamic wiring with interested observers (see Figure 3.3). This kind of refactoring is basically shifting the focus from coding to designing. The architecture might change, or it might stay the same. The question is whether we could consequently follow the path and provide refactoring to other layers of abstractions or other disciplines.

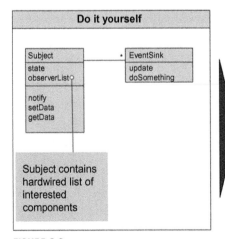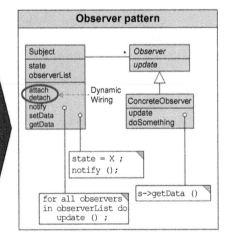

FIGURE 3.3

It is often a better choice to apply the *observer* pattern than to provide a proprietary solution for the same problem.

It is important to mention in this context that, due to its nature, a refactoring tactic can be understood and applied in both directions without changing semantics. In the example above, developers could remove the *Observer* design pattern and use hard-wiring instead. A good reason for this might be the support for embedded or real-time devices that need to avoid any kind of dynamic wiring. This example also shows that the desired requirements and qualities should influence all refactoring decisions. Refactoring should never be applied for its own sake or that of a software architect.

3.5 THE MOTIVATION FOR SOFTWARE ARCHITECTURE REFACTORING

If refactoring can be applied to code, why shouldn't it be applicable to other software engineering artifacts as well (e.g., to database schemas, Unified Modeling Language (UML) design diagrams, or state machines)? In fact, software architecture denotes a potential area for refactoring activities due to its continuous growth and evolution (also known as piecemeal growth). Hence, software architecture assessment [12, 13] and refactoring should happen regularly, in all iterations (see Figure 3.4).

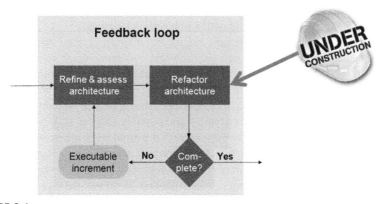

FIGURE 3.4

Architecture assessment and improvement (refactoring) happens in each iteration.

3.6 ARCHITECTURAL SMELLS

The challenge of refactoring comprises identifying areas that architects potentially should improve. For code refactoring, the authors of [1] introduced "code smells" to name such potential improvement areas. In the same manner, architecture smells represent indicators for architectural problems. Some common examples are illustrated in the following list without providing complete coverage or completeness:

- *Duplicate design artifacts*: If the same responsibilities are assigned to different architecture components, the DRY (don't repeat yourself) principle might be violated. As aspect-oriented software development demonstrates, common tasks should be modularized. The difficulty is to decide what amount of replication is acceptable or beneficial, and what kind of repetition should be considered an architecture issue. There is no straight answer for this question. It depends on the problem context whether the DRY principle should be applied or not.

- *Unclear roles of entities*: In a telecommunications project, the development team introduced both a *conference organizer* and a *conference manager*. Project managers were confused about the differentiation between these components. The names of components should explain their responsibilities so that stakeholders can easily understand the design. In addition, responsibilities should be assigned to individual components and not spread across multiple components. Otherwise, proven principles like separation of concerns will inevitably suffer. Likewise, a component should only have one single responsibility. In other words, it should do one thing and do this one thing well.

- *Inexpressive or complex architecture*: Accidental complexity leads to unnecessary abstractions. These abstractions lead to complex and inexpressive software systems. For example, architecture entities might have unclear or misleading names, superfluous components or dependencies, or too fine or too coarse a granularity, all of which make the architecture difficult to understand. Software architecture should be as simple as possible without becoming simplistic.

- *Everything centralized*: Software engineers may be biased to centralized approaches, even when self organization and decentralization would be more appropriate. One example is the application of the *mediator* pattern resulting in a *hub and spoke* architecture where the communication patterns and dependencies are hidden behind a single component. This approach introduces a single point of failure—the mediator or hub—and possibly reduces scalability because all traffic is routed through the mediator. If the problem is inherently decentralized, then a decentralized architecture approach is more appropriate.

- *Home-grown solutions instead of best practices*: Software engineers might reinvent the wheel instead of using proven solutions. However, there is often a high probability that well-known solutions or patterns are superior to home-grown solutions. For example, the *observer* pattern offers a smart solution for many event notification problems. However, home-grown solutions sometimes are preferable. For example, the *observer* pattern is not applicable in real-time environments due to its dynamism. In that case, engineers might come up with their own solution using predefined and hard-coded references to observers.

- *Over-generic design*: Patterns such as the *strategy* design pattern allow deferring variability to later binding times. However, if they are overused, maintainability and expressiveness suffer. An example is the overuse of the *open-closed* principle applying patterns like *strategy*, *observer*, or *interceptor*. When engineers open their system for change and modification in many—even unsuitable—places, the software architecture will become difficult to configure, evolve, and maintain. An architecture design should be as specific as possible and only as generic and configurable as necessary.

- *Asymmetric structure or behavior*: Symmetry is often an indicator for high internal architectural quality, while asymmetry may indicate potential architectural issues. There are two kinds of symmetry: behavioral symmetry, and structural symmetry. Behavioral symmetry mainly deals with functionality for beginning and starting activities, such as an open-method that also requires a close method, a begin transaction which also requires a commit or rollback method, or a fork that requires a join. In other words, every opening bracket also requires a closing bracket. Structural symmetry implies that identical problems are always solved using identical patterns, such as applying the *observer* pattern when event notification is required. While symmetry is often an indicator of high architectural quality, asymmetry—respectively, the breaking of symmetry—may be preferable or even necessary in some cases (e.g., when allocation and deallocation of resources needs to be conducted by different components). Thus (a)symmetry is not necessarily proof of good or bad architecture.

- *Dependency cycles*: Dependency cycles among architectural components indicate a problem because they might cause negative impact on testability, modifiability, or expressiveness. For example, an architect cannot simply modify or test a component in a dependency cycle without analyzing all other components in the cycle.

- *Design violations*: Violation of design policies, such as using relaxed layering instead of strict layering, should be avoided; otherwise, different engineers in a project might resolve the same kind of problem with different solutions in an uncontrolled way, which reduces visibility and expressiveness.

- *Inadequate partitioning of functionality*: Inadequate mapping of responsibilities to subsystems is another cause of accidental complexity. In general, constituents of a subsystem should reveal high cohesion, while the coupling between subsystems should be low. Otherwise, this might indicate a wrong partitioning of functionality into subsystems. The existence of a very large or a very small number of subsystems can be indicative for such a smell. Software engineers may leverage coupling or cohesion metrics to identify such problems.

- *Unnecessary dependencies*: To reduce complexity, the number of dependencies should be minimized. All additional and unnecessary (i.e., accidental) dependencies might affect performance and modifiability. For example, whenever the McCabe Cyclomatic Complexity metrics rise significantly between two iterations, this could indicate that some dependencies or abstractions should be removed.

- *Implicit dependencies*: When the implementation of a software system contains dependencies that are not available in the architectural models, this may cause many liabilities. Developers could create a drift between desired and implemented architecture when they add implicit dependencies in the implementation without informing anyone else about these new dependencies. Some changes will break the implementation because software engineers might not be aware of those implicit dependencies. An example of such implicit dependencies is the frequent use of global variables, such as those introduced by the *singleton* pattern. Another example is the breaking of "higher" layers within architectures that apply a strict layering approach. If the higher user interface layer breaks whenever the lower level persistence layer is changed, then this might be caused by implicit dependencies.

There is one caveat, though: as seen in the descriptions of various smells, architecture smells do not represent proofs of architectural problems. They are just indicators that such problems *might* exist. A design might use asymmetry due to the kind of required behavior, as mentioned earlier. Over-generic design, such as instantiating the *strategy* pattern frequently, could be necessary when developing a product-line platform [11]. It depends on the concrete problem context whether an architecture smell represents an architectural issue. The same holds for software.

3.7 A REAL-WORLD EXAMPLE

In a warehouse management system(see Figure 3.5) with rectangular shapes modeling architecture components, software architects came up with the abstraction called *abstract storage* that represents all kinds of storages where items can be added or

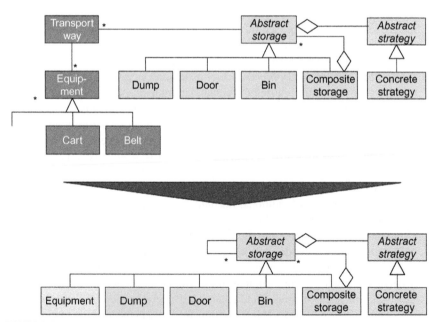

FIGURE 3.5

Adding a new abstraction in a warehouse management system resulted in higher complexity, which could be reduced by applying a refactoring pattern.

retrieved using a specific algorithm (strategy). For dealing with the transportation of items between different locations, architects introduced a new abstraction: *transport way*. Obviously, the addition of *transport way* led to a more complex software design with additional components and relationships. After rethinking the problem and considering the problem domain more deeply, it became obvious that transport ways also resemble abstract storages with the associated strategy defining their concrete kind of transport. Thus, the *transport way* abstraction could be eliminated by considering transport equipment as a special kind of storage. Through this strategy, the warehouse architecture improved significantly in terms of configurability (e.g., configuring concrete storages) and changeability (e.g., exchanging a concrete storage or strategy).

If the architects had not applied the refactoring early, then abstractions such as *transport way* would have been extended and refined in succeeding design phases, leading to increasing proliferation of additional artifacts (a.k.a. *big ball of mud*). Trying to get rid of the problem in a later phase will get more and more expensive as a consequence. The main reason for this design erosion is the introduction of new dependencies in subsequent iterations. New artifacts might depend upon or refine the *transport way* abstraction, and the *transport way* abstraction might add additional dependencies. Like quality assurance (QA) by testing, there is no viable alternative to systematic and early refactoring.

This refactoring tactic can be generalized to a common solution for a whole family of similar problems. Whenever new abstractions are introduced by subsystems, components, or interfaces, software architects should check whether these abstractions are necessary or could be avoided by restructuring the design.

The refactoring tactic is applicable in a specific context (whenever a design is extended with a new abstraction), solves a recurring problem with the solution balancing various forces, and suggests a concrete solution. In other words, a refactoring solution that represents a proven solution for a specific problem family should be considered a structural transformation pattern (see Figure 3.6), or refactoring pattern, as we will call it hereafter.

This chapter illustrates why architecture refactoring should be considered an application of architecture transformation patterns that help improve the quality of a system in a specific problem context. The problem may be specified using architecture smells, quality attributes, and forces. In addition, pattern descriptions make it easier to organize refactoring in catalogs and identify the right refactoring patterns for a particular problem.

The patlet[a] in the example only illustrates some of the constituents of a pattern. Of course, we would need to add sections like Consequences, Implementation, or Variants to a complete pattern description (see Ref. [4]).

---

[a]A patlet denotes a distilled description of a pattern (e.g., using only a single page). Patlets are often used within pattern catalogs or pattern almanacs.

Name: Remove unnecessary abstractions in abstraction hierarchies
- Context
  - Removing unnecessary design abstractions after system extension
- Problem
  - Minimalism is an important goal of software architecture, because minimalism increases simplicity and expressiveness
  - If the software architecture comprises abstractions that could also be considered abstractions derived from other abstractions, then it is recommendable to remove these abstractions
- General solution idea
  - Determine whether abstractions/design artifacts exist that could also be derived from other abstractions
  - If this is the case, remove superfluous abstractions and derive dependent from existing abstractions
- Caveat
  - Don't generalize too much (such as introducing one single hierarchy level: "All classes are directly derived from Object")

FIGURE 3.6

Common refactoring tactics represent transformation patterns.

3.8 QUALITY IMPROVEMENT

It is important to understand that there are two kinds of architecture quality. On one hand, internal architecture quality measures structural aspects, such as symmetry, coupling, and cohesion; software metrics and architecture assessment tools help disclose internal quality. On the other hand, external quality refers to quality attributes, such as those defined by ISO/IEC 25010. Architecture quality indicators primarily address internal quality. However, they are also capable of improving external qualities, such as performance. An example would be when architects remove unnecessary indirection layers from their architecture design.

The application of refactoring must always serve one specific goal: to improve the qualities of the software system under construction. As mentioned, software architects need to address two distinct areas in this context: architectural quality indicators (internal quality), and quality attributes (external quality) [5]. Internal quality improvements require thorough analysis regarding their impact on external quality.

Refactoring and refactoring patterns help increase different internal architecture qualities:

- *Economy*: Following the Keep it simple, stupid! (KiSS) principle, a software architecture should contain those artifacts that are required to achieve the development goals. That is, the architecture should be simple but not simplistic.
- *Visibility*: All parts of the architecture should be easily comprehensible, which also implies that all architectural components and dependencies must not be implicit.

- *Spacing*: Good separation of concerns is important to map responsibilities efficiently and effectively to architectural entities.
- *Symmetry*: There are two variations of symmetry: Behavioral symmetry means that for each "open," there needs to be a "close" statement, and for each "begin transaction," there needs to be a "rollback" or "commit." Structural Symmetry requires that for the same problem, architects always provide the same solution in software system. Lack of symmetry indicates that there might be problems in the design.
- *Emergence*: The whole is more than the sum of its parts. It is more effective to rely on simple constituents from which complex functionality can emerge than to centralize the same functionality in complex, heavyweight artifacts.

As with architecture smells, architecture quality indicators point to possible problems. However, an indicator is not a proof of bad internal quality. Architects should keep that in mind when they discover these indicators.

A refactoring can improve both developmental qualities, such as modifiability, and operational qualities, such as performance. For example, unnecessary abstractions or dependencies will inevitably decrease modifiability. Applying refactoring patterns to get rid of these unnecessary artifacts will help improve modifiability. Unnecessary indirection layers might also cause performance penalties. If a refactoring pattern can make the indirection layer obsolete, its application will increase performance. Architects should explicitly keep track of sensitivity points and tradeoff points, because these are potential risk areas. Applying refactoring patterns that affect tradeoff points especially requires thorough considerations.

3.9 THE PROCESS OF CONTINUOUS ARCHITECTURE IMPROVEMENT

All refactoring activities should be conducted iteratively in a systematic way (see also Figure 3.4). Note that for the sake of brevity, we are introducing only a rough outline of such a process:

1. *Architecture assessment*: Identify architecture smells and design problems—for instance, the architecture's ability to meet its quality attributes. A design issue is architectural when it addresses strategic design, or the fundamental framework used for tactical design, such as variability. As a result, create a list of identified architectural issues. For this purpose, code quality management and architecture assessment tools, as well as architecture review methods, are useful.
2. *Prioritization*: Prioritize all identified architectural issues by determining the priority of the affected requirements. For example, all problems related to strategic design should be solved before addressing tactical areas, and all artifacts associated with high-priority requirements should be covered before those with lower priorities. As a result, order the architecture issues with respect to their priorities and scope. If prioritization is not considered, architects might end up focusing on

local optimizations instead of focusing on strategic parts first. As the old saying goes, unsystematic optimization is the root of all evil.

3. *Selection*: For each problem in the list (starting with higher priorities), conduct the following activities (note: some of the problems might be resolved by higher-prioritized refactoring activities):
   a. Select appropriate refactoring patterns. In this context, "appropriate" means that the refactoring patterns solve the problem at hand considering both internal and external quality.
   b. If more than one refactoring pattern exists, choose the one which reveals consequences appropriate for the system under design. For this purpose, also consider its impact on external qualities.
   c. If no such patterns exist, fall back to conventional architectural (re-)design.
4. *Quality assurance*: For each refactoring application, check whether it changes the semantics of the system by accident. There are three possible ways for QA:
   a. Formal approach: Prove with formal methods that the structure transformation did not change the behavior. Formal methods are particularly useful for safety-critical systems.
   b. Architecture Assessment: Perform architecture or design reviews to check the quality. Code reviews might be valuable if an implementation already exists.
   c. Testing: If the software architecture is already implemented, existing test strategies and test levels will help with QA. Also apply software-quality metrics to measure internal architecture quality. For example, a big jump in coupling could be indicative of a problem.

Despite the current lack of tools that directly support architecture refactoring, we can at least use existing tools for some of the phases of the refactoring process. For instance, architecture assessment applications and metrics help with identifying architecture smells in the analysis phase.

While the refactoring process is applicable to all kinds of development process models, it is particularly useful in the context of agile development. For example, in a Scrum process, architecture refactoring can be integrated by adding refactoring activities in the sprints (iterations). Architects need to (re)check their architecture, testers and product owners need to validate that the system still meets its specifications after refactoring activities. After the implementation of user stories in a particular sprint, software architects conduct an architecture assessment to identify architecture smells and other quality issues during the rest of the sprint.

In contrast to code refactoring, which developers need to consider their daily job, architecture refactoring should only be conducted once per iteration. If done more often, the architecture might be subject to uncontrolled and frequent change. If done less often, eliminating architecture problems involves more time and complexity.

Refactoring of uncritical architecture issues should not be applied immediately before release date. However, if a specific refactoring is not applied in the iteration for that reason, it becomes subject to design debt [6] and needs to be resolved in the next iteration. In a Scrum setting, architecture problems that are not dealt with in the current sprint should be stored and maintained in the backlog.

3.10 SHALLOW AND DEEP REFACTORING

Applying a software architecture refactoring (pattern) always requires the same approach—at least in theory. In practice, its application depends on whether the affected part of the architecture is already implemented or not.

- If the architecture is available only as a set of models (i.e., views), architecture refactoring only implies model refinement and modification. In this case, software architects check the correctness of such shallow architecture refactoring by architecture assessment methods (e.g., using architecture assessment tools and software metrics).
- Otherwise, it is necessary to apply deep architecture refactoring, which will not be constrained to architectural models but also address the implementation itself (i.e., applying a software architecture refactoring pattern will also require code refactoring). Consequently, the writer of an architecture refactoring pattern should recommend appropriate code refactoring patterns the same way architecture patterns refer to design patterns. Note that refactoring might also have an impact on further artifacts, such as documentation, database schemas, and reference architectures. For deep architecture refactoring, additional QA can be achieved by testing.

3.11 ADDITIONAL EXAMPLES OF ARCHITECTURE REFACTORING PATTERNS

3.11.1 Breaking dependency cycles

In a telecommunication management network, centralized monitors allow operators to retrieve the current state of hardware and software equipment. On each observed network node, agent components monitor and control the underlying equipment. Agents report problems using event-based communication. One important constituent of these event messages is a time stamp. But how can agents assign unique time stamps to their events, considering the asynchrony of clocks in a distributed environment? Unfortunately, the project architects decided to move the responsibility of generating time stamps to the monitors (see Figure 3.7), introducing a dependency cycle.

This problem can be solved in various ways. For instance, architects could try to invert one (or more) of the dependencies. They could also introduce dependency injection mechanisms. Another proven solution is to reassign responsibilities by adding additional architecture components, like the dedicated date component in the example.

A patlet is introduced in Figure 3.8.

3.11.2 Splitting subsystems

Coupling and cohesion are examples of architectural metrics. Within an architectural subsystem, the coupling between its constituents should be rather tight, thus leading to high cohesion. On the contrary, the coupling between subsystems should be loose.

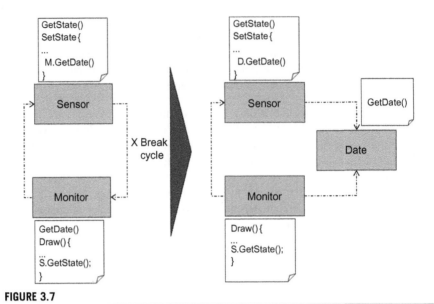

FIGURE 3.7

A dependency cycle as illustrated on the left side, which must be removed as it reduces manageability, testability, and modifiability.

- Context
  - Dependencies between subsystems
- Problem
  - Your system reveals at least one dependency cycle between subsystems
  - Subsystem A may either depend directly or indirectly on subsystem B (e.g., A depends on C which depends on B), which is why we always need to consider the transitive hull
  - Dependency cycles make systems less maintainable, changeable, reusable, testable, understandable
  - Thus, dependency hierarchies should form DAGs (directed acyclic graphs)
- General solution idea
  - Get rid of the dependency cycle by removing one of the dependencies

FIGURE 3.8

Patlet for the architecture refactoring pattern *break dependency cycle*.

If this is not the case, it might indicate that some components are bound tightly together which shouldn't be—and vice versa—as the following example illustrates. In the development of a proprietary container infrastructure subsystem for a unified communication system, almost all components revealed a high degree of cohesion—with one notable exception. The communication middleware itself was only loosely

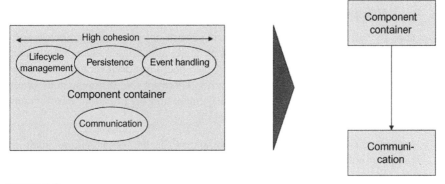

FIGURE 3.9

If components within an architectural subsystem are only loosely coupled with the other components, this indicates a potential split into multiple subsystems.

coupled with the rest of the container. Thus, architects decided to split the subsystem into two subsystems: one for the actual container, and another one for the distribution middleware (see Figure 3.9). By separating container responsibilities and communication responsibilities, the architects could even exchange and extend the communication infrastructure later on without further impact on business and container logic.

In general, the degree of coupling and cohesion can be used as an indication of when to split or merge subsystems. A patlet for the architecture refactoring pattern *split subsystem* is shown in Figure 3.10.

- Context
  - Cohesion within a subsystem
- Problem
  - Within a subsystem, the interdependencies (cohesion) should be high
  - Between two subsystems in a software architecture, the degree of coupling should be rather loose
  - If the cohesion between some parts is loose, then some design decisions seem to be questionable
  - It is recommendable to change this to obtain better modularization and understandability
  - Another potential problem is subsystems/components with too many responsibilities
- General solution idea
  - Loose cohesion within a subsystem implies that the functionality can be split into multiple subsystems
  - Thus, determine areas with high cohesion in a subsystem. All those areas with low cohesion are candidates for becoming subsystems of their own

FIGURE 3.10

Patlet for the architecture refactoring pattern *split subsystems*.

3.12 KNOWN OBSTACLES TO ARCHITECTURE REFACTORING

The need for software architecture refactoring seems obvious, but nonetheless software architects have to cope with different obstacles as soon as they try to introduce refactoring to their organization. Of course, they could just do it for their own sake, but then they typically lose a lot of the benefits. There are four different areas where objections or obstacles might appear: management and organization, development process, technology and tools, and applicability.

- *Management and organization*: Stakeholders in the organization, such as product or project management, often consider new features the most important software engineering assets. Considerations such as "the software architecture design should be done correctly in the first place so that no problems might ever appear" ignore the fact of continuous change in all but trivial projects. Firstly, software architects do not initially know all requirements—at least not in full detail. Thus, their decisions can only take existing knowledge into account. As soon as the knowledge deepens, previous decisions need to be checked and refined. Secondly, big design up front does not work—which leads to piecemeal growth as the only viable alternative. However, piecemeal growth requires constant QA of all design artifacts and thus also needs architecture refactoring. A common problem in this context is that architecture refactoring, like testing, can typically prove its value only after project completion. There might not be any immediate return on investment, but experience has shown that neglecting QA is much more expensive than introducing regular quality checks and improvements. Test-driven design (TDD) is a common answer to this problem, because it enables early detection of quality problems. Another known challenge is the inappropriateness of organizations. According to Conway's law, organization often drives architecture. Hence, bad organization may lead to bad architecture. If the responsibilities are spread inappropriately across organizational units, almost all architecture refactoring activities might force the organizational units to cooperate in a tight fashion—which might not be feasible, for instance, when organizational units are geographically distributed or follow different goals.
- *Development process*: The refactoring process needs to be explicitly integrated into the overall development process. Otherwise, project management will not plan sufficient resources for refactoring purposes. In addition, it is necessary to explicitly assign responsibilities for refactoring to different stakeholders, such as testers or software architects. For instance, test managers should be aware of architecture refactoring so that they can check the correctness of refactoring and the quality of the software system.
- *Technology and tools*: On one hand, due to lack of tools directly supporting software architecture refactoring, the refactoring process must be done manually—which is often tedious and error-prone. On the other hand, finding and coping with architectural problems in later phases is even more tedious

and error-prone. If a catalog or system of refactoring patterns is available, software architects can improve the software architecture much more efficiently. If such a collection is not available, the organization might spend some efforts to build their own one.

- *Applicability*: If design erosion of a software system has progressed in such a way that tactical refactoring activities can only cure the symptoms, not the causes, reengineering or even rewriting might be more appropriate and efficient. An indication for such a scenario could be whenever refactoring activities cannot improve the quality to a larger extent (such as measured by bug rates or architecture metrics). Contexts where it is mainly the behavior of a system that must be modified also indicate that refactoring would not be the right choice. As illustrated in the refactoring process, it is important that refactoring activities be prioritized. If, for instance, refactoring of tactical design is applied before refactoring of strategic design, architects might optimize tactical parts that are eliminated anyway as soon as the strategic parts are addressed. A further challenge is the integration of third party components. Refactoring patterns that require the modification of such components might not be applicable if the organization is not in control of these components.

Proof of concept—that is, collecting, documenting, and applying established architecture refactoring patterns—is an issue the software architects should focus on to extend and improve current refactoring practices. The software architecture refactoring concepts described in this chapter have already been applied in real projects at Siemens. They are not carved in stone, but subject to continuous improvement like all patterns should be. For example, architecture refactoring patterns have been applied in a project for industry automation, in the design of a VoIP client, in a warehouse management system, and in a software application for spectrometers. In most cases, the software architects involved leveraged the refactoring process and the catalog of refactoring patterns [7]. Many of these projects helped in extending the refactoring catalog. In fact, the availability of such a catalog was considered essential by project participants. The application of architecture refactoring could actually increase the architectural quality and reduce costs.

3.13 COMPARING REFACTORING, REENGINEERING, AND REWRITING

Software architecture refactoring helps improve architecture design in a local scope—that is, on the tactical level. If software systems have already suffered from significant and untreated design erosion, they might bear so many design challenges that addressing them with refactoring would only cure the symptoms—not the root problems. Software engineers can recognize such situations, when even intensive refactoring does not lead to substantial improvement. In such cases, refactoring

Table 3.1 Comparing Refactoring, Reengineering, and Rewriting

	Refactoring	**Reengineering**	**Rewriting**
Scope	▪ Many local effects	▪ Systemic effects	▪ Systemic or local effects
Process	▪ Structure transformation ▪ Behavior/semantics preservation ▪ Possible change of architecture qualities	▪ Disassembly/ reassembly	▪ Expensive replacement of whole system with new implementation
Results	▪ Improved structure ▪ Mostly Identical behavior	▪ New system	▪ New system or new component
Improved qualities	▪ Developmental	▪ Functional ▪ Operational ▪ Developmental	▪ Functional ▪ Operational ▪ Developmental
Drivers	▪ Complicated design/ code evolution ▪ When fixing bugs ▪ Upon design and code smells	▪ Refactoring is insufficient ▪ Bug fixes cause rippling effect ▪ New functional and operational requirements ▪ Changed business case	▪ Refactoring and reengineering are insufficient or inappropriate ▪ Unstable code and design ▪ New functional and operational requirements ▪ Changed business case
When	▪ Part of daily work ▪ At the end of each iteration ▪ Dedicated refactoring iterations in response to reviews ▪ It is the third step of TDD	▪ Requires a dedicated project	▪ Requires dedicated effort or a dedicated project, depending on scope

should not serve as the main tool for architecture recovery. Software architects might apply reengineering or rewriting instead (see Table 3.1).

In contrast to refactoring, a reengineering project (see [8]) always implies systemic effects on the underlying software system. In the first phase, the complete system is reverse-engineered and its components are evaluated using a SWOT (Strengths, Weaknesses, Opportunities, and Threats) analysis. Software engineers will adapt components they consider valuable and thus reusable. In the subsequent phase of reengineering, these components will become part of a freshly designed and built software system. In this scenario, refactoring is often applied for component adaptation.

If the effort of refactoring a system or component exceeds that of rebuilding it, rewriting often is the only choice left. It should be considered a last resort if refactoring and reengineering would not work.

3.14 SUMMARY

Systematically extending and evolving a software system is only one side of the coin. Software architects are also responsible for keeping the complexity of the existing software architecture small by avoiding accidental complexity. For this purpose, they should leverage architecture assessment and testing. Software architecture refactoring is an additional activity, which improves the architectural structure of a system without changing its intended semantics. It is generally applicable when architecture smells are found in an architecture assessment. Consequently, architecture refactoring should become a mandatory process, conducted before or after adding new (major) architecture artifacts to a software system, or when architects identify critical problems. This way, wrong or inappropriate design decisions can be detected and eliminated early, thus assuring high quality in the software architecture. In an agile or iterative/incremental development process, architecture refactoring is an activity that should be conducted at least once per iteration. Refactoring in general is considered mandatory in TDD.

Unfortunately, unsystematic refactoring activities can cause more harm than good. Some examples of this were introduced in Section 3.12 (e.g., applying an inadequate refactoring pattern that does not consider architecturally relevant quality attributes, such as real-time aspects). Consequently, refactoring itself requires a systematic process.

Refactoring patterns offer proven solutions to recurring refactoring problems. Using these patterns increases the productivity of software architects, because they can rely on proven practice instead of reinventing the wheel.

Although code refactoring has already become a commodity for software development (in contrast to software architecture refactoring), there are still many areas for future research in software architecture refactoring, such as:

- The availability of substantial catalogs or even systems of refactoring patterns would provide a sound foundation for architecture refactoring. Currently, such pattern catalogs are not sufficiently available in literature—at least not publicly. As a first approach, software architects and developers might leverage the refactoring books by Martin Fowler [1], Joshua Kerievsky [2], and Scott Ambler [9]. Martin Lippert and Stefan Roock provide further refactoring examples in their book on refactoring large systems [10]. The author of this chapter provides a document that includes a catalog of such architecture refactoring patterns [7]. In addition, interested software engineers could establish a public or company-local catalog.
- It is necessary to better investigate the combination and relation between architecture and code refactoring. Some tactics for code refactoring also address architecture design. Architecture refactoring can also have an impact on implementation, which implies that architecture refactoring and code refactoring are interleaved activities.
- Detecting architecture smells is already part of existing architecture assessment tools that use software metrics for this purpose, but so far no tool support is available for actually refactoring the architecture of a software system.

- Refactoring platforms of software product lines leads to additional issues. For example, refactoring core assets of a product-line architecture potentially influences all applications, not just one.

Research in software engineering should also investigate refactoring for further disciplines, such as refactoring of test plans, documents or development processes, and their interdependencies, to name just a few.

As the size and complexity of software systems are still increasing, software architecture refactoring is an important tool to manage this complexity. If applied regularly and systematically, it can provide a kind of safety net for software architects by keeping their software systems in good shape.

References

[1] Fowler M, Beck K, Brent J, Opdyke W, Roberts D. Refactoring: improving the design of existing code. Reading, MA: Addison-Wesley; 1993.
[2] Kerievsky J. Refactoring to patterns. Reading, MA: Addison-Wesley; 2004.
[3] Gamma E, Helm R, Johnson R, Vlissides J. Design patterns: elements of reusable object-oriented software. Reading, MA: Addison-Wesley; 1995.
[4] Buschmann F, Meunier R, Rohnert H, Sommerlad P, Stal M. Pattern-oriented software architecture: a system of patterns. New York: Wiley; 1996.
[5] Bass L, Clements P, Kazman R. Software architecture in practice. 2nd ed. New York: Addison-Wesley; 2004.
[6] For more details on design debt and technical debt read http://en.wikipedia.org/wiki/Design_debt.
[7] Stal M. Architecture refactoring foundation incl. a refactoring pattern catalog: https://dl.dropbox.com/u/2228034/ArchitectureRefactoringCatalog.pdf.
[8] Demeyer S, Ducasse S, Nierstrasz O. Object-oriented reengineering patterns. San Francisco, CA: Morgan Kaufmann; 2002.
[9] Ambler SW, Sadalage PJ. Refactoring databases: evolutionary database design. Reading, MA: Addison-Wesley; 2006.
[10] Lippert M, Roock S. Refactoring in large software projects: performing complex restructurings successfully. New York: Wiley; 2006.
[11] Bosch. Design and use of software architectures: adapting and evolving a product-line approach. New York: Addison-Wesley; 2000.
[12] Clemens P, Kazman R, Klein M. Evaluating software architectures: methods and case studies. New York: Addison Wesley; 2002.
[13] Maranzano J, Rozsypal S, Zimmermann G, Warnken G, Wirth P, Weiss D. Architecture reviews: practice and experience. Washington, DC: IEEE Software; 2005.

Driving Architectural Design and Preservation from a Persona Perspective in Agile Projects

4

Jane Cleland-Huang, Adam Czauderna and Mehdi Mirakhorli

DePaul University, Chicago, IL, USA

CHAPTER CONTENTS

4.1 INTRODUCTION

A software-intensive system must deliver the functionality needed by its stakeholders while also satisfying their quality concerns. Such concerns come in many different shapes and sizes [1–3]. A safety-critical avionics system must guarantee levels of safety through performance and dependability requirements, while a mobile phone service must provide reliable hand-over as a subscriber moves across various towers, must deliver high-quality voice and data service, and must provide fast response times for placing calls and sending text messages [4]. These kinds of concerns are considered "architecturally significant." They exhibit very diverse impacts upon the system and must therefore be specified in quite different ways. For example, performance requirements are often specified in terms of response time or throughput, availability requirements are specified in terms of allowed downtime, while accessibility requirements can be specified in terms of standards or specific features.

Architects must understand stakeholders' quality concerns and design a solution that balances their potentially complex interdependencies and tradeoffs. Unfortunately, some evidence suggests that project stakeholders, whether in agile or non-agile projects, are not very good at eliciting and understanding quality concerns. Franch et al. conducted a survey of elicitation techniques for architecturally significant requirements (ASRs) in 13 different software projects [5] and found that in many cases they were not documented at all. This led to misunderstandings between architects and developers. For example, in one case, a customer assumed that a web page would load in less than 2 s but never explicitly expressed this requirement. The customer was not happy when the page loaded more slowly and the unspoken requirement was unmet.

While many techniques exist for capturing and documenting ASRs [6–8], these are typically perceived as too heavyweight for an agile project. For example, Robertson and Robertson's Volere approach describes how to capture and specify a broad range of quality requirements [8]. Gilb's Planguage method goes a step further by providing a template for rigorously quantifying measures to be achieved for each of the qualities [6]. On the other hand, there has been very little discussion focused on quality concerns in agile projects. An exception to this is the work by Cohen, who describes an approach for specifying constraints in the form of user stories [9].

In a point-counterpoint article that appeared in IEEE Software [10], Alistair Cockburn articulately countered Tom Gilb's argument for concretely specifying quality concerns and argued that qualities should be allowed to emerge as the project progresses. Similarly, in an interview conducted for IEEE Software's special edition on the Twin Peaks of Requirements and Architecture [11], Jan Bosch outlined the growing acceptance of designing and constructing a system incrementally and allowing both functional and non-functional requirements to emerge. He acknowledged that this practice assumes that refactoring the architecture to accommodate newly discovered requirements is an acceptable cost of doing business in an agile project.

On the other hand, industrial architects attending the Twin Peaks workshop hosted at the IEEE International Requirements Engineering Conference stressed that even though architectural design may not be an official upfront activity in an agile project, a good architect will have a clear architectural vision for the solution in his or her head before embarking on actual development. Nevertheless, it is important for this architectural vision to be based on stakeholders' actual needs.

Unfortunately, the agile mantra of "no big upfront design" is often used to justify a less-than-effective exploration of quality requirements during early phases of the software development lifecycle, thereby increasing the likelihood of later costly refactoring efforts. In this chapter, we introduce the notion of architecturally savvy personas (ASPs) [12,13] as a means of exploring and documenting stakeholders' quality concerns in a lightweight manner well suited to the agile project environment.

The approach we describe in this chapter emerged from our own experiences in the TraceLab project [14], a US$2 Million endeavor funded by the US National Science Foundation and developed by researchers at DePaul university, the College of William and Mary, Kent State University, and the University of Kentucky. The core part of the project involved developing an experimental environment in which researchers can design experiments using a library of pre-existing and user-defined components, execute their experiments, and then comparatively evaluate results against existing benchmarks.

Early in the project, it became apparent that there were some challenging and conflicting quality goals that would impact both the time to market and the long-term adoption of the system. To fully explore and understand the impact of early architectural decisions, we developed a set of personas, such as the one shown in Figure 4.1. Each persona represented distinct sets of users' needs, especially those needs which impacted major architectural decisions. The personas were initially developed through a series of brainstorming activities by the core project team. They were then presented to collaborators from all participating universities as part of the

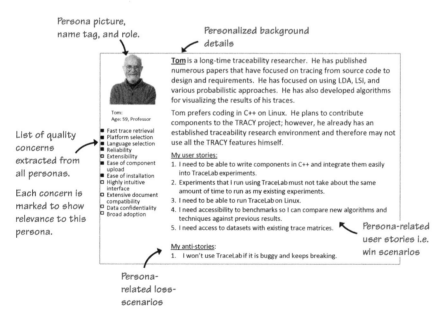

FIGURE 4.1

Lightweight personas used as part of the agile development process to highlight quality concerns (i.e., nonfunctional requirements). Personas are used to drive architectural design and to evaluate and validate candidate design solutions. (For color version of this figure, the reader is referred to the online version of this chapter.)

initial project launch, and iteratively refined until all meeting participants were satisfied that the personas provided a realistic and relatively complete representation of TraceLab users' quality concerns. The personas were then used throughout the remainder of the project to guide and critically evaluate architectural design decisions. More recently, we have applied the approach as part of an industrial research project to develop a prototype for a Mechatronics Traceability system that supports systems-level traceability at the enterprise level [12].

In this chapter, we describe our use of personas for capturing ASRs, driving and evaluating candidate architectural designs, and finally, establishing on-demand traceability between real stakeholders, architectural decisions, and the implementation of those decisions in the code. Several elements of our approach have appeared in previous publications. The concept of ASPs has been described in two earlier publications [12,13], and an example of using them to create traceability from stakeholders to code was also described in a previous workshop paper [15]. However, in this chapter we focus on the integration of our approach into agile projects for purposes of requirements discovery, architectural design, and long-term architectural preservation. Furthermore, we extend our previously published ideas by providing a more extensive set of personas from a broader set of projects.

4.2 PERSONAS IN THE DESIGN SPACE

The notion of a *persona* first emerged in the field of human-computer interaction. Initially introduced by Cooper as a means of integrating user goals and perspectives into the design process [16], a persona is a realistic, life-like, archetypical person, designed to represent an important group of users. A persona description often includes personal details related to the pysche, background, emotions and attitudes, and personal traits of a fictitious person [17,18]. In most of the literature and practice, a persona is created following a fairly rigorous set of user analysis activities including surveys and interviews, slicing of users into categories, data collection and analysis to determine whether candidate slices create distinguishable user groups, analysis of potential usage patterns within the groups, persona design, and ultimately the writing of scenarios that describe how the identified scenario might interact with the system. The created personas are then used to evaluate the design of the system. As a rule of thumb, most systems are represented by only about 5-8 personas. The goal is therefore not to create different personas for each and every user group, but to find an ideal way of slicing users into cohesive and unique categories that capture key ways in which actual users might interact with the system.

The use of personas has also been explored for supporting requirements elicitation. Dotan et al. evaluated the idea of using personas to communicate users' goals and preferences to project members as part of a 2-day design workshop for the APOSDLE project [19]. Similarly, Robertson et al. discussed using personas to discover requirements when actual stakeholders were not available [8]. In both cases, the focus was on eliciting a general set of requirements and/or goals.

However, to the best of our knowledge, there has been no prior application of personas to architectural design. While both user-interaction design and architectural design are inherently creative activities there are obvious differences between them. In particular, a user interface can easily be modified to reflect ongoing user feedback, whereas inadequate or even incorrect architectural solutions can be difficult and costly to refactor. Using personas in the architectural design space can reduce these missteps simply by focusing attention on issues that should be considered in the project's early stages.

In the following sections, we describe our approach for engaging personas in the tasks of discovering ASRs, sketching out the architectural design, and the long-term preservation of architectural knowledge and system qualities. Our approach is illustrated with examples drawn from our TraceLab project. In later sections of this chapter, we provide additional examples in which ASPs are used across a broader swathe of projects.

4.3 DISCOVERING ASRs

Requirements discovery is best accomplished by including a broad and representative group of stakeholders. Feature requests can be collected using online forums or through engaging stakeholders in brainstorming activities and/or interviews. Our ASP process takes feature requests as a starting point for creatively identifying a set of personas, each of which represents a distinct perspective on the architecturally significant concerns of the system. Each persona is personalized with a name and other descriptive characteristics, and also by a set of architecturally significant user stories. The idea is that the persona must become "real" to the team members so that they can relate to his or her needs during ongoing design and development. Feature requests are matched to personas, and the personas are then evaluated for coverage and distinctness.

The process can be summarized by the four activities of feature collection, persona creation, persona enrichment, and documentation, all of which are depicted in Figure 4.2. In the following sections, we describe the main activities of extracting architectural concerns from feature requests, transforming them into user stories, and then creating architecturally significant personas.

4.3.1 From features to architectural concerns

Most projects are driven by a collection of feature requests. While there is a tendency for project stakeholders to focus on systems' functionality, feature requests provide a good starting point for eliciting critical architectural concerns. Questions such as "how fast?," "how secure?," or "how available?" are a helpful starting point.

We illustrate our approach by presenting a subset of feature requests, and the subsequent quality concerns that were identified for our TraceLab project. The

a Collect feature requests, organize them into groups, identify architecturally significant ones.

c Assign user stories to each persona. Add detailed personalized information to bring the persona to life.

b Select pictures for candidate personas.

d If desired, create a project-wide repository of personas. This will aid communication throughout the remainder of the project.

FIGURE 4.2

The process for exploring architecturally significant user stories and creating meaningful personas. (a) Collect feature requests, organize them into groups, identify architecturally significant ones. (b) Select pictures for candidate personas. (c) Assign user stories to each persona and add detailed, personalized information to bring the persona to life. (d) If desired, create a project-wide repository of personas. This will aid communication throughout the remainder of the project. (For color version of this figure, the reader is referred to the online version of this chapter.)

requirements discovery process for TraceLab initially focused on eliciting feature requests, of which a small selection is shown in Table 4.1. This table uses a numbering scheme that reflects the contributing stakeholder (i.e. JD = John Doe) and then the feature request itself. A feature such as "JC1: Runtime Plug and play of components" is clearly architecturally significant. Similarly, a feature such as "JM1: Run fast" represents a high-level quality concern that is likely to exhibit a major impact upon the architectural design once it is more succinctly elaborated.

By examining the set of feature requests, we can identify and extract a set of architectural concerns. For example, the following concerns were identified for TraceLab.

Table 4.1 A Representative Sample of Initial Feature Requests Showing the Initials of the Contributing Stakeholder (SH)

SH	Feature Request	SH	Feature Request
JC1	Runtime plug and play of components	JC2	Write components in C#, Java, Python
JC3	Users create their own components	AS1	Drag and drop components into an experiment
AC1	Save and retrieve experiments	DP1	Share experiments
DP2	Share datasets	JH1	Provide standard datasets
DP2	Reuse data	DP3	Run experiments against the same data
JM1	Run fast	JM2	Execute on linux
JH2	Run on Windows	UP1	I need this to work on Windows
PM1	My lab uses Linux	AZ1	I want to run this on my Mac
UP2	There should be a basic library of components available	DP3	Researchers should be able to share algorithms
DP4	I would like to reproduce experiments from previous papers	JC4	Baseline results from experiments
JM2	Needs to run as fast as my own experiments	SA1	Experiments may be complex
JC5	Cut and paste parts of experiments	EK1	Exchange data between components
AC2	Components written by one researcher and used in one experiment should be easily reused	AC3	Creating new components should be very simple
UP3	New researchers should be able to get started quickly	SG1	Must be downloadable onto my own desktop
UP4	Needs to be secure	BB1	Proprietary data must be protected
EK2	Must scale to work on large datasets	MH1	Experiments should support hundreds of different components
JH4	Installation must be simple	SG2	I would like to share components
SG3	I would like to be able to reuse other peoples' components	GL1	Must provide a visual interface
AC5	Must tell me if there are mistakes in the design of an experiment	AC6	Must provide runtime debugging information
JC6	The interface must be professional looking	EK3	Razzle dazzle of the user interface
EM1	Must be fast	EK3	Must protect my environment when I run other people's components

Plug and Play:
- Visual interface to support plug and play
- Interchangeable components
- Experiments comprised of multiple components (perhaps created using different languages)

Multiplatform:
- Must run on Linux, Windows, Mac

Multi-Language and Integration:
- Must support creation of components in a variety of languages, including C#, C++, Java, Python
- Must integrate with 3rd party tools, such as Stanford Parser, Weka, GATE, MatLab, etc.

Security:
- Confidentiality of proprietary data
- Protection from malicious components

Performance:
- Scalability (large datasets, many components)
- Fast experiment runtime (should have only a minor performance penalty over non-TraceLab experiments)

User Interface/Appearance:
- Razzle-Dazzle
- Professional

Debugging Support:
- Runtime debugging of plug-and-play components

4.3.2 Embedding architectural concerns into personas

Our persona-centric approach assigns the responsibility of representing quality concerns to a carefully defined set of personas. While persona design is a creative process and there is no single "right" or "wrong" way to allocate quality concerns to each persona, we adopted a greedy approach in which we first identified important types of users and/or other stakeholders, merged similar ones together, and then represented each of these groups as a persona. Meaningful, architecturally significant user stories were then assigned to each of the personas. Finally, the complete set of user stories were evaluated to ensure complete coverage of the most important quality concerns.

In the TraceLab project, requirements were gathered in an initial joint application design session and augmented through a series of subsequent brainstorming meetings. Given the competing nature of user requirements and their architectural significance, the principle investigator (PI) of the project developed a set of personas and wrote a series of architecturally significant user stories for each one. The user stories were primarily architectural in nature and addressed issues related to performance, security, reliability, and so on.

Six personas were created for the TraceLab project. The first persona, "Tom," is depicted in Figure 4.1. Tom is a seasoned traceability researcher who has already established an effective research environment on the Linux/C++ platform. His particular concerns include (1) the ability to create components in C++, which is the language of choice in his research group, and then to integrate them easily into TraceLab experiments, (2) the need for TraceLab experiments to run as fast as his current experiments, (3) the need to run TraceLab on Linux, (4) the need to be able to easily compare results from existing experiments against benchmarks, and finally (5) the need for publicly available data sets. Tom represents quality concerns related to language selection, platform selection, and ease of sharing experiments and components across research group boundaries. We also created five additional personas. Jack and Karly are shown in Figure 4.3. For space purposes, we provide only a summarized form of the remaining personas—Glen, Wayne, and Mary—in Figure 4.4.

Karly is a new PhD student. She is interested in tracing requirements to software architecture.

She has contacts with a local company who will allow her to access their data for her experiments; however, this data is proprietary (i.e. protected by an NDA) and so she cannot share it with anyone else.

She predicts that it will take her about 6 months to set up her traceability environment, but then she discovers TraceLab. Karly is quite a good programmer, but is much more interested in the process side of her research.

Karly
Age: 26, PhD Student

☐ Fast trace retrieval
■ Platform selection
■ Language selection
☐ Reliability
■ Extensibility
☐ Ease of component upload
☐ Ease of installation
☐ Highly intuitive interface
☐ Extensive document compatibility
■ Data confidentiality
☐ Broad adoption

My user stories:
1. I need to be able to maintain confidentiality of my data.
2. I need to be able to create my own components and integrate them with existing experiments.
3. I need to be able to set up new benchmarks for comparative purposes.
4. I need to be able to program my new components in C#.
5. I need TraceLab to run on Windows.
6. I need visual components to display quickly to the users.

Jack is married and has two young children. He has recently been hired by the TRACY project into the role of software architect/developer. He has 6 years of experience as a software developer and 2 years as a lead architect in a successful gaming company. He has taken a job on the TRACY project because he is excited by the challenge of working in a research-oriented project.

Jack is very motivated to build a high-quality product. Jack has never worked in an academic research setting before. He is very collaborative and is looking forward to working with the other developers, academics, and students on the project.

Jack, 34
Architect

☐ Fast trace retrieval
■ Platform selection
■ Language selection
☐ Reliability
☐ Extensibility
☐ Ease of component upload
☐ Ease of installation
☐ Highly intuitive interface
☐ Extensive document compatibility
☐ Data confidentiality
☐ Broad adoption

My user stories:
1. I need to develop the TraceLab framework in a language which supports rapid prototyping.
2. I need the framework language to easily interface with, and call, components written in other languages.
3. I need the platform to provide natural support for the separation of model and view components.
4. I need libraries to be available for supporting GUI development.

FIGURE 4.3

Two additional personas identified for the TraceLab project. (For color version of this figure, the reader is referred to the online version of this chapter.)

Tom

Karly

Jack

Glen
Age: 23
MS Student

Glen is an MS student who will help his advisor build TraceLab components. This is his first experience of working on an open source project. Glen is looking forward to working with the other researchers on the project.

User Stories:
1. I need it to be simple to get started with my first TraceLab experiment.
2. I want my experiments to run on both Windows (at work) and Mac (at home).
3. I need to be able to create new components in C# and integrate them easily into existing experiments.
4. I need to be able to make calls to external products, such as MatLab.

Wayne
Age: 46
Project Mgr
ABC Corp

Wayne is the technical manager for a very large systems engineering project. He prides himself in keeping an eye out for good ideas that could help his organization. Wayne wants to improve the efficiency of traceability practices in his organization and is interested in using TraceLab.

User Stories:
1. I need to be able to install TraceLab behind my firewall.
2. I need TraceLab to run on Windows.
3. I need the GUI to be industry-ready and professional.
4. TraceLab must be almost entirely bug free.
5. TraceLab must provide fast processing of very large datasets.

Mary
Age: 51
Funding Officer

Mary is the funding officer for the grant. She is concerned that the project delivers on time and ultimately meets all major goals in terms of adoption, research advancements, and technology transfer.

User Stories:
1. I would like to see broad buy-in of TraceLab from the traceability community.
2. TraceLab must provide reduced investment costs for new traceability research, enabling productivity much earlier in the research cycle.
3. As we cannot see into the future of traceability research, TraceLab must be able to evolve to support new ideas so that it doesn't become irrelevant after a few years.

FIGURE 4.4

Complete set of personas identified for the TraceLab project. (For color version of this figure, the reader is referred to the online version of this chapter.)

The six personas were presented to TraceLab team members at our project launch in the fall of 2010 and used to confirm, modify, and prioritize the quality concerns for the system. Team members came from five different universities and also included two industrial consultants.

Once ASR-related user stories were identified for each persona in the project, they were compiled into a project-wide list containing quality concerns from all the personas and then summarized in a succinct format as shown on the left-hand side of Figure 4.1. A simple classification process was then used to mark each quality concern as *high* (black), *medium* (gray), or *low* (white) importance for each of the personas.

Our approach takes steps to ensure that the created personas provide full coverage of important architectural concerns, but does not guarantee this. As depicted in Table 4.2, a quick analysis of the user stories assigned to each persona versus the quality concerns extracted from the feature requests shows that the personas are distinct and provide reasonable coverage of the quality concerns. However, personas do not need to be entirely static. As initial versions of the software are released, the feedback elicited from real stakeholders can be used to expand or modify the personas' goals and their user stories, or even to add entirely new personas.

From our initial experiences using personas, we found that they provided an effective way to communicate our current understanding of stakeholder needs and

Table 4.2 Informal Coverage Analysis Shows That the Personas' User Stories Provide Basic Coverage of all Architecturally Significant Concerns Expressed by the Project Stakeholders

	Tom	Karly	Jack	Glen	Wayne	Mary
Plug and Play		•		•		
Multiplatform	•					
Multi-Language & Integration	•	•	•	•		
Sharing	•					
Security		•			•	
Performance	•	•			•	
User Interface/ Appearance					•	
Fast Development						
Getting Started	•			•		•
Framework			•			
Extensibility						•

served as a starting point for discovering additional constraints, determining priorities, analyzing tradeoffs, and exploring architectural design solutions. In the following section, we discuss the role of personas in these design activities.

4.4 PERSONAS FOR DRIVING ARCHITECTURAL DESIGN

Architectural design activities can be conducted individually by project developers and/or an architect or could be performed collaboratively. In either scenario, the personas are useful for helping drive the design process. Our approach involves four primary activities, all of which can be executed concurrently and iteratively as part of an agile process. The first activity includes transforming quality concerns—as depicted by the personas' user stories—into soft goals [2], and then reasoning about their tradeoffs (see Figure 4.5a). The second activity involves brainstorming, sketching, and evaluating candidate architectural solutions (see Figure 4.5b). Candidate solutions are transformed back into candidate operationalizations (i.e. possible solutions) in the goal graphs. The third activity, conducted concurrently with the first two, involves evaluating the selected architectural solution against each of the personas (see Figure 4.5c).

Finally, as depicted in Figure 4.5d, the architectural sketches, goal graphs, and architectural design decisions can be documented either by taking photographs to capture the output of the design session or through the use of case tools. Documenting these models in case tools establishes the infrastructure needed to allow actual stakeholders to register their interests in specific personas and/or architectural concerns.

a Transform quality concerns (captured as architecturally significant user stories) into softgoals, and model them and their tradeoffs.

c Evaluate satisfaction of personas against architectural design decisions.

b Sketch out and analyze candidate architectural solutions.

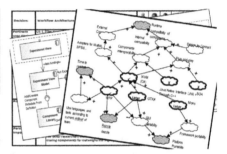

d Document architectural decisions and supporting rationales (either informally through photos, or more formally using case tools).

FIGURE 4.5

Personas and their role in architectural design and analysis. (a) Transform quality concerns (captured as architecturally significant user stories) into softgoals, and model them and their tradeoffs. (b) Sketch out and analyze candidate architectural solutions. (c) Evaluate satisfaction of personas against architectural design decisions. (d) Document architectural decisions and supporting rationales (either informally through photos or more formally using case tools). (For color version of this figure, the reader is referred to the online version of this chapter.)

As a side note, while we include goal analysis under the general umbrella of design activities, there is no real division between requirements and architectural design in agile projects. Requirements must be understood and analyzed within the context of potential and existing architectural solutions. This synergy between requirements and architecture is discussed in various papers including Nuseibeh's Twin Peaks model [20].

4.4.1 Goal analysis

There are many different approaches for analyzing quality concerns and their trade-offs. These range from informal techniques, such as the thought process that goes on inside the head of a single architect, to a more deliberate process in which goals are modeled and tradeoffs are analyzed with respect to specific architectural solutions.

In the TraceLab project, we modeled quality goals, tradeoffs, and subsequent architectural decisions using a Softgoal Interdependency Graph (SIG) [2]. In keeping with the agile nature of our project, these SIGs were sketched informally on a whiteboard. An SIG includes two primary kinds of nodes. Quality goals and sub-goals are represented as softgoals, while candidate design solutions are represented as operationalizations (shown with bolded borders). Design decisions are depicted by marking the selected operationalizations with check marks. An SIG supports four different contribution structures between nodes, depicting the extent to which a lower-level node contributes towards "satisficing" (i.e. sufficiently satisfying) its parent node. These contribution structures are depicted qualitatively as + helps, ++ makes, − hurts, −− breaks, or ? unknown. Traditionally, SIGS do not show contributions between operationalizations; however, we included these arcs to show how various design solutions support each other.

The SIGs depicted in Figures. 4.5a, 4.6, and 4.8 were all sketched on a whiteboard and used to analyze tradeoffs and potential solutions for the TraceLab project.

4.4.2 Generating and evaluating architectural solutions

Our approach loosely follows SEI's Attribute-Driven Design process [21], which is an incremental, scenario-driven design technique that involves identifying quality attribute scenarios and then proposing and evaluating candidate architectural solutions.

Each candidate architecture is evaluated to determine the extent to which it satisfies (or satisfices) persona concerns. We adopt a template for each primary concern. The template lists all relevant persona user stories, evaluates the extent to which each user story is addressed in the solution, and lists pertinent architectural risks and planned mitigations. Instances of templates are provided in Figures 4.7 and 4.9.

4.4.3 Examples

As it is difficult to separate out goal analysis from architectural design and evaluation, we illustrate our approach with two all-inclusive examples taken from the TraceLab project.

Example 1: Achieving Multi-Language Compatibility and Portability. Several TraceLab personas expressed the need to achieve *multi-language compatibility* and *platform portability*. The SIG in Figure 4.6 shows three primary languages that were considered for developing the TraceLab framework. Among other responsibilities, the TraceLab framework loads components at runtime, executes experiments, and displays results. Candidate framework languages included C# with C++ / CLI (to support integration of components written in other languages), Java with JNI, and an SOA solution. A C++ solution was also considered, although not shown, in the SIG. The SOA solution was rejected because we believed that TraceLab experiments would include numerous fine-grained components, and that SOA would introduce too much overhead. Following extensive prototyping of other potential solutions,

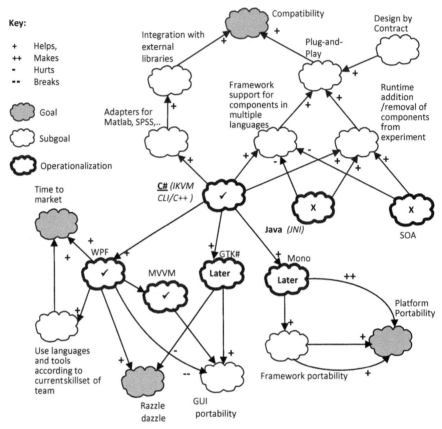

FIGURE 4.6

SoftGoal interdependency graph showing major tradeoffs and decisions for achieving compatibility, portability, time to market, and other project goals. Note that this SIG was initially sketched informally on a whiteboard and only transformed into a more formal model for purposes of this chapter. (For color version of this figure, the reader is referred to the online version of this chapter.)

the C# option was selected as the leading contender. Unfortunately, this solution was not immediately conducive to supporting cross-platform portability.

Additional factors were therefore taken into consideration for the language choice, such as the skill set of the development team (WPF and C#), and the desire to rapidly produce appealing GUIs. Ultimately, a decision was made to focus on current needs first by delivering an initial Windows-based solution using C# and WPF. However, to support the planned port to Linux and Mac environments, we adopted the Model View ViewModel (MVVM) architecture and actually split the code in the view layer into code that could be recompiled on Mono for porting purposes and code that would need to be reprogrammed using either GTK# or Windows Forms.

Decision:	Platform/Language		Tom	Janet	Karly	Jack	Mary	Wayne
Pertinent user stories:	US 1.	The system must run on multiple platforms	●	●	●		●	
	US 2.	Users must be able to write and integrate components from multiple languages	●	●	●		●	
	US 3.	The source language of each component must be invisible at runtime				●		
	US 4.	The selected language/platform must support rapid framework prototyping				●		
	US 5.	The selected GUI must deliver "razzle dazzle"	●			●		●
Architectural Decisions	AD 1.	Build framework using VisualStudio.net and C#.						
	AD 2.	Develop the initial Windows-specific GUI in WPF.						
	AD 3.	Utilize MVVM (model view view model) architectural pattern, so that (a) the GUI view is loosely coupled and can be later implemented using GTK or Windows forms and compiled for multiple platforms, and (b) the TraceLab engine can be compiled using Mono for porting to Linux and Mac environments.	½	✓	✓	✓	½	✓
Risks	R 1.	The Mono library may not support latest features of C#. Better support for Linux than Mac.	Long-running OS project. Initial tests showed adequate support. Mitigate risk through frequent Mono compiles throughout the project.					
	R 2.	Build first for Windows solution may lead to multiple GUIs to maintain in the long run.	Decision is deferred as to whether the WPF version will be maintained or discarded in favor of a multi-platform GUI over the long term.					
Personal Impacts	PI 1.	Tom & Mary's needs are partially met through this solution. In the long-term, researchers will be able to use TraceLab in Linux, but early releases will run on Windows only.						
	PI 2.	All other personas impacted directly by platform/language decisions are positively impacted by this decision.						

FIGURE 4.7

Architecturally significant user stories related to the platform/language issue. Subsequent architectural decisions and their impact upon the personas are shown. (For color version of this figure, the reader is referred to the online version of this chapter.)

Team members met over a period of 2-3 weeks to brainstorm and prototype potential architectural solutions for addressing these quality concerns. Serious consideration was given to three different framework languages: C++ (as this was the preferred language of at least one of our developers), Java (which would be intrinsically portable), and C# (which from the perspective and experience of the overall

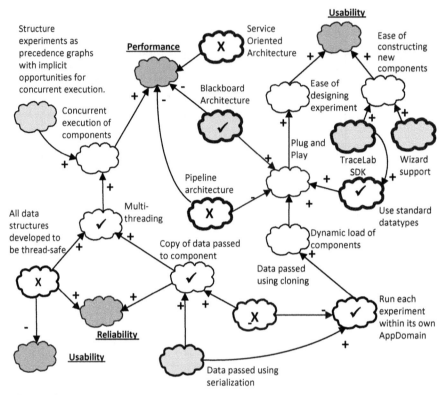

FIGURE 4.8

A second architecturally significant issue related to the way in which components should be built into an experimental workflow. (For color version of this figure, the reader is referred to the online version of this chapter.)

development team was the easiest language for development). C++ was discarded due to the learning curve needed by most of the developers and its anticipated lower productivity.

A series of architectural spikes were created to test the benefits of using a C# framework versus a java framework to support the integration of components from multiple source languages. The results from this phase showed that it was far simpler to make calls from C# to components written in other languages than vice versa, which suggested developing the TraceLab framework in C# and then later compiling it to Mono so it could run on other platforms. Future portability issues were addressed through a series of architectural decisions. For example, the VisualStudio.net environment provides intrinsic support for the MVVM architectural pattern and integrates closely with WPF. WPF supports rapid prototyping of professional GUIs, while the use of MVVM provides a clear separation between view and model and facilitates future reimplementation in GTK# or Windows Forms for porting to Linux and Mac platforms. Our design also separated out the WPF code in the views layer

Decision:	Workflow Architecture	Tom	Janet	Karly	Jack	Mary	Wayne
Pertinent user stories:	US 1. The TraceLab environment must support plug and play.	●	●	●			●
	US 2. The performance penalty of using TraceLab must be low (i.e., close to runtime of non-TraceLab experiments).	●	●	●			●
	US 3. Components should be reusable across research groups and experiments.	●				●	
	US 4. Components should run concurrently whenever feasible.	●					
Architectural Decisions	AD 1. Utilize a blackboard architecture.						
	AD 2. Create standard data types for exchanging data between components.						
	AD 3. Construct the experiment around the concept of a workflow.	½	✓	✓			✓
	AD 4. Support concurrent execution of components.						
	AD 5. Trust the TraceLab users to create a viable workflow. Provide basic type checking only.						
Risks	R 1. Performance may suffer as data is exchanged between components via shared memory.	Keep the data cache in the same app space as the experiment to avoid excessive data marshalling. Stream only critical data, not entire data structure class.					
	R 2. If TraceLab users proliferate the creation of data types, then plug-and-play ability will be lost.	Use community governance to increase the likelihood of shared use of data types.					
Personal Impacts	PI 1. All personas are satisfied with the plug-and-play solution.						
	PI 2. The performance penalty will be felt more by Tom, as he already has a functioning tracing environment. For other researchers, the benefits of the plug-and-play environment and the use of previously defined tracing components far outweighs the slight performance penalty.						

FIGURE 4.9

Architecturally significant user stories and architectural decisions, risks, and impacts related to the design of the workflow. (For color version of this figure, the reader is referred to the online version of this chapter.)

(which would need to be rewritten for porting purposes) from the non-WPF code, which could be compiled using Mono.

Example 2: Achieving a plug and play workflow. Because TraceLab was planned as a plug-and-play environment, the second iteration focused on exploring the architectural solutions for achieving a plug-and-play experimental workflow. The quality goals, subgoals, and candidate architectural decisions were modeled in the SIG, depicted in Figure 4.8. In this SIG, the usability goal of ease of designing an experiment is explored in more depth.

TraceLab experiments are composed from a series of pre-defined and/or user-defined components, and therefore the TraceLab architecture needs to support communication between components and to control their execution. Relevant user stories extracted from the personas included the following:

1. "The TraceLab environment must incorporate plug and play." *(Tom, Janet, Karly, Wayne)*
2. "The performance penalty of using TraceLab must be low (i.e., close to runtime of non-TraceLab experiments)." *(Tom, Janet, Karly, Wayne)*

3. "Components should be reusable across experiments and research groups." *(Tom, Mary)*

4. "Components should run concurrently whenever feasible." *(Tom)*

To achieve high performance (i.e. fast execution times), one of the strategies explored was the use of concurrency through multithreading. One solution for achieving thread-safety is for all individual data structures to be thread-safe; however, this is a risky assumption given that individual users can create their own data structures. It also assigns a significant programming burden onto the users. Instead, the architectural decision was made for each executing component to be given a copy of the data and for access to the data to be coordinated through designing the experiment as a precedence graph. Two alternate options were considered for achieving this goal. Cloning was ruled out because it had a negative impact upon a previous decision to enable dynamic loading of components by running each experiment in its own AppDomain. As clones cannot be passed across AppDomains without serializing them, the basic data serialization option was chosen.

Although this discussion only briefly describes the rationales for the architectural decisions, it provides a second example that illustrates how personas were taken into consideration throughout the architectural design process. These user stories and associated architectural decisions are documented in Figure 4.9. Three different high-level architectural patterns were considered for connecting components in an experiment. An early consultant on the project proposed a service-oriented approach based on his industrial experience as an SOA architect. However, this option was ruled out because we anticipated that some individual experiments might include over 50 fine-grained components (a supposition that has since proven to be correct). The overhead of calling so many services in a SOA environment was deemed to be prohibitively expensive. The second somewhat intuitive candidate architecture was the pipe-and-filter architectural pattern [21]. However, while this approach seemed to initially fit the concept of data flowing through the experiment, an initial analysis demonstrated that many filters (i.e. components) would in fact be assigned responsibility for the task of transferring data that they did not actually use. While this problem could be partially mitigated by having all components accept a composite message (containing self-describing datasets), this approach has the known flaw of creating ambiguous interfaces that cannot be understood without looking at the inner workings of the code. Furthermore, this approach would pass on the complexity of handling data typing to the component builders and could result in relatively large amounts of data being passed from one component to another. For these reasons, the pipe-and-filter approach was rejected.

The final architectural pattern we considered, and adopted, was the blackboard architecture. In this approach, all data is transferred in standard datatypes representing domain-specific concepts such as trace matrices, artifact collections, and/or metric containers. Each component retrieves a copy of the data from a shared memory space (i.e. the blackboard), processes the data, and then returns the results in standard data formats back to the blackboard for use by other components. The TraceLab experimental graph represents a precedence graph, and the blackboard controller is responsible for dispatching components once the components preceding them in the graph have completed execution. This design supports parallel computation and therefore also addresses performance concerns. In fact, once deployed, we found that performance was still below expectations, but we were able to modify the data-marshaling functions to achieve Tom's performance goals. Some of the architectural decisions that contributed to satisfying the workflow requirements are shown in Figure 4.9.

The Architectural Issues Template shown in Figure 4.9 also documents specific risks and their mitigations. For example, the decision to defer porting to the Linux and Mac environments is potentially impacted by Mono's ability to compile framework code correctly. This risk was partially mitigated through testing Mono on a variety of projects and through frequent compiles of the growing TraceLab framework into Mono.

Finally, the proposed architectural decisions were evaluated against the ability of the delivered architecture to meet each of the persona goals. In this case, four of the personas would be fully satisfied with the solution, while Tom and Mary would need to wait until later in the project for the port to Linux and Mac environments. However, this solution was determined to be an acceptable trade-off in light of the tight delivery constraints of the project, the need to build rapid prototypes to address the difficulty of potentially changing requirements in such a novel research instrumentation project, and the ease by which C# code was able to invoke components written in other languages.

As a follow-up to this decision, it is interesting to note that the solution has now been successfully ported to the Linux and Mac environments.

4.5 PERSONAS AND ARCHITECTURAL PRESERVATION

Agile development projects are highly iterative. Even though an architecture may be planned in advance, it is subject to refactoring and change and is therefore likely to be implemented and delivered incrementally. One of the primary challenges in a constantly evolving agile environment is to ensure that architectural decisions, and subsequently the quality of the design, are preserved.

While just-enough design is an underlying principle of agile development, there is a tendency in all software systems for the design to degrade over time. Engaging relevant stakeholders in ongoing discussions can therefore be very beneficial during the change process—especially if new conflicts or potential tradeoffs emerge, or if existing architectural decisions need to be revisited or new decisions need to be made.

Facilitating round-trip traceability between quality concerns, architectural decisions, rationales, and relevant areas of the code provides critical support for several aspects of the software engineering process, including change impact analysis, requirements validation, safety-case construction, and long-term system maintenance. For example, practice has shown that architectural erosion often occurs when developers make changes to the code without fully understanding the underlying architectural decisions and their associated quality concerns [22]; however, if trace links are available, they can be used to keep developers informed of underlying architectural decisions in order to reduce the likelihood of undermining previous strategic design decisions [23,24]. It is particularly important to trace architectural decisions in safety-critical systems because these decisions often help mitigate potential risks and ensure that the system will operate safely [25].

To be most effective, architectural preservation needs effective tool support. We present two different tools here. As depicted in Figure 4.10, we first instrument the agile environment to provide support for event-based traceability (EBT) [26], and second we introduce our tool *Archie*, which establishes traceability between code and architectural decisions and is used to keep developers informed of underlying architectural concerns during the change maintenance process. Together, these

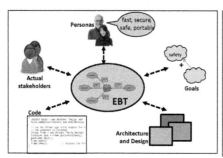

a Create lightweight and flexible trace links using Event Based Traceability (EBT) subscriptions.

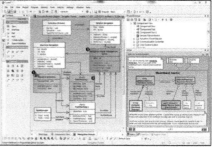

c Instrument the environment. Here, our Archie tool is used to monitor architecturally critical areas of the code.

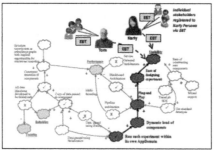

b Use trace links to support development tasks, such as change impact analysis.

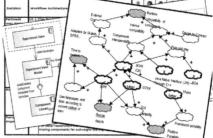

d Maintain lightweight strategic documentation of personas, concerns, and goals as changes occur.

FIGURE 4.10

Personas and their role in architectural preservation. (a) Create lightweight and flexible trace links using Event Based Traceability (EBT) subscriptions. (b) Use trace links to support development tasks, such as change impact analysis. (c) Instrument the environment. Here, our Archie tool is used to monitor architecturally critical areas of the code. (d) Maintain lightweight strategic documentation of personas, concerns, and goals as changes occur. (For color version of this figure, the reader is referred to the online version of this chapter.)

two techniques provide lightweight round-trip traceability between stakeholders, personas, key architectural decisions, design, and code, which can effectively be used to preserve architectural knowledge and to maintain the underlying qualities of a software-intensive system.

4.5.1 Trace by subscription

EBT enables a stakeholder, or even an object, to subscribe to any registered artifact to receive notifications when a change event occurs. EBT provides a very lightweight and flexible approach for establishing strategic trace links. While traditional traceability methods tend to introduce unwanted overheads into agile projects, a registration-based scheme such as EBT enables the strategic creation of useful links. For example, if a stakeholder feels a particular connection with any of the personas, he/she can subscribe to that persona and change notifications will be sent to the stakeholder if the persona or its interests are impacted by a change. In turn, the persona or its individual user stories could subscribe to an architectural decision, and an architectural decision could subscribe to specific sections of code. Using this approach, there is no attempt at full trace coverage; instead, useful trace links are established using a lightweight approach. Our Archie tool [15,27] is implemented as an Eclipse plugin and provides full lifecycle traceability between stakeholders, goals, and code. If used strategically, Archie can send alerts to developers if they start to implement changes in architecturally sensitive areas of the code.

4.5.2 Generating persona-centric perspectives

By instrumenting the project environment, it is possible to use EBT links to generate interesting and useful views of the system. For example, Figure 4.11 shows a top-down view of parts of the system (including goals and implementation) that are of interest to Tom. Similarly, Figure 4.12 (discussed shortly), provides a bottom-up perspective that originates with a proposed change to a specific area of code and that bubbles up to show the personas' quality concerns that are potentially impacted by the change. Furthermore, the subscriptions of real stakeholders to personas means that actual stakeholders can be identified and, if necessary, engaged in the discussions.

4.5.3 Examples

To illustrate these points, we present two concrete examples of changes which were considered and/or ultimately implemented in TraceLab, and then describe how the change impact analysis was supported through our use of personas.

Change Proposal 1: Eliminating an Architecturally Significant Requirement. Given our initial decision to build for Windows first, and based on our observation that almost all of our early adopters had managed to work effectively in the Windows environment, one of the lead developers asked us to consider abandoning the

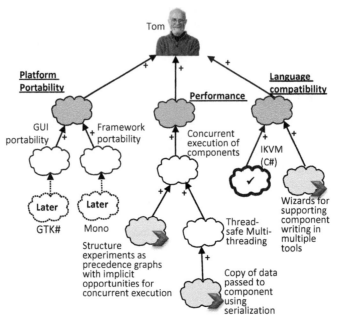

FIGURE 4.11

Utilizing trace links to demonstrate how the system addresses stakeholder /persona concerns. (For color version of this figure, the reader is referred to the online version of this chapter.)

requirement to port to Linux and Mac platforms. The EBT system allowed us to quickly and simply identify all stakeholders who had registered an interest in the decision "Windows first, port later," and garner their feedback. The fact that five different personas (i.e. Tom, Karly, Glen, Jack, and Wayne) had user stories related to the choice of platform suggested that this was an impactful issue. By tracing the contribution structures back to the originating stakeholders (JH, JM, PM, etc.) and asking these stakeholders for their opinions, we determined that porting to Mac and Linux was still of the highest priority. In fact, we found that Linux and Mac users were feeling slightly disenfranchised with the Windows-only version. The multiplatform port was therefore reprioritized and in fact became the focus of the final phases of the project.

Issue 2: Creating a cross-platform GUI. To support the cross-platform port, we needed to re-implement the WPF code in either WinForms or GTK#. Our existing architectural design had already separated the View code into two distinct layers (i.e., code that could be compiled in Mono, and code that needed to be reprogrammed). We ran several tests (i.e., architectural spikes) to ascertain the degree of compatibility both candidate solutions would have with various platforms and found that only GTK# worked seamlessly in our application. WinForms had some

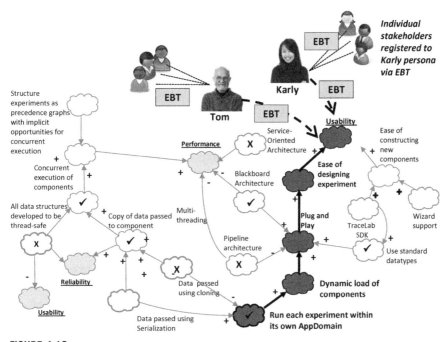

FIGURE 4.12

A traceability view which utilizes goal sketches, personas, and EBT to retrieve the rationale behind the separate "AppDomain" decision. This information enables architects and/or developers to make informed decisions during the maintenance process. (For color version of this figure, the reader is referred to the online version of this chapter.)

problems running on the Mac that were related to our use of dynamic loading, the separation of the framework, and the running experiment into two AppDomains.

On the other hand, it was much harder to achieve our "razzle dazzle" goal using GTK#. We traced this concern back to a single stakeholder (EK), who happened to be a developer and not an actual user. It turned out that our actual users were far more interested in functionality than in "razzle dazzle," and that the GTK# GUI fully met our users' needs.

4.6 ASPs IN OTHER PROJECT DOMAINS

To date, we have used ASPs in the TraceLab project and in a Mechatronics Traceability Project [28]. We have also introduced the concept into our requirements engineering and software architecture classrooms where our students have developed personas for a broad range of application domains. In this section, we therefore present the personas that were created for three additional projects in order to demonstrate the broader applicability of our approach.

4.6.1 Mechatronics traceability

The Mechatronics Traceability project was conducted by a team at DePaul in conjunction with our industrial collaborators [28]. In mechatronics systems, core concepts and designs are often documented across multiple systems engineering models, each of which might depict a single viewpoint or perspective of the system. Models include requirements, software components (e.g., design, code, and test cases), electrical components, thermodynamics, and mechanical components. Furthermore, although each of these perspectives is modeled in isolation from one another, they often interact to produce the final behavior of the mechatronics system. For example, electronic sensors might monitor temperatures or fluid movements in a thermodynamic model and generate digitized messages that are processed by a software component to produce signals that control the behavior of mechanical components. In this type of complex mechatronics environment, changes in one part of the system can have significant and sometimes adverse impacts in other parts of the system.

By capturing dependencies and associations across various models as traceability links, it is possible to support engineers as they evaluate the potential impact of proposed changes in requirements or in one of the design or simulation models. Although it is quite possible to achieve this through creating and maintaining traceability matrices, this task can add significant overhead to the project and is therefore unlikely to be a viable option on the scale needed for effective mechatronics systems.

Furthermore, in mechatronics systems the traceable documents are likely to be distributed across multiple tools. Each tool may store the model in its own proprietary format, using domain specific notations, and may be located on separate, and perhaps remotely located, servers. These realities create challenges related to coordination, data access, and query formulation. First, trace links need to be coordinated across multiple, potentially dispersed models. Second, data stored in proprietary formats needs to be accessed and shared in either a centralized or distributed model. Finally, trace queries need to be formulated and then interpreted by individual case tools so correct results can be retrieved.

To better understand the quality concerns and to ensure that the architectural solution would meet stakeholders' needs, we created the four personas depicted in Figure 4.13. Elaine is a mechanical engineer who frequently uses Pro/e to create physical models. She plans to use the mechatronics traceability system to help ensure that her models are in compliance with numerous regulatory codes. She is particularly concerned with performance because she knows that the requirements for her system are stored in a remote repository, and she doesn't want to slow down her modeling activities waiting for search results to be returned. She is also concerned

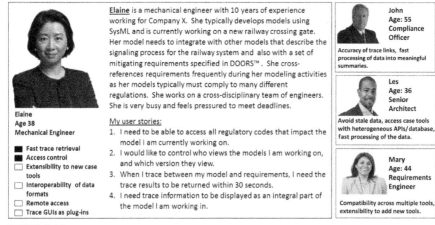

Elaine is a mechanical engineer with 10 years of experience working for Company X. She typically develops models using SysML and is currently working on a new railway crossing gate. Her model needs to integrate with other models that describe the signaling process for the railway system and also with a set of mitigating requirements specified in DOORS™. She cross-references requirements frequently during her modeling activities as her models typically must comply to many different regulations. She works on a cross-disciplinary team of engineers. She is very busy and feels pressured to meet deadlines.

Elaine
Age 38
Mechanical Engineer

■ Fast trace retrieval
■ Access control
☐ Extensibility to new case tools
☐ Interoperability of data formats
☐ Remote access
☐ Trace GUIs as plug-ins

My user stories:
1. I need to be able to access all regulatory codes that impact the model I am currently working on.
2. I would like to control who views the models I am working on, and which version they view.
3. When I trace between my model and requirements, I need the trace results to be returned within 30 seconds.
4. I need trace information to be displayed as an integral part of the model I am working in.

John
Age: 55
Compliance Officer

Accuracy of trace links, fast processing of data into meaningful summaries.

Les
Age: 36
Senior Architect

Avoid stale data, access case tools with heterogeneous APIs/database, fast processing of the data.

Mary
Age: 44
Requirements Engineer

Compatibility across multiple tools, extensibility to add new tools.

FIGURE 4.13

Four personas from the mechatronics traceability project. This project involved building a prototype enterprise-wide tracing tool that provided trace retrieval services across heterogeneous systems engineering modeling environments. Primary concerns were extensibility (to integrate with new case tools), performance, and security. (For color version of this figure, the reader is referred to the online version of this chapter.)

with access control. While she needs to access the baselined version of the requirements specification, she wants to maintain strict control over who accesses her current models. John is a compliance officer whose interests include gathering and collating up-to-date, correct information into a variety of reports. Les is the lead architect for the project and has concerns related to performance, security, and adaptability. In particular, he realizes that the system must grow with the changing enterprise and must support new case tools as they are adopted by various engineers. Finally, Mary is a requirements engineer responsible for eliciting, specifying, and managing requirements. These requirements are central to the mechatronics traceability system. Together, these four personas brought a rich overview of quality concerns to the design process.

Figure 4.14 explores one of the key decisions in building a centralized solution in which traceable data is regularly pushed by its owners to the trace engine server. A set of architecturally significant user stories raised performance issues related to data retrieval, processing of data, and visualization of the results. The analysis showed that the proposed architectural solution satisfies all four personas' quality concerns.

One interesting observation is that the quality concerns that emerged for the mechatronics traceability system are quite different from those that emerged for the TraceLab project. While TraceLab concerns focused around platform portability and programming language support, the mechatronics system concerns focused on confidentiality of data, extensibility, and trace query response time.

Goal		Achieve fast trace query response time	Elaine	John	Les	Mary
Pertinent user stories:	US 1.	Results from trace queries must be returned within 30 seconds.	•	•	•	•
	US 2.	The trace engine must process queries against very large datasets (see assumptions for size).			•	
	US 3.	The trace query engine must allow a single query to access multiple datasets and collate the results.			•	
	US 4.	The trace engine will be integrated with globally distributed 3rd party case tools.			•	
	US 5.	Trace results must be displayed in a visual way using forms and graphs.	•			•
	US 6.	Trace data must be exchanged across heterogeneous tools which store their data in a variety of ways (such as heterogeneous databases) and have individual APIs.			•	
	US 7.	Access to trace data must be controlled at the model level.	•		•	•
Architectural Decisions impacting this goal	AD 1.	The system will be built around a single centralized trace engine with a supporting data repository.	✓	✓	✓	✓
	AD 2.	Data will be pushed to a centralized trace repository as new model versions become base-lined.				
	AD 3.	Indexed data will be updated as new traceable data is received by the trace engine.				
	AD 4.	Access to trace data will be controlled by the central Trace server.				
Risks	R 1.	The data may become stale. Engineers may need to trace against the current model (even if not yet base-lined).	More frequent updates for certain models. Feature for refresh request.			
	R 2.	Bottleneck, single point of failure.	Expected query load is not excessive. Downtime is tolerable.			

FIGURE 4.14

Architectural solutions for achieving fast response time in the mechatronics traceability system are evaluated with respect to the created personas. (For color version of this figure, the reader is referred to the online version of this chapter.)

4.6.2 Online trading

The second example covers the domain of online trading (Figure 4.15). For this project, we created personas but did not design or develop the corresponding system. It was created as part of a class exercise and is based on a real case study of the Mitsuho trading company in Japan [29]. Four personas were created representing quality concerns of transaction control, ability to undo an incorrect transaction, rigorous UI controls to prevent bad transactions, real-time monitoring, confidentiality, and non-repudiation.

4.6.3 Bond, James Bond

Our last example, shown in Figure 4.16 and created as part of a class exercise, presents a set of personas for an imaginary communication device for Spies R Us. Quality concerns include look-and-feel, accuracy of GPS, accuracy of speech recognition, and platform issues. Again, the system was neither designed nor developed, but the personas demonstrate the viability of applying our approach across yet another domain.

Nielson is married and has four children. After three years of working for the Australian Embassy in Japan, Neilson joined the Tokyo Stock Exchange as Manager of Operations. He has been working with TSE for seven years now. Nielson monitors the interactions of investment banks and brokerage firms with TSE to ensure that transactions are completed correctly.

Nielson is a highly educated individual with two master's degrees in economics and business administration, as well as a PhD in finance. He thrives on hard work and executes it with great precision. He believes that there is no room for mistakes in his line of work.

Nielson
Stock Market Manager
of Operations

☐ +30% transaction alert.
☐ Confirmation screen
☐ Cancel transaction
☐ +30% transaction clearance
☐ Auto outgoing calls
☐ Monitor broker screens
■ Halt error sales
☐ System demo
■ On-time transaction
☐ "what if" exchange

My user stories:
1. I need the TSE system to deliver on-time transactions from investment banks.
2. I need the TSE system to inform me of any transactions (selling/buying) at 30% or less of market prices.
3. I need the TSE system to display broker information and contact numbers for any investment bank selling/buying at less than 30% of the market value.
4. I need to be able to immediately stop the sale of stocks when an error is discovered.

My anti-stories:
1. I will not use a system that is unable to cancel erroneous transactions.

Tim
Trader

Enter buy/sell orders on Fidessa, GUI control to prevent sell/buy errors, fast transaction cancellations.

Mark
Investment Banking Professor

Alerts when sell/buy < 30% market price, real -time monitor trans. on brokers screens.

Marta
Developer

Exchange analytics engine. Security. Non-repudiation of trades. Fast response time when trade is placed.

FIGURE 4.15

Personas for a financial trading application created by Niza Alahmadi as part of requirements engineering coursework at DePaul University. (For color version of this figure, the reader is referred to the online version of this chapter.)

Mel is the head of the Spies R Us Secret Service. Her job requires that she have the very latest intelligence data possible to help her make informed decisions. She also has a deep desire to keep track of her greatest asset, James, by being able to locate him anywhere in the world. She is counting on the HMR-TOE* System to provide this, as well as the ability to communicate with James in real-time when necessary.
Mel is not always at the office, so her piece of the HMR-TOE system must be accessible from her mobile device.

Mel
Head of Spies R Us

■ Fast data retrieval
■ Highly intuitive interface
■ Secure communications
■ Data security
☐ Reliability
☐ Ruggedness
■ Ease of use
■ Real-time location data
☐ Watch-like appearance
■ Voice Recognition
■ Extensive map data
■ OS X Compatible
■ IOS Compatible
☐ Android OS Compatible

My users stories:
1. I need the system to be able to track James' location with ultra-high precision.
2. I don't want to have to type commands. Barking orders is what I do, so that's what the system bloody well should understand.
3. I need the system to provide real-time communication.
4. While I need to be able to use from anywhere, I would prefer using it on my MacBrook Pro or from my iPad.

My anti-stories:
1. I will never approve of this system if it is not secure. I cannot afford to have the enemy listening in on my conversations with James.
2. I want to be able to either have the data made easier to read, or have it read to me. My eyes aren't what they used to be.

James

Look-and-feel (like ordinary watch), accurate response to voice commands, accurate GPS, physically robust.

Hugh

Fast data delivery, accurate speech recognition, compatible with OSX, IOS, and Android, <5 sec recovery from failure, run on quantum HW.

Mindy Penny

Run on GOOGLE Nexus 10 tablet, earpiece must be clear, accuracy of maps, real-time GPS location, reliability.

FIGURE 4.16

Personas for an imaginary spyware communication device created by Eric Benedict as part of requirements engineering coursework at DePaul University. (For color version of this figure, the reader is referred to the online version of this chapter.)

4.7 CONCLUSIONS

In this chapter, we have introduced the notion of using ASPs as an integral part of the architectural design process within a highly iterative agile development process. ASPs were used to prioritize ASRs, and then to drive and evaluate the architectural design. ASPs originated from practices we adopted in our own agile project where they proved useful for exploring quality concerns, tradeoffs, and for proposing and evaluating architectural design solutions.

Like all design techniques, our ASPs are more applicable to some projects than others. ASPs are most useful in projects with clearly defined stakeholders, potentially conflicting quality concerns and tradeoffs, and where the best architectural solution is not entirely obvious at the start of the project. We suspect that our approach would have far less value in domains for which architectural solutions and their tradeoffs are well understood. On the other hand, our approach is ideally suited to agile development processes because it provides a lightweight technique for "just enough," "just in time" exploration of architectural concerns while allowing the architecture to be constructed and delivered incrementally throughout the lifetime of the project.

Acknowledgments

The ideas discussed in this chapter were developed in part by work conducted under National Science Foundation grants CCF-1265178 and CCF-0959924.

References

[1] Chen L, Babar MA, Nuseibeh B. Characterizing architecturally significant requirements. IEEE Softw 2013;30(2):38–45.

[2] Chung L. Non-functional requirements in software engineering. Norwell, MA: Kluwer Academic Publishers; 2000.

[3] Glinz M. A risk-based, value-oriented approach to quality requirements. IEEE Softw 2008;25(2):34–41.

[4] Mirakhorli M, Cleland-Huang J. Tracing non-functional requirements. In: Cleland-Huang J, Gotel O, and Zisman A, editors. Software and systems traceability. London: Springer-Verlag; 2011.

[5] Ameller D, Ayala CP, Cabot J, Franch X. How do software architects consider non-functional requirements: an exploratory study. In: RE; 2012. p. 41–50.

[6] Boehm BW, Egyed A, Port D, Shah A, Kwan J, Madachy RJ. A stakeholder win-win approach to software engineering education. Ann Software Eng 1998;6:295–321.

[7] Gilb T. How to quantify quality: finding scales of measure. ICSOFT, vol. 1; 2006.

[8] Robertson S, Robertson J. Mastering the requirements process. Boston: Addison Wesley; 2006.

[9] Cohen M. Non-functional requirements as user stories. Mountain Goat Software, http://www.mountaingoatsoftware.com/blog/non-functional-requirements-as-user-stories.

[10] Gilb T, Cockburn A. Point/counterpoint. IEEE Softw 2008;25(2):64–7.

[11] Mirakhorli M, Cleland-Huang J. Traversing the twin peaks. IEEE Softw 2013;30(2): 30–6.

[12] Cleland-Huang J. Meet Elaine: a persona-driven approach to exploring architecturally significant requirements. IEEE Softw 2013;30(4):18–21.

[13] Cleland-Huang J, Czauderna A, Keenan E. A persona-based approach for exploring architecturally significant requirements in agile projects. In: REFSQ; 2013. p. 18–33.

[14] Keenan E, Czauderna A, Leach G, Cleland-Huang J, Shin Y, Moritz E, et al. Tracelab: an experimental workbench for equipping researchers to innovate, synthesize, and comparatively evaluate traceability solutions. In: ICSE; 2012. p. 1375–8.

[15] Cleland-Huang J, Mirakhorli M, Czauderna A, Wieloch M. Decision-centric traceability of architectural concerns. In: Traceability in emerging forms of software engineering; 2013.

[16] Cooper A. The inmates are running the asylum. In: Software-Ergonomie; 1999. p. 17.

[17] Nielsen L. Personas—user focused design. Human-computer interaction series, vol. 15. London: Springer; 2013.

[18] Putnam C, Kolko BE, Wood S. Communicating about users in ictd: leveraging hci personas. In: ICTD; 2012. p. 338–49.

[19] Dotan A, Maiden NAM, Lichtner V, Germanovich L. Designing with only four people in mind?—a case study of using personas to redesign a work-integrated learning support system. INTERACT, vol. 2; 2009. p. 497–509.

[20] Nuseibeh B. Weaving together requirements and architectures. IEEE Computer 2001;34 (3):115–7.

[21] Bass L, Clements P, Kazman R. Software architecture in practice. Upper Saddle River, NJ: Addison Wesley; 2003.

[22] Eick SG, Graves TL, Karr AF, Marron JS, Mockus A. Does code decay? Assessing the evidence from change management data. IEEE Trans Softw Eng 2001;27(1):1–12.

[23] Cleland-Huang J. Towards improved traceability of non-functional requirements. In: Traceability in emerging forms of software engineering; 2005.

[24] Mirakhorli M, Shin Y, Cleland-Huang J, Çinar M. A tactic-centric approach for automating traceability of quality concerns. In: ICSE; 2012. p. 639–49.

[25] Cleland-Huang J, Heimdahl M, Huffman Hayes J, Lutz R, Maeder P. Trace queries for safety requirements in high assurance systems. In: International working conf. on requirements eng.: foundation for software quality; 2012.

[26] Cleland-Huang J, Chang CK, Christensen MJ. Event-based traceability for managing evolutionary change. IEEE Trans Softw Eng 2003;29(9):796–810.

[27] Mirakhorli M, Cleland-Huang J. Using tactic traceability information models to reduce the risk of architectural degradation during system maintenance. In: Proceedings of the 2011 27th IEEE international conference on software maintenance, ICSM'11. Washington, DC: IEEE Computer Society; 2011. p. 123–32.

[28] Czauderna A, Cleland-Huang J, Berenbach B. Just-in-time mechatronics traceability. Siemens White Paper 2010;1–56.

[29] Tamai T. Social impact of information system failures. IEEE Computer 2009;42 (6):58–65.

Architecture Decisions: Who, How, and When?

Jan Salvador van der Ven[*] **and Jan Bosch**[†]

[*]*Factlink, Groningen, The Netherlands*
[†]*Chalmers University of Technology, Gothenburg, Sweden*

CHAPTER CONTENTS

5.1 INTRODUCTION

In the past decade, the creation of software systems has changed rapidly. Traditionally, long-lasting waterfall projects (>2 years) were standard, whereas now rapid development (<3 months) with fast-changing requirements is becoming the norm for creating software products. In both cases, the architecture of the system has to be taken into account, although when, how, and who is responsible differs significantly. Formerly, experienced architects created models and documentation for the system beforehand, so the development team had a solid base of decisions on which to build. Nowadays, in more agile projects, the architectural decisions are made just in time by the development team itself, often assisted by a participating architect. Alternatives for heavy template-based documentation, like wikis or photos, are used to document the decisions.

This leads to a change in responsibilities, and in the role, of the architect. The responsibilities for the architectural decision process shift from the formal architect on one hand to the development team on the other hand. The architect takes on more of an advisory servant role within the project, often participating in the development team as a designer or developer. This difference, and thereby the newly needed alignment between agile and architecture is the topic of this chapter.

In recent research, architecture in agile software development has been a topic of hot debate [1,2]. While some authors emphasize the importance of architecture with Agile [3], others have described their experiences with Agile in product lines [4,5]. This chapter contributes to the debate by presenting a framework that helps in identifying alignment problems in agile and architecture. Our framework is validated by case studies.

We have conducted a literature search on architectural decisions, the role of the architect, and how these decisions are documented. On the basis of this search, together with our own experiences, we constructed our Triple-A (Agile, Architecture, Axes) Framework. This framework identifies three different axes. The first axis describes the person making the decision (often called the architect). The second axis shows the way in which the architectural decisions are communicated (e.g., the artifacts used). The third axis describes the length of the decision feedback loop, the periodicity of a decision. We show that these axes can be used to profile a project or case study and that positions on these axes can be indicators for the success of a project.

The contribution of this chapter is twofold. First, we present a framework that helps project teams and software development organizations understand how they handle architecture. Second, we provide case study material that shows the effects when changing the architecture decision process. This helps organizations that are gaining agility identify what points of their architecture process need improvement.

The next section describes the research methodology used, followed by a description of our Triple-A Framework. Then our industrial cases are described. On the basis of our evaluation of the shifts in these cases and their resulting effects on business, the Tripe-A Framework is validated in Section 5.5. This chapter ends with related work, reflections on further research, and conclusions.

5.2 RESEARCH METHODOLOGY

We took the following steps to create the theory presented in this chapter. (1) During our participation in the industrial cases, we iteratively discovered changes in our case studies (for the good or the bad). (2) To emphasize the changes (described as shifts in Section 5.4), we have taken two points in time per case study and described the differences at each. We made the discovered changes explicit and categorized them. (3) Triggered by our experience while working on our cases, we conducted a thorough literature search of related projects and models. By generalizing our research and experiences, we created the axes that are the core of our Triple-A Framework. (4) We validated our framework with our case study material. (5) Finally, we identified several problems that occurred in our case studies and related them to changes in our model.

In our case studies, we used comparative multicase analysis methodology [6]. Our initial theory building and measurement is done as an iterative process during the full period of all the case studies. We used longitudinal case studies for a period of time ranging from 9 to 48 months, where the qualitative data obtained by the participant observer complemented, in some cases, interviews with key participants in the project or product development team. In other cases the qualitative data was discussed with participants of the projects to validate the findings.

For each case, the research started with a discussion about what happened during the case, resulting in the descriptions in Section 5.4. Two phases were identified, resulting in shifts that were rated according to business impact. While some of the cases involved positive shift, other cases showed a negative shift between the phases. These shifts were used to validate our research-based Triple-A Framework.

To determine the business impact of the shifts in the case studies, three success factors were used:

- The return on investment (profit minus investment cost)
- The speed of the project (whether the project progressed as scheduled and finished on time)
- The quality of the delivered project (whether the customer and the team were satisfied with the quality)

The return on investment is measured by the success of the projects: Did the project actually deliver? What were the investments and the cost? This evaluation was done after the fact and based on estimations of the researchers who participated in the project because first-hand financial data was not available to them. The speed of the project was measured by the speed of delivery of functionality (or changes in case of bugs) as perceived by the participant observer. The researchers based their quality assessment on discussions with customers and project team members.

The cases we use as a basis of our theory are not selected at random. From our experience, other cases could have been chosen. However, as stated in Ref. [6], in case study research it is "neither necessary nor preferable to randomly select cases." We have selected the cases that contained the clearest shifts, as described in Section 5.4. The cases are similar in that they all involved relatively small, collocated teams facing complex, real-life problems, but they involve a variety of situations— from a small product company (case Epsilon), to small projects at large companies (case Beta), to moderate-size projects at large customer sites (cases Alpha and Gamma), to a large company changing its way of working (case Delta). Three of the cases primarily involved the development of new products (Alpha, Beta, Gamma), whereas two involved evolution and maintenance of the running system (Delta, Epsilon) in addition to the creation of new functionality.

5.3 THE AGILE ARCHITECTURE AXES FRAMEWORK

In software architecture literature, many models are used to describe the software architectural decision process. For example, different models [7], templates [8], or ontologies [9] are used to describe architectural knowledge. Several authors have compared the ability of available models to process architectural design decisions. For example, De Boer et al. [7] describe a "core model" for architectural knowledge. They present a model and validate it through interviews and by testing it against existing models in the literature. Bu et al. [10] analyzed nine different approaches for describing design decisions. Such topics are beyond the scope of this chapter; however, we have seen that there are three essential aspects of the architecture creation process that are rarely thoroughly described

- *The Architect.* In architectural knowledge literature, the architect is referred to as the person responsible for the architecture, or the person who makes the architectural decisions. However, who this person is and what his or her skills are, are rarely discussed. And the effects of these skills on the results of the project are also seldom written about.
- *Artifacts.* This term is often used as an abstraction of all things that are created during the architecture development process. Examples of artifacts that are mentioned are documents, models, or source code. However, the effects of the types of artifacts used on the outcome of a project are rarely researched.

- *Periodicity*. The "decision loop" [7] describes how decisions lead to new decisions based on the alternatives chosen. However, the periodicity of the decisions is rarely described. What is the length of time between the actual decision and the resulting validation of that decision in the quality attributes that the system needs to comply to?

The Triple-A Framework consists of three axes for describing where the decision process can differ in projects or companies. Each axis focuses on a different aspect of the architecture decision process as described above. In the following subsections, each axis is discussed by first describing relevant literature, followed by the points that we identified on the axis.

5.3.1 Who makes the architectural decisions?

Although there has been some debate about the role of the architect [11], in most literature concerning architectural design decisions or architectural knowledge the term *architect* is used but not well defined. For example, in the survey about architectural knowledge [7], the term *architect(s)* is used 11 times, without defining who this person is or mentioning this person in the described core model. In another survey [10], the term is only used three times, again without a definition or explanation. In [12], the work of architects is described, based on a survey conducted with a large group of architects. The authors mention that they included architects of different types in their research ("...including software, IT, solution, enterprise, and infrastructure architects"), but do not mention what the exact skills are or what effect a certain architect could have on the project. Kruchten [11] emphasizes that the architect has a broader role than just making the architectural decisions. In this chapter, we focus on the actual decision-making, not on the other things architects do.

Often, we have seen that people other than the formally assigned architects make architectural decisions. For example, the product owner (customer or domain-related decisions) and the development team (technical decisions) are heavily involved in, and sometimes responsible for, the architecture decision process. We have extended the scopes for architects described in [13] (Enterprise, Domain, Application) with two additional roles we encountered in our industrial cases (Management, Development Team). Note that the described roles are not one-to-one mappings to position names. They should be interpreted more as baskets for skills that a person with this role possesses.

- *Management*: Management can consist of company or project managers. Managers can have significant influence on the architecture decision process. However, the main focus of management is on project properties (on-time, in-scope). Typically, management lacks knowledge of the actual technical background of the system or the customer's specific functional demands. Because management often has a high position in the hierarchy of the organization, its decisions are hard to debate.

- *Enterprise Architect*: Enterprise or solution architects are typically responsible for the decisions at enterprise scope [13]. They often have a thorough background in theory and sometimes in practice.
- *Domain Architect*: Domain architects [13] are often customer-employed people who have thorough understanding of what the customer actually needs. The role of product owner is typically existent in Scrum [14] projects. This person functions like a domain expert, but is not necessarily part of the customer organization, and is often close to the team. Domain experts or product owners are often responsible for architectural decisions that have a high functional impact.
- *Application Architect*: The application architect [13] is typically an architect that also writes code as a team member. To make the right technical architectural decisions, he or she must have up-to-date knowledge. Typical role names that we encountered for these people are senior developer or technical architect.
- *Development Team*: The development team consists of the people involved in the actual designing, coding, testing, and deploying of the system. This includes people with architecting skills. The responsibility of the decisions lies with the whole team, in contrast to the previous roles.

Although often more than one role is involved in the decision process, in our experience there usually is one (sometimes assigned) role that has the formal or informal responsibility for making the decisions. The "who" axis describes who the main responsible person (or persons) is (are) for the architecture decision process.

5.3.2 What artifacts are used to document the decision?

Architectural design decisions are often traceable to, or represented in, artifacts. Many authors use the term *artifact* [7,9] to describe that the decisions have a representation somewhere. Some authors emphasize that the decisions themselves should be first-class entities or artifacts in the design [15], or provide templates to make the artifacts for design decisions [8]. As described in [16], knowledge can be shared personally (remembering, talking, etc.), or more formally (documenting, modeling). We have identified the following points, ordered from heavy to lightweight documentation approaches:

- *Mandatory Template-based Documentation*: These artifacts are architecture documents that have to be created because they are part of an offer, agreement, or project plan. Examples of these documents are the functional and technical design documents.
- *Facultative Template-based Documentation*: The Rational unified Process (RuP) [17] has a very extended set of document templates that can be used in software projects. An example of an architectural deliverable is the software architecture document. Because they are not mandatory, it is easier to decide not to use one of the documents. The templates add to the unnecessary complexity of writing down architectural decisions. On the other hand, templates can help to make sure certain aspects of a design are not forgotten.

- *Ad hoc Documentation*: This documentation type consists of all the random documentation that is present in almost every software development project that does not comply with a template. It can be structured on a common share or (semantic) wiki [18], or unstructured by e-mail or *ad hoc* sharing. Because they don't have to follow a template, they are typically quicker to write—but with the risk of forgetting important aspects.
- *Meeting Notes (sketches, photos, etc.)*: Meeting notes, in written or visual form, can be used to create very lightweight documentation of design meetings or open spaces. This method has the advantages of being very quick and the fact that the details of a meeting are easier to remember when seeing the drawings from the meeting. However, it can be difficult for people who were not involved in the meeting to understand the decisions.
- *Direct Communication*: Direct communication is the tacit "documentation" that takes place every day. This can be in a chat, on the phone, or face-to-face. Direct communication is the richest form of communication because it is bidirectional (it is possible to ask for explanation) and multiple senses can be used.

Projects usually do not use just one of these communication approaches. However, there is usually one medium for reading and writing architectural decisions that tends to be preferred by the team. We use the items mentioned above as points on our "how" axis.

5.3.3 What is the feedback loop of an architectural decision?

During both the initial development and the evolution of the system, architectural decisions are made with a goal in mind. Often, these decisions are made to confirm nonfunctional requirements or the quality attributes to a certain level. However, sometimes the confirmation of the suitability of the decision takes a long time. Kruchten [11] describes antipatterns where architects are disconnected from the actual team. In our opinion, these patterns show what happens if the feedback loop from the decision to the actual validation of the decision becomes too long. Some authors have suggested the use of templates with "states" [9] or "status" information [8] to be able to document where the decision is in the feedback loop. However, neither of these representations of the state of the decision describes when a decision is actually implemented and validated.

To get a better idea of the validity of a decision, assessment methods like Architecture Tradeoff Analysis Method (ATAM) [19] are used to increase the confidence level for the decision. However, final validation occurs when the decision is implemented in the system and is being measured by the usage. Typically three points in time are relevant for an architectural decision: the time the decision was made ("Decided" in [9] and [8]), the realization of the decision, and the validation that it was a correct decision (the latter two are nonexistent in the described literature). We take the time between the initial decision and the validation as elements for the periodicity of the decision.

- *Long (>6 months)*: In long-running projects or offers, sometimes architectural decisions are made before the project starts. It can take several years before the decision is implemented and validated.
- *Medium (1-6 months)*: Often, a proof of technology or proof of concept (POC) is used to validate whether an architectural design decision has the desired result. These decisions are typically validated quicker than the long-running project decisions.
- *Short (<1 month)*: In more agile settings, the validation of decisions can be much quicker. Especially when the technical infrastructure for continuous delivery is in place, the time between decision-making and validation can be decreased. The shortest cycle can be achieved during refactoring, where the decision is changed on the existing code base.

Of course, some decisions cannot be validated in the short term. Also, a typical project has more than one decision point. However, projects tend to lean more towards one point on this axis, characterized by the organization style of the project. We use these three points in our framework as the "when" axis.

5.3.4 Summary of the axes

To summarize, we have identified three axes that can be used to describe the architecture decision process in projects. In Figure 5.1, we visualize our Triple-A Framework in a radar plot.

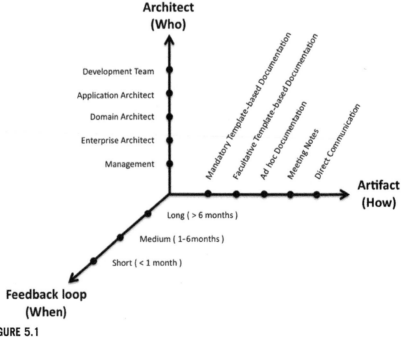

FIGURE 5.1

The Triple-A Framework.

In the following section, five industrial cases are introduced. All of the cases have a representation on the Triple-A Framework, which is evaluated in Section 5.5.

5.4 INDUSTRIAL CASES

This section describes the industrial cases that are used in this chapter. In all of the cases, one of the researchers was involved as a team member within the studied company. As authors, at least one of us was involved in all the described industrial cases over an extended period of time. This allowed us to study the response of the case organizations to the changes that we saw. This chapter focuses on issues related to the work of software architects, although we studied the cases more broadly including other software development aspects. The cases are anonymized to protect the companies and customers involved. The roles that the researchers had in the cases varied from developer, architect, and team lead, to being part of the management of the organization.

For every case, the description starts with an introduction of the context, the customer, and the domain of the case. This is followed by a summary of project characteristics: the technology used, the type of architectural challenges that were tackled, the number of people involved, the duration of the project, and the process(es) used. Then a separate description of the two different phases is given. Every case description finishes by noting the shifts that occurred, and the business impact on these shifts. After the description of the shifts, the differences between the phases are summarized.

5.4.1 Case Alpha

Case Alpha involved the construction of a software system that had to replace a legacy geographic information system. The new system had to be coupled with several legacy back-office systems. The customer, a large harbor company in the Netherlands, initiated the project. The solution was service oriented, and consisted of several systems communicating with each other through an enterprise service bus (ESB). Most of the software was written in (Oracle) Java. This coupling was one of the most challenging issues in the project. This case consisted of a POC and a realization phase, 3 and 6 months, respectively. Ten to twenty people were involved during the various phases of the project. In the POC phase, a lightweight, iterative approach was used, whereas RuP [17] was adopted in the realization phase.

5.4.1.1 Phase one

During the first phase of case Alpha, an iterative approach was followed. The first deliverable of the project was a POC that had to be ready on a predefined time-line. During this period, functionality was delivered every 2 weeks. In every iteration, new architectural challenges were tackled (e.g., how to process the data of the legacy system via the chosen ESB to the user interface, or how to correctly merge the real-time data from the ships' locations to the static cargo data provided in one of the legacy systems). The customer was very happy with the result—a running technological

POC—and the supplier company was invited to participate in the execution of the next phase of the project.

5.4.1.2 Phase two

In the second phase, the organization of the project radically changed. This was done because there was the potential that the project would need to be scaled up in team size. The result was that a group of eight architects from different companies was formed, assisted by a team of five project managers. They conducted thorough work in documenting all the possible situations, interfaces with other systems, etc. The development team that was involved in the initial POC was rarely consulted, and was colocated on the other side of the Netherlands. The main results of this phase were the documents that were created: use case descriptions, architectural documentation, project plans, and more.

5.4.1.3 Shifts

The following were the most striking shifts that took place in case Alpha:

- Because of fear of making the wrong decisions, the focus was more on documentation and less on making working software.
- The iterations were longer (from 2-week iterations to half-year release).
- Because the system had to be connected to the deprecated systems that were running, there was a tendency to over-think the architecture to prevent making mistakes.
- There was no longer a structural feedback loop from the development team to the architects and customers and vice versa.

By making the decision process more heavyweight and focusing on documentation, the project was slowing down so much that it became paralyzed. After 6 months during the second phase, almost no working software was produced (one use case was realized). The project was discontinued because the customer no longer had confidence in it.

5.4.2 Case Beta

The product developed in case Beta was an administrative case management system for a department of the Dutch national government. This system had to handle (changing) regulations, and was to be used by various departments who had different demands for it. There was a multidisciplinary team of five to ten people involved for two periods of 6 months. The system was based on the Oracle Collaboration Suite, and the UI was developed with Java technology. The main architectural challenge in this project was the mapping of the desired functionality onto the technical infrastructure that was already in place at the customer site. The tradeoff between the specific solution and the generic components was also considered a major architectural challenge. The customer organization assisted the team with their operations and architecture teams. During the first phase of the project, an agile approach was used: high customer involvement, iterative delivery, and constant adaption of the product. In the second phase of the project, a more traditional approach was chosen, based on the Prince II [20] project management technique.

5.4.2.1 Phase one

Case Beta is split up in two phases that differed mainly in organization of the project. Phase one was facilitated by a very light RuP approach. The main goal of the project was to prove that case-based working, on an extendable technical solution, was applicable for the organization. There was a practical attitude towards documentation, and a focus on working software. Biweekly iterations were used to get the customer involved and to get feedback quickly. The results of this phase were a proof of technological validity of the solution and a first working version of the case management system. The customer was enthusiastic about the results and decided that a second phase should be initialized to complete the case management system for a specific department.

5.4.2.2 Phase two

In the second phase, the team remained mostly the same, but the project management methodology changed because a new project manager was assigned. This phase was managed strictly in Prince II, by a project manager and a steering committee formed mostly of higher management from the customer and supplier organizations. The goal of this phase was to extend, customize, and implement the techniques from the first phase for a very small department in the organization. As prescribed by the development methodology used, the first aim of the project was to get the functionality and the architecture of the proposed system written down completely (functional design, technical design).

5.4.2.3 Shifts

The following shifts occurred in case Beta:

- In phase two, more emphasis was on (mandatory) documentation instead of working software.
- There was increased complexity of the organization around the development team.
- The architectural decisions needed to be made earlier in the design process, and the decisions were never validated.

Because the customer was afraid of missing something in the description and design, it took about half a year to complete the documentation. The results were so detailed and complex that the architect board that had to monitor the design was unable to determine if the resulting documentation guaranteed that the resulting software could be created. The project became paralyzed because of the amount of documentation generated. Therefore, no value was delivered to the customer in the second phase.

5.4.3 **Case Gamma**

Case Gamma was conducted at a medium-sized product company in the Netherlands. The project involved a new administrative software system for specific departments in Dutch hospitals. Changing regulations and different working environments needed to be taken into account from the beginning. The project was executed by a multidisciplinary team of seven people, assisted by the architect of the company. A Java stack (JSF, Spring, Eclipselink) was used to create this product from scratch, while a different team of approximately seven people developed a part of the back end separately. This separate development was one of the most challenging architectural parts of the project. Product development took place over 12 months. The team used Scrum [14] with biweekly iterations to show results while being able to adopt to changes in functionality.

5.4.3.1 *Phase one*

The company involved in case Gamma had the vision to create a reusable architecture for its products. This generic, reusable architecture was implemented in parallel to the development of the system. This generic software was also used by another product at the same time. Architects in cooperation with the company's management made these architectural decisions (and the resulting interrelationship of the projects) before the project started. The development team was notified about the decisions, but the concerns they had were never seriously heard. During the first phase of the development of the system, the team felt that they had no influence on the decision process. Therefore, the atmosphere in the development team became less constructive. The reusable architecture was blamed for every defect in the system, as well as causing the system's slow development.

5.4.3.2 *Phase two*

The shift in this case came when the project team decided to take over responsibility and make the product independent of the decisions made before the project started. This included stubbing certain parts of the application, and sometimes even building functionality that was to be replaced by the generic software in the (near) future. New decisions were made within the development team, and the company architect was kept informed but was not held responsible anymore. Because the connection with the other projects stayed, the validation of the decisions was still delayed, but the decision loop was shortened significantly.

5.4.3.3 *Shifts*

The following shifts were identified for case Gamma:

- The responsibility for the architectural decision-making shifted from the management and architect to the development team.
- There was a quicker architecture decision process because the responsible persons were always present.
- There was less dependency on other projects within the company.
- There was less architectural documentation, and the documentation used was more lightweight.

Although the change caused the project to take more time in creating functionality (some functionality had to be made twice—once by the project team and once by the platform team), the overall speed of the project enhanced (more functionality was produced), and the team was much more committed to the result and the product, which increased its quality.

5.4.4 Case Delta

Case Delta is a Fortune 500 company developing software products and services operating primarily on personal computers. The company's products address both consumer and business markets and the company releases several products per year, including new releases of existing products and completely new products. The products developed by the company range in multi- to tens of millions of lines of code and tend to contain very complex components that implement national and international regulations. Although significant opportunities for sharing between different business units (BUs) exist, the company has organized its development based on a BU-centric approach. The products developed by each BU are typically based on a software product line. The company employs agile teams. It has new product development teams (who have no interdependency with other teams) and component teams for large established products in both North America and Asia.

The management and evolution of product architectures have been organized through architect teams that mentor and coach agile development teams. The organization arrived on this structure after falling into several traps around architecture and development efficiency. These traps included an overly complex software architecture for certain products, and software architects who had stopped coding and consequently had lost connection with the reality of software development that the team faced. The latter caused teams to be unvested in the architectural design decisions; the software architecture documentation and the system deviated rapidly. Finally, there were some signs of architecture work that was done for the architects, rather than for the benefit of the team or customer.

5.4.4.1 Phase one

In the situation of case Delta, the company used software architects as liaisons between general management, product management, and the development teams. The architects' role was to translate business needs into top-level architecture decisions before development of new products or the next (yearly) release of existing products started. Because of their role, architects spent very little time actually building systems and would often make decisions based on outdated understanding of technology and the implemented product architecture. This resulted in architectures that were more complex than necessary, due to the need to bring the designed and real, implemented software architectures together in one system. A second consequence was that teams were not committed to the designed architecture, because it had limited bearing on reality and the architecture work was viewed as being done for the architects' sake.

5.4.4.2 Phase two

The organization realized the challenges and made four main changes. First, architects returned to coding and spent a significant part of their time developing software together with the teams. Second, the teams got more autonomy and interacted much more with customers, and system-level architects started to act more in a coaching and mentoring role. Third, the organization accepted that "life happens" and that it often is better to refactor the architecture of products when the need arrives than to try to predict everything beforehand. Finally, the latter also changed the perception around the importance of documentation and the organization focused much more on maintaining a stable product team that collectively holds the architectural knowledge in their heads.

5.4.4.3 Shifts

To summarize, the following shifts took place in case Delta:

- The architecture team got more connected to the development team.
- Customers were explicitly heard during the development.
- Architectural decisions were made more quickly, and were checked against the working software.
- Documentation was used less and more emphasis was put on the tacit knowledge of team members.

The shift in case Delta resulted in features that were better suited to the needs of customers, which was a significant benefit. In addition, because of agile development practices, customers could get access to features much earlier than in the traditional development model. Finally, the significantly shortened feedback cycles resulted in higher quality of the overall system, because customers reported issues quickly and the team had the mechanisms to address their issues promptly.

5.4.5 Case Epsilon

A small startup company that creates a web-based product for the consumer market was the scene for case Epsilon. The project contained high-risk technological challenges; the architecture needed to be flexible in the beginning, to be able to handle the expected high number of users. The application was created in Ruby/Rails with a NoSQL back end based on MongoDB and Redis. The main architectural challenges were to be able to potentially scale up the application when lots of consumers are using the system, and being able to adapt the system to changing requirements from the customer. There was one development team of seven people that conducting (bi) weekly iterations (using Scrum) over a period of 12 months.

5.4.5.1 Phase one

In case Epsilon, the architecture was not fixed from the beginning, the main architect was an experienced developer, and the product owner had significant influence on the decision process. Architecture decisions were made before the implementation phase of any iterative development methods. The architect also helped the team with the coding of the software. After 3 months, the architect moved and was unable to participate in the project anymore, while the product owner got less involved in the actual development.

5.4.5.2 Phase two

This started the second phase of the project, where no formal architect was with the team. All of the team members felt responsible for the architecture. No large architecture documentation was written—architectural decisions were made when needed and summarized in the wiki, or photos of meetings were shared in the internal chat. Important architectural issues were formulated as functionality and put on the backlog as user stories, often after debating them with everyone interested. Simplicity guided the architecture. The result of the project was a working closed Beta version of the product.

5.4.5.3 Shifts

The following shifts occurred in case Epsilon:

- Responsibility for the architectural decisions process changed from one architect to a team responsibility.
- There was a quicker decision process because the right people were always on-site.
- There was extremely lightweight documentation of architectural decisions and a focus on direct communication.

Although the change was not as severe as in the other cases, a definite change in the flexibility of the team was noticed. This resulted in quicker responses to bug or feedback reports and more predictable delivery of functionality (both quality aspects).

5.4.6 Overview

As an overview of the case studies used, Table 5.1 describes the characteristics of them all: the period, the team sizes, and the team experience.

Table 5.1 Overview of Case Studies

Case	Domain	Period	Team Size	Experience of Team
Alpha	Harbor	9 months	10-20 FTE	Experienced team and architects
Beta	Government	12 months	5-10 FTE	Moderate team and architects
Gamma	Hospital	12 months	7-14 FTE	Moderate team, experienced architects
Delta	Product company	12 months	>50 FTE	Experienced teams and architects
Epsilon	Consumer product	12 months	5-8 FTE	Moderate team, experienced architect

In the following section, the case studies are mapped against the Triple-A Framework, followed by an analysis of the problems that can be generalized from the case studies.

5.5 ANALYSIS

In this section, we will provide an analysis of the results by correlating them to problems that occur in software development. First, we will show how the cases can be mapped to the Triple-A Framework. From this, we will analyze what problems have been addressed in our work.

5.5.1 Mapping the cases to the Triple-A Framework

To illustrate the value of the Triple-A Framework, we show that the changes in the cases from Section 5.4 can be seen as shifts among the axes of the Triple-A Framework. In this section, we identify what effects shifting along the axes have on the efficiency of the whole case.

All five cases have been mapped on the Triple-A Framework. In the Appendix, a visual representation of the mapping is given. The results of the cases are summarized in Table 5.2. In this table, the cases are described and the shifts on the axes are visualized by: "−" shift toward the center, "+" shift away from the center, and "++" a radical shift away from the center. The results are split into the three parts that were discussed above: Return on Investment (RoI), Speed, and Quality. In the result columns, the "−" means that the result was worse in the second phase, and the "+" means the results were better in the second phase. Empty fields indicate no difference has been found.

Generally, we saw that the shifts towards the center of the Triple-A Framework (cases Alpha and Beta) increased complexity and tended to decrease productivity and speed. In the other cases (Gamma, Delta, and Epsilon), the shift to the edges of the axis resulted in increased quality and development speed.

Table 5.2 Mapping the Cases on the Triple-A Framework

	Axes			Result		
Case	Who	How	When	RoI	Speed	Quality
Alpha	−	−	−	−	−	
Beta		−	−	−	−	
Gamma	++	+	+		+	+
Delta	++	++	+	+	+	+
Epsilon	+	+	+		+	+

5.5.2 Identified problems

As we have seen in our cases, organizations seek to improve agility because of real business benefits that can be achieved. Companies invest in software architecture and software architects for the same reasons. Unfortunately, as we discussed in the introduction, these areas are occasionally combined in ways that cause the organization to fail in its ambitions. From the experience of the described cases, we have identified six main problems. They are discussed below. With every problem, we indicate which cases involved the specific problem, what axes are affected and a short description of the identified problem.

Architects as single point of failure
Cases involved: Alpha, Gamma
Axis affected: Who

The architect(s) often represent a single point of failure. The architect has to be the one that (a) talks to the customer to understand the vision and the most significant requirements, (b) creates the main structure of the system, (c) makes sure the solution is future-proof—especially concerning the nonfunctional requirements—and (d) makes sure the development team creates software conforming to the architectural decisions made. These tasks are hard for one person to do, especially in larger projects. A project being dependent on one person presents a high risk.

Complexity instead of simplicity
Cases involved: Alpha, Beta, Gamma, Delta
Axes affected: Who and When

Architects are assumed to be the cleverest people in the team; therefore, they often create smart solutions that are more complex than they need to be to solve the problem at hand. The pressure from management and customers on the architect to create a "future-proof" architecture often enhances this effect. When groups of architects get too large compared to the rest of the team, the results look nice—but sometimes they are hard to implement. This is a typical example of the "create a perfect architecture, but too hard to implement" antipattern described by Kruchten [11].

Outdated software architects
Cases involved: Alpha, Gamma, Delta
Axis affected: Who

Often, the architectural decision-makers are not involved in developing the software anymore. This creates a lack of hands-on experience in the technology they are designing for. Because of this, their decisions are based on outdated assumptions and experiences, and because the decision-makers have no direct experience with any important design flaws, there is no incentive to change the design when necessary.

Uncommitted teams
Cases involved: Gamma, Delta, Epsilon
Axis affected: Who

If many important decisions are made solely by the architect(s), the development team does not feel primarily committed to the decisions made. If this happens, there is a lack of support for the decisions. In the worst case, the team opposes the decisions made and undermines the actual development of the system. This is a typical consequence of what Kruchten calls the "architects in their ivory tower" [11].

Static architectural decisions
Cases involved: Beta, Epsilon
Axis affected: When

As customer demands, technology, and organizations change, architectural decisions also need to change. Therefore, architectural decisions do not last forever. During the development and evolution of a system, architectural decisions are made and revised constantly. As architects in traditional settings are involved primarily in the earlier stages of development, the tendency is to make decisions earlier on and to keep to them for a long time. This makes it hard to adapt the system to new challenges.

Illusion of documentation
Cases involved: Alpha, Beta, Delta
Axis affected: How

It is very tough to have good documentation when it is used as a communication medium. Often, documentation is out of date and is badly read. Since architecture documentation especially needs to be created manually, it is typically outdated within weeks—if not days or hours. In addition, very few people, even architects, actually read architecture documentation. This is both because of its obsoleteness and because it fails to help the reader build a relevant understanding of the system. However, these symptoms are rarely acknowledged—and when things don't go as planned, often more documentation is mandated.

5.5.3 Summary

The description of the problems above can help teams identify problems and understand which change (shift on a axis) could help improve the project. Based on this set of problems, we can conclude that the who axis affected four problems, the how axis affected only one problem, and the when axis affected two problems. This is an indication that the who axis could be the most influential one.

5.6 REFLECTION

This section reflects on the findings from the previous section and discusses questions on the validity of this research.

5.6.1 Findings

As with many solutions in software engineering research, the Triple-A Framework proposed in this chapter is no silver bullet. Often, the situation greatly influences the possibilities of companies, projects, teams, and individuals. However, the described axes can be used to see how responsibilities, timing, and communication methods can influence the results of a project. And, if a project or organization needs to change, the Triple-A Framework can help in identifying where the change can be made, by analyzing the current decision process and focusing on one of the axes where change can be achieved.

Some of the changes that derive from the Triple-A Framework have a big influence on how a project is run. When a project stops using certain templates, makes other people responsible for the decision process, or waits for design issues to occur, there is always the concern of trust involved. We have experienced that trusting people to do the right things is often very tough, especially within large organizations or large contract structures (as seen in cases Alpha, Beta, and Delta).

In traditional organizational setups, architects come in three archetypes that, although overlapping in some cases, have different responsibilities. The first type of architect acts as the bridge between the business strategy and customers on one side and the software development team on the other side. Secondly, with highly complex systems, architects often have the responsibility for the end-to-end quality requirements of the system and coach individual engineers to make sure that new features and functionality do not violate system properties. Finally, some organizations share responsibility for the team between a project manager focusing on milestones and people management and an architect who acts as the technical lead for the team. In our experience, and this is the position that we take in this chapter, there is a fourth archetype. In this type, the architect becomes the coach for the development team responsible for facilitating architectural decision-making. In an age where teams become increasingly self-selected, -directed, and -managed [21], it is important that architects move away from traditional hierarchical, formal leadership roles and adopt meritocracy-based leadership styles. This can be done in an iterative way by accurately shifting along the axes of the Triple-A Framework.

5.6.2 Questions of validity

Several matters raise questions on the validity of our research.. First of all, the participant/observer method does imply some subjectivity. The results are qualitative (not quantitative), and based on the experience of the researchers participating in the project. However, this is one of the accepted ways to gather case study material in software engineering research, and all of our cases involved real-life industrial software projects that could not have been studied in any other way.

Although we have identified three axes that influence the results of the case study projects, it is possible that these are not the only parameters affecting the results of the cases studied. Due to the nature of our research, and the fact that it was conducted in real industrial settings, it is likely that there were other factors involved. However, we have seen that in all of the cases the shifts did occur in the same direction along the defined axis.

We have used only five cases, which involved mainly small project teams. As such, the degree to which this research can be generalized is restricted to projects of this type. However, as seen in the context of case Delta, the axes also show impact in larger organizations.

5.7 RELATED AND FUTURE WORK

In the research community, there is currently a debate on the usefulness of agile software development. The trend is to say that there are enough stories of successful and failed projects done with various methodologies, but insufficient (empirical) evidence to found a conclusion [2,22]. This chapter contributes in this debate by describing additional case study results.

There has been much attention given to documenting software architectures [23,24], as well as documentation templates [17] and computational modeling [25] for documenting relevant architectural knowledge. Recently, there has been a trend toward using semantic wikis [18], and some research experiments show promising results [26].

Another topic that is being discussed is the role of the architect [12]. Here, often the architect is responsible for creating and maintaining the architecture documentation. In this chapter, we have shown the importance to collaborative multidisciplinary decision-making of identifying who makes the decisions in projects.

In the architecture design decision research hierarchical structures are used to model architectural knowledge [3] or design decisions [15,27]. This research often emphasizes the recording of decisions and the extraction of decisions later in the development process. This chapter focuses on the decision process itself.

The agile community often doesn't explicitly describe the role of architects' architectural documentation or architectural decisions when explaining what they do [14,28]. Although there have been brave initiatives for merging the two [3], most of the agile community still has an aversion against architects and architecture documentation. Some authors emphasize the importance of architecture even in agile settings [29]. In this chapter, we have shown changes for software architecture in agile software development.

In future research, we would like to extend our validation of the Triple-A Framework to other industrial cases, specifically to larger-sized projects and distributed settings where direct communication is more complicated. Second, we will conduct more research on other possible axes that influence the architecture decision process. Third, we would like the Triple-A Framework to be based on a more discrete scale, to be able to score teams or companies.

5.8 CONCLUSIONS

From our industrial cases, we have seen a trend take shape. First, we have seen that leaning heavily on architects as the persons that should solve the architectural problems leads to unproductive teams, or even no working software at all. Second, we have experienced that when the focus is too much on large (architectural) documentation, the speed and quality of the project decreases. Third, we have seen that making important architectural decisions early on in the project leads to architectural problems during development. Although the agile community makes these claims, this is rarely backed up by case material. We contribute to this debate by presenting initial case study material.

In this chapter, we have followed two steps toward a better understanding of what happens around architectural decision-making. First, based on our experience and existing literature, we have generalized the Triple-A Framework for assessing how the architecture is handled in projects or organizations. Second, we have described five industrial cases, and we have identified shifts in these cases. We have shown that these changes can be mapped to the three axes that we created within the Triple-A Framework. We have seen that the successes and failures of the cases were influenced by the shifts that were made. These axes can be used to help teams that are becoming more agile to align their architecture practices.

From our research conducted at the five case studies presented in this chapter, we can conclude that moving on the axes of the Triple-A Framework influences the success of a project. This means that by moving away from the center (development team, direct communication and short feedback loop), the projects became more successful (Gamma, Delta, Epsilon), while by moving towards the center (management, mandatory templates, long feedback loop), the cases became less successful (Alpha, Beta). We are planning to use our framework on additional cases to further validate our findings.

APPENDIX A VISUAL REPRESENTATION OF THE CASE STUDIES MAPPED ON THE TRIPLE-A FRAMEWORK

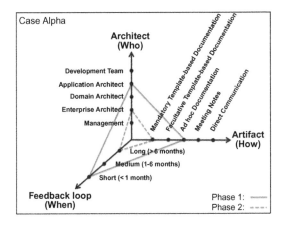

Continued

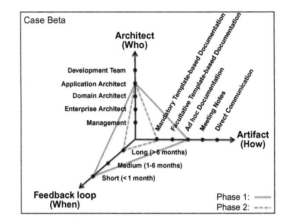

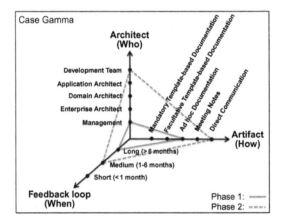

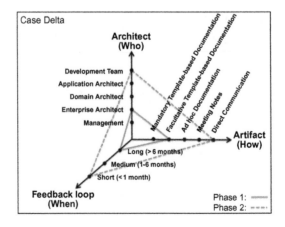

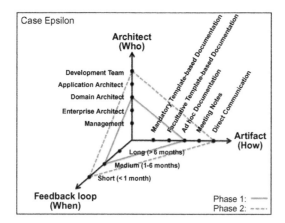

Case Epsilon

References

[1] Abrahamsson P, Babar MA, Kruchten P. Agility and architecture: can they coexist? IEEE Softw 2010;27(2):16–22.

[2] Breivold HP, Sundmark D, Wallin P, Larsson S. What does research say about agile and architecture? In: Proceedings of the 2010 fifth international conference on software engineering advances; 2010.

[3] Coplien J, Bjørnvig G. Lean architecture: for agile software development. Chichester: Wiley; 2010.

[4] Ali Babar M, Ihme T, Pikkarainen M. An industrial case of exploiting product line architectures in agile software development. In: Proceedings of the 13th international software product line conference; 2009.

[5] Bosch J, Bosch-Sijtsema PM. Introducing agile customer-centered development in a legacy software product line. Softw Pract Exper 2011;41(8):871–82.

[6] Eisenhardt KM. Building theories from case study research. Acad Manage Rev 1989;14 (4):532–50.

[7] de Boer RC, Farenhorst R, Lago P, van Vliet H, Clerc V, Jansen A. Architectural knowledge: getting to the core. In: Proceedings of the quality of software architectures 3rd international conference on software architectures, components, and applications; 2007.

[8] Tyree J, Akerman A. Architecture decisions: demystifying architecture. IEEE Softw 2005;22(2):19–27.

[9] Kruchten P. An ontology of architectural design decisions in software intensive systems. In: 2nd Groningen workshop software variability; 2004.

[10] Bu W, Tang A, Han J. An analysis of decision-centric architectural design approaches. In: Proceedings of the 2009 ICSE workshop on sharing and reusing architectural knowledge; 2009.

[11] Kruchten P. What do software architects really do? J Syst Softw 2008;81(12):2413–6.

[12] Farenhorst R, Hoorn JF, Lago P, van Vliet H. The lonesome architect. J Syst Softw 2011;84(9):1424–35.

[13] Malan R, Bredemeyer D. Less is more with minimalist architecture. IT Professional 2002;4(5):46–7, pp. 48.

[14] Kniberg H. Scrum and XP from the trenches: enterprise software development. C4Media; 2007. www.Lulu.com. ISBN: 9781430322641.

[15] Jansen AGJ, Bosch J. Software architecture as a set of architectural design decisions. In: Proceedings of the 5th IEEE/IFIP working conference on software architecture (WICSA 2005); 2005.

[16] Hansen MT, Nohria N, Tierney T. What's your strategy for managing knowledge? Harv Bus Rev 1999;77(2):106–16.

[17] Kruchten P. The rational unified process: an introduction. Reading, MA: Addison-Wesley; 2003.

[18] Happel H-J, Seedorf S. Ontobrowse: a semantic wiki for sharing knowledge about software architectures. Boston, MA: SEKE; 2007.

[19] Kazman R, Klein M, Barbacci M, Longstaff T, Lipson H, Carriere J. The architecture tradeoff analysis method. In: Proceedings of the fourth IEEE international conference on engineering of complex computer systems (ICECCS); 1998.

[20] Hedeman HB, Vis van Heemst G, Fredriksz H. Project management: based on Prince2 2009: Best Practice Series. Zaltbommel, Netherlands: Van Haren Publishing, 2010. 254 pp. ISBN: 9087534965, 9789087534967.

[21] Appelo J. Management 3.0: leading agile developers, developing agile leaders. Reading, MA: Addison Wesley; 2010.

[22] Petersen K, Wohlin C. A comparison of issues and advantages in agile and incremental development between state of the art and an industrial case. J Syst Softw 2009;82 (9):1479–90.

[23] Clements P, Garlan D, Bass L, Stafford J, Nord R, Ivers J, et al. Documenting software architectures: views and beyond. Boston, MA: Pearson Education; 2002.

[24] Hofmeister C, Nord R, Soni D. Applied software architecture. Reading, MA: Addison-Wesley; 2000.

[25] Group OMG. UML specification, version 2.0. Online at: http://www.omg.org/spec/UML/; 2012.

[26] de Graaf KA, Tang A, Liang P, van Vliet H. Ontology-based software architecture documentation. In: WICSA/ECSA; 2012.

[27] van der Ven JS, Jansen A, Nijhuis J, Bosch J. Design decisions: the bridge between rationale and architecture. In: Rationale management in software engineering. Berlin: Springer; 2006. p. 329–48.

[28] Rasmusson J. The agile samurai: how agile masters deliver great software. 1st ed. Pragmatic Bookshelf; 2010 ISBN-10: 1934356581; ISBN-13: 978-1934356586.

[29] Kruchten P. Software architecture and agile software development: a clash of two cultures? In: Proceedings of the 32nd ACM/IEEE international conference on software engineering—volume 2, ICSE 2010; 2010.

Managing Software Architecture in Agile Projects

Supporting Variability Through Agility to Achieve Adaptable Architectures

Matthias Galster * **and Paris Avgeriou** †

University of Canterbury, Christchurch, New Zealand
†*University of Groningen, Groningen, The Netherlands*

CHAPTER CONTENTS

6.1 INTRODUCTION

Variability plays an important role in defining and managing parts of a software architecture that may vary. Variability is needed when a number of similar but not identical systems from different usage or deployment scenarios are developed [1]. Traditionally, variability is interpreted as "anticipated and preplanned change."

Many of today's software systems are designed with variability in mind. Examples include software product lines or families, self-adapting systems, open platforms, or service-based systems that support the dynamic composition of web services.

Variability is reflected in and enabled through the software architecture. Therefore, handling variability during software architecture design is important. Here, *handling* variability refers to all activities related to identifying, constraining, implementing, and managing variability. In software architecture, variability is described in terms of variation points (i.e., locations in the architecture where change might occur) and variants (i.e., options to resolve variation points). Depending on the architectural representation, variation points and variants can occur in the form of components, connectors, decisions, and so on. Consequently, variability handling requires up-front planning of what variability will exist and how it will affect the software architecture.

Another paradigm that embraces change and adaptation is the *agile paradigm*. The agile paradigm is an umbrella concept for methods that are based on the Agile Manifesto [2]. Agile methods are defined in terms of values (or ideals), principles (i.e., the application of ideals to industry), and practices (i.e., principles applied to a specific type of project) [2]. All agile methods implement iterative, incremental life cycles and share similar values and principles. The agile paradigm accepts the reality of change instead of aiming for complete and rigid software requirements and software architectures. For most projects, accepting the existence of frequent changes can cost less than aiming for requirements or architectures that will never change. Furthermore, agile methods usually focus on delivering value to customers through early and continuous delivery [2]. Besides these common principles of agile methods, each agile method (e.g., XP, Scrum) defines its own practices (e.g., sprints in Scrum, pair-programming in XP).

Variability facilitates the design of software systems for contexts or for customers' needs, which are not fully known during early design. Similarly, agile development starts with building software solutions before the desired product is fully understood. The goal of this chapter is to combine the agile paradigm and handling variability; we leverage the agile paradigm in the context of architecture-centric variability handling to propose an approach for handling variability at the software architecture level. The benefit of combining agility and variability is threefold:

1. It helps achieve less heavyweight variability handling because the agile paradigm claims to reduce the overhead introduced by many software development processes.
2. It allows quick feedback about required variability in the software product and the architecture to be obtained from customers.
3. It helps incorporate changing variability requirements in the architecture (e.g., new variation points or variants or a new deployment context that a system must support). Thus, facilitating variability through agility can improve the evolution of variability.

By integrating the agile paradigm and variability at the architectural level (i.e., as part of the architecting process), adaptable and flexible software architectures are achieved. Variability described in the architecture then makes variability-related information available at other development stages, such as implementation or testing. We believe that the proposed approach is suitable for production-focused projects and therefore is useful for projects with short schedules, tight deadlines, and frequently changing requirements. This approach focuses on working software, with other activities (such as up-front planning) being of lower importance. Therefore, our approach offers a way to handle variability with less time and effort and with little architecture design when a heavyweight process cannot be used.

In Section 6.2 of this chapter, we discuss background related to variability and agility. In Section 6.3, we present related work on combining variability and agility. In Section 6.4, we discuss challenges that occur when combining variability and agility, before we elaborate on arguments for combining variability and agility in Section 6.5. In Section 6.6, we present an approach for variability handling that uses concepts from agile development. In Section 6.7, we introduce an industrial example that is used to illustrate the individual steps of our approach in Sections 6.8–6.15. We conclude this chapter with Section 6.16.

6.2 BACKGROUND
6.2.1 Variability

Variability is understood as the ability of a software artifact to be adapted (e.g., configured, extended) for a specific context in a preplanned manner [3]. Thus, we interpret variability as planned change rather than change due to errors, maintenance, or unanticipated customer needs. Variability specifies parts of the system and its architecture that remain variable or are not fully defined during design time. Variability allows the development of different versions of an architecture or system. Variability in the architecture is usually introduced through variation points (i.e., locations in the architecture where change might occur). Variants describe options to resolve variability at these variation points. Variability occurs in different phases of the software life cycle [4]. Design time variability resolves variability at the time the architecture is designed. Runtime variability resolves variability while the system is running (e.g., after design, implementation, and so on).

Handling variability requires explicitly representing variability in software artifacts throughout the life cycle of a software product. Please note that we use the term *handling* variability rather than *managing* variability. As argued by Svahnberg et al. [5], managing variability is only one of several activities in the context of handling variability. Managing variability comprises managing dependencies between variables, maintenance and continuous population of variant features with new variants, removing features, the distribution of new variants to the installed customer base, and more. Additional activities involved in handling variability include identifying variability (i.e., determining where variability is needed), reasoning, representing, and implementing variability (i.e., using a variability realization technique to resolve variability at variation points and to implement a certain variant) [5].

Variability has mainly been addressed in the software product line domain and in product line architectures. However, most product line approaches are rather heavyweight. A product line architecture assumes the existence of a product line infrastructure, including related processes (e.g., core asset development, product development, management) [6]. This is rarely the case for many software architectures that should support variability.

6.2.2 Agility

The agile paradigm is an umbrella concept for methods that are based on the Agile Manifesto [2]. The Agile Manifesto (www.agilemanifesto.org) values "individuals and interactions over processes and tools," "working software over comprehensive documentation," "customer collaboration over contract negotiation," and "responding to change over following a plan." The Agile Manifesto defines 12 principles, which are listed in Table 6.1.

Table 6.1 Principles in the Agile Manifesto (www.agilemanifesto.org)

Principle	Description
1	The highest priority is to satisfy the customer through early and continuous delivery of valuable software.
2	Changing requirements are welcomed, even late in the development (agile processes harness change for the customer's advantage).
3	Working software should be delivered frequently, with a preference to shorter timescale delivery.
4	Business people and developers must work together daily throughout the project.
5	Projects should be built around motivated individuals and in an environment that supports their needs and facilitates trust to get the job done.
6	The most efficient and effective method of conveying information within/across development teams is face-to-face communication.
7	Progress is measured based on working software.
8	Agile processes promote sustainable development. Sponsors, developers, and users should maintain a constant pace indefinitely.
9	Agility is enhanced through continuous attention to technical excellence.
10	Maximizing the amount of work not done is essential.
11	The best architectures, requirements, and designs emerge from self-organizing teams.
12	Software development teams should reflect on how to become more effective, and adjust their behavior accordingly.

6.3 **RELATED WORK**

Work on combining the agile paradigm with variability handling is quite limited. Most work has been conducted in the context of agile product line engineering. In product line engineering, variability is treated as a key concept. In 2006, the First International Workshop on Agile Product Line Engineering [7] was held, which concluded that it is feasible to combine agility and product line engineering. More recently, literature reviews on agile product line engineering have been published [2,8]. These reviews discuss reasons for combining agility and product line engineering (e.g., to reduce costs during domain engineering, to deal with volatile business situations, or to handle situations in which a domain is not well understood up-front), what agile methods are used in product line engineering, and present open research challenges (e.g., provide more support for evolving variability). Most proposed approaches for agile product line engineering introduce agility in existing software product lines [1]. Other works suggest that the competing philosophies of agile software development (little up-front planning) and software product line engineering (heavy up-front planning) make their integration difficult [9]. Instead, agile development and product line engineering should be tailored so that both can "retain their basic characteristics" [1].

In contrast to these literature reviews, an industrial study on agile product line engineering has been presented by Hansen and Faegri [10]. This study concluded that introducing agile product lines involves multiple disciplines (e.g., product planning, knowledge management, organizational aspects, and innovation), and is thus a long-term effort. Similarly, Pohjalainen describes experiences in agile modeling of a product line [11], including a lightweight method for feature modeling. Additional examples of combining agility and product line engineering include agile product line planning that focuses on product line engineering as a highly collaborative process [12], or an agile process for building product lines using a lightweight feature model [13], similar to Pohjalainen. Furthermore, Ghanam et al. proposed reactive variability management in agile development [1] and used acceptance tests from test-driven development to elicit variability in requirements [14]. All these efforts show that combining agile development and product line engineering is feasible. However, thorough up-front planning is traded against faster development and more flexibility throughout the development process.

Even though product lines are only one type of variability-intensive systems, not much work on combining variability and agility can be found outside the domain of product lines. Furthermore, software architecture has not been the focus when studying the impact of combining agility and variability.

Although our work can be related to dynamic architectures and adaptive architectures, these two concepts are beyond the scope of this chapter. We do not focus on systems that are self-adaptive during runtime, but investigate how variability can be enabled to develop different product versions more easily. Dynamic architectures, on the other hand, are architectures that provide adaptability of systems during runtime. Many approaches utilize service-based computing to dynamically adapt systems, such as Shokry and Ali Babar [15] or Hallsteinsen who explored dynamic product lines [16], Fiadeiro and Lopes who proposed dynamic reconfiguration of service-oriented architectures [17], or Parra et al. who explored dynamic service-based product lines that are context-aware. Oreizy et al. proposed an architecture-based approach for self-adaptive software [18].

6.4 CHALLENGES WHEN COMBINING VARIABILITY AND AGILITY

We identified several challenges when integrating variability and the agile paradigm in the context of software architecture design:

- To identify variability (i.e., commonalities and variations) between software products and the variability needed in the architecture, a comprehensive analysis is conducted up-front. We determine what requirements in a product may vary, including the sources of variation and the allowed options to resolve this variation. This also includes investigating how the architecture can facilitate the required variability. In agile development, however, the focus is on developing software systems that satisfy customers by minimizing up-front investment and process overhead [1]. This is in fact a direct conflict with handling variability, because it requires up-front analysis to anticipate change.
- Documentation of variability is essential to communicate architecture knowledge between stakeholders. Thus, the architecture must properly represent variability. When handling variability, designers usually plan and document extensively, and each designer has a specific responsibility [19]. In contrast, agile development tries to reduce overhead caused by excessive documentation but relies on implicit or light-weight documentation (e.g., through documentation in source code or story cards). As a result, in agile development, designers use a lot of tacit knowledge and share responsibilities.
- In agile development, fast and frequent delivery is a key for quick customer satisfaction and feedback. This is difficult to achieve in variability-intensive systems: variability is analyzed before delivering any product to provide a flexible infrastructure, which is later configured and deployed [13]. The agile principle of "simplicity" and implementing functionality that satisfies current instead of future requirements could contradict the need to support different variation points in the architecture. In agile development, not a lot of effort is put into designing the architecture beyond the current iteration [19].
- Agile methods focus on quick response to requirement changes with short iterations and small increments. This requires direct customer collaboration and participation in the whole software project lifecycle [19]. When handling variability at the software architecture level, communication between stakeholders is important. However, collaboration takes place not as extensively as in a typical agile development setting, and customers are rarely on site.

- One assumption of variability is that target application domains in which a system is deployed are stable and do not change much. In contrast, in agile environments, application domains are unstable and domain boundaries change. However, stable domains would reduce risks when pre-developing software assets for later (re-)use. Consequently, while there is no emphasis on reuse in agile development, variability puts special emphasis on maturity and reliability of reused artifacts [19].
- Agile methods emphasize simple and efficient tools (e.g., paper-based or virtual story cards, web-based tools for test-driven development) where technology only affects the current project [19]. To handle variability, robust, heavyweight, and powerful tools (e.g., Gears[a] or Pure::variants[b]) are used.

6.5 ARGUMENTS FOR COMBINING VARIABILITY AND AGILITY

Despite the different natures of variability and the agile paradigm, there are some common principles between these two concepts that justify their combination, as proposed in this chapter. Such principles include the following:

- Agile methods and handling variability are about vague or changing (or adapting) requirements. Agility even encourages change and handles it when it happens, whereas variability is about anticipating change (or adaptations) during the design phase. Consequently, the architecture is "enriched" with variation points in its design. This not only allows handling anticipated change, but also allows handling unanticipated change better than approaches which do not consider variability. This is because some of the unanticipated changes will coincide with variation points [9]. It is easier to make changes to the architecture and add new variants than it is to introduce changes in the architecture for which no provision for change has been made.
- Agile development and variability handling require collaboration. Agile methods are based on collaboration between stakeholders (e.g., customer, product users, and developers) [9]. Similarly, to handle variability, there is a need for various stakeholder groups (e.g., architects, product users) to be involved in scoping variability. During both agile development and variability handling, collaborations serve the purpose of a feedback circuit [9].
- Agile development and variability handling are assumed to operate within a scope. The scope of variability defines what the range of adaptation can be [9].
- Agility and variability handling aim at minimizing work to be done. Agility is about postponing work until it is needed, while variability is about systematically anticipating what will be needed in the future and then creating reusable common artifacts for specific purposes within the specific scope.

---

[a]www.biglever.com
[b]www.pure-systems.com

6.6 AGILE-INSPIRED VARIABILITY HANDLING

In this section we outline an approach for agile-inspired variability handling (Figure 6.1). The approach is proactive, rather than reactive. "Proactive" means that we prepare the architecture for adaptation and anticipate change during up-front analysis, rather than only dealing with change when change (or the need for adaptation) occurs. This up-front analysis (Phase 1 of our approach, see Figure 6.1) prepares the architecture for variability and makes variability handling at a later stage more lightweight, because less rework will be required (Phase 2 of our approach). Our approach maps to generic architecture design activities proposed by Hofmeister et al. [20] and extended by Tang et al. [21]:

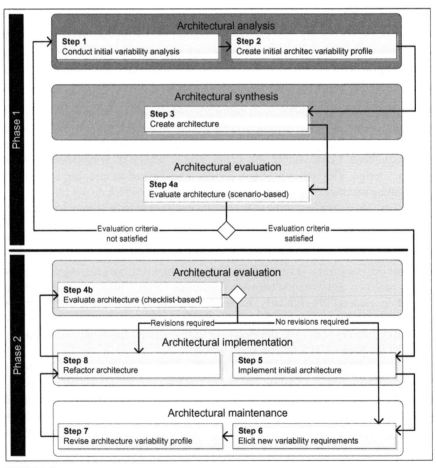

FIGURE 6.1

Overview of the approach.

- *Architectural analysis* defines the problem that a system architecture must solve. During this activity, architectural concerns and the context of the system are examined to define a set of architecturally significant requirements.
- *Architectural synthesis* proposes architecture solutions (i.e., architecture candidates) for the architecturally significant requirements identified during architectural analysis. Synthesis can result in several architecture candidates or candidate decisions for one architecturally significant requirement.
- *Architectural evaluation* examines candidate architectural decisions against the architecturally significant requirements. Based on the outcome of the evaluation, the architecture can be revised by going back to architectural analysis/synthesis.
- *Architectural implementation* realizes the architecture—by passing it on to designers to proceed with the detailed design, and further on to implementers for writing the code.
- *Architectural maintenance* accommodates changes once the initial system is deployed.

As mentioned before, the proposed approach comprises two phases (see Figure 6.1). Each phase requires a number of steps that take place within the aforementioned five generic architecture design activities. The first phase is about creating an initial architecture that is "prepared" for accommodating adaptations. As can be seen in Figure 6.1, Phase 1 usually requires some iterations to properly understand the problem domain and to define a sound variability profile and architecture. Steps in Phase 2 are repeated every time new requirements are established and make it necessary to evolve variability. Consequently, Phase 1—the up-front analysis—is performed once, whereas Phase 2 is a continuous activity along the life cycle of a product. Phase 2 also utilizes agile principles and ensures an adaptable architecture (hence the highly iterative nature), whereas Phase 1 prepares the architecture with variability to facilitate easier adaptation. Phase 2 utilizes ideas from Kanban [22], which argues for continuous incremental and evolutionary changes to a current system (architecture in our case) to achieve improvements. Instead of going back to analysis and synthesis, our approach only revises the architecture variability profile and refactors the architecture. An overview of the proposed approach and how it relates to software architecture design activities is shown in Figure 6.1. Please note that in our approach, the architecture does not fully emerge during development (as claimed in agile development). Instead, our approach creates an architecture that supports variability. This architecture then evolves throughout development (just like in agile development).

The approach is not prescriptive about when and how to apply certain techniques within the different steps. A technique is used when it seems appropriate, and it is not used when it does not help anymore. Thus, the approach can be considered a framework because it defines what is important to achieve, but does not specify when and how to use a technique. Furthermore, the proposed approach focuses on variability handling at the *software architecture level*. Thus, it addresses four architecture-related activities for handling variability [5,23]:

- *Identify variability*: When variability is identified, decisions are made about what variability is needed and where. This requires the definition of what architecture elements are variable. Depending on the architecture's representation and granularity, architecture elements could be components, connectors, decisions, and so on.
- *Constrain variability*: Constraining variability is about making sure that just enough flexibility is provided in the architecture to meet current and future needs.
- *Implement variability*: When implementing variability, suitable realization techniques to implement variability are selected. Examples include architectural refactoring, the inclusion of optional architecture components, or the specialization of variant components.
- *Manage variability*: Managing variability includes evolution, maintenance, and continuous addition of features and variants. For example, new components could be added, components could be replaced, decisions could be changed, and so on.

Table 6.1 shows how the steps of the approach relate to the architecture-related variability-handling activities introduced above. Details on the mapping will be discussed when introducing the individual steps in the following subsections. Note that Steps 4a and 4b (evaluation) are not related to any architecture-related variability-handling activity.

Although the process includes many steps, we have kept individual steps lightweight. Furthermore, Phase 1—which includes up-front analysis and may be considered heavyweight in agile methodologies—is only conducted once to prepare the architecture for easier variability handling later on. Consequently, Phase 1 is more similar to traditional variability handling, whereas Phase 2 integrates agile mechanisms (such as refactoring). In the following, we detail each step and illustrate them using the example of variability in a Dutch e-government system. This system and its context are described in the next section.

6.6.1 Industrial context: Dutch e-government

The Dutch e-government system in our example supports municipalities in performing their business processes (e.g., processing social services or requests for building permits). The software is based on a service-oriented architecture (SOA). In local Dutch e-government, variability occurs because of the differences between municipalities. Dutch municipalities are autonomous when implementing laws that have been approved by the national government. In the Netherlands, there are more than 400 municipalities. These municipalities implement different business processes to support the same law. For example, let us look at the Dutch law for social support (so-called WMO law): One municipality might require a dedicated assessment from an approved health care practitioner to determine whether or not a citizen is eligible for a subsidized home modification to improve accessibility. On the other hand, another municipality might simply rely on the self-assessment of a citizen. Another example is that some municipalities charge citizens for certain services (e.g., a taxi pass for senior citizens), while some municipalities do not. Please note that this example is merely used to show how our approach could be applied in a realistic case; the real system was developed without using our approach.

6.6.2 Step 1: conduct initial variability analysis

Similar to [12], variability analysis requires the identification of and the agreement upon the relevant scope of an application and the required variability. To determine the scope of an application and required variability, we have to gain access to domain and business knowledge and interact with customers to define short- and long-term requirements. Thus, initial variability analysis is related to *identifying variability* to find out what variability is needed and where. The outcome of variability analysis is an agreed-upon list of initial functionality and variability to be implemented in an architecture. Furthermore, during variability analysis, special attention has to be paid to identifying architectural variability [24]. Here, architectural variability is understood as variability in the architecture that is required due to variability in functionality. Understanding the business of an organization, the problem domain being addressed, common and variable features, and so on, are in line with agile methods. For example, in feature-driven development [25], a project starts with a high-level walkthrough of the scope of a system and its context and the gathering of a list of mandatory features.

The initial variability analysis for the Dutch e-government system leads to an agreed-upon list of initial functionalities to be implemented in the architecture. However, instead of defining a complete architecture, a preliminary architecture blueprint is created. The domains in the case of the e-government system are different municipalities. The functionality is prescribed by the WMO law. Furthermore, variability is identified in business processes or in the IT infrastructure of municipalities. This variability would be specified in the architectural variability profile created in Step 2.

6.6.3 Step 2: create initial architecture variability profile

An architectural variability profile describes all variation points, their variants, the type (s) of variability, and resolution time (see Table 6.2). By defining variants, we *constrain variability*. The variability profile ensures that just enough flexibility is provided in the architecture to meet current and future needs based on the initial variability analysis. This type of profile is different from known variability models—such as feature models, which focus on the description of commonalities and differences in systems. It is introduced to ensure that the right changes can be made easier, as recommended by some agile methods, such as Kanban [22]. The format of the variability profile is a generalized version of the business process variation point model introduced in our previous work [26]. Consequently, the variability profile can be integrated into

Table 6.2 Mapping of Steps to Variability Handling Activities

Step	Identify Variability	Constrain Variability	Implement Variability	Manage Variability
1	✓	–	–	–
2	–	✓	–	–
3	–	–	✓	–
4a + 4b	–	–	–	–
5	–	–	✓	–
6	✓	–	–	✓
7	–	✓	–	–
8	–	–	✓	–

an architectural viewpoint for describing variability in software architecture [26]. Variability profiles can be used as part of the story cards frequently used in agile development. Furthermore, in contrast to known variability models' (e.g., feature models) variability profiles can be extended more easily with new concepts.

For the example of Dutch e-government, Table 6.2 shows the initial architectural variability profile. It shows five variation points in the business architecture of the e-government system, their variants, the types, and when the variability in the architecture would be resolved. "Yes/no" as variants for the variation point "Quick procedure" mean that "Quick procedure" is a binary variation point (i.e., a quick procedure to provide WMO services is either implemented in a software system or not). Furthermore, variability types (as defined in the e-government case) are sub-processes, or activities within a process/sub-process. In the context of implementing the WMO law, we do not deal with dynamic or runtime adaptation. Thus, all variation points are resolved at design time (Table 6.3).

6.6.4 Step 3: create architecture

The creation of the architecture is the first step towards *implementing variability*. As mentioned earlier, architectural synthesis would consider several candidates for architecturally significant requirements. The selection of candidates is driven by assessing them against architecturally significant requirements. Our goal is to create highly adaptable architectures and to prepare the architecture for variability. Thus, we define the capability of the architecture to be adapted for different environments—without applying actions or means "other than those provided for this purpose for the architecture considered" [27]—as the key driver when selecting candidates for addressing architecturally significant requirements. Besides this key driver, there can be additional key drivers in a project (e.g., performance, availability, etc.).

Table 6.3 Initial Architectural Variability Profile in the Dutch E-Government Example

Variation Point	Variant	Type	Resolution
Quick procedure	Yes	Sub-process	Design
	No	Sub-process	Design
Clarification of request	Request advice	Sub-process	Design
	Home visit	Sub-process	Design
	Phone conversation	Sub-process	Design
	Personal meeting	Sub-process	Design
Investigation of claims	Home visit	Sub-process	Design
	Dossier research	Activity	Design
	Personal meeting	Sub-process	Design
	External advice	Sub-process	Design
Budget phase	In-house	Sub-process	Design
	Outsourced	Activity	Design
Payment phase	In-house	Sub-process	Design
	External provider	Activity	Design

To avoid the architectural approach becoming too heavyweight, and to keep the architectural description up-to-date more easily, the architecture is expressed with simple component-connector diagrams. However, the architects are free to use any language, notation, or tool of their own taste, based on their preference and experience. Furthermore, for the same reason we do not differentiate application-independent models (such as models used in product line architectures) and application-specific models (such as models used in the architecture of product instances of a product line). The architectural description then evolves throughout the development project.

Figure 6.2 shows a partial architectural candidate for a real multi-tenant solution from a software vendor in Dutch e-government that is intended to implement variability according to the variability profile shown in Table 6.2. Cornered boxes indicate architectural components, whereas rounded boxes indicate architectural variation points and variants. The dotted arrow indicates the connection to the rest of the architecture, which is not shown in this figure. Please note that multi-tenancy is a solution chosen only for this particular project. Here, multi-tenancy refers to a principle in software architecture where one instance of the system runs on a server, serving multiple client organizations (so-called "tenants") [28].

6.6.5 Steps 4a and 4b: evaluate architecture

Thorough architecture evaluation and testing are usually not part of agile development practices. However, we include explicit architecture evaluation in our approach. Here, we split the evaluation into two parts. One evaluation is conducted during Phase 1, and

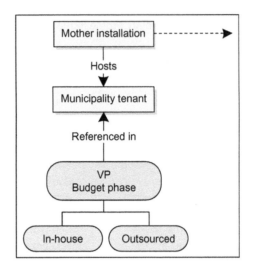

FIGURE 6.2

Partial architecture candidate.

another (continuously performed) evaluation is conducted during Phase 2. The architecture evaluation during Phase 1 is more conventional and can use scenario-based evaluation (e.g., PBAR, a pattern-based architecture review method that targets agile and lightweight projects [29]) but focuses on adaptation scenarios. Based on the outcome of this evaluation, the architecture can either be revised, or, if evaluation criteria are met, accept this architecture as input for Phase 2 of our approach. It is then considered as "prepared" for accommodating variability. Evaluation criteria are subjective. This means that as soon as the architect is satisfied with the outcome of the scenario-based evaluation, the architecture is accepted. In addition to the scenario-based evaluation, mechanisms for evaluating architecture evolvability [30] can be used.

As variability introduces additional complexity into software architectures, we integrate lightweight architecture evaluation into Phase 2 of our approach. As this evaluation is conducted continuously and therefore may incur significant effort, we suggest the use of a checklist as in other architecture review methods [31]. This checklist is structured based on potential stakeholders with an interest in variability in the architecture. Compared to conventional architecture evaluation as done in Phase 1, a checklist is more lightweight. Furthermore, the checklist provides questions that can be reused throughout different reviews. The questions could even be used to evaluate the architecture as part of every design iteration (e.g., a sprint when using Scrum). However, they may not replace a full-fledged architecture evaluation. Some questions overlap to obtain more complete evaluation results. The checklist can be adjusted for specific projects. Aspects covered by the checklist relate to the form of the description of the architecture and to its content. To answer questions in the checklist, any of the architectural artifacts (variability profile, etc.) may be used. The checklist is as follows:

All stakeholders:

- Does the architecture clearly state its stakeholders and concerns?
- Does the architecture clearly state stakeholders of instantiated systems, and their concerns?
- Does the selected architecture representation frame the concerns of the stakeholder of the architecture?
- Does the selected architecture representation frame the concerns of the stakeholders of the instantiated architecture?
- Does the selected architecture representation include concerns that are not concerns of domain stakeholders?
- Is the architecture consistent with domain practices and standards?
- Is it feasible for the architecture to be instantiated in concrete product architectures within the time and budget available?

Architect:

- Has the binding time of each variation point been clearly defined?
- Are variability dependencies and product constraints clearly defined and traceable?
- Are common and specific requirements separated and easily identifiable?
- Is there a description of potential contexts in which architectures are instantiated?
- Are there guidelines for architects and developers for how to resolve variability?

Domain expert:

- Are domain goals that the system must satisfy clearly prioritized?
- Is it clear how domain goals determine the requirements?
- Is there traceability between domain goals and technical solutions (i.e., is it possible to navigate from domain goals, to architecturally significant requirements, to technical decisions)?
- Are there criteria to determine of the architecture supports domain goals?

Software manager:

- Is the architectural description sufficient to make an estimate of the effort to implement it?
- Is it possible to determine development dependencies between different parts of the architecture?
- What resources are required to instantiate the architecture?
- Is there a schedule for implementation and integration?

Designers and integrators:

- Do you understand the variation points and variants in the architecture?
- Can you determine approaches for implementing variability?
- Can you determine success criteria for testing?
- Is it possible to identify "representative" challenges that occur for testing the architecture?

Using this checklist, we can ask questions not only about the architecture, but also about the architectural variability profile. For example, the binding time for each variation point is clearly defined in the variability profile.

In the e-government example, domain experts and software managers come from municipalities. Architects, designers, and integrators come from software vendors. Questions related to all stakeholders usually require a discussion amongst stakeholders.

6.6.6 Step 5: implement initial architecture

The initial architecture undergoes detailed design and is implemented based on the initial architecture. After architecture evaluation, the architectural cycle continues with architectural implementation. During this step, the architecture is realized by designers who create a detailed design. This step goes beyond software architecture, and is therefore not discussed further in this chapter.

6.6.7 Step 6: elicit new variability requirements

New variability requirements (see Section 6.1) are elicited and documented whenever requests from customers arrive. This step is about evolution, maintenance, and continuous addition of variation points and variants. Similar to initial variability analysis, this step involves *identifying variability*. This step is also part of *managing variability*. New variability requirements are passed on to Step 7 to revise the architectural variability profile. This step fits into requirements management in agile approaches. For example, in agile approaches, such new variability requirements can be added to a backlog (Scrum) or be defined as user stories (XP) for another iteration of Phase 2 of our approach.

New requirements in the Dutch e-government example mean that different municipalities have different requirements and adapt these requirements. For example, a new variation point can be added to determine the age requirement for certain social services.

6.6.8 Step 7: revise architecture variability profile

After each iteration, the variability profile has to be revised with regard to new variability requirements (see Step 6) and changes in variation points and variants caused by new variability requirements. Similar to the initial variability profile, revising the profile and variants *constrains variability*. A revised variability profile is important for facilitating communication between all stakeholders through the development process and for tracing variability to the architecture. Traceability to the architecture is ensured by using the revised variability profile as input for architectural refactoring. Revising the architecture variability profile is part of constraining variability to accommodate flexibility in the architecture to meet current and future needs. Change

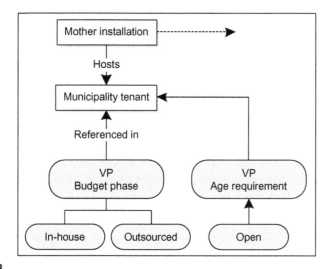

FIGURE 6.3

Refactored architecture.

to existing variability is handled by revising the variability profile of a variation point or variant that is changed, or by adding new variation points or variants.

For example, the new variation point "Age requirement" could be added to the variability profile in the Dutch e-government example, with variability type "Activity," resolution time "Design," and open variants. This is because age requirements for social support are determined by municipalities.

6.6.9 Step 8: refactor architecture

To implement the new variability profile, the architecture might need to be refactored. For example, new architecture layers might be introduced to further abstract common aspects, or to handle variable aspects. Refactoring the architecture is an iterative step to *implementing variability*.

Based on the revised variability profile, the architecture is refactored. The refactored architecture for our Dutch e-government example and the revised variability profile is shown in Figure 6.3. We added the variation point "Age requirement," which has no predefined variants (i.e., it is "open").

6.7 SUMMARY AND CONCLUSIONS

We presented an agile-inspired lightweight approach for handling variability in software architectures. This approach combines ideas from the agile paradigm and variability. Referring to the 12 principles from the Agile Manifesto presented in the introduction of this chapter, our approach addresses these principles as follows:

- Principle 1 (the highest priority is to satisfy the customer through early and continuous delivery of valuable software): Our approach facilitates continuous delivery through iterative development.
- Principle 2 (changing requirements are welcomed, even late in the development): Our approach harnesses change for the customer's competitive advantage. We systematically elicit and process newly arriving requirements to be implemented in the architecture.
- Principle 3 (working software should be delivered frequently, with a preference to shorter timescale delivery): Similar to principle 1, frequent delivery is ensured though iterative development in Phase 2 of our approach.
- Principle 4 (business people and developers must work together daily through the project): This principle is met mainly in Phase 2 of our approach. New requirements are analyzed by business people and discussed with developers to clarify if it is feasible to implement them. Furthermore, the checklist to evaluate the architecture requires communication between different stakeholders.
- Principle 5 (projects should be built around motivated individuals and in an environment that supports their needs and facilitates trust to get the job done): This principle is not explicitly facilitated by our approach, but would depend on the organization in which our approach is applied.
- Principle 6 (the most efficient and effective method of conveying information within and across development teams is face-to-face communication): Similar to principle 5, this principle is not explicitly facilitated by our approach but would depend on the organization in which our approach is applied.
- Principle 7 (progress is measured based on working software): With each iteration of Phase 2, our approach produces the architecture for the implementation of a working software product.
- Principle 9 (agility is enhanced through continuous attention to technical excellence): This principle is supported by having continuous evaluation of the architecture with regard to its support for variability.
- Principle 10 (maximizing the amount of work not done is essential): This principle is partially supported. By preparing the architecture for variability in Phase 1, less work is required to implement variability in Phase 2.

Principles 8, 11, and 12 are of an organizational nature and thus not directly affected by our approach.

Although we discussed some benefits of this approach, we acknowledge that it is not applicable in all situations. There are basically three criteria to decide if an environment is suitable for combining agility and variability. First, there should be enough commonalities and differences between products that systematic handling of variability would be justified. Otherwise, we should rather implement separate, custom-built products. Second, the more rapidly a domain changes, the more an agile, variability-handling approach becomes useful. This is because the frequency of newly arriving variability requirements increases. The third criterion is magnitude [9]. Magnitude includes the size of products, involved teams, the organization which develops a software system, and the organization that will be using the system. Small-scale product development usually benefits from lightweight processes, because they do not require the discipline and rigor prescribed by heavyweight processes. This is particularly true because variability already increases complexity and communication efforts in a software development project.

Future work to expand the proposed methodology is related to detailed architecture evaluation in the context of agile projects. This includes the definition of a more detailed checklist for architecture evaluation with regard to variability. The checklist would be applied at different steps of the presented methodology to ensure that the architecture supports variability in a continuous manner, rather than only as part of Steps 4a and 4b of our approach.

Acknowledgments

This research has been partially sponsored by NWO SaS-LeG, contract no. 638.000.000.07N07.

References

[1] Ghanam Y, Andreychuk D, Maurer F. Reactive variability management in agile software development. In: AGILE conference. Orlando, FL: IEEE Computer Society; 2010. p. 27–34.

[2] Diaz J, Perez J, Alarcon PP, Garbajosa J. Agile product line engineering—a systematic literature review. Softw Pract Exper 2011;41:921–41.

[3] Bachmann F, Clements PC. Variability in software product lines. Technical report, SEI CMU; 2005.

[4] Aiello M, Bulanov P, Groefsema H. Requirements and tools for variability management. In: 4th IEEE workshop on requirement engineering for services (REFS 2010). Seoul, South Korea: IEEE Computer Society; 2010. p. 245–50.

[5] Svahnberg M, van Grup J, Bosch J. A taxonomy of variability realization techniques. Softw Pract Exper 2005;35:705–54.

[6] Clements P, Northrop L. Software product lines—practices and patterns. Boston, MA: Addison-Wesley; 2001.

[7] Cooper K, Franch X. APLE—1st international workshop on agile product line engineering. In: 10th international conference on software product lines. Baltimore, MD: IEEE Computer Society; 2006. p. 205–6.

[8] de Silva IF, da Mota Silveira Neto PA, O'Leary P, de Almeida ES, de Lemos Meira SR. Agile software product lines: a systematic mapping study. Softw Pract Exper 2011;41:899–920.

[9] McGregor JD. Agile software product lines, deconstructed. J Object Technol 2008;7:7–19.

[10] Hanssen G, Faegri TE. Process fusion: an industrial case study on agile software product line engineering. J Syst Softw 2008;81:843–54.

[11] Pohjalainen P. Bottom-up modeling for a software product line: an experience report on agile modeling of governmental mobile networks. In: 15th international software product line conference. Munich, Germany: IEEE Computer Society; 2011. p. 323–32.

[12] Noor MA, Rabiser R, Gruenbacher P. Agile product line planning: a collaborative approach and a case study. J Syst Softw 2008;81:868–82.

[13] Paige RF, Wang X, Stephenson Z, Brooke PJ. Towards an agile process for building software product lines. In: 7th international conference on eXtreme programming and agile processes in software engineering (XP). Oulu, Finland: Springer Verlag; 2006. p. 198–9.

[14] Ghanam Y, Maurer F. Using acceptance tests for incremental elicitation of variability in requirements: an observational study. In: AGILE conference. Salt Lake City, UT: IEEE Computer Society; 2011. p. 139–42.

[15] Shokry H, Ali Babar M. Dynamic software product line architectures using service-based computing for automotive systems. In: 2nd international workshop on dynamic software product lines. Limerick, Ireland: Lero International Science Centre; 2008. p. 53–8.

[16] Hallsteinsen S, Jiang S, Sanders R. Dynamic software product lines in service-oriented computing. In: 3rd international workshop on dynamic software product lines, San Francisco, CA; 2009. p. 28–34.

[17] Fiadeiro JL, Lopes A. A model for dynamic reconfiguration in service-oriented architectures. In: 4th European conference on software architecture. Copenhagen, Denmark: Springer Verlag; 2010.

[18] Oreizy P, Gorlick MM, Taylor RN, Heimbigner D, Johnson G, Medvidovic N, et al. An architecture-based approach to self-adaptive software. IEEE Intell Syst 1999;14: 54–62.

[19] Tian K, Cooper K. Agile and software product line methods: are they so different? In: First international workshop on agile software product line engineering, Baltimore, MD; 2006. p. 1–8.

[20] Hofmeister C, Kruchten P, Nord RL, Obbink H, Ran A, America P. Generalizing a model of software architecture design from five industrial approaches. In: 5th working IEEE/IFIP conference on software architecture. Pittsburgh, PA: IEEE Computer Society; 2005. p. 77–88.

[21] Tang A, Avgeriou P, Jansen A, Capilla R, Ali Babar M. A comparative study of architecture knowledge management tools. J Syst Softw 2010;83:352–70.

[22] Anderson DJ. Kanban: successful evolutionary change for your technology business. Sequim, WA: Blue Hole Press; 2010.

[23] Capilla R, Ali Babar M. On the role of architectural design decisions in software product line engineering. In: Second European conference on software architecture. Paphos, Cyprus: Springer Verlag; 2008. p. 241–55.

[24] Santos AL, Koskimies K, Lopes A. A model-driven approach to variability management in product-line engineering. Nordic J Comput 2006;13:196–213.

[25] Palmer SR, Felsing JM. A practical guide to feature-driven development. Upper Saddle River, NJ: Prentice Hall; 2002.

[26] Galster M, Avgeriou P. A variability viewpoint for enterprise software systems. In: Joint 10th working IEEE/IFIP conference on software architecture (WICSA) and 6th European conference on software architecture (ECSA). Helsinki, Finland: IEEE Computer Society; 2012. p. 267–71.

[27] ISO/IEC: software engineering—product quality—part 1: quality model, vol. ISO/IEC 9126-1, Geneva, Switzerland; 2001.

[28] Pathirage M, Perera S, Kumara I, Weerawarana S. A multi-tenant architecture for business process executions. In: IEEE international conference on web services. Washington, DC: IEEE Computer Society; 2011. p. 121–8.

[29] Harrison N, Avgeriou P. Pattern-based architecture reviews. IEEE softw 2011;28:66–71.

[30] Breivold HP, Crnkovic I, Eriksson P. Analyzing software evolvability. In: 32nd IEEE international computer software and applications conference (COMPSAC). Turku, Finland: IEEE Computer Society; 2008. p. 327–30.

[31] Nord R, Clements P, Emery D, Hilliard R. A structured approach for reviewing architecture documentation. Technical report, SEI CMU; 2009.

Continuous Software Architecture Analysis

7

Georg Buchgeher[*] **and Rainer Weinreich**[†]

[*]*Software Competence Center Hagenberg (SCCH), Hagenberg, Austria*
[†]*Johannes Kepler University Linz, Linz, Austria*

CHAPTER CONTENTS

7.1 INTRODUCTION

There is no one specific activity termed software architecture analysis. Instead, software architecture analysis covers a wide range of activities and aims, which are supported by different methods and tools. Examples are scenario-based evaluation methods like the Software Architecture Analysis Method (SAAM) [1] and the Architecture Tradeoff Analysis Method (ATAM) [2], different kinds of reviews, dependency analysis with architecture management tools (AMTs), architecture prototyping, and model-based analysis approaches using formalized architecture description languages (ADLs). Most of these approaches have been developed for rather traditional, plan-driven, and nonagile development processes with dedicated points in the development process where specific process results, such as a finished architecture design, are available for analysis.

In agile processes, however, architecture design is typically performed incrementally and continuously. This means that the architecture design is inherently incomplete and continuously evolving. Architecture analysis methods not only have to deal with incomplete architecture design, but must themselves be performed incrementally and continuously to align with the development process. Existing methods for architecture analysis need to be adapted to support these new requirements, and new approaches to architecture analysis need to be developed.

In this chapter, we take a closer look at continuous software architecture analysis (CSAA). We start by defining software architecture analysis and discussing related terms such as *architecture evaluation*, *validation*, *verification*, and *architecture assessment*. We then give an overview of existing and well-known architecture analysis methods and tools. After discussing important terms and approaches, we look at CSAA as a means for software architecture analysis in agile development processes. We identify the core requirements of CSAA by looking at agile principles and at approaches for continuous quality control (CQC) in agile processes. The identified requirements serve as the basis for discussing the suitability of existing approaches to CSAA and for discussing specific architecture analysis goals in the context of CSAA. This general discussion of the topic is then followed by the presentation of experiences with an approach to CSAA. The approach currently mainly supports continuous structural and conformance analysis, though we will argue that these kinds of analysis also provide the basis for other forms of architecture analysis, particularly for architecture evaluation. On the basis of these experiences, we discuss what has worked and what has not worked so far and identify challenges and potential topics for future research.

7.2 SOFTWARE ARCHITECTURE ANALYSIS

Software architecture analysis activities are the counterparts of the constructive activities of architecture design and implementation [3,4]. Taylor et al. [5] define architecture analysis[a] as "as the activity of discovering important system properties using the system's architectural models." Kazman et al. [8] state that "in software architecture analysis, the software architecture is evaluated against some criteria." In most cases, software architecture analysis is used as means of quality control and risk reduction [9]. However, economic considerations like cost/benefit relations are also among the drivers of architecture analysis [10].

---

[a]Taylor et al. [5] use the term "architectural analysis." Since this term also describes a phase of the architecture life cycle (see Hofmeister et al. [6] and Tang et al. [7]), we use the term "architecture analysis."

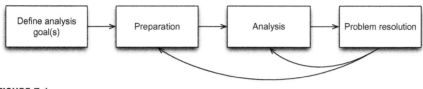

FIGURE 7.1

Software architecture analysis process.

The software architecture analysis process is depicted in Figure 7.1. It can be roughly partitioned into four phases/activities: goal definition, preparation, analysis, and problem resolution. First, the analysis goals need to be defined. Next, architectural models and documentation required for performing analysis need to be prepared, and organizational activities—like the selection of reviewers, the review schedule, and the selection of analysis techniques—need to be performed. After having defined the analysis goals, and finished all preparation activities, the actual analysis can be performed. If the analysis is performed as a means for quality control, each step of the analysis is followed by activities for problem resolution. After resolving detected problems, the architecture typically has to be reanalyzed to check whether the problems have been resolved correctly.

Terms that are closely related and often used synonymously with architecture analysis are *architecture validation and verification, architecture evaluation,* and *architecture assessment.*

Validation and verification is "is the process for demonstrating that a program meets its specifications (verification) and the real needs of its stakeholders (validation)" [11]. The central difference between validation and verification is that validation checks if a created artifact "conforms to the needs of its users" [12], whereas verification checks if "a created artifact corresponds to some other artifacts created earlier or being used as source data" [12]. As noted by Sommerville [11], the users' needs are not always specified in the form of documents. Therefore, validation is a less formal and more general activity than verification. Validation and verification are often performed in parallel.

The aim of architecture evaluation is "to analyze the software architecture to identify potential risks and verify that the quality requirements have been addressed in the design" [13]. This means that architecture evaluation is architecture analysis with a specific analysis goal, which is to determine whether the architecture design satisfies the requirements that are defined as architecturally significant requirements [6,14].

Architecture assessment is the process of analyzing an architecture against specified criteria like standards, guidelines, and certain quality attributes to determine the quality of a system's architecture with regard to the specified criteria [15].

Architecture analysis can be performed manually, automatically, and semiautomatically [5]. Manual analysis means that stakeholders perform architecture analysis without the use of dedicated tools. Automatic analysis means that architecture analysis is performed without human interaction. Semiautomatic analysis means that the analysis is performed partially manually and partially automatically.

The definition of one or more analysis goals is the starting point of each analysis. Often the analysis goal is implicitly defined by the analysis method used. An overview of different analysis goals in the context of software architecture analysis is provided by Taylor et al. [5]. They classify analysis goals into four categories: completeness, consistency, compatibility and correctness.

Completeness analysis comprises external completeness (whether all system requirements have been addressed in architectural design) and internal completeness (whether all necessary architectural elements have been defined and whether all design decisions have been made). An example of a particular kind of internal completeness analysis is determining whether all necessary elements have been defined with respect to a particular modeling notation.

Consistency analysis means checking whether the defined architecture contains contradicting information or not. Examples of inconsistencies are inconsistent names, interfaces, and refinements of architectural elements.

Compatibility analysis is used for checking whether an architecture adheres to design guidelines and constraints defined by architectural styles, reference architectures, and standards.

Correctness analysis is always performed with respect to some artifact of reference. Important kinds of correctness analysis are the determination of whether the architecture is correct with regard to the specified system requirements (architecture evaluation), and whether the system implementation conforms to its defined architecture (architecture/implementation conformance).

Aside from analysis goals, Taylor et al. [5] list additional important properties of different kinds of architecture analysis, including analysis scope (e.g., local vs. global), analysis concerns, the formality of architecture models, the type of analysis (static vs. dynamic), the degree of automation, and the kind of stakeholders involved.

7.3 APPROACHES TO SOFTWARE ARCHITECTURE ANALYSIS

Approaches to architectural analysis range from manual approaches like architecture reviews, scenario-based evaluation methods, and *ad hoc* analysis, to automated analysis using ADLs and AMTs. In the following, we give an overview of the main characteristics of these methods. Later in this chapter, we will discuss them again in the context of CSAA.

7.3.1 Architecture reviews

Architecture reviews are a static analysis technique. They are typically performed manually, based on informal or semiformal architecture documentation and on the experience and expertise of the reviewers.

Architecture reviews can be separated into heavyweight and lightweight reviews [16]. Heavyweight reviews, like technical reviews [17] and inspections [17], are based on rigorously defined, long-running processes and on comprehensive documentation. Lightweight reviews, like walkthroughs [17], active design reviews [18], and the Tiny Architectural Review Approach (TARA) [19], are associated with simple and short-running processes and can be performed with no or only a small amount of architecture documentation.

In terms of analysis aims, architecture reviews are primarily used for architecture evaluation (correctness) and for checking architecture/implementation conformance. Aside from correctness, analysis aims may be consistency, completeness, and compatibility.

Walkthroughs are typically performed by internal technical stakeholders while technical reviews and inspections are intended to be performed by external technical stakeholders. External reviewers provide an independent perspective [20,21]; this is known as independent quality control [22].

7.3.2 Scenario-based evaluation methods

Scenario-based architecture evaluation is a specific kind of architecture review, which is based on the notion of a scenario. A scenario is a "short statement describing an interaction of one of the stakeholders with the system" [23]. Each identified scenario is then checked to determine whether it is supported by a system's architecture or not. Well-known examples of scenario-based evaluation methods are ATAM [2] and SAAM [1]. An overview of other existing scenario-based analysis methods can be found in Refs. [24] and [25].

Scenario-based architecture analysis is typically performed as a one- or two-day workshop, where ideally all system stakeholders participate in the review. The workshop includes the explanation of the architecture, the identification of the most important scenarios, the analysis of the identified scenarios, and the presentation of the results.

Like other review-based methods, scenario-based evaluation methods are a static and manual analysis approach.

7.3.3 Architecture description languages

ADLs are formal languages for describing the architecture of a software system [26,27]. Each ADL defines a notation with precise syntax and semantics in which architecture models can be expressed, and provides a corresponding toolkit for working with the language.

ADLs include general purpose languages like xADL [28] and ACME [29], and domain-specific languages (DSLs) [30] like Koala [31], the *Architecture Analysis and Design Language* [32], and AUTOSAR [33]. A survey of available ADLs can be found in [30]. Many ADLs are academic research projects.

ADLs support the description of structural and selected behavioral aspects. An ADL describes a system at the component and connector abstraction level. A system is a configuration of components and connectors. Components are units of computation and data stores. Connectors describe interactions between components and the rules that govern these interactions [30]. The supported behavioral aspects are different for each ADL. For example, Wright [34] can be used for identifying interface incompatibilities and deadlocks.

ADLs primarily support architecture evaluation of selected quality attributes. In addition, architecture models can be analyzed for completeness with respect to a modeling notation, and for consistency. Some ADLs, like ACME, also support compatibility analysis [35].

ADL-based architecture analysis is performed automatically using dedicated analysis tools. ADL-based architecture descriptions can also be used to simulate system behavior [5].

The creation of ADL-based architecture models is sometimes difficult and requires technical stakeholders with specific expertise [5]. This may be one reason why ADLs have not yet found their way into mainstream software development. Additional reasons are listed by Woods and Hilliard [36] and include the restrictive nature of ADLs, the lack of multiple views, lack of good tool support, their generic nature, and the lack of domain concepts.

In addition to ADLs, DSLs can be used to describe software architectures. Architecture-centric DSLs are typically developed for a particular domain or even a particular system and support the automatic generation of the system implementation and specific kinds of automatic analysis [37].

7.3.4 Dependency analysis approaches and architecture metrics

Dependency analysis approaches can be used for extracting and analyzing static dependencies from code and for comparing the actually implemented architecture with the intended architecture. Early dependency analysis approaches have been developed by Murphy et al. [38] (software reflection models) and by Tran et al. [39]. Today, dependency analysis can be performed with software architecture management tools (AMTs) like Lattix [40], Sotograph [41], and Structure 101 [42].

Architecture models of the actually implemented system are automatically extracted from the system implementation, while models of the intended architecture need to be defined manually. Dependency analysis approaches target technical stakeholders. Analysis can be performed by members of the development organization and by external consultants.

Many AMTs also integrate code quality management (CQM) functionality. CQM tools support the calculation of architecture metrics from the system implementation and support metric-based analysis [43]. Metrics can be used for detecting bad smells like cyclic dependencies and tight coupling.

7.3.5 Architecture prototyping

An architecture prototype is a functional subset of a system created to get early feedback from the stakeholders [44,45]. Prototypes are used for performing dynamic (but also static) analysis [46] based on an executable (but incomplete) system implementation. The strength of prototypes is that they permit architecture analysis under close-to-real conditions. Prototypes are used for answering questions that cannot be sufficiently answered by other analysis approaches like architecture reviews.

The prototyping process includes the selection of functionality to be analyzed, the construction (implementation) of the prototype, the analysis of the prototype, and, optionally, the further use of the prototype. Prototypes are typically used for analyzing performance, modifiability, and buildability [47]. They are created and analyzed by technical stakeholders, like developers and architects [47].

7.3.6 *Ad hoc* analysis

Ad hoc analysis means that architecture analysis is performed implicitly as part of architecture design and implementation activities based on experience, expertise, and argumentation [15]. Experience-based, informal architecture analysis is one of the most often-used analysis techniques [48,49]. *Ad hoc* analysis supports all kinds of architecture analysis goals and can be performed with both formal and informal architecture documentation, or without any documentation at all. The analysis is performed manually by technical stakeholders, like software architects and developers.

7.4 CONTINUOUS SOFTWARE ARCHITECTURE ANALYSIS

The discussed approaches for software architecture analysis have mostly been developed for plan-driven processes. This is mainly because architecture is the primary means for planning [50] and risk reduction [23] in such processes. An architecture is usually defined, fully documented, and evaluated before the implementation phase [5,23]. Architecture evaluation is thus a critical and thorough activity in plan-driven processes, which requires a significant amount of time and human resources [51]. For example, an ATAM review may require up to 30 person-days [9].

In agile processes, however, typically no complete up-front architectures are defined. Either a core architecture is created in early iterations of an agile software development process, or the architecture emerges as part of subsequent iterations. Risk reduction is inherent to the process itself [52]: software is developed in iterations and planning can be adjusted at the beginning of each new iteration to anticipate changes late in development. The focus of agile processes is on early and continuous delivery of customer value in the form of working software. This is achieved, for example, through valuing working software over documentation and communication over processes and tools [53].

Whether plan-driven methods with an up-front architecture or agile methods with little or no up-front architecture are the appropriate means for development depends on the kind of project [54,55]. But there is no doubt that the role and means for architecture analysis are different in agile and lean processes than in plan-driven processes with big up-front design. This leads us to the question of the potential role, the suitability, and the requirements of architecture analysis and architecture analysis methods in agile and lean processes.

Since in agile processes architecture design is also a continuous activity that spreads across the entire development process, architecture analysis needs to be performed continuously, too. The concept of analyzing the complete architecture design at a dedicated time in the development process does not hold for agile processes. Also, other assumptions of existing analysis methods—like comprehensive architecture documentation, external stakeholders, and long-running, resource-intensive processes—do not align with agile principles. This raises the questions, "Which kinds of analysis and analysis approaches are useful in agile processes?" and, "How do existing analysis approaches need to be adapted?"

7.4.1 CSAA and different kinds of architecture analysis

Different kinds of analysis, in terms of analysis goals, were discussed in Section 7.2. Continuous releases in agile processes require means for continuous quality control (CQC) to ensure that a system possesses the required quality for each release.

In terms of architecture analysis, continuous compatibility analysis ensures that the (implemented) architecture conforms to company-wide standards, reference architectures, and guidelines.

Continuous analysis of architecture/implementation conformance can be used to prevent architectural drift. In agile processes, it can be used to ensure that the implementation conforms to architectural core decisions and structures defined in previous iterations.

Consistency analysis is important if architectural models are used for capturing these core architectural decisions in agile processes. In this case, continuous consistency analysis ensures that the consistency of such models is preserved over time.

Completeness analysis plays a minor role in agile processes, since the architecture design evolves continuously. It is thus reduced to completeness analysis of potentially used architectural models, since these models need to be complete if they are to be used for other kinds of analysis or for the generation of implementation artifacts.

We assume that the role of architecture evaluation will also change significantly in agile processes, though we lack reports on the role and importance of this kind of analysis in this context. In plan-driven processes, evaluation is an important means of risk reduction, while in agile processes, risk reduction is inherent to the process itself. In plan-driven processes architecture, evaluation is based on a complete architecture design, but in agile processes, architecture evaluation will be rather incremental and selective, focusing on specific parts of an architecture. Our assumption is that architecture evaluation will still play a role, though we assume that it is less important in agile processes than in plan-driven ones. We also assume that evaluation will require more lightweight methods to support the principles of agile software development.

In the following, we take a look at other approaches to CQC in agile processes to derive requirements for CSAA and to discuss the suitability of current approaches for CSAA in the following sections.

7.4.2 **Approaches for continuous quality control (CQC)**

Approaches for CQC in agile processes include continuous testing [56], continuous code analysis [57], continuous integration (CI) [57], continuous refactoring [52,58], and pair-programming [52].

Continuous testing is a combination of techniques and tools like *test-driven development* (TDD) and *regression testing* [56]. TDD [59] is essentially a method for continuously developing test-cases as part of software design. It is thus also seen as a design approach, because it ensures that the system is testable by applying good design principles [60]. Regression testing, on the other hand, is the process of retesting software after modifications to ensure that the new version of the software has retained the capabilities of the old version and that no new defects have been introduced [61]. Both TDD and regression testing are well integrated into the development process. Tools for creating and executing test cases are integrated with development tools and environments and provide test automation, which is important due to the principle of constant change in agile processes.

Continuous code analysis as provided by static code analysis tools like PMD,[b] Checkstyle,[c] and FindBugs™[d] are either directly integrated in an Integrated Development Environment (IDE) or in the build infrastructure and can thus be applied automatically and on a regular basis.

CI [57,62] also provides automation using a dedicated build infrastructure (build server). It promotes the principle of early build and delivery. Builds are typically performed on a daily basis. Building a system usually incorporates the execution of test cases and of static code analysis.

Continuous refactoring [52], on the other hand, focuses on problem resolution rather than analysis, though analysis activities need to precede refactoring activities. In the ideal case, refactoring is also performed continuously [58], because it is easier to make several smaller changes throughout the development process than to make larger changes later in development. However, large refactorings cannot always be avoided [43]. Refactoring support is often part of modern IDEs.

Finally, *pair programming* [52] is an example for continuous *ad hoc* analysis during development. Code is developed collaboratively by two developers sitting in front of one machine. Analysis during development is *ad hoc* and thus not easily repeatable.

7.4.3 **Characteristics of CQC approaches**

If we look at the main characteristics of the above approaches, we see integration and continuous application as prominent properties, which are typically not present in approaches for quality control in plan-driven processes.

---

[b]http://pmd.sourceforge.net/
[c]http://checkstyle.sourceforge.net/
[d]http://findbugs.sourceforge.net/

Integration takes place not only at the level of the development process, but also at the level of the development tools and the development team. *Process integration* makes it possible to assess a system's quality as part of the daily development work, which is necessary to detect and resolve problems early. *Tool integration* permits seamless switching between constructive and quality control activities, and it also permits performing quality control in response to changes in the implementation. This results in fast feedback of analysis results. Finally, quality control is typically performed by members of the development team—either by developers themselves, or by integrating other stakeholders, like testers, with other team members.

Continuous application of quality control activities means their frequent and repeated application during development. The actual meaning of "frequently" depends on the CQC approach used and can vary between *instantly* (on each modification), *multiple times a day*, *on a daily* or *weekly basis*, or *in each iteration*. Repeatability, on the other hand, is important because in agile development processes a system—including requirements, design, and implementation—is continuously extended and modified. Continuous modifications require reanalysis of already-analyzed system parts after system modifications.

In addition, we should note that an important aspect of continuous application is support for problem resolution. In agile processes, it is not only important to detect problems as early as possible, but also to resolve the detected problems as part of the CQC activities used. Therefore, problem resolution is typically, and often implicitly, part of CQC activities.

To summarize, integration and continuous application are main characteristics of approaches for CQC. It can be observed that continuous application in many CQC approaches is facilitated through automation and tool support. For example, continuous testing, continuous code analysis, and CI would not be possible without automation because these approaches encompass activities that would be tedious, time-intensive, and error-prone if performed manually. However some approaches, like refactoring and pair programming, do not rely on automation but rather on process and team integration.

7.4.4 CSAA process

The main activities of a CSAA process align with the typical activities of the software architecture analysis meta-process outlined in Section 7.2: goal definition, preparation, actual analysis, and problem resolution. The main extension is the continuous application of these activities. This is illustrated in Figure 7.2.

The figure shows that the original architecture analysis process from Section 7.2 is now a cyclic process. It also starts with the definition of analysis goals—a step that is optional—because once defined, the goals need not be defined anew in subsequent iterations. This is followed by a step for creating and maintaining architectural information as a basis for performing the actual analysis. Preparing architectural information is a major activity in plan-driven analysis approaches, and thus it consumes significant resources. In a CSAA process, it is important that this activity can also

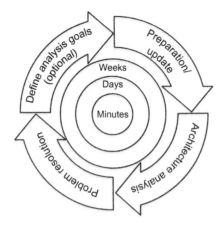

FIGURE 7.2

Continuous software architecture analysis process.

be performed with as little effort and resources as possible and as an integrated activity of the development process. This means that it is not possible to create complete and extensive documentation, which has to be maintained in subsequent iterations. Instead, this effort needs to be reduced by restricting the created information selectively to the analysis task at hand and by automatically generating architectural information from other artifacts (e.g., by extracting architecture from code). In subsequent iterations, the available architecture documentation (e.g., architecture models) need to be incrementally updated as part of the development process. This means the preparation phase of the original architecture analysis process is not mainly concerned with creating architectural information, but with updating and maintaining the existing documentation. Finally, problem resolution is an integrated activity of continuous analysis to support the principle of continuous delivery in agile processes.

7.5 CSAA IN EXISTING APPROACHES

Having identified central characteristics of approaches for CQC, and thus for CSAA, we now examine how well CSAA is supported in existing approaches for software architecture analysis. Specifically, we examine the aspects of integration, frequency, and repeatability as discussed in the previous section.

Heavyweight architecture reviews, like inspections and technical reviews, are long-running processes that span multiple weeks [20] and require a significant amount of human resources. This makes it impossible to use heavyweight architecture reviews as a frequent and integral part the development process. Also, heavyweight architecture reviews are typically intended to be performed by personnel outside the development organization [20,21], not by the development team.

Lightweight architecture reviews, like walkthroughs, are performed by the development team and can be integrated into the development process at regular intervals.

They can be performed frequently (i.e., weekly or in each iteration) by, for example, only analyzing new and modified system parts.

Scenario-based architecture evaluation methods, like SAAM [1] and ATAM [2], define long-running processes covering multiple weeks, which are intended to be performed isolated from development. Analysis is performed by external consultants [63] together with all stakeholders of the system [23]. Because of the required resources, scenario-based evaluation methods are not easily repeatable and cannot be performed frequently. Dedicated tool support for scenario-based architecture evaluation is considered important [64], but most scenario-based methods lack adequate tool support [25].

Architecture prototyping approaches can be partially integrated in the daily development process, depending on the kind of prototype and on the resources required for prototype creation and analysis. Architecture prototyping is typically performed by members of the development team [47]. Because of the effort involved in prototype creation, architecture prototyping cannot be performed frequently and it is not easily repeatable.

Dependency analysis and metric-based analysis can be integrated in the daily development process, and dependency analysis tools are usually integrated well with IDEs and the build infrastructure. Because of the high degree of automation, analysis can be performed at a high frequency and is easily repeatable. Analysis can be performed by members of the development team [41]. Some dependency analysis tools also provide support for problem resolution, such as support for virtual refactoring [65].

ADLs are not well integrated into processes and teams. This is attributed to the formal and sophisticated nature of ADLs [66], the resulting complexity in using ADLs [67], and the lack of support of various stakeholder concerns through different viewpoints [67]. Some ADL toolkits, like ArchStudio 4[e] and AcmeStudio,[f] are integrated with development tools, but a tight integration between ADL the toolkit and IDE functionality is typically missing. Because analysis is performed automatically, analysis is repeatable. However, performing ADL-based analysis at a high frequency is difficult because of the required resources for creating and maintaining the required architecture models. Architecture-centric DSLs are better integrated with the development process and team. Such languages can even be developed by the development team itself according to their specific needs.

Ad hoc analysis can be seamlessly integrated into architecture design and implementation activities because it is an implicit activity. *Ad hoc* analysis is usually performed by members of the development team. Since analysis is performed implicitly, it can be performed at a high frequency and as part of architecture design activities. However, since it is performed as part of other activities, it is not easily repeatable. *Ad hoc* analysis does not build upon any specific tool support other than available design and implementation tools.

---

[e]http://www.isr.uci.edu/projects/archstudio/
[f]http://www.cs.cmu.edu/~acme/AcmeStudio/

Support for CSAA in existing architecture analysis approaches is summarized in Table 7.1. Heavyweight review-based approaches and scenario-based methods are intended to be performed by external stakeholders at specific points in the development process and have not been designed for tight integration as required in agile processes. Lightweight reviews, dependency analysis approaches, *ad hoc* analysis, and architecture prototyping can be performed by internal stakeholders and can be integrated in the development process. Integration of ADL-based analysis remains rather unclear due to the lack of experiences of using ADLs in practice. ADL tools also lack integration with other development tools. Currently, only dependency analysis approaches provide tight tool integration.

Heavyweight review-based approaches and scenario-based evaluation methods cannot be applied continuously. They suffer from high demand for resources in terms of the time needed for review and required stakeholders, which makes frequent application and repeatability infeasible. Lightweight reviews require fewer resources and can thus be performed more frequently (e.g., on a weekly basis, or in each iteration). The resource demand is lower because lightweight reviews typically only analyze selected parts of a system's architecture.

ADLs seem like perfect candidates for continuous application because of their support for automatic analysis. ADL-based analysis is easily repeatable because of automation, but it cannot be performed at a high frequency due to the effort required to create and maintain architecture descriptions, and because of the need for the stakeholders involved to possess specific, formal skills (or because of the high learning curve for acquiring those skills; see Ref. [5], p. 220).

The best support for continuous application is currently provided by dependency analysis approaches. They provide a high degree of automation and tool support, which permits short-running analysis processes that can be integrated in the daily development process. Further, analyses can be performed frequently and are easily repeatable. They also typically provide support for problem resolution.

To summarize, approaches with a high resource demand in preparation, analysis, and resolution are not well suited for CSAA. This includes heavyweight reviews and scenario-based analysis, but also ADLs.

7.6 CSAA AND ANALYSIS GOALS

There is also a relation between the suitability of an analysis method for continuous architecture analysis and the supported kind of analysis. Many analysis goals are supported by multiple analysis methods. The efforts required for analysis differ between these methods. In general, analysis methods that require few resources are desirable for CSAA because they can be applied more frequently. Required resources can be reduced if analysis methods provide automation and tool support in all phases of the analysis process. In this section, we discuss which analysis goals can benefit from automation and tool support being used to help keep required resource demands low.

Table 7.2 gives an overview of analysis methods and typically supported analysis goals (we use the classification of analysis goals as presented in Section 7.2).

Table 7.1 Architecture Analysis Approaches and CQC Requirements

		Heavyweight Reviews	Lightweight Reviews	Scenarios	Dependency Analysis	ADLs	Architecture Prototyping	Ad hoc Analysis
Integration	Process	--	+	--	++	?	o	++
	Tool	--	--	--	++	-	o	na
	Team	o	++	-	++	?	++	++
Continuous Application	High Frequency	--	o	--	++	--	-	o/+
	Repeatability	--	o	--	++	++	o/-	--
	Problem Resolution	--	--	--	o	-	--	--

++, excellent; +, good; o, partially; -, poor; --, none; ?, don't know; na, not applicable.

Table 7.2 Analysis Approaches and Analysis Goals

Analysis Goals		Heavyweight Reviews	Lightweight Reviews	Scenarios	Dependency Analysis	ADLs	Architecture Prototyping	Ad hoc Analysis
Completeness	Requirements	×	×	×				×
	Architecture Design	×	×	×				×
	Model (Notation)	×	×			×		×
Correctness	Requirements/ Architecture	×	×	×		×	×	×
	Architecture/ Implementation	×	×	×	×		×	×
Compatibility		×	×	×		×		×
Consistency		×	×			×		×

Completeness analysis refers to completeness with regard to the defined requirements (external completeness) and to the completeness of the design (internal completeness). As shown in the table, these kinds of analysis are typically part of review-based architecture evaluation approaches and *ad hoc* analyses. Since they are based on the experience and expertise of the software architect, they are hard to automate and therefore must be analyzed manually.

Internal completeness with regard to a modeling notation, consistency, and the compatibility of architecture models (like the compatibility to reference architectures) can be analyzed manually as part of review-based approaches, but also automatically by formalizing the models and rules for completeness, consistency, and compatibility. Provided that the effort for creating and maintaining the architecture models is kept at a minimum, these kinds of analysis goals are suitable for continuous architecture analysis.

Correctness with regard to defined requirements also cannot easily be automated, since this requires formal specifications, which are expensive both to create and to maintain. Correctness analysis is currently either part of architecture evaluations using review-based methods, or part of ADL approaches. The former require manual effort and resources; the latter suffer from the effort involved in creating and maintaining the necessary formal models.

Finally, the conformance of architecture models to external artifacts, like the architecture implementation, can also be automated—at least for architectural information that can be extracted from an implementation. In this case, two formalized artifacts—the architectural model and the system implementation—are available.

In summary, automation facilitates continuous architecture analysis. However, automation requires formalization, and the feasibility of automating architecture analysis goals depends on the effort required to create and maintain such models during the development process. Analysis goals that perform some kind of structural analysis based on formally defined architecture models (i.e., analysis of the completeness of an architecture model with respect to a modeling notation, analysis of consistency and compatibility, conformance between architecture models and the system implementation) can be automated more easily than semantic analyses that typically require manual interpretation based on experience and expertise. While some of the structural analyses can be considered rather fine-grained and low-level, these kinds of analyses can be seen as foundational and prerequisite for more semantic kinds of analysis, like architecture evaluation. Structural analyses and conformance analyses ensure that architecture descriptions required for analysis are complete and consistent. Without complete and consistent architecture descriptions, architecture analysis may be difficult or even impossible [68].

7.7 EXPERIENCES WITH AN APPROACH TO CSAA

In the previous section, we argued that architecture analysis goals that support some kind of structural analysis are candidates for automatic, continuous architecture analysis. In the following, we report on experiences with automatic architecture analysis as supported by the LISA (Language for Integrated Software Architecture) approach. The approach supports the continuous analysis of *model completeness* and *consistency*, and of *architecture/implementation conformance*.

In general, LISA is a model-based approach for managing and analyzing the architecture of heterogeneous, component-based software systems [69]. It supports activities like architecture design, architecture extraction, architecture documentation, architecture knowledge management, and architecture analysis. The approach is based on a single formalized architecture model, which is used for architecture representation throughout the whole software architecture life cycle. This central model, which we call the LISA model, integrates and connects requirements, design decisions, architectural abstractions, and implementation artifacts [70], and information needed for both manual and automatic architecture analysis [71]. The nature of architectural abstractions and implementation artifacts in the LISA model can be compared to UML structure diagrams (e.g., class diagram and component diagram). Requirements and design decisions are described informally, but can be linked other requirements, design decisions, and architectural structures to support tracing and impact analysis.

The LISA Toolkit (see Figure 7.4) provides a set of integrated tools for working with LISA-based architecture models. The toolkit provides support for defining, editing, and visualizing LISA-based architecture models via multiple views, for extracting architectural information from a system implementation [69], and for automatic tracing of decisions to architecture and implementation [72].

CSAA support in LISA is provided by a framework for continuously analyzing LISA-based architecture models, which is part of the LISA Toolkit (see Figure 7.3). The framework performs architecture analysis after each modification of a system to support immediate problem detection. Analysis is performed automatically via an extensible set of rules that check architecture description and system implementation

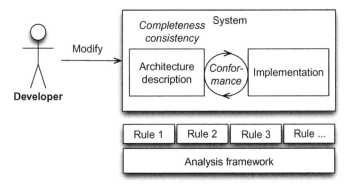

FIGURE 7.3

CSAA approach overview.

for problems. Rules are evaluated incrementally; this means that only those parts of an architecture model that have actually been modified are analyzed, and that only rules that are effected by a certain modification are evaluated. If problems are detected, they are immediately reported to the developers by annotating the architecture diagrams and the system implementation with problem markers, in a manner similar to how IDEs report compile errors (see Figure 7.4).

The resolution of problems is partially supported via automatically suggested resolution actions, which are called "quick fixes." A quick fix either automatically resolves a problem by making changes to architecture and/or implementation, or it guides the user through the problem resolution process. For example, a quick fix may prompt the user for missing information and automatically add this information to both architecture and implementation. Quick fixes can also be used for automatically creating component definitions, ports, and component instances in the architecture model, based on information found in the system implementation.

Currently, the LISA Toolkit mainly provides rules for analyzing the completeness and consistency of architecture models and for analyzing the conformance of the architecture model and system implementation (see Figure 7.3).

Completeness rules check whether the architecture model contains all required elements and whether these elements possess all required properties. Examples include rules for checking whether a component possesses one or more ports,

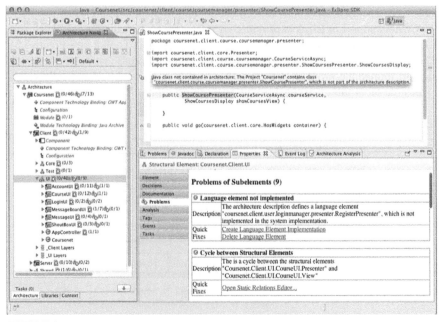

FIGURE 7.4

CSAA with LISA.

whether a port has a name, and whether a component is linked to an implementation artifact. The completeness of the architecture model is a prerequisite for other kinds of architecture analysis. For example, architecture/implementation conformance can only be analyzed if a component provides a link to an implementation artifact.

Consistency rules check whether architecture elements and their properties are consistently defined. For example, the system checks whether a component contains a valid reference to its definition and whether a connection is defined from a reference port to a service port (in case of a request-response style). In agile development processes, inconsistencies may easily arise as architecture and implementation evolve continuously.

Architecture/implementation conformance rules check whether architecture elements defined in the architecture model are also part of the system implementation, and vice versa. This includes checks like whether classes found in the system implementation are part of the architecture model and whether components found in the architecture model are implemented as components in the system implementation, and vice versa. Architecture/implementation conformance analysis aids not only in avoiding problems like architectural drift and erosion, but also in keeping architecture models up to date throughout the development process.

Architecture/implementation conformance analysis is provided for architectural information that is contained in both architecture description and system implementation. We provide conformance rules for code structures (classes, packages, dependencies), for component definitions, and for configuration structures. Components are identified in the system implementation based on heuristics using either provided metadata (annotations), extended and/or implemented classes and interfaces, and information available from configuration files and deployment descriptors.

7.7.1 **Validation**

We monitored the application of our approach in an industrial software development project (P1) and in several student projects (P2-P6). The developers of project P1 had multiple years of development experience. The project was medium-sized with about 350,000 lines of code, and was based on Eclipse. Developers in projects P2-P6 were students in computer science and business informatics classes. Projects P2-P6 varied between 5000 and 13,000 lines of code and included web applications based on the Google Web Toolkit and mobile applications based on Android. Developers were asked to use the LISA Toolkit to document their architectures and to keep this documentation up to date during the development process by using architecture/implementation conformance analysis. In each project, the architecture descriptions consisted of implementation structures, higher-level component structures, requirements, and design decisions.

All projects used an agile development process with iterations of 3-4 weeks. During the development process, we supported the developers by answering questions and discussing the usage of the LISA Toolkit at the end of each iteration.

We wanted to know whether the approach was applied continuously and whether it was integrated in the daily development process as outlined in Section 7.4. Relevant data was collected over a period of 3-8 months with a logging component that transparently recorded analysis-related data like detected and resolved analysis problems over time.

For making statements regarding continuous application, we first investigated the frequency of analysis during development. Usually, analysis is performed on each change in the system under investigation. However, analysis rules can be deactivated, which may lead to larger analysis intervals, or may deactivate analyses completely. We derived the analysis frequency from the logged analysis problems. As a frequency measure, we aggregated all detected problems within 1 h intervals and counted the average number of intervals with new problems per day. This resulted in a problem detection rate (number of intervals with new problems) of 2.3 in project P1. In the student projects the average problem detection rates were 1.7 (P2), 1.6 (P3), 1.9 (P4), 1.3 (P5), and 2.0 (P6), respectively (see Table 7.3). These results indicate that in all projects, architecture analysis has at least been performed on a daily basis. Further, in all projects there have been days with a detection rate of 3-5 times per day. All in all, this is a clear indication of high analysis frequency in all examined projects.

As described in Section 7.4, continuous application also requires the continuous resolution of problems to assess that a system retains its required quality. For this reason, we further analyzed the lifespan of problems to find out when detected problems were resolved—that is, whether they were resolved immediately, whether they were resolved later in the development process, or whether they were not resolved at all. For calculating the lifespan of a problem, we subtracted the time of first problem detection from the time of (last) problem resolution.[g] We classified the lifespan of problems into six categories: problems that were resolved within 5 min, within 1 h, within 1 day, within 1 week, within 1 month, and problems that existed for over 1 month.

Figure 7.5 provides an overview of the average lifespan of the detected problems in the analyzed projects. As shown in the figure, in all projects at least 49% of all detected problems were resolved within 5 min, and more than 62% of all problems were resolved within 1 h. Finally, between 68.2% and 96.9% of all problems were

Table 7.3 Overview of Problem Detection

	P1	P2	P3	P4	P5	P6
Avg. Detection Times per Day (1 h Interval)	2.3	1.7	1.6	1.9	1.3	2
Maximal Detections per Day	5	4	4	5	3	5

[g]Since analysis is performed on each modification of a system in our approach, problems are detected multiple times.

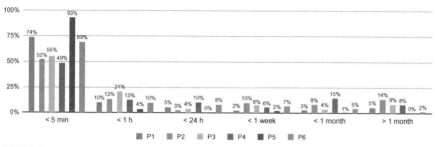

FIGURE 7.5

Average lifespan of problems.

Table 7.4 Problems That Have Been Resolved Within One Day						
	P1 (%)	P2 (%)	P3 (%)	P4 (%)	P5 (%)	P6 (%)
Problems Resolved Within One Day	89.1	68.2	79.9	71.3	96.9	86.9

resolved within 1 day. We should also note that in all projects a small number of problems had a lifespan of over 1 month. This shows that the majority of problems were resolved continuously, with about 50% even being resolved within 5 min and about 70% within 1 day (see Table 7.4).

The high frequency of the performed analyses (at least 1.4 times per day) and the short lifespan of most problems already indicate that analysis has been performed continuously and as an integral part of the development process in all projects. We further analyzed the aspect of process integration by taking a closer look at the problem resolution process. In particular we investigated the role of quick fixes for problem resolution. Quick fixes are (semi)automated resolution actions that are provided in architecture diagrams and source code editors and support the direct and immediate resolution of problems during architecture design and implementation activities. There is not always a one-to-one relationship between the execution of a quick fix and the resolution of a problem, which makes drawing conclusions from the analyzed data more difficult. The execution of a single quick fix might resolve multiple problems at once. Contrarily, not every execution of a quick fix necessarily resolves a problem. Therefore, we divided quick fixes into two categories: quick fixes that eventually resolved a problem and quick fixes that only assisted in problem resolution.

Table 7.5 shows the number of quick fixes that were executed in each project. Between 58% and 90% of all executed quick fixes definitely resolved a problem, while the other executed quick fixes assisted in problem resolution but did not directly resolve a problem. The data shows that in all projects, quick fixes have been used for problem resolution. Given the overall number of detected problems in each

Table 7.5 Quick Fix Execution Overview

	P1	P2	P3	P4	P5	P6
Executed Quick Fixes	604	156	123	406	239	171
Number of Quick Fixes That Resolved Problems	543	92	76	295	140	100
Number of Quick Fixes That Resolved Problems (%)	89.9	59.0	61.8	72.7	58.6	58.5
Problems	1682	528	390	552	280	203
Problems Resolved via Quick Fixes (%)	32.3	17.4	19.5	53.4	50.0	49.3

project, between 17.4% and 53.4% of all problems have at least been resolved via quick fixes. The actual number of problems resolved via quick fixes might be higher because the execution of a single quick fix may resolve multiple problems at once. It should also be noted that we have not developed quick fixes for all kinds of problems. Therefore the number of problems that can be resolved via quick fixes could be improved by providing additional quick fixes in the future. This shows that while quick fixes have been used in all projects for problem resolution, we cannot conclude that they are a prerequisite for continuous problem resolution.

7.8 FINDINGS AND RESEARCH CHALLENGES

Our experiences with the LISA approach are currently restricted to continuous analysis of the structural aspects of an architecture description and to conformance analysis. The data collected from the case studies presented in the previous section shows that this kind of analysis can be applied continuously in an agile setting, which means that developers were able to keep the architecture model up to date during development through conformance analysis. The analyzed data also shows a high number of detected conformance problems, even for the smaller projects. This indicates that even for smaller systems the architecture documentation (i.e., the architecture model) may easily become out of date in an agile process. We further found that many problems have been resolved within 5 min. This shows that conformance and inconsistency problems can be fixed rather quickly if analysis is performed continuously. Despite these findings, it is still too early to draw general conclusions for even these restrictive kinds of analysis. Further validation in additional projects— especially larger industrial ones—is needed.

Continuous model completeness and consistency analyses as provided in the LISA approach are useful during architecture design for indicating where architecture elements and required properties are still missing and/or inconsistent. This is especially valuable for the creation of formalized models with precise syntax and semantics. The provided benefits are similar to what is provided by compilers for programming languages and architecture-centric DSLs. Continuous conformance analysis not only aids in the creation and maintenance of a valid architecture description over time, but is also an important means for preventing architectural drift and erosion.

While CSAA seemed to work for the discussed kinds of analysis in the presented approach, we assume that less structural and more semantic kinds of analysis, like architecture evaluation, require a different approach for CSAA. Such kinds of analysis cannot easily be automated. Automatic evaluation requires formalization of both requirements and architecture—which is still too costly, at least for general use. Many well-known manual evaluation methods are too resource- and time-intensive and have so far not been adapted for use in agile settings. The resource demand can be reduced either by limiting the scope of analysis by analyzing only selected parts of a system's architecture, or by automating single steps/activities of the analysis process, like the creation and maintenance of architecture documentation. Lightweight reviews might be a possible approach for continuous architecture evaluation, but we lack documented experiences with lightweight reviews in agile processes.

Still we see the structural and conformance analysis as provided in the LISA approach as a possible foundation and as a first step for continuous architecture evaluation support. A strength of the LISA approach is its support for extracting architecture information from a system implementation and keeping this documentation up to date during the development process. The possibility of linking requirements and design decisions with solution structures further aids in using the resulting architecture model for manual and *ad hoc* architecture evaluation. Further, we can image that the formalized nature of the LISA model can help to identify modified parts of the architecture that need to be reevaluated.

Finally, we still need to clarify the role and the degree of architecture evaluation in agile processes. While architecture evaluation is an important means for risk reduction in plan-driven processes, this role may be less important in projects at the agile side of the spectrum because risk reduction is implemented as part of the process itself. Projects are often somewhere between strictly agile and strictly plan driven, so we assume that architecture evaluation will still have its place in many agile projects. We still need data on the actual use and the benefits of architecture evaluation in agile projects.

7.9 CONCLUSION

Architecture analysis is a broad topic, which is addressed by a large number of different analysis methods and techniques. Available analysis approaches differ considerably in various aspects, including process, stakeholders, and in the supported analysis goals. Many of the existing approaches for architecture analysis are currently not well suited for being applied continuously in an agile setting. This is mainly because they have been developed for rather plan-driven processes, with dedicated points of analysis in the process and external analysis processes. Approaches for quality control in agile processes show that integration, low resource demand, and/or automation are main requirements for CSAA. If we look at existing approaches for architecture analysis, we see that very few provide sufficient support for these requirements throughout all analysis activities, including preparation, analysis, and resolution.

Our own experiences with an approach for CSAA showed that automated CSAA works well in structural and conformance analyses. Automation-based approaches for other kinds of analysis, specifically for architecture evaluation, remain a challenge because of the effort involved in creating and maintaining the required formally defined models. Also, architecture evaluation includes not only checking whether an architecture design addresses the requirements correctly, but also comparing different alternatives and selecting the most suitable one by weighing the benefits and drawbacks of different solutions. This means that large parts of architecture evaluation are based on experience and cannot be automated. Lightweight architecture reviews might be a possible approach, but we still lack experiences with lightweight reviews in agile processes.

We conclude that continuous architecture evaluation in agile processes remains an open research question. Continuous analysis of semantic analysis goals based on experience can be performed using lightweight architecture reviews, which reduce resource demand by analyzing only selected parts of an architecture and do not require explicit architecture documentation. Further, structural analysis as provided by the approach presented in this chapter can be used for automating single activities of the analysis process like the creation and maintenance of architecture documentation. Providing an architecture description that is always up to date and support for lightweight capturing of architectural documentation (e.g., through architectural knowledge) might help to make architectural evaluation more explicit and manageable in such processes. To answer these questions, we need studies of the state of practice of architecture evaluation in agile processes, new approaches for automating specific tasks of architecture evaluation with reasonable effort, and suggestions for improving manual reviews in environments with constraints on time and other resources.

References

[1] Kazman R, Bass L, Abowd G, Webb M. SAAM: a method for analyzing the properties of software architectures. In: Proceedings. 16th international conference on software engineering (ICSE-16); 1994. p. 81–90.

[2] Kazman R, Klein M, Barbacci M, Longstaff T, Lipson H, Carriere J. The architecture tradeoff analysis method. In: Proceedings. Fourth IEEE international conference on engineering of complex computer systems (ICECCS '98); 1998. p. 68–78.

[3] Bass L, Clements P, Kazman R, Klein J, Klein M, Siviy J. A workshop on architecture competence. tech. note CMU/SEI-2009-TN-005, Software Engineering Institute, Carnegie Mellon University; 2009.

[4] Endres A, Rombach D. Illustrated edition: a handbook of software and systems engineering: empirical observations, laws and theories. Reading, MA: Addison Wesley; 2003.

[5] Taylor RN, Medvidovic N, Dashofy EM. Software architecture: foundations, theory, and practice. New Jersey: Wiley; 2009.

[6] Hofmeister C, Kruchten P, Nord R, Obbink H, Ran A, America P. A general model of software architecture design derived from five industrial approaches. J Syst Softw 2007;80:106–26.

[7] Tang A, Avgeriou P, Jansen A, Capilla R, Babar MA. A comparative study of architecture knowledge management tools. J Syst Softw 2010;83:352–70.

[8] Kazman R, Bass L, Klein M, Lattanze T, Northrop L. A basis for analyzing software architecture analysis methods. Software Qual J 2005;13:329–55, Kluwer Academic Publishers.

[9] Bass L, Clements P, Kazman R. 2nd ed. Software architecture in practice. Boston, MA: Addison-Wesley Professional; 2003.

[10] Kazman R, Asundi J, Klein M. Quantifying the costs and benefits of architectural decisions. In: International conference on software engineering. Colorado: IEEE Computer Society; 2001. p. 297+.

[11] Sommerville I. 8th ed. Software engineering: update, Boston, MA: Addison Wesley; 2006.

[12] Karpov A. Verification and validation, Intel® Software Network Software Blogs; 2010.

[13] Kazman R, Bass L, Abowd G, Webb M. Analyzing the properties of user interface software. Pittsburgh, PA: Carnegie Mellon University; 1993.

[14] Obbink H, Kruchten P, Kozaczynski W, Hilliard R, Ran A, Postema H, et al. Report on software architecture review and assessment (SARA); 2002.

[15] Bosch J. Design and use of software architectures: adopting and evolving a product-line approach. Boston, MA: Addison-Wesley Professional; 2000.

[16] Harrison N, Avgeriou P. Pattern-based architecture reviews. IEEE Softw 2011; 28:66–71, IEEE Computer Society Press.

[17] IEEE 1028-2008 IEEE standard for software reviews and audits. Institute of Electrical and Electronics Engineers, 2008.

[18] Parnas DL, Weiss DM. Active design reviews: principles and practices. In: ICSE '85: proceedings of the 8th international conference on software engineering. Washington, DC: IEEE Computer Society Press; 1985. p. 132–6.

[19] Woods E. Industrial architectural assessment using TARA. In: Proceedings of the 2011 ninth working IEEE/IFIP conference on software architecture. Boulder, CO: IEEE Computer Society; 2011. p. 56–65.

[20] Maranzano JF, Rozsypal SA, Zimmerman GH, Warnken GW, Wirth PE, Weiss DM. Architecture reviews: practice and experience. IEEE Softw 2005;22:34–43, IEEE Computer Society.

[21] Abowd G, Bass L, Clements P, Kazman R, Northrop L, Zaremski A. Recommended best industrial practice for software architecture evaluation. tech. note CMU/SEI-96-TR-025, Software Engineering Institute, Carnegie Mellon University; 1997.

[22] Balzert H. Lehrbuch der Softwaretechnik: Softwaremanagement (German Edition). 2nd Aufl. Heidelberg: Spektrum Akademischer Verlag; 2008.

[23] Clements P, Kazman R, Klein M. Evaluating software architectures: methods and case studies. Reading, MA: Addison-Wesley Professional; 2001.

[24] Dobrica L, Niemela E. A survey on software architecture analysis methods. IEEE Trans Softw Eng 2002;28:638–53, IEEE Computer Society.

[25] Babar MA, Zhu L, Jeffery R. A framework for classifying and comparing software architecture evaluation methods. In: ASWEC '04: proceedings of the 2004 Australian software engineering conference. Washington, DC: IEEE Computer Society; 2004. p. 309+.

[26] Clements P. Formal methods in describing architectures. In: Monterey workshop on formal methods and architecture; 1995.

[27] Clements PC. A survey of architecture description languages. In: IWSSD '96: proceedings of the 8th international workshop on software specification and design. Washington, DC: IEEE Computer Society; 1996.

[28] Dashofy EM, van der Hoek A, Taylor RN. A comprehensive approach for the development of modular software architecture description languages. ACM Trans Softw Eng Methodol 2005;14:199–245, ACM Press.

[29] Garlan D, Monroe R, Wile D. Acme: an architecture description interchange language. In: CASCON '97: proceedings of the 1997 conference of the centre for advanced studies on collaborative research. Toronto, Ontario: IBM Press; 1997.

[30] Medvidovic N, Taylor RN. A classification and comparison framework for software architecture description languages. IEEE Trans Softw Eng 2000;26:70–93, IEEE Press.

[31] van Ommering R, van der Linden F, Kramer J, Magee J. The koala component model for consumer electronics software. Computer 2000;33:78–85, IEEE Computer Society Press.

[32] Feiler PH, Gluch DP, Hudak JJ. The Architecture Analysis & Design Language (AADL): an introduction. tech. note CMU/SEI-2006-TN-011, Software Engineering Institute, Carnegie Mellon University; 2006.

[33] Heinecke H, Schnelle K-P, Fennel H, Bortolazzi J, Lundh L, Leflour J, et al. Automotive open system architecture—an industry-wide initiative to manage the complexity of emerging automotive E/E architectures. In: Convergence international congress & exposition on transportation electronics; 2004. p. 325–32.

[34] Allen RJ. A formal approach to software architecture. Pittsburgh, PA: Carnegie Mellon University; 1997.

[35] Schmerl B, Garlan D. AcmeStudio: supporting style-centered architecture development. In: Proceedings of the 26th international conference on software engineering. Washington, DC: IEEE Computer Society; 2004. p. 704–5.

[36] Woods E, Hilliard R. Architecture description languages in practice session report. In: WICSA '05: proceedings of the 5th working IEEE/IFIP conference on software architecture. Washington, DC: IEEE Computer Society; 2005. p. 243–6.

[37] Völter M. Architecture as language. IEEE Softw 2010;27:56–64, IEEE Computer Society Press.

[38] Murphy GC, Notkin D, Sullivan KJ. Software reflexion models: bridging the gap between design and implementation. IEEE Trans Softw Eng 2001;27:364–80, IEEE Press.

[39] Tran JB, Godfrey MW, Lee EHS, Holt RC. Architectural repair of open source software. In: IWPC '00: proceedings of the 8th international workshop on program comprehension. Washington, DC: IEEE Computer Society; 2000. p. 48.

[40] Sangal N, Jordan E, Sinha V, Jackson D. Using dependency models to manage complex software architecture. SIGPLAN Not 2005;40:167–76.

[41] Bischofberger W, Kühl J, Löffler S. Sotograph – A pragmatic approach to source code architecture conformance checking. In: Oquendo F, Warboys BC, Morrison R, editors. Software Architecture. Lecture notes in Computer Science, vol. 3047. Berlin: Springer; 2004. p. 1–9. ISBN: 978-3-540-22000-8, http://dx.doi.org/10.1007/978-3-540-24769-2_1.

[42] Sangwan RS, Vercellone-Smith P, Laplante PA. Structural epochs in the complexity of software over time. IEEE Softw 2008;25:66–73.

[43] Lippert M, Roock S. 1st ed. Refactoring in large software projects: performing complex restructurings successfully, New York: Wiley; 2006.

[44] Floyd C. A systematic look at prototyping. Approaches to prototyping, Berlin: Springer; 1984. p. 1–18.

[45] Rozanski N, Woods E. Software systems architecture: working with stakeholders using viewpoints and perspectives. Boston, MA: Addison-Wesley Professional; 2005.

[46] Beregi WE. Architecture prototyping in the software engineering environment. IBM Syst J 1984;23:4–18, IBM Corp.

[47] Christensen HB, Hansen KM. An empirical investigation of architectural prototyping. J Syst Softw 2010;83:133–42.

[48] Babar MA, Gorton I. Software architecture review: the state of practice. Computer 2009; 42:26–32, IEEE Computer Society.

[49] Garland J, Anthony R. Large-scale software architecture: a practical guide using UML, Chichester, NY: Wiley; 2003.

[50] Paulish DJ. Architecture-centric software project management: a practical guide. Boston, MA: Addison-Wesley Professional; 2002.

[51] Rozanski N, Woods E. Software systems architecture: working with stakeholders using viewpoints and perspectives. Upper Saddle River, NJ: Addison-Wesley; 2012.

[52] Beck K. Extreme programming explained: embrace change, Reading, MA: Addison-Wesley; 2000.

[53] Beck K, Beedle M, van Bennekum A, Cockburn A, Cunningham W, Fowler M, et al. Manifesto for agile software development; 2001. Website: http://agilemanifesto.org/.

[54] Boehm B, Turner R. Using risk to balance agile and plan-driven methods. Computer 2003;36:57–66, IEEE Computer Society.

[55] Boehm B. Get ready for agile methods, with care. Computer 2002;35:64–9, IEEE Computer Society Press.

[56] Rady B, Coffin R. Continuous testing with ruby, rails, and JavaScript. Dallas, TX: Pragmatic Bookshelf; 2011.

[57] Duvall PM, Matyas S, Glover A. Continuous integration: improving software quality and reducing risk. Boston, MA: Addison-Wesley Professional; 2007.

[58] Stamelos IG, Sfetsos P. Agile software development quality assurance. Hershey, PA: Idea Group Inc; 2007.

[59] Beck K. Test-driven development: by example. Boston, MA: Addison-Wesley; 2003.

[60] Hibbs C, Jewett S, Sullivan M. The art of lean software development: a practical and incremental approach. Sebastopol, CA: O'Reilly Media; 2009.

[61] Burnstein I. Practical software testing : a process-oriented approach. New York: Springer; 2003.

[62] Fowler M. Continuous integration, http://martinfowler.com; 2006.

[63] Kazman R, Nord R, Klein MH. A life-cycle view of architecture analysis and design methods. tech. note CMU/SEI-2003-TN-026, Software Engineering Institute, Carnegie Mellon University; 2003.

[64] Kazman R, Carrière SJ, Woods SG. Toward a discipline of scenario-based architectural engineering. Ann Softw Eng 2000;9:5–33J. C. Baltzer AG, Science Publishers.

[65] Merkle B. Stop the software architecture erosion. In: Proceedings of the ACM international conference companion on object oriented programming systems languages and applications companion. New York: ACM; 2010. p. 295–7.

[66] Inverardi P, Muccini H, Pelliccione P. DUALLY: putting in synergy UML 2.0 and ADLs. In: WICSA '05: proceedings of the 5th working IEEE/IFIP conference on software architecture. IEEE Computer Society; 2005. p. 251–2.

[67] Kandé MM, Crettaz V, Strohmeier A, Sendall S. Bridging the gap between IEEE 1471, an architecture description language, and UML. Softw Syst Model 2002;1:113–29.

[68] Albin S. The art of software architecture: design methods and techniques. John Wiley & Sons, Inc.; 2003.

[69] Weinreich R, Buchgeher G. Towards supporting the software architecture life cycle. J Syst Softw 2012;85:546–61.

[70] Weinreich R, Buchgeher G. Integrating requirements and design decisions in architecture representation. In: Proceedings of the 4th European conference on software architecture. Springer-Verlag; 2010. p. 86–101.

[71] Buchgeher G, Weinreich R. An approach for combining model-based and scenario-based software architecture analysis. In: Fifth international conference on software engineering advances (ICSEA 2010); 2010. p. 141–8. http://dx.doi.org/10.1109/ICSEA.2010.29.

[72] Buchgeher G, Weinreich R. Automatic tracing of decisions to architecture and implementation. In: 9th working IEEE/IFIP conference on software architecture (WICSA 2011); 2011. p. 46–55. http://dx.doi.org/10.1109/WICSA.2011.16.

Lightweight Architecture Knowledge Management for Agile Software Development

8

Veli-Pekka Eloranta and Kai Koskimies

Tampere University of Technology, Tampere, Finland

CHAPTER CONTENTS

8.1 INTRODUCTION

The tension between agile software development and software architecture (see Refs. [1–3]) is reflected and even emphasized in architecture knowledge management (AKM). We define AKM as methods to support sharing, distributing, creating, capturing, and understanding a company's knowledge of software architecture [4,5].

The Agile Manifesto [6] downplays the significance of activities aimed at comprehensive knowledge codification, including architectural knowledge. Still, it is generally agreed (see [7,8]) that systematic codification of architectural knowledge is required for many kinds of systems (e.g., for systems that are used and maintained for decades or have legislative viewpoints). If agile approaches are used in the context of such systems, AKM must be integrated with agile development.

On the other hand, we strongly believe that AKM is not necessarily a burden for agile development in general, but rather a practice that can support agile methods in the long run by improving communication between stakeholders—especially in large-scale and possibly distributed agile projects—and by helping to maintain the systems developed. In particular, we argue that by integrating a carefully tuned, lightweight AKM as part of the process, the agile development paradigm can largely avoid the maintenance problems originating from scarce documentation.

To fit with agile approaches, AKM itself must be lightweight. The central property of lightweight AKM is minimal additional cost in terms of human work; neither producing nor consuming architectural knowledge should introduce significant activities that are related to AKM itself, rather than to the direct support of product development. We aim for AKM that is next to invisible for the stakeholders, thus affecting the agile characteristics of the work as little as possible. In this chapter, we propose possible ways to make both producing and consuming architectural knowledge lightweight while preserving the main benefits of AKM.

From the viewpoint of architectural knowledge codification, an attractive approach would be to populate the architectural information repository (AIR) as a side effect of some activity that creates new architectural information or makes architectural knowledge explicit. This can be accomplished by integrating the tools used in those activities with the AIR. Examples of such tools are requirement engineering tools (creating architecturally significant requirements (ASRs)), architecture modeling tools and Integrated Development Environments (IDEs), architectural evaluation tools, and reverse engineering tools. In particular, we advocate the use of lightweight architectural evaluations for codifying architectural knowledge; during architectural evaluations, a significant amount of architectural knowledge emerges and becomes explicit, such as architectural decisions, high-level designs, ASRs, and business drivers. If a bookkeeping tool used in the evaluations is integrated with the AIR, a large body of valuable architectural knowledge can be codified virtually effortlessly. In particular, tacit architectural knowledge [9] is not captured in documents during the development process, but it does typically emerge during the discussions of architecture evaluation. Thus, architecture evaluation is a natural context in which to make tacit architectural knowledge explicit.

From the viewpoint of consuming architectural knowledge effortlessly, the main problem is that the information in the AIR is typically structured according to a conceptual metamodel rather than the needs of the stakeholders [10–12]. Consequently, without more high-level, need-oriented support, stakeholders have to express their needs using general query and navigation mechanisms, which can be tedious in many cases. In this chapter, we propose augmenting the AIR with a need-oriented interface that is able to generate information packages that satisfy particular anticipated needs of stakeholders. In this way, the stakeholders do not have to use time and energy screening the relevant information from a mass of architectural knowledge. An earlier description of this kind of tool support is given by Eloranta et al. [13].

There are many ways to develop software in an agile way. We explore the realization of the above proposals in the context of Scrum [14], which is by far the most popular agile approach applied in today's industrial software development projects [3]. According to a recent survey [15], Scrum and Scrum hybrids have a 69% market share of agile methods in the software industry. Scrum combines agile principles [6] with a lean manufacturing philosophy [16]. Essentially, Scrum defines how the work is broken down into tasks; how the tasks are ordered, managed, and carried out; what the roles of the project members are; and how persons in these roles interact during the development process. A central concept of Scrum is a sprint—a working period during which the team produces a potentially shippable product increment.

On the other hand, there are also many ways to do architecture-related work in Scrum. Eloranta and Koskimies [17] investigated software architecture work practices used with Scrum in the software industry. While some of these practices are more in line with Scrum than others, they are all motivated by reasons that emerge in real life, and they all have their merits. The main contribution of this chapter is a proposal for integrating existing architecture evaluation and documentation techniques with these practices to establish lightweight AKM in Scrum. Since the proposal is based on observations of agile projects in industry concerning software architecting practices, we expect that the proposal is feasible in practice. In addition, to understand in more detail the flow of architectural information in real-life agile projects, we carried out a study in which we interviewed practitioners in industry to identify the artifacts carrying architectural information and the ways they are produced and consumed. The approach draws on the first author's experiences with software architecture documentation challenges in agile projects, which are summarized in the next section.

In Section 8.3, we briefly introduce techniques that serve as constituent parts of our proposal for lightweight AKM for agile software development, architectural evaluation methods, and automated document generation. In Section 8.4, we give a short summary of Scrum and discuss the findings of an earlier study on architectural practices in Scrum in industry. In Section 8.5, we discuss the results of an interview carried out in industry to identify the architectural information flow in real-life agile projects. In Section 8.6, we propose models to integrate Scrum with lightweight AKM, based on the observed architectural practices and architectural information flow in Scrum. Finally, we conclude with a formulation of lightweight AKM principles for agile software development as we now see them, and with some remarks on future work.

8.2 CHALLENGES OF AGILE ARCHITECTURE DOCUMENTATION

The Agile Manifesto [6] guides the reader to value working software over comprehensive documentation, but it also explicitly states that documentation can be valuable as well. Unfortunately, the Agile Manifesto is often misread as a permission to overlook documentation. In small, short projects, documentation may be less important.

However, in large projects, the need for communication exceeds the limits of face-to-face communication—both spatially and temporally. When hundreds or even thousands of developers and other stakeholders are involved in the project, some documentation practices must be established to distribute the information efficiently throughout the organization. Similarly, if the life span of a software system is several decades, then documentation is needed to bridge the communication gap between several generations of architects and developers. On the other hand, there may even be compelling legal reasons that dictate documentation. In particular, safety-critical systems must often pass certifications that are largely based on reviewing documents.

It should be emphasized that documentation should not replace face-to-face communication when the latter is more appropriate. According to Coplien and Bjørnvig [18], all documentation (including architectural) is written for two reasons: to remember things, and to communicate them. However, documentation is one-directional communication and, as stated by Cockburn in Ref. [19], it is not a very efficient way of communicating between two persons. The most efficient way of communicating is two persons talking face to face at the whiteboard. The main motivation to produce architectural documentation is to record the design and its rationale as a kind of collective memory.

To better understand the problems of architectural documentation in agile industrial project contexts, the first author participated actively in an industrial project for about 18 months with the responsibility of developing the project's software architecture documentation practices. The company was a global manufacturer of work machines with embedded control systems. From this experience, we recognized three major challenges related to software architecture documentation:

- *Size*. One of the main concerns was that the amount of required documentation is rather large. The architecture document soon became unreadable and non-maintainable as its size grew. To solve the problem, the document was split into smaller chunks. However, this led to the problem that it was hard to find the right document. Furthermore, the splitting of the document resulted in synchronization problems (how to ensure that the different documents constitute a consistent and complete description of the architecture).
- *Fragmentation*. In general, fragmentation of architectural information was found to be a major problem. A lot of existing architectural information was fragmented in different places (e.g., presentation slides, e-mails, meeting memos, etc.). The reason for this was that people had to make notes in the meetings, give presentations, send e-mails, and so on, but no one was responsible for compiling all of this information and updating the documents on any critical path towards the completion of backlog items. This resulted in an unpleasant situation: architectural information existed but nobody was sure where it was, or whether it was the most current information.
- *Separated architecture documentation*. Architectural information was produced throughout the development, but architecture documentation took place only at certain major milestones. This caused a delay in the recording of architectural information, and led to loss of information. Architectural information was mostly

produced in the beginning of the project in the form of rough designs and decisions, but during Scrum sprints more detailed design information was produced and more architectural and design decisions were made. To make the codifying of architectural knowledge more efficient and precise, the codifying should take place immediately when the knowledge is available.

The conclusions drawn from the experience were the following:

• Architectural information should be presented in small information packages that address stakeholders' specific needs, rather than in conventional all-purpose, comprehensive architecture documents. The consistency of such information packages should be guaranteed by the underlying infrastructure rather than relying on manual updating.
• The storing of architectural information should be centralized in a common architectural repository to be sure where the current version of the information resides.
• The codifying of architectural knowledge should be seamlessly integrated with the agile process so that architectural knowledge is largely codified as a side effect of those activities that create the knowledge, without notable additional effort.

These conclusions can be viewed as (fairly ambitious) high-level requirements for lightweight AKM for agile software development. In this chapter, we propose approaches which constitute a partial solution for these requirements, but also leave many issues open. In particular, the integration of the AKM practices with an agile process is a challenging problem for which we offer a specific solution, namely exploiting (lightweight) architectural evaluation as a means to codify architectural knowledge without extra effort.

8.3 SUPPORTING TECHNIQUES FOR AKM IN AGILE SOFTWARE DEVELOPMENT

In this section, we discuss existing techniques that can be used to support lightweight AKM in agile software development, which we will explore in the next section. First, we discuss the role of architecture evaluation from the viewpoint of AKM and briefly introduce two architecture evaluation methods—the architecture trade-off analysis method (ATAM) [20], and the decision-centric architecture review method (DCAR) [21]. The former is the most widely used architecture evaluation method, while the latter is a new method especially aiming at lightweight and incremental evaluation. Both can be used to produce core architectural information in a repository as a side effect of the evaluation. We use ATAM as an example of a holistic evaluation method; several other architecture evaluation methods, such as Software Architecture Analysis Method (SAAM) [22], Pattern-Based Architecture Review (PBAR) [23], or Cost Benefit Analysis Method (CBAM) [24] could replace ATAM in the discussion of this chapter. As the second topic, we outline existing techniques to expose the architectural information in the form of focused information packages and to populate the AIR [13].

8.3.1 Architecture evaluation methods, agility, and AKM

Software architecture is typically one of the first descriptions of the system to be built. It forms a basis for the design and dictates whether the most important qualities and functionalities of the system can be achieved. Architecture evaluation is a systematic method to expose problems and risks in the architectural design, preferably before the system is implemented.

ATAM is a well-known, scenario-based architecture evaluation method used in industry [20]. The basic idea of a scenario-based architecture evaluation method is to refine quality attributes into concrete scenarios phrased by the stakeholders (developers, architects, managers, marketing, testing, etc.). In this way, the stakeholders can present their concerns related to the quality requirements. The scenarios are prioritized according to their importance and expected difficulty, and highly prioritized scenarios are eventually used in the architectural analysis. The analysis is preceded by presentations of the business drivers and of the software architecture.

Architectural evaluations not only reveal risks in the system design, but also bring up a lot of central information about software architecture. The authors have carried out approximately 20 full-scale scenario-based evaluations in the industry, and in most cases the industrial participants have expressed their need for uncovering architectural knowledge as a major motivation for the evaluation. A typical feedback comment has been that a significant benefit of the evaluation was communication about software architecture between different stakeholders, which otherwise would not have taken place. Thus, software architecture evaluation has an important facet related to AKM that is not often recognized.

Essential architectural information emerging in ATAM evaluations include ASRs (and scenarios refining them), architectural decisions, relationships between requirements and decisions, analysis and rationale for the decisions, and identified risks of the architecture. Since the issues discussed in the evaluation are based on probable and important scenarios from the viewpoint of several kinds of stakeholders, it is reasonable to argue that the information emerging in ATAM (and other evaluation methods) is actually the most relevant information about the software architecture. Furthermore, this information is likely to actually be used later on and is therefore important to document.

From the viewpoint of agile development, the main drawback of ATAM (and scenario-based architecture evaluation methods in general) is heavyweightness; scenario-based methods are considered to be rather complicated and expensive to use [25–27]. A medium-sized ATAM evaluation can take up to 40 person-days covering the work of different stakeholders ([28], p. 41). In our experience, even getting all the required stakeholders in the same room for 2 or 3 days is next to impossible in an agile context. Furthermore, a lot of time in the evaluation is spent on refining quality requirements into scenarios and on discussing the requirements and even the form of the scenarios. Most of the scenarios are actually not used (as they don't get sufficient votes in the prioritization), implying notable waste in the lean sense [16]. On the other hand, although communication about requirements is beneficial, it is often time-consuming as it comes back to the question of the system's purpose. In an agile context, the question about building the right product is a central concern that is taken care of by fast development cycles and incremental development, allowing the customers to participate actively in the process. Thus, a more lightweight evaluation method that concentrates on the soundness of the current architectural decisions, rather than on the requirement analysis, would better serve an agile project setup.

Techniques to boost architecture evaluation using domain knowledge have been proposed by several authors. So-called "general scenarios" [29] can be utilized in ATAM evaluation to express patterns of scenarios that tend to reoccur in different systems in the same domain. Furthermore, if multiple ATAM evaluations are carried out in the same domain, the domain model can be utilized to find the concrete scenarios for the system [30]. In this way, some of the scenarios can be found offline before the evaluation sessions. This will speed up the elicitation process in the evaluation sessions and create significant cost savings because less time is required for the scenario elicitation. However, even with these improvements, our experience and a recent survey [47] suggest that scenario-based architecture evaluation methods are not widely used in the industry because they are too heavyweight—especially for agile projects.

Another problem with integrating ATAM with agile processes is that ATAM is designed for one-off evaluation rather than for the continuous evaluation that would be required in Agile. ATAM is based on a holistic view of the system, starting with top-level quality requirements that are refined into concrete scenarios, and architectural approaches are analyzed only against these scenarios. This works well in a one-off evaluation, but poses problems in an agile context where the architecture is developed incrementally. The unit of architectural development is an architectural decision, and an agile evaluation method should be incremental with respect to this unit, in the sense that the evaluation can be carried out by considering a subset of the decisions at a time.

The lack of incrementality in ATAM is reflected in the difficulty to decide on the proper time for architectural evaluation in an agile project. If the architecture is designed up-front, as in traditional waterfall development, the proper moment for evaluation is naturally when the design is mostly done. However, when using agile methods, such as Scrum, the architecture is often created in sprints. Performing an ATAM-like evaluation in every sprint that creates architecture would be too time-consuming. On the other hand, if the evaluation is carried out as a post-Scrum activity, the system is already implemented and the changes become costly.

A recent survey shows that architects seldom revisit the decisions made [25]. This might be because the implementation is ready and changing the architectural decisions would be costly. Therefore, it would be advisable to do evaluation of the decisions right after they are made. This approach can be extended to agile practices. If the architecture and architectural decisions are made in sprints, it would be advisable to revisit and review these decisions immediately after the sprint.

Partly motivated by this reasoning, a new software architecture evaluation method called DCAR was proposed in [21]. DCAR uses architectural decisions as the basic concept in the architecture evaluation. Another central concept in DCAR is a *decision force*—that is, any fact or viewpoint that has pushed the decision in a certain direction [31]. Forces can be requirements, or existing decisions (e.g., technology choices, previous experiences, political or economical considerations, etc.). A force is a basic unit of the rationale of a decision; essentially, a decision is made to balance the forces. In DCAR, a set of architectural decisions is analyzed by identifying the forces that have affected the decisions and by examining whether the decision is still justified in the presence of the current forces. Besides the evaluation team, only architects and chief developers are assumed to participate in the evaluation.

DCAR is expected to be more suitable for agile projects than scenario-based methods because of its lightweightness: a typical system-wide DCAR evaluation session can be carried out in half a day, with roughly 15-20 person-hours of project resources [21]. Thus, performing a DCAR evaluation during a sprint is quite feasible—especially when developing systems with long life spans or with special emphasis on risks (e.g., safety-critical systems). On the other hand, since DCAR is structured according to decisions rather than scenarios, it can be carried out incrementally by considering a certain subset of decisions at a time. If the forces of decisions do not change between successive DCAR evaluations, the conclusions drawn in previous evaluation sessions are not invalidated by later evaluations. Thus, in Scrum, decisions can be evaluated right after the sprint they are made in. If the number of decisions is relatively small (say, <10 decisions), such a partial evaluation requires less than 2 h and can be done as part of the sprint retrospect in Scrum.

If new information emerges in the sprints, the old decisions can be revisited and reevaluated. DCAR makes this possible by documenting the relationships between decisions. If a decision needs to be changed in a sprint, it is easy to see which earlier decisions might be affected as well and (re-)evaluate them. Additionally, as the decision drivers (i.e., forces) are documented in each decision, it is rather easy to see if the emergent information is going to affect the decision and if the decision should be reevaluated.

From the AKM viewpoint, a particularly beneficial feature of DCAR is that the decisions are documented as part of the DCAR process, during the evaluation. This decision documentation can be reused in software architecture documentation as such. If a tool is used in DCAR to keep track of the evaluation and to record the decision documentation, this information can be immediately stored in the AIR without extra effort.

8.3.2 Advanced techniques for managing architectural repositories

Even for a medium-sized system, the AIR can grow large, containing several hundreds or even thousands of information elements. This can easily lead to an information bloat problem: a stakeholder that has specific information needs faces a mass of information with complicated structure, not directly addressing his or her needs. Typical AKM tools (e.g., [32]) provide search and navigation mechanisms to find the relevant information, but their utilization requires understanding of the AIR structure and experience in its usage. Introducing such a tool concept in an agile development process is difficult, as the agile philosophy explicitly tries to avoid heavy tools.

In Ref. [13], this problem is addressed by providing a need-oriented high-level interface for consuming the information in the AIR, essentially hiding the AIR from the consumer. This could be seen analogical to an informaticist who has knowledge about the kinds of specialized documents that are probably needed and who is able to produce the desired type of document on the basis of the contents of the AIR. If such a document is not sufficient, the stakeholder may use the conventional search and navigation mechanisms of the AIR, but since new document types can be introduced when needed, it is expected that eventually the predefined document types cover most of the needs of stakeholders. The tool, called TopDocs, has been implemented on top of Polarion [33], a commercial life cycle management system.

Currently, TopDocs supports the generation of specialized architectural documents on the basis of a certain quality aspect, a certain part of the system, or a certain maintenance scenario. For example, a developer can ask for a component-oriented architectural document, showing everything he or she needs to know about the component when developing it (e.g., interfaces, dependencies, internal design, architectural contexts, related decisions, etc.). In addition, the tool can generate a conventional, comprehensive software architecture document or an architecture evaluation document. The tool can also generate documents on different granularity levels—allowing, for example, the generation of very high-level architectural documents for managers. TopDocs differs from other repository-based AKM tools such as EAGLE [34] or ArchiMind [10] in that it has the capability to generate specialized, focused architectural documents for a particular requirement in our approach.

These documents correspond closely to the *view* concept in ISO/IEC 42010 [35], defining a view as a work product expressing the architecture of a system from the perspective of specific system concerns. Architecture viewpoint [35], in turn, establishes the conventions for the construction, interpretation, and use of architecture views to frame specific system concerns. Thus, a viewpoint is realized in TopDocs by defining and implementing a new document type for a new concern. In principle, any AKM tool that provides the capability to define new viewpoints and generate views according to viewpoints could be used in our approach.

It is also important to provide automated support for populating the AIR. Centralized AIR offers a common place where all architectural information can be recorded immediately when it emerges. For example, instead of writing separate memos in meetings and hoping that this information eventually finds its way to the architecture document, a stakeholder can directly write the memo into the AIR where its information immediately contributes to the reports produced from the AIR contents. Similarly, a bookkeeping tool for ATAM and other evaluation methods should be integrated with the AIR so that the tool automatically populates the AIR immediately when architecturally relevant information emerges. TopDocs provides such a tool interface for ATAM and DCAR evaluations, making it possible to store all architectural information appearing in an evaluation session directly to the AIR without extra effort. Assuming that this captures the relevant information about the software architecture that is probably used in the future, automated evaluation-based feeding offers an attractive solution to the problem of populating the AIR.

From the agile viewpoint, hiding the complexity of the AIR from both the producing side and the consuming side is of crucial importance. Ideally, the stakeholders should not be aware of the underlying AKM infrastructure, and just use tools that are targeted to the activities related to the actual development work. Under the surface, these tools should then populate the AIR with the new architectural information. TopDocs is a step in that direction, demonstrating that especially architectural evaluation tools, which are integrated with the AIR, can greatly assist in the feeding of the AIR. In a truly lightweight AKM, the architectural information is collected automatically, and the information needs of stakeholders are satisfied with automated generation of targeted information packages.

8.4 ARCHITECTURE PRACTICES IN AGILE PROJECTS

In this section, we lay groundwork for later discussion on how to align lightweight AKM with Scrum. We start by briefly describing the main elements of the Scrum framework. In Section 8.4.2, we will summarize the results of a recent survey on how organizations build architectures while using Scrum.

8.4.1 Scrum framework

Scrum is an iterative and incremental framework for agile project management [14,36]. Figure 8.1 illustrates the structure of the Scrum process. The process is divided into three central parts: analysis phase (sometimes called pregame), development phase, and review phase.

In the analysis phase, the requirements are collected and analyzed. This analysis leads to product backlog, which is a collection of all features and properties that the software to-be-built may have. For example, an item in the product backlog could say, "Rework the component so that it has better scalability." The product backlog is ordered so that the most valuable items are on top of the list while taking dependencies into account. Items at the top of the list will be implemented in the next sprint.

The original Scrum paper [14] states that high-level architecture design is part of the pregame. However, descriptions about software architecture and Scrum are left open in [14]. Many later descriptions of the Scrum framework do not describe the analysis phase in detail at all.

After the analysis phase, the actual implementation of the system starts. Implementation is time-boxed into periods of 2-4 weeks called sprints. In the beginning of the sprint, development teams take items from the top of the product backlog and split them into tasks that they commit to finish within the sprint.

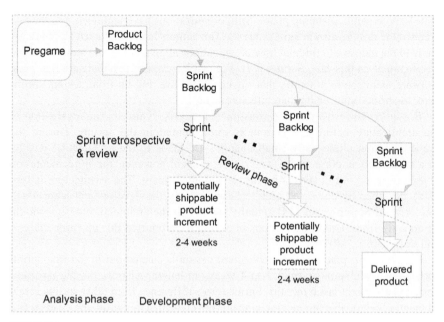

FIGURE 8.1

Scrum framework.

After the sprint, there are review sessions where the customer accepts the results of the sprint. There is also an assessment of whether the goals set for the sprint were met. At this stage, the software should be tested and ready to be shipped to the customer. In the review phase, the team also has a lessons-learned session where they discuss how they could improve their work practices.

8.4.2 **Architecting while using Scrum**

Software architecture can be seen as the result of a set of complex system of architectural design decisions depending on each other [37,38]. These decisions are typically made during an iterative and incremental process. The process of architecture design has been divided into three common, recurring activities by Hofmeister et al. [39]: architectural analysis, synthesis, and evaluation. *Architectural analysis* consists of identifying and analyzing concerns and business contexts to produce ASRs. *Architectural synthesis* is an activity where solutions satisfying ASRs are found. Finally, *architectural evaluation* ensures that the architectural decisions are solid. This is done by evaluating candidate solutions from the synthesis phase against ASRs.

Aligning these activities with an agile software development process has raised a lot of concerns [1–3]—it has even been said that agile and architecture is a clash of two cultures [2]. Architecture has traditionally been perceived as a plan for how the system will be built. However, in agile methods, change should be embraced and there is no separate planning phase. Still, organizations have architects and they do architecture design, also in agile contexts. The authors have conducted an interview study in the industry to find out how organizations align architecture work and agile development (in this case, Scrum) [17]. The results revealed that there are four main software architecture practices that organizations use: big-up-front design, sprint-zero, in-sprints, and separate-architecture-team.

Big-up-front-design practice constitutes analysis, synthesis, and evaluation of the architecture before the system is implemented in the sprints. During the implementation phase, only small changes are made to the architecture design. In a sense, this is close to the waterfall approach; however, the implementation phase is carried out in sprints by the development team. The architecture is typically designed by dedicated architects and not by the development team itself. The original Scrum paper [14] actually states that the architecture design should be done up-front. Later descriptions of Scrum have omitted this up-front analysis and design (e.g., [40]).

In *sprint-zero* practice, the architecture design is carried out in the first sprint: sprint-zero. This sprint is from 2 to 4 weeks in length, whereas the big-up-front-design phase might last 6 months. Sprint-zero's difference from other sprints is that a potentially shippable product increment is not created in the sprint-zero. This sprint is dedicated to design and setting up the development environment. In other words, analysis and synthesis are done in sprint-zero. Sometimes, evaluation is also carried out within the sprint or right after it. The main differences from big-up-front-design approach are that the length of the design phase is radically shorter, and the design is carried out by the development team itself.

In-sprints practice builds the architecture within the sprints. The architecture work is carried out by the development team. Architecture is designed and refactored within the sprints whenever the need arises. This requires very a skillful development team with good domain knowledge. As stated in [17], without an experienced team with good domain knowledge, this approach is doomed to fail. In this approach, analysis is partially made by the product owner outside sprints and partially by the team within the sprints. Architectural synthesis takes place in the sprints. This approach does not offer a natural place for architectural evaluation, because the architecture is evolving all the time. Of course, at some point the architecture design stabilizes and the sprints focus on finishing the functionality of the system. At this point, it might be possible to carry out architectural evaluation—especially in a lightweight form. However, changes to the architecture at this stage of the development can already be expensive to make.

In *separate-architecture-team* approach, there is a separate team that designs the architecture. The members of this team might be from different development teams. Additionally, there might be an architect who acts as a part of this team. Typically, a separate-architecture-team gathers up whenever necessary and analyses the next release ASRs and designs the architecture (synthesis). The actual implementation of the system is then carried out by development teams. Architectural evaluation can be carried out when the architecture team releases a new version of the design.

8.5 ARCHITECTURAL INFORMATION FLOW IN INDUSTRY

In this section, we present the results of an interview survey concerning architecture knowledge flow in the industry. The first section briefly describes the interview setup. In Section 8.5.2, the main results of this survey are presented. Additional general remarks of interviewees are presented and discussed in Section 8.5.3. Finally, Section 8.5.4 describes the limitations of this survey.

8.5.1 Interview setup

To study the actual flow of architectural information in industry using Scrum, we interviewed three teams (represented by six persons) in two companies that are global manufacturers of large machines and automation systems exploiting Scrum in their projects. The goal was to find out what kind of architectural knowledge is produced, why and for whom it is produced, and at what stages of the project the information is produced and consumed. In this way, we expected that we could explore architectural information flow in a realistic industrial context and ensure that our proposal for lightweight AKM was consistent with the actual architectural information flow in the company. Although the number of teams interviewed was small, this study was expected to provide at least a rough picture of architectural information flow followed in real-life Scrum work.

The following is a breakdown of the interview questions:

- What is meant by software architecture in your company?
- How is software architecting carried out while using Scrum?

These questions revealed the architectural approach used by the teams, which were assumed to fall into one of the four types discussed in the previous section. The next question,

- What kind of architecture information is utilized in your company?

resulted in a list of artifacts (or types of architectural information), such as ASRs, designs, design patterns, component descriptions, and so on. For each of these artifacts mentioned by an interviewee, the following set of questions was presented:

- Who is the producer of this architectural information?
- In which stage of the project is this kind of architectural information produced?
- Why is this information produced?
- Who uses this information?
- In which stage of the project is this architectural information utilized?
- How does the producer communicate this information to the consumer?
- How often does this communication take place?

Interviewers utilized the architectural knowledge metamodel presented in [13] to make sure that interviewees did not forget some relevant type of architectural information. The interviewers did not mention any specific stakeholder groups, but just collected the stakeholders the interviewees brought up.

8.5.2 Results

The three interviewed teams each used a different approach to carry out architecture work: big-up-front-design, sprint-zero, and in-sprints approach. The separate-architecture-team approach was not used by these teams. The results are presented in Figures 8.2 and 8.3. The figures are structured according to the main three phases of Scrum: analysis phase, development phase, and review phase [14]. Figure 8.2 summarizes the architectural information flow in teams using big-up-front-design and sprint-zero approaches; these approaches coincide from the viewpoint of architectural information flow, viewing the first sprint in the sprint-zero approach as part of the analysis phase. Figure 8.3 shows the architectural information flow in the in-sprints approach in the same way. Arrows in the figures show what information a stakeholder produces (exiting arrow) and consumes (entering arrow) in a certain phase. Arrows to both directions mean that the architectural information is both produced and consumed by the participating stakeholders.

The figures exhibit fairly expected information flow. The differences in the information flow between big-up-front-design/sprint-zero and in-sprints are clearly visible: in the former, architectural decisions are produced in the analysis phase by several stakeholders and mostly consumed in sprints, while in the in-sprints approach only an initial architecture design is produced by the architect in the analysis phase,

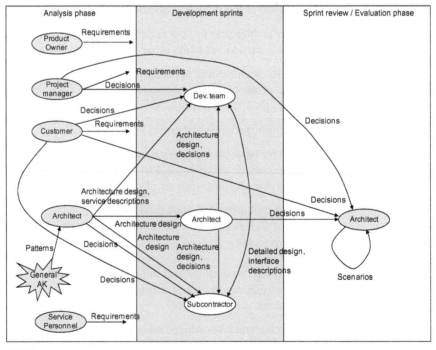

FIGURE 8.2

Architectural information flow in big-up-front-design and sprint-zero approaches.

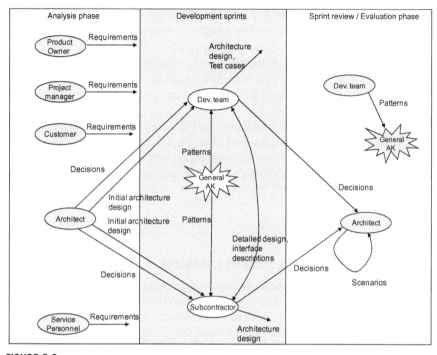

FIGURE 8.3

Architectural information flow in in-sprints approach.

and most of the architectural decisions and designs are produced during the sprints. A noteworthy observation is that ASRs are produced in the analysis phase, but not consumed explicitly in the development phase, as one could expect (the arrows going nowhere). An explanation could be that the ASRs are reflected in the architectural decisions and designs and consumed in this form during the development. Another possible explanation is that while using Scrum, the requirements are reflected in product backlog items (in user stories, in use cases, etc.), so no one is explicitly using requirements and the stakeholders have a feeling that they are using product backlog items rather than requirements.

Patterns were used by the architect in the analysis phase (big-up-front-design) and by the development team in the development phase (in-sprints). The interviewees also reported that they have their own in-house patterns, but they are rarely documented. Sometimes patterns were discussed during the review to find out which pattern really worked and which ones caused problems. So, the team was refining the general architectural knowledge in this phase. However, this information was not written down, either. In all approaches, architects mentioned that they use decisions and scenarios in the architecture evaluations and also exploit them in the sprint review phase. Decisions are typically discussed in the sprint review during the lessons-learned sessions. One observation was that architectural designs are not used in sprint reviews as such, but the discussion focuses on the decisions. Scenarios were produced and consumed by the architect in the architecture evaluation.

Even in big-up-front-design/sprint-zero approaches, interfaces were only specified in the development phase. In the interviews, an architect mentioned that it is not reasonable to specify interfaces up-front, but instead one should just describe what services the interface should provide, because the exact interface design will always change during the implementation.

In the in-sprints approach, architecture designs were produced by subcontractors and development teams but not consumed by any stakeholder. The explanation is that the products the interviewed teams were working on were not released yet. The architecture design was produced and documented for later use (i.e., for the maintenance phase of the product). However, normally this information would probably be used by the teams themselves.

8.5.3 General comments from interviewees

The interviewees confirmed the difficulty to align architecture and agile development. In Scrum, for instance, there is no explicit architect role and still many organizations do up-front design and have architects. This creates the need to communicate the design to the development team, which is hard. Architectural design cannot be completely communicated using traditional architecture documents because it is, in many cases, lacking *why* something is designed as it is. For example, the implementation might be in line with the design and function properly when the system has order of 100 parameters. But when the number of used parameters grows significantly during the life cycle of the product, the same implementation does not scale anymore. So it is crucially important to provide the development team with a rationale for the design and explicitly mention the main concerns in the design. (E.g., in the aforementioned example, it is important to have efficient parameter handling, but it is even more important that the implementation is scalable and the efficiency is not lost when the amount of parameters increases.)

In general, if the design is carried out without simultaneous implementation, there is a high possibility that the design needs to be changed. New information emerges during the implementation, making the design invalid. Often a customer may also change his or her mind, and the current design cannot handle those changes.

In interviews, the architects also mentioned that there is a lot of architectural knowledge that should be communicated. In many cases, the development teams are experienced with the domain and with similar systems, so all the knowledge does not need to be communicated from the architect to the team. However, if there is a lot of subcontracting involved or the development teams change once in a while, the architectural knowledge needs to be communicated. In this process, architectural documentation can help but not completely replace face-to-face communication. Furthermore, if the development team is implementing just one component of a large system, they may lose touch with the architectural context and may not be able to take into account all information that concerns the component.

The interviewees reported that the communication of architectural information is most prevalent in the beginning of the sprints (e.g., in-sprint planning sessions). The interviewed teams had used architecture evaluation methods like ATAM to evaluate the architecture. The experience was that evaluations are beneficial when the project size is large. If the project is small, the workload caused by the evaluation was considered to be too heavy.

8.5.4 Limitations

The number of interviewed teams and persons was small, limiting the reliability and generalizability of the results. On the other hand, an interview allowed for clarification of the work practices and more detailed answers than, for example, a questionnaire-based study would allow. Further, one of the architectural practices in Scrum, separate-architecture-team, was not addressed at all in the interview. Still, since the interviewed teams already had years of experience in using Scrum for software development projects, we believe that the results give a representative snapshot of the architectural information flow in industry, to be used as a guideline for proposing lightweight AKM practices.

8.6 AKM IN SCRUM

In this section we present a model to produce and consume architectural information in Scrum, exploiting the existing techniques for software architecture evaluation (ATAM, DCAR), architectural information repositories, and architectural document generation, as reviewed in Section 8.3. We discuss the architectural practices presented in Section 8.4 separately; however, we discuss separate-architecture-team case only briefly as we don't have empirical data about the architectural information flow in that case. We also merge big-up-front-design and sprint-zero approaches, since they are similar from the AKM viewpoint. We make use of the types of architectural information identified in the study of Section 8.5, showing the Scrum phases when a particular type of information can be fed to the AIR and when a particular information package should be generated from the AIR to support the stakeholders.

8.6.1 Big-up-front-architecture and sprint-zero architecting approaches

In the big-up-front-architecture approach, most of the architectural decisions are made and a comprehensive architecture design is produced in the analysis phase (or, in the case of sprint-zero, in the first sprint), before the development sprints. Still, it is realistic to assume that during the development sprints, architecture has to be modified, and some new decisions are made by the Scrum team or by the architect. The AKM process for the big-up-front-architecture (and sprint-zero) case is depicted in Figure 8.4. For the sprint-zero case, the only essential difference is that the analysis

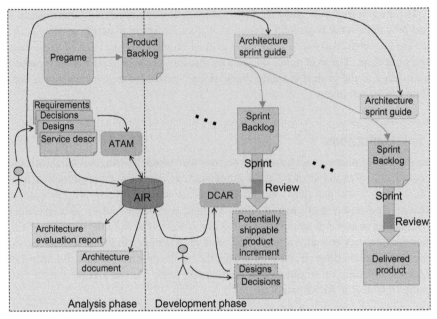

FIGURE 8.4

AKM for big-up-front-architecture (sprint-zero) case.

phase extends to the first sprint, so that most of the architectural designs and decisions are produced in that sprint.

Since a major concern in the big-up-front-architecture and sprint-zero approaches is to ensuring that the architecture satisfies all the essential quality requirements coming from different viewpoints, a natural evaluation method for this case is a scenario-based one (e.g., ATAM [20], possibly in a lightened form). With a suitable scribe tool (e.g., [13]), the information emerging in ATAM can be immediately stored in the AIR without additional effort. Since ATAM is based on the idea of discussing the most relevant architectural aspects of the system from the viewpoint of various stakeholders, it is reasonable to assume that the architectural information emerging in ATAM actually captures the most useful portion of architectural knowledge. On the other hand, an example of an information type not appearing in ATAM is service descriptions, reported in the interview in Section 8.5. Service descriptions have to be manually inserted into the AIR.

For evaluating the decisions made during the development sprints, ATAM or similar evaluation methods would be inappropriate. Instead, DCAR can be used for lightweight evaluation of the individual decisions possibly made during a sprint—for example, in the context of the retrospective. A suitable DCAR bookkeeping tool, built on top of AIR, allows for the completion of the AIR contents with the new architectural information emerging in DCAR. DCAR does not directly support the documentation of design, and introducing heavy design tools would not be appropriate in Scrum. However, lightweight practices for capturing design information during team meetings (e.g., taking photos of whiteboard drawings) and attaching this information to the decisions in DCAR would make it possible to add this information to the AIR without notable extra effort.

As discussed in [13], it is possible to exploit the AIR to generate a (possibly on-line) software architecture document, showing the current architectural design to the stakeholders in a conventional form. This will presumably be used in the composition of the product backlog, and also used as a guideline throughout the project, always reflecting up-to-date architectural information. In addition, the information related to the ATAM evaluation can be extracted from AIR and shown in the form of an evaluation report, possibly affecting some of the decisions.

The usage of the AIR enables the generation of focused architecture guides to be consumed during a sprint, collecting architectural information that is supposed to be relevant for the backlog items under work in the sprint. Assuming that backlog items (or requirements) are linked to decisions and designs, the required architectural information ("architecture sprint guide") can be filtered and compiled automatically from AIR, in the style of the customized documents in [13].

8.6.2 In-sprints architecting approach

If the architecture work follows the in-sprints architecting practice, architectural decisions are made primarily during the development sprints as part of the elaboration of the sprint backlog items. In this case there will presumably be more architecture-related sprints in the beginning of the project. Regardless of the character of the sprint, all architectural decisions made during a sprint can be evaluated with DCAR in the retrospective phase of the sprint. If a DCAR scribe tool has been built on top of the AIR, the decisions can be again recorded in the AIR as a side effect of DCAR, possibly augmented with design drawing photos from whiteboards. An evaluation report ("Sprint architecture evaluation report") can be generated from the AIR, to be reviewed in the sprint review meetings and possibly affecting the product backlog and the next sprint backlog. At any time, the contents of the AIR can be used to generate a comprehensive architecture document (e.g., to be used in communication with customers or off-shore teams). The AKM flow in the in-sprints architecting case is depicted in Figure 8.5.

As observed in the interview in Section 8.5, some initial design and basic architectural decisions can be produced already in the analysis phase. A natural way to both validate these decisions and store them to the AIR would be again to use DCAR, in principle in the same way as during the sprints. Note that ASRs are associated with decisions as forces in DCAR, and will be stored in the AIR along with the decisions.

8.6.3 Separated-architecture-team architecting approach

In the case of a separated-architecture-team, architectural decisions are made outside of the Scrum loop by an architecture team consisting of members of the Scrum teams or external architects (or both). In this approach, the AIR can serve as an architectural communication interface between the architecture team and the Scrum team.

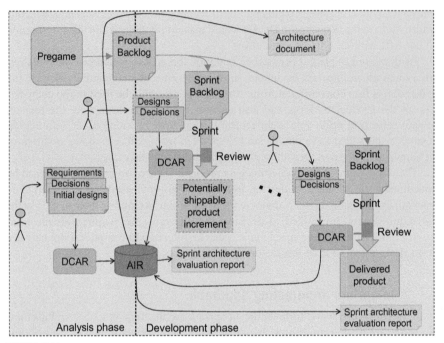

FIGURE 8.5

AKM for in-sprints architecting case.

Architectural decisions are recorded by the architecture team, and these decisions can be evaluated by DCAR in suitable intervals, generating evaluation reports that may affect product backlog and sprint backlog. The evaluation may also lead to reconsideration of some of the decisions.

In the separated-architecture-team case, a major issue is the communication between the architecture team and the Scrum team. For each sprint, the Scrum team should get the architectural information relevant for the sprint in a condensed form. Similarly to the big-up-front-architecture case, this can be accomplished by generating a customized sprint architecture guide containing the information in the AIR related to the backlog items under work in the sprint.

8.7 RELATED WORK

Even though the clash between agile software development and software architecture (e.g., [1–3]) has been recognized by multiple authors, there is surprisingly little written about aligning the software architecture process with agile development processes, and practically nothing about adjusting AKM for agile software development, to the best of our knowledge. For example, in a recently edited book on AKM [4], the agile viewpoint is completely missing. There are few proposals from agilists on how to scale up Scrum and agility, e.g., [41]. However, typically these proposals focus only on big-up-front-design architecture, neglecting other types of practices.

Babar [42] describes the software architecture process as a set of activities producing the architecture: architecture analysis, synthesis, evaluation, implementation, and architectural maintenance. Basically, the same set of activities is presented by Tang et al. [32]. Although this model applies as such for agile architecting as well, the faster cycles of the development essentially change the nature of architecture work. If the big-up-front-design approach is used, architecture design can be much like in traditional waterfall development [43]. However, if architecture design is carried out in sprints, ASRs need to be analyzed, design has to be finished and documented, and the architecture needs to be evaluated within a sprint. Using traditional tools and techniques, this might be next to impossible to carry out.

Two strategies of how organizations can manage their (architectural) knowledge have been identified: codification and personalization [7,44]. In addition, a third approach combining these two has been proposed [45]. In the codification strategy, as much information as possible is made explicit, for example, by writing it down to the documents. In the personalization strategy, the majority of the information is tacit knowledge in persons' minds. There might also be some advice concerning who is the right person to ask from, when the need for the knowledge emerges.

Although agile approaches in many cases overlook the importance of documentation, we believe that the key to successful AKM while using Scrum is to find the sweet spot between codification and personalization. Agile approaches tend to favor personalization, but in large projects it might not work. Especially if the development is distributed or there are subcontractors involved, the software process becomes highly knowledge-intensive [45] and requires efficient means of communication. Codification is too laborious and time-consuming in many cases, especially without proper tools.

We suggested exploiting an existing technique to generate targeted information packages to satisfy the information needs of agile stakeholders [13]. Somewhat similar ontology-based documentation approach has been proposed by de Graaf et al. [10].

General requirements for AKM infrastructure have been proposed by Liang et al. [46] in the form of a covering set of possible use cases for AKM tools, many of them applying to agile contexts as well. Furthermore, Farenhorst et al. [34] present seven desired properties of architectural knowledge-sharing tools. Some of these properties are particularly important in agile contexts, like easy manipulation of content and sticky in nature.

8.8 CONCLUSIONS

We have demonstrated that by exploiting state-of-the-art techniques related to software architecture evaluation and automated document generation, Scrum can be augmented with lightweight AKM with reasonable cost. The most significant additional activity is architectural evaluation. When architecture evaluation is required in sprints, a decision-based, lightweight evaluation technique can be used. If a simple bookkeeping tool is used to assist the evaluation, the architectural information can be stored in a repository with virtually no extra effort.

The proposed AKM approach, despite of its lightweightness, may not be suitable for all projects. For small projects it might still be too laborious, and the benefits of the approach do not necessarily outweigh the amount of work that has to be put into codifying the architecture knowledge, unless there is a definite need for covering technical documentation. However, for large and mid-sized projects in which the information sharing needs exceed the limits of personal communication, a systematic AKM approach aligned with Scrum is justified, even though there are no explicit requirements to produce technical documentation.

Research on AKM has produced a lot of advanced tools for codifying and presenting architectural knowledge. However, in our view, many of these approaches have been developed with the mindset that the software development process is expected to be adjusted for these tools, rather than the other way around. We are afraid that this may be a critical hindrance to the adoption of AKM in the industry in large scale. To be successful, an AKM approach should be possible to be introduced in a project with close to zero cost, and with clearly visible and significant benefits.

To make things more explicit, we postulate the essence of lightweight AKM for agile software development as the following manifesto.

1. *The producing and consuming of architectural information in AKM should not require extra effort.* There should be no activities that are related only to AKM itself during the software system life cycle.
2. *AKM should be invisible from the viewpoint of information producers and consumers.* The producers and consumers should not need to be aware of AKM. AKM should be seamlessly integrated with usual knowledge-sharing activities like documentation, reviews, and project meetings.
3. *Only potentially useful architectural information should be stored in AKM.* All stored information is expected to be used in the context of a probable development or evolution scenario. The burden of useless information surpasses the possible benefit of coincidental usage.

In this chapter, we have taken steps in the direction of the above principles, although many open questions still remain. In particular, although the proposed integrated collection of lightweight AKM practices are founded on findings in industrial studies, the actual application of the combination of AKM practices in Scrum calls for extensive empirical research that falls beyond the scope of this chapter.

Acknowledgments

The authors would like to thank the industrial participants of Sulava project: Metso Automation, Sandvik Mining and Construction, Cybercom, Wapice, Vincit, and John Deere Forestry. This work has been funded by the Finnish Funding Agency for Technology and Innovation (TEKES), under project Sulava.

References

[1] Abrahamsson P, Ali Babar M, Kruchten P. Agility and architecture: can they coexist? IEEE Softw 2010;27(2):16–22.

[2] Kruchten P. Software architecture and agile software development: a clash of two cultures? In: Proceedings of the 32rd international conference on software engineering (ICSE). IEEE CS; 2010. p. 497–8.

[3] Nord RL, Tomayko JE. Software architecture-centric methods and agile development. IEEE Softw 2006;23(2):47–53.

[4] Ali Babar M, Dingsøyr T, Lago P, van Vliet H, editors. Software architecture knowledge management—theory and practice. Berlin: Springer; 2009.

[5] Avgeriou P, Lago P, Kruchten P. Towards using architectural knowledge. ACM SIG-SOFT Software Eng Notes 2009;34(2):27–30.

[6] Agile alliance: manifesto for agile software development. Available at: http://agilemanifesto.org [retrieved 10.01.2012].

[7] Ali Babar M, de Boer RC, Dingsøyr T, Farenhorst R. Architectural knowledge management strategies: approaches in research and industry. In: 2nd workshop on sharing and reusing architectural knowledge—architecture, rationale, and design intent (SHARK/ADI '07). Minneapolis, USA: ACM; 2007.

[8] Weyns D, Michalik B. Codifying architecture knowledge to support online evolution of software product lines. In: Proceedings of the 6th international workshop on sharing and reusing architectural knowledge (SHARK '11). New York, NY: ACM; 2011. p. 37–44.

[9] Farenhorst R, Boer RC. Knowledge management in software architecture: state of the art. In: Ali Babar M, Dingsøyr T, Lago P, van Vliet H, editors. Software architecture knowledge management—theory and practice. Berlin: Springer; 2009. p. 21–38.

[10] de Graaf KA, Tang A, Liang P, van Vliet H. Ontology-based software architecture documentation. In: Proceedings of joint working conference on software architecture & European conference on software architecture (WICSA/ECSA). Helsinki: IEEE CS; 2012. p. 191–5.

[11] Jansen A, Avgeriou P, Ven J. Enriching software architecture documentation. J Syst Softw 2009;82(8):1232–48.

[12] Vliet H, Avgeriou P, Boer RC, Clerc V, Farenhorst R, Jansen A, et al. The GRIFFIN project: lessons learned. In: Ali Babar M, Dingsøyr T, Lago P, van Vliet H, editors. Software architecture knowledge management—theory and practice. Berlin: Springer; 2009. p. 137–54.

[13] Eloranta V-P, Hylli O, Vepsäläinen T, Koskimies K. TopDocs: using software architecture knowledge base for generating topical documents. In: Proceedings of the joint working conference on software architecture and European conference on software architecture (WICSA/ECSA). Helsinki: IEEE CS; 2012. p. 191–5.

[14] Schwaber K. Scrum development process. In: Proceedings of the 10th annual ACM conference on object oriented programming systems, languages and applications (OOPSLA); 1995. p. 117–34.

[15] Version one: 6th annual state of agile survey. Available at: http://www.versionone.com/pdf/2011_State_of_Agile_Development_Survey_Results.pdf; 2011 [retrieved 29.08.2012].

[16] Poppendieck M, Poppendieck T. Lean software development: an agile toolkit. Boston: Addison-Wesley Professional; 2003.

[17] Eloranta V-P, Koskimies K. Software architecture practices in agile enterprises. In: Mistrik I, Tang A, Bahsoon R, Stafford JA, editors. Aligning enterprise, system, and software architectures. Hershey, PA: IGI Global; 2012. p. 230–49.

[18] Coplien J, Bjørnvig G. Lean architecture for agile software development. Chichester: Wiley; 2010.

[19] Cockburn A. Agile software development: the cooperative game. 2nd ed. Reading, MA: Addison-Wesley; 2007.

[20] Kazman R, Klein M, Clements P. ATAM: method for architecture evaluation. Report, Software Engineering Institute, Carnegie Mellon University. Available at: http://www.sei.cmu.edu/publications/documents/00.reports/00tr004.html; 2000.

[21] van Heesch U, Eloranta V-P, Avgeriou P, Koskimies K, Harrison N. DCAR—decision-centric architecture reviews. IEEE Soft 2013; to appear.

[22] Kazman R, Bass L, Webb M, Abowd G. SAAM: a method for analyzing the properties of software architectures. In: Proceedings of the 16th international conference on software engineering (ICSE). IEEE CS; 1994. p. 81–90.

[23] Harrison N, Avgeriou P. Pattern-based architecture reviews. IEEE Softw 2010;99:1.

[24] Kazman R, Asundi J, Klein M. Quantifying the costs and benefits of architectural decisions. In: Proceedings of the 23rd international conference on software engineering (ICSE). IEEE CS; 2001. p. 297–306.

[25] van Heesch U, Avgeriou P. Mature architecting - A survey about the reasoning process of professional architects. In: Proceedings of the working IEEE/IFIP conference on software architecture (WICSA). IEEE CS; 2011. p. 260–9.

[26] Maranzano J, Rozsypal S, Zimmerman G, Warnken G, Wirth P, Weiss D. Architecture reviews: practice and experience. IEEE Softw 2005;22(2):34–43.

[27] Woods E. Industrial architectural assessment using TARA. In: Proceedings of the 9th working IEEE/IFIP conference on software architecture (WICSA). IEEE CS; 2011. p. 56–65.

[28] Clements P, Kazman R, Klein M. Evaluating software architectures. Boston, MA: Addison-Wesley; 2002.

[29] Bass L, Klein M, Moreno G. Applicability of general scenarios to the architecture tradeoff analysis method software engineering institute. Carnegie Mellon University, Pittsburgh, Pennsylvania, CMU/SEI-2001-TR-014. Available at: http://www.sei.cmu.edu/library/abstracts/reports/01tr014.cfm.

[30] Eloranta V-P, Koskimies K. Using domain knowledge to boost software architecture evaluation. In: Proceedings of European conference on software architecture (ECSA'10). Heidelberg: Springer; 2010. p. 319–26.

[31] van Heesch U, Avgeriou P, Hilliard R. Forces on architecture decisions—a viewpoint. In: Proceedings of joint working IEEE/IFIP conference on software architecture and European conference on software architecture (WICSA/ECSA). Helsinki: IEEE CS; 2012. p. 101–10.

[32] Tang A, Avgeriou P, Jansen A, Capilla R, Ali Babar M. A comparative study of architecture knowledge management tools. J Syst Softw 2010;83(3):352–70.

[33] Polarion software: application lifecycle management, requirements & quality assurance software solutions. Available at: http://www.polarion.com [retrieved 28.08.2012].

[34] Farenhorst R, Lago P, van Vliet H. Effective tool support for architectural knowledge sharing. In: Oquendo F, editor. LNCS. Software architecture, vol. 4758. . Berlin: Springer; 2007. p. 123–38.

[35] ISO/IEC WD4 42010, IEEE P42010/D9 Standard draft. Available at: http://www.iso-architecture.org/ieee-1471/docs/ISO-IEC-IEEE-latestdraft-42010.pdf; 2011 [retrieved 12.12.2012].

[36] Schwaber K, Beedle M. Agile software development with scrum. Upper Saddle River, NJ: Prentice-Hall; 2001.

[37] Jansen A, Bosch J. Software architecture as a set of architectural design decisions. In: Proceedings of working IEEE/IFIP conference on software architecture (WICSA). Los Alamitos, CA: IEEE CS; 2005. p. 109–20.

[38] Ven J, Jansen A, Nijhuis J, Bosch J. Design decisions: the bridge between rationale and architecture. In: Dutoit AH, McCall R, Mistrík I, Paech B, editors. Rationale management in software engineering. Berlin: Springer; 2006. p. 329–48.

[39] Hofmeister C, Kruchten P, Nord R, Obbink H, Ran A, America P. A general model of software architecture design derived from five industrial approaches. J Syst Softw 2007;80(1):106–26.

[40] Sutherland J, Schwaber K. The Scrum guide—the definitive guide to Scrum: the rules of the game. Available at: http://www.scrum.org/storage/scrumguides/Scrum_Guide.pdf; 2011 [retrieved 7.06.2012].

[41] Leffingwell D. Scaling software agility: best practices for large enterprises. Upper Saddle River, NJ: Addison-Wesley Professional; 2007.

[42] Ali Babar M. Supporting the software architecture process with knowledge management. In: Ali Babar M, Dingsøyr T, Lago P, van Vliet H, editors. Software architecture knowledge management—theory and practice. Heidelberg: Springer; 2009. p. 69–86.

[43] Royce W. Managing the development of large software systems. Proc of IEEE WESCON 1970;26:1–9.

[44] Hansen MT, Nohria N, Tierney T. What is your strategy for managing knowledge? Harv Bus Rev 1999;77(2):106–16.

[45] Desouza K, Awazu Y, Baloh P. Managing knowledge in global software development efforts: issues and practices. IEEE Softw 2006;23(5):30–7.

[46] Liang P, Avgeriou P. Tools and technologies for architecture knowledge management. In: Ali Babar M, Dingsøyr T, Lago P, van Vliet H, editors. Software architecture knowledge management—theory and practice. Berlin: Springer; 2009. p. 91–111.

[47] Dobrica L, Niemelä E. A survey on software architecture analysis methods. IEEE Trans Softw Eng 2002;28(7):638–53.

Bridging User Stories and Software Architecture: A Tailored Scrum for Agile Architecting

Jennifer Pérez, Jessica Díaz, Juan Garbajosa, and Agustín Yagüe
Universidad Politécnica de Madrid (Technical U. of Madrid), Madrid, Spain

CHAPTER CONTENTS

9.1 INTRODUCTION

The role of software architecture in agile software development (ASD) has been extensively discussed over the past few years [1,2]. The tension between architecture and agility is a controversial issue, with many advocates for and opponents against giving architecture the importance in ASD that it has in other development approaches.

Among others, the Agile Manifesto [3] establishes the following principles: "Working software is the primary measure of progress," and, "Deliver working software frequently, from a couple of weeks to a couple of months, with a preference to the shorter timescale." These two agile principles imply that the time it takes developers to construct a working product should be limited and it should be mainly invested in coding to satisfy the delivery deadline. Therefore, agile practitioners often consider the upfront design and definition of software architecture an invest-ment in time and effort that may not pay off. In fact, hard opponents perceive effort devoted to architecture as wasted effort, "equating it with big design up-front (BDUF)—a bad thing—leading to massive documentation and implementation of YAGNI (you ain't gonna need it) features" [1]. In fact, the literature is full of refer-ences that advocate against architecture in ASD, because customers rarely appreciate the value that architecture delivers. A common belief is that if you are sufficiently agile, you do not need architecture; you can always refactor it on the fly. Hence, agile projects pay as much attention as possible to user needs and requirements at hand, which are often represented as *user stories* [4,5]. Agile project planning is based on prioritized product backlogs and sprint backlogs composed of user stories and does not take software architecture into account.

Dyba and Dingsoyr [6] illustrated that the lack of focus on architecture is bound to engender suboptimal design decisions; Bowers et al. [7] argued that inaccurate architectural design leads to the failure of large software systems, and a significant amount of refactoring might create significant defects. Therefore, it is possible to conclude that "refactoring on the fly" is not sufficient to meet the agile principle "Continuous attention to technical excellence and good design enhances agility" [3], and software architecture is necessary.

These arguments, along with the fact that software architecture enables commu-nication and accountability for design decisions [8], stress the pivotal role of soft-ware architecture in the development process. In fact, it is even more crucial when agile methodologies are applied to the development of large and complex software systems [9]. The work of Cockburn [10] revealed that agile methods may be infeasible in large projects and life-critical systems, and Babar and Abrahamsson [2] stated that software architecture may also be essential to scale up ASD in large software-intensive systems—especially to achieve quality goals [1]. Therefore, agile scalability has become the key point that has forced the agile community to consider the need to architect in an agile way. As a consequence, the agile community is making an effort to adopt agile methodologies for large-scale software development projects. Agile practitioners realize that the iteration planning works for small projects, whereas multiple teams on large projects usually lose sight of the entire system and the real implications of their decisions in planning each iter-ation [11]. Therefore, when ASD is applied to large-scale products, many authors propose an analysis of the product vision and product requirements at a higher abstraction level than user stories [4,11–13], and the construction of the product soft-ware architecture [4,12,13], because it is risky to assume that a large architecture will naturally emerge as a result of continuous refactoring [4]. In addition, Cockburn [10] stated that it should be assumed that architectural practices can be valuable to cus-tomers, and Kruchten [14] concluded that despite the fact that software architecture means cost, it also means value for Agile. Finally, large-scale ASD also requires trac-ing how the analysis of requirements is related to the software architecture to not to lose sight of the entire system. As Leffingwell [4] set out, it is critical to understand the effect of new agile requirements on architecture.

Therefore, the obstacles that hinder agile practitioners from designing software products using software architecture must be avoided, and mechanisms for designing software architecture in Agile without renouncing its values and principles should be defined. Bosch [15] mentioned the need to increase the speed in designing software architecture to approximate agile methodologies, stating, "The way software is developed has changed as well, especially focusing on short development cycles and frequent, or even continuous, deployment." To do that, these design mechanisms should also be integrated into the agile process and should provide value for guiding the design decision process in each agile iteration. One of the most extended agile methodologies to support the agile process is Scrum [16].

In this chapter, a tailored Scrum for agile architecting in large-scale development projects is described. This tailored Scrum for agile architecting is based on a set of mechanisms that smoothly bridge user stories and software architecture through the features product vision. These mechanisms consist of: (1) highly flexible architecture that allows agile practitioners to design their corresponding working architecture [17,18] together with working products, (2) feature pools and feature trees to identify the working product features that the working architecture must cope with, (3) traceability mechanisms for bridging user stories and software architecture through features and design, and (4) change impact analysis (CIA) [19] of each feature on the working architecture to assist agile practitioners in the prioritization of features and their user stories, as well as in the effort estimation of user stories. All of these mechanisms are described in detail in this chapter, followed by a description of how they should be applied to this tailored Scrum for agile architecting and how they should be smoothly integrated.

Finally, the usage of the tailored Scrum for agile architecting is demonstrated in this chapter. Details are given of our experience on putting its mechanisms into practice in a case study that has been deployed in a software factory set up in collaboration between the Technical University of Madrid (UPM) and the company Indra [20].

9.2 AGILE ARCHITECTING

Recently, there has been a growing recognition of the importance of paying more attention to effective architecture design in ASD [2]. Cockburn [10] claimed that the issue between architecture and Agile is not whether architecture should be used; rather, the issue is how much effort should be invested in architecture, assuming that the architecture can be valuable to the customer. In their survey of 72 IBM software developers, Falessi et al. [8] found that agile practitioners perceive software architecture as relevant.

Advocates of a balance between architecture and agility propose that the architecture emerges gradually, iteration after iteration, as a result of successive, small refactoring [9,21]. The initial insights on how to align software architecture and Agile are provided by Kruchten [14] and Booch [22], among others, who propose the iterative and incremental evolution of the architecture to reduce the big up-front design and keep the system in sync with changing conditions. Several approaches present successful cases of agile architecture [23] or iterative architecture [24] in specific domains, such as mobile and security-based applications, respectively. An iterative architecture is defined as "one that develops with the system, and includes only features that are necessary for the current iteration or delivery. The architecture is a working vision for developers, which encapsulates important features of the existing design" [24]. However, how this incremental architectural design should be performed and which general-purpose architectural mechanisms support it is, in fact, one of the main challenges already identified by Abrahamsson et al. [1].

The work of Falessi et al. [8] presents the most relevant qualities of software architecture for agile practitioners, including (1) communication and understanding of software systems, (2) the rationalization of previous design decisions, (3) the documentation of rationale, assumptions, constraints, and other dependencies, (4) the scaling of agile practices to large projects, (5) the documentation of flexibility, and (6) system planning and budgeting. To deal with this general-purpose agile architecting, and to leverage these qualities of software architecture in ASD, it is necessary to provide agile practitioners with mechanisms to incrementally design architecture (i.e., agile architecting). This incremental design implies that software architecture will be flexible and open to changes in such a way that they will be constructed by means of small increments in each agile iteration.

However, an incremental design is not enough to support agile architecting in large-scale projects. Agile architecting must be completely integrated with the rest of the agile process, and the trace of requirements and architecture should be supported in an agile way. Leffingwell [4] pointed out the relationship between a product's vision and its architecture, involving both in the *portfolio*. The portfolio consists of the main big blocks to connecting product requirements and architecture. There are three big blocks: (1) the definition of a product's vision through the portfolio vision in terms of large-scale initiatives that realize the product's value, (2) the *architectural runway*, which is "an architecture with the infrastructure to allow the incorporation of current and anticipated requirements without excessive refactoring" [13], and (3) the portfolio backlog, which is later refined as the well-known product backlog. Leffingwell proposed an agile process to make agile architecting feasible. However, the mechanisms for agile architecting, tracing the artifacts (e.g., features, releases, user stories, architecture), and suitably integrating them are not detailed.

9.3 CASE STUDY: METERING MANAGEMENT SYSTEM IN ELECTRICAL POWER NETWORKS

This chapter uses a case study to introduce and illustrate, step by step, how to apply the described tailored Scrum for agile architecting. The case study involves the development of a metering management system in electric power networks. It is part of a development project called OPTIMETER, in which various proofs of concept of large data storing technologies for a metering management system were developed.

OPTIMETER is part of a larger project called the intelligent monitoring of power networks (IMPONET) [25]. IMPONET focuses on supporting complex and advanced requirements in energy management, specifically electric power networks that are envisioned as Smart Grids [26].

Smart Grids are composed of an aggregation of a broad range of energy resources, from large generating systems (traditional sources like nuclear power plants and hydro power plants) to smaller generating systems (called microsources, like small solar farms and distributed wind generators), operating as a single system providing both power and heat [26,27]. They promote the integration of renewable energy resources and their distributed, open, and self-controlled nature. Therefore, IMPONET aims for the following: (1) continuous monitoring and bidirectional communication with customers to promote sustainability, and (2) facilities and operational systems to prevent congestions, faults, and peak loads in real time. The main result of IMPONET is a flexible and innovative platform that facilitates the continuous monitoring of the network with real-time data processing and automation capabilities, supporting a wide range of devices, protocols, and technologies. Hence, this platform includes features and services that will enable consumers to configure their consumption profile, to monitor its evolution, and to make decisions based on this information. One of the main parts of this platform is the metering management system, which efficiently captures and manages meter data from a large number of distributed energy resources.

The metering management system developed in the project OPTIMETER (see metering management system, Figure 9.1) has the main goal of providing metering management with real-time data processing. To select the data-storing technology, it is necessary to account for performance when loading the large amounts of energy data coming from the meter capturing processes, as well as performance when querying these data. The project has been divided into four releases; each one consists of one proof of concept to select the most suitable data storage technology. Specifically,

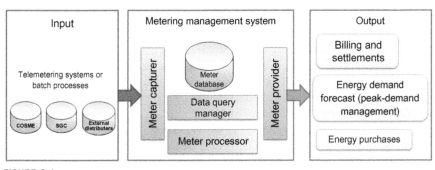

FIGURE 9.1

Metering management system.

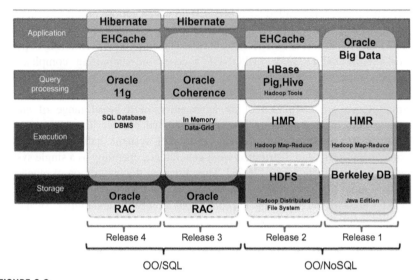

FIGURE 9.2

OPTIMETER releases.

the presented case study focuses on the first release, called OPTIMETER I—which was started with Oracle Big Data, the large object-oriented NoSQL data storing technology (see Release 1, Figure 9.2).

OPTIMETER I implements the following three processes of the metering management system—meter capturing, meter processing, and meter providing—using the Oracle Big Data Database Manager:

1. *Meter Capturing.* This involves integrating all meter capturing processes that are currently being supported by telemetering systems and batch processes that collect measurements at substations (see meter capturer, Figure 9.1). This entails reading metering data from different energy resources, periods of time (quarterly, hourly, daily, and monthly), and intervals. The obtained metering data are text files with a specific date that must be stored. This storage involves the data loading of historical metering data associated with 1 month and the storage of these metered data. Oracle Big Data uses Berkeley DB for storing data and Hadoop Map-Reduce for supporting the execution of queries, insertions, deletions, and updates throughout the database with high performance (see Release 1, Figure 9.2). Therefore, these text files are stored in the Berkeley DB.

2. *Meter Processing.* This consists of handling raw data to obtain optimal data by performing three operations: (1) the validation of meter data according to an established validation formula, (2) the calculation of the optimal vector for a measuring point for a type and period of energy data, and (3) the estimation of energy data according to an established estimation formula (see meter processor, Figure 9.1).

3. *Meter Providing.* This involves defining the interface with information client systems, such as billing and settlements, energy demand forecast, and energy purchases, to exchange data with them (see meter provider, Figure 9.1). It is a graphical user interface (GUI) that facilitates these data and interacts with the database in an intuitive way.

9.4 AGILE ARCHITECTING MECHANISMS

Agile architecting must be supported during the agile process through the systematic application of a set of concrete mechanisms. They should be part of the agile process, and their systematic application should help agile practitioners to see them as another agile technique, such as pregame, product backlog construction, estimation, or prioritization. This section describes those mechanisms that can help us to make agile architecting feasible and how they can be integrated into the entire agile process.

9.4.1 Feature pool and feature tree of user stories

Scaling Agile requires the product to be analyzed as a whole to ensure that it has long-term implications [11]. It is necessary to identify the needs of the customer at the highest level of expression in terms of functionality and delivered value [4]. When identifying and analyzing users' requirements, a big up-front design must be avoided. It should work similarly to what Leffingwell [4,13] or Smits [11] among others, proposed—a multilevel approach to planning activities that incorporates the current holistic view. The feature pool and feature tree are two levels of planning above user stories that this multilevel approach follows.

A feature is a product's characteristic—either a key value or a key differentiator of the product in regard to the rest of the market. As Leffingwell set out in [28], features are above requirements and bridge the gap between users' needs and the specific requirements that represent these needs.

A feature description consists of an identifier, a title, and a statement that describes the feature in terms of the desired product. For example, the feature *Meter Reading* of the OPTIMETER I case study is described in Figure 9.3a. In this project, the identifier is defined by the letter *F* and a unique number, so the identifier of the feature is *F1*, the title is *Meter Reading*, and the description is *Reading metering data from different energy resources, periods of time, and intervals.* Each project can use a different identification mechanism that will be convenient and suitable.

The characteristic of the product that a feature defines can be functional or nonfunctional. Most features are expressed in terms of functional requirements, because the customer easily appreciates functional needs. However, there are non-functional requirements, such as performance, reliability, security, and industry standards that are critical for the quality of the product [13] and its success in the market [11]. Therefore, it is important to work with customers to identify those nonfunctional needs that are relevant for them that they usually assume and do not verbalize.

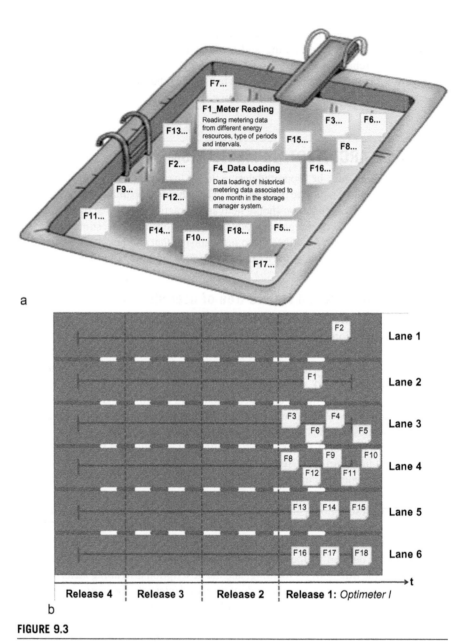

FIGURE 9.3

Feature pools: (a) Feature pool and (b) Feature olympic pool.

These needs are also features that are critical for the product and have to be described in the same way as the functional features. For example, the feature *F6_HighPerformanceDataAccessing* (see Figure 9.4) is a nonfunctional feature that is critical for OPTIMETER and, in the case of OPTIMETER I, deals with using the clustering technique.

Features are identified through brainstorming between the people involved in a product's development. The description is immediately created through a brief statement without considering any issues regarding timing, dependencies, or priorities among them. Features are entered into the feature pool as soon as their description is finished (see Figure 9.3a). The feature pool is a repository where the features of a product are stored, and the people involved in a particular project can access and view it at any moment. The feature pool constitutes the portfolio of the project at a high level of abstraction [4,11,13] and represents the product vision.

Once the pool has been constructed, it is time to analyze the possible relationships between the different features in the pool. Some features can be a refinement of others, and some can be dependent on others. Making these dependencies visible facilitates the definition of priority and the estimation of timing or complexity that the features' development may imply. These dependencies can easily be described graphically through a simple hierarchical tree-like structure as other approaches propose [29]. Figure 9.4 shows the feature tree of OPTIMETER.

A feature tree is constructed as a tree hooking the features to a *root feature*, which represents the product that is going to be developed. For example, in the case study, the root feature is called OPTIMETER (see Figure 9.4). The features can be hooked to each other through relationships to denote their dependency. For example, the feature *F3_MeterDataAccess* depends on the complete development of the features *F4_DataLoading*, *F5_DataQuerying*, and *F6_HighPerformanceDataAccessing*.

In addition to the feature pool or the feature tree, large-scale projects need to define the releases and the value that is going to be delivered in each release [11,30]. They constitute a project's roadmap, which is crucial in large-scale projects because it is required for the project's development. This roadmap must establish the releases, when they are going to be provided, and which value is going to be delivered in each one of them. Therefore, it is necessary to refine the features when planning a project. Hence, the pool of features is extended and structured following the analogy of an *Olympic pool*. The pool is horizontally divided into lanes, each representing a different priority level. The features are grouped into these lanes following the customer's priorities as a criterion. Those features with higher priority are launched in lane 1, and those with less priority are launched in lane 6 in the case of OPTIMETER I (see Figure 9.3b). The number of lanes varies depending on the identified levels of priority for the project. The feature tree may help with this prioritization. The visualization of dependencies among features, which the feature tree provides, helps to time and prioritize the features. It indicates that the features that depend on others must be previously developed. For example, the features *F9_EnergyDataValidating* and *F12_IntegratedProcessing* depend on the features *F10_RawData* and *F11_OptimalData* to be completely developed (see Figure 9.4). Releases

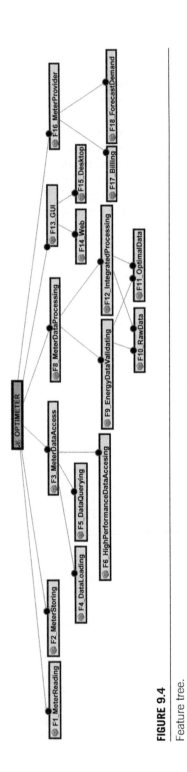

FIGURE 9.4

Feature tree.

are delimited by vertical dashed lines and identified by a name and the date when the release will be delivered. For example, in the case of OPTIMETER, OPTIMETER I and all of its features constituted the first release of OPTIMETER. Figure 9.3b illustrates only the features of OPTIMETER I, prioritized into lanes and grouped into its release. As a result, it can be concluded that the feature pool is a simple mechanism to identify features (what), whereas the feature Olympic pool is based on the feature pool to prioritize features and define releases (when). Finally, the feature tree is also based on the feature pool to identify feature dependencies (how).

This high-level description of features must be refined into user stories [4] to be included in the product backlog [4,16,31]. These user stories can be too big (known as "epics") at first if they are cross-grained, or they can be user stories by definition [5]. A user story is fine-grained when it is described following the INVEST model (Independent, Negotiable, Valuable, Estimable, Small, and Testable) and verifying the 5 Ws (Who, What, When, Where, and Why) [31], and any epic must be broken down into user stories when it is introduced into the sprint backlog for its implementation.

The feature Olympic pool and the original product backlog of Agile provide the basis for easily constructing a tailored product backlog based on releases and features, as Leffingwell indicated in [13] and later refined into user stories. This product backlog represents the fact that features are realized by user stories that agile teams use to implement the functionality of the first ones [4]. The product backlog of OPTIMETER I is illustrated in Figure 9.5 by showing the title of each user story, its estimation in story points, and the release and feature to which the user story belongs.

9.4.2 **Flexibility in software architecture design**

One of the four agile values is "Responding to change over following a plan" [3]. Changeability makes it possible to respond to change and is therefore critical for ASD. Changeability is defined as "the ability of a software system to, throughout its lifespan, accommodate to changes and enhancements in requirements and technologies that influence the system's architectural structure, with the least possible cost while maintaining the architectural integrity" [32]. Agile architecting can be feasible if software architecture design supports changeability. Changeability includes flexibility (i.e., the ability to deal with changes that can be either anticipated or planned), and adaptability (i.e., the ability to deal with changes that can neither be anticipated nor foreseen) [33]. This chapter focuses on flexibility, which is directly related to the variability definition at a given point of time [34]. Taking this into consideration, agile methodologies can take advantage of variability mechanisms to flexibly adapt software architecture and to incrementally develop it together with a working product [17]. Although variability has primarily been addressed in the domain of software product line engineering [34], variability is also a relevant characteristic of the architecture enabling *the last responsible moment for a decision*, the planned evolutionary software development, or quality attributes such as changeability [35]. In fact, several authors distinguish *product-line variability* from

Release	Sprint	Feature	User Story	Estimation (story points)
Optimeter I	Sprint 1 (18sp)	F2	US1. Installation of the database manager (BerkeleyDB)	8
			US2. Configuration of the database manager (BerkeleyDB)	5
			US3. Proof of concept	5
	Sprint 2 (21sp)	F1	US4. Reading textfiles of metering data	2
			US5. Processing the previously read data to form pairs of key/value	4
		F4	US6. Data loading of pairs key/value associated to quarterly data	3
			US7. Data loading of pairs key/value associated to hourly data	3
			US8. Data loading of pairs key/value associated to daily data	3
			US9. Data loading of pairs key/value associated to monthly data	3
		F5	US10. Data query of an energy resource	3
	Sprint 3 (21sp)	F6	US11. Hadoop installation and configuration	8
			US12. Hadoop clustering	3
			US13. Map/reduce of quarterly data	2
			US14. Map/reduce of hourly data	2
			US15. Map/reduce of daily data	2
			US16. Map/reduce of monthly data	2
			US17. Map/reduce of data from an energy resource	2
	Sprint 4 (20sp)	F9-F10	US18. Validating metering raw data	4
		F9-F11	US19. Validating metering optimal data	4
		F12-F10	US20. Calculating optimal vectors from raw data	6
		F12-F11	US21. Calculating optimal vectors from optimal data	6
	Sprint 5 (21sp)	F14	US22. Form to select an energy resource	2
			US23. Web graphical application to show meter data from an energy resource	15
			US24. Secure web application	4
	Sprint 6 (20sp)	F15	US25. Panel to select an energy resource	2
			US26. Graphical UI to show meter data from an energy resource	12
			US27. Authenticate user from LDAP	6
	Sprint 7	F17	US28. Data provider for billing	10
			US29. Interface billing systems	2
	Sprint 8	F18	US30. Data provider for forecast demand	14
			US31. Interface forecast systems	2
Optimeter II		Fa-Fz	......	... ...
Optimeter III		Fa-Fz	......	... ...
Optimeter IV		Fa-Fz	......	... ...

FIGURE 9.5

Feature-user story product backlog (Some of the user stories defined here are epics and were therefore decomposed. We use this abstraction level to focus on relevant details.).

software variability (i.e., mass customization versus "the ability of a software system or artifact to be efficiently extended, changed, customized, or configured for use in a particular context") [36]. Therefore, Agile can take advantage of variability to efficiently change software architecture in each iteration to fit requirement changes. Reinertsen [37] defined eight key themes that provide guidance for Lean; one of them states, "Understand and exploit variability," by promoting the addressing and exploitation of variability instead of avoiding it. As Leffingwell set out in [4], "it is easy to view XP, Scrum, and others as software instances of Lean." Therefore, XP, Scrum, and others also should exploit and address variability. Plastic partial components (PPCs) and working architecture mechanisms have been constructed based on variability support to make flexibility feasible during the agile development of software architecture. These two mechanisms are presented in the following subsections.

9.4.2.1 Plastic partial components

The notion of PPC [18] was defined not only to specify variability in software architecture configuration, but also to define variations inside components. PPCs can effectively support the internal variation of architectural components. A PPC is a specialization of a component and inherits all of its properties and behavior. PPCs' variability mechanisms are based on invasive software composition principles [38]. The variability of a PPC is specified using variability points, which hook fragments of code to the PPC known as variants, and weavings, which specify where and when extending the PPCs using the variants. Two examples of PPCs are the components *DataLoader* and *DataQuery* of the software architecture OPTIMETER (see Figure 9.6).

Variants implement specific features of a software product, and it is desirable that variants can be easily reused by different PPCs. The variant *hadoop/MAPREDUCE* implements the operations for clustering and distributing work around a cluster using Hadoop to improve data accessing performance (see Figure 9.6). To that end, variants are unaware of the linking context because of how the weavings between the PPC and the variants are defined. The weaving is defined in the variability point, not in the variant. The specification of a variability point must include the definition of the weavings between the PPC and the variants. Therefore, the PPCs *DataLoader* and *DataQuery* have a variability point called *clustering* that hooks these two PPCs with the variant *hadoop/MAPREDUCE* (see Figure 9.6).

PPCs' variability mechanisms are used in Agile to flexibly add, remove, and modify variants throughout the iterations of an Agile life cycle. Variability mechanisms behave as extensibility mechanisms to flexibly compose pieces (variants, components) of software as if software architects were building a puzzle. As a result, PPCs get closer and closer to meeting customers' needs by means of specifying variants only when they are strictly required by a working product. In this way, PPCs are presented as the mechanism that make *architectural runway* feasible (i.e., "the ability to implement new features without excessive refactoring") [13]. The two characteristics of PPCs, partial and plastic, enable them to meet agile principles and values:

- Partial: PPCs are partial because they can be incompletely specified. They can be working components delivered and refined in each iteration as part of the working product. Therefore, PPCs allow the incremental development of

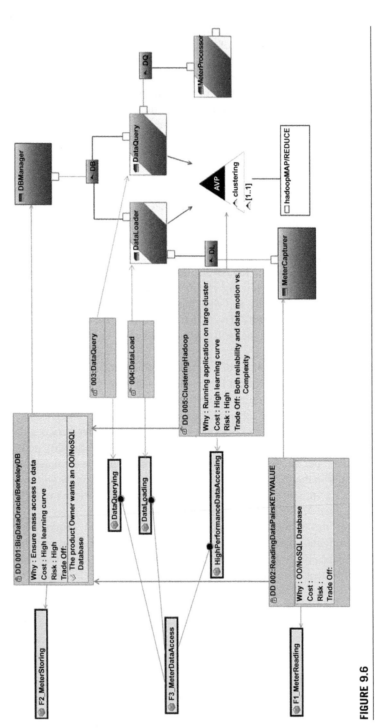

FIGURE 9.6

Working architecture of OPTIMETER-Sprint III.

architectural components by only taking the required functionality for each iteration into account and to construct them on time for the working product.

- Plastic: PPCs are plastic because they are highly malleable. This is a result of their extensibility mechanisms, which allow the flexible adaptation of software components by easily adding or removing fragments of code. As a consequence, they are ready to be extended or modified at any moment.

Therefore, the *DataLoader and DataQuery* components of the OPTIMETER software architecture are PPCs; they are incrementally developed, iteration after iteration, in a flexible way.

9.4.2.2 Working architecture

PPCs allow the iterative and incremental development of architectural design in each iteration, and by extension, the software architecture that they make up. This architecture is incrementally and iteratively designed in each iteration by adding/removing (1) variants to/from its PPCs and (2) components and connections to/from the architecture. From this proposal, a new concept in software architecture emerges, called *working architecture*.

Working architecture is iteratively and incrementally designed together with a working product. This idea was also proposed in [21,39] as *continuous architecting*, and in [4] as an *architectural runway*. Continuous architecting permits the tackling of architecture degradation and keeps the system in sync with changing conditions. All of the architecture's components are PPCs because they are incrementally developed on time for the working product. The PPCs of the architecture constitute the new concept of working architecture.

During the construction of a working architecture, a distinction is made between the findings in the first iteration and the others. This is because in the first iteration there is no previous architecture, whereas in the rest of the iterations, there is a working architecture resulting from previous iterations.

In each iteration, user stories are selected following the priority and effort estimation of the backlog. Selection can also be guided and supported by the working architecture obtained from the previous iteration—except for the case of the first iteration, in which there is no previous architecture. This architecture guidance is available because software architecture not only helps to determine the feasibility of the software systems' development, but it can also help to determine which requirements are reasonable and viable [40], and by extension, which user stories could be selected. Different selection criteria can be assisted by architecture knowledge, such as scalability, reusability, and the impact of changes. Therefore, the knowledge of a working architecture can enrich the agile process. Once the user stories have been selected for each iteration, their architecture design and implementation can be started by analyzing the user stories and features to identify the following:

1. PPCs/Components: Units of basic functionality, also known as major software components [41]. They are candidate components of a working product's software architecture. They make up the working architecture.

2. Variants: Features that are not relevant enough to be major software components, that constitute additional functionality for the final product, and that are susceptible to being removed over time. Thus, they are part of the functionality that a PPC provides.
3. Architectural Connections: Connections to coordinate PPCs that configure a working architecture.

As a result, a new version of the working architecture is obtained from each iteration. After completing the last iteration, the final software architecture is obtained as part of the final product.

9.4.3 Agile design decisions: CIA support

Continuous improvement is one of the two pillars of Lean, and also a key issue of XP, Scrum, and other agile methodologies [4]. One guide to achieving continuous improvement is to "make decisions slowly by consensus, thoroughly considering all options; implement decisions rapidly" [4]. Therefore, techniques to analyze different options and make the most suitable decision are required in Agile.

CIA [42] determines the potential effects that a proposed change can have on a system, possibly estimating the effort/cost to implement the change [43] and the potential risks involved [44]. This analysis can then be used to make better evolutionary decisions, such as whether or not a change should be carried out based on the economic viability of software evolution or other risks, such as software system degradation. CIA also allows trade-offs between a group of candidate/alternative solutions and can be used to select the most beneficial solution among them [45]. In fact, extensive work has been done on CIA to support software evolution [46,47], and Mens et al. [44] identified change impact as one of the future challenges (timeframe of 2015 and beyond). As a result, we defined a CIA technique to support agile architecting and to introduce changes in the architecture iteration by iteration, paying special attention to continuous improvement [19].

This CIA technique considers architectural knowledge to aid CIA. This architectural knowledge consists of the design decisions, the dependencies between these design decisions, and the rationale driving the architecture solution. Agile architects can take advantage of this technique to support the change decision-making process.

Four kinds of design decisions [48] have been defined to capture the knowledge of adding feature increments or changing features in each agile iteration. The CIA technique is based on these four kinds of design decisions:

- *Closed Design Decisions (Closed DDs)*: These DDs are completely closed (or bound) in a given iteration and support the realization of those features that can be completed in one iteration and that architects considered unchanging over time. The decision to use Oracle Big Data in OPTIMETER I and its Berkeley Database is an example of a closed DD, *DD001BigDataOracle/BerkeleyDB* (see Figure 9.6).

- *Open Design Decisions (Open DDs)*: These DDs are intentionally left open (or delayed) and support the realization of those features that cannot be completed in one iteration and that architects plan to complete iteration after iteration. Open DDs consist of a set of optional design decisions. The decision to use the clustering technique of Hadoop in OPTIMETER I is an example of an open DD, *DD005ClusteringHadoop* (see Figure 9.6).
- *Optional Design Decisions (Optional DDs)*: These DDs support each of the increments in each agile iteration of an open DD.
- *Alternative Design Decisions (Alternative DDs)*: These DDs support the alternatives of open and closed DDs.

These four types of DDs offer complete support for the documentation of knowledge derived from the agile architecting process. They store rationale, assumptions, constraints, and design items. For example, *DD001BigDataOracle/BerkeleyDB* stores its rationale: (1) why it was selected, (2) the risk involved in using this DD, and (3) the cost of its deployment (see *DD001*, Figure 9.6). DDs completely or partially realize features effecting multiple architectural components and connectors, and they often become intertwined with other DDs [49]. As a result, DDs are traceability links between the features they realize and the architectural components/connectors they effect. For example, *DD001BigDataOracle/BerkeleyDB* establishes a traceability link between the feature *F2_MeterStoring* and the component *DBManager* by means of two arrows that connect them (see *DD001*, Figure 9.6). In this way, the architectural knowledge is stored as DDs associated with the traceability links between features and architecture [19].

The CIA technique is based on this architectural knowledge representation to obtain the maximum amount of knowledge to incorporate changes iteration after iteration. It consists of a traceability-based algorithm and a rule-based inference engine, which traverse features, DDs, and architectural elements through the traceability links and a set of propagation rules. The process that this CIA technique [19] implements consists of two main steps described below:

1. Given a change in features (adding, deleting, or updating), the traceability-based algorithm determines (1) the first-order DDs that are involved with the feature to be changed, (2) the n-order DDs that depend on the first-order DDs, and (3) the first-order architectural elements (PPCs, components, and connectors) that are involved in each (first- and n-order) DD. The algorithm traverses the traceability links that bridge features and architectural elements, as well as the dependency relationships between design decisions.
2. Given a change in the working architecture that realizes the change in features, the rule-based inference engine fires propagation rules. The execution of these rules returns the change propagation in the working architecture. Namely, when a modification over the working architecture is applied, propagation rules are executed to simulate the effects on the rest of the working architecture. Thereby, the n-order architectural elements that are impacted by the change are obtained.

For example, OPTIMETER selected the feature *F6_HighPerformanceData-Accessing* (see Figure 9.4) for their implementation using clustering. The CIA algorithm retrieves the design decisions and components that could be impacted as a consequence of adding the new feature on the current working architecture delivered from the previous sprint (see Figure 9.6). The feature *F6_HighPerformanceData-Accessing* is a subfeature of feature *F3_MeterDataAccess* (see Figure 9.4), and F3 has the subfeatures *F4_DataLoading* and *F5_DataQuerying* (see Figure 9.4), which are implemented by the PPCs *DataQuery* and *DataLoader*, respectively (see the traceability links *003DataQuery* and *004DataLoad* that connect the two features with the two PPCs, Figure 9.6). As a result of applying the CIA algorithm, the PPCs *DataQuery* and *DataLoader* were retrieved as potential candidates to be impacted by the high-performance feature increment. The more updates the working architecture undergoes and the higher its complexity, the more vital CIA is for determining the impact of changes. In subsequent OPTIMETER releases, the CIA algorithm will propagate the database change and find the ripple-effects that may cause the dependences between design decisions *DD002* and *DD001*, and *DD005* and *DD001* (see Figure 9.6).

In addition, the CIA algoritm also supports design decisions when user stories are eliminated, updated, or added from/to the product backlog. Since the tailored Feature-User Story Product Backlog (see Figure 9.5) stores which feature realizes each user story, it is possible to determine which architectural elements could be impacted by changes in user stories through features.

9.5 A TAILORED SCRUM FOR AGILE ARCHITECTING

In this chapter, we describe a tailored Scrum development process in which agile architecting is considered a key activity in preparing the iteration (a.k.a. sprint). This tailored Scrum takes advantage of the mechanisms described in this chapter to systematically apply agile architecting to both small- and large-scale products.

Successful agile architecting requires the role of the architect in the agile team to be defined. Therefore, the agile team has a group of members that play the role of architects in this defined tailored Scrum for agile architecting (see Figure 9.7). This group of members is in charge of being aware of the architecture. They interact with the rest of the members of the agile team during the decision-making process by tracking architectural concerns and balancing them with business priorities. Thereby, architects can also improve communication (one of the agile values), and increase the knowledge shared between the members of the agile team. It is important to emphasize that those members of the agile team that play the role of architects can perform part-time architectural activities and part-time developing activities in the agile team.

The first step of this tailored Scrum for agile architecting entails capturing the product owner's requirements from the product vision (features) and packaging them into releases with an established date. The aim of this tailored Scrum *pregame phase*

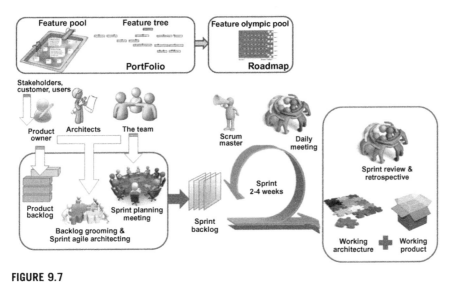

FIGURE 9.7

Agile architecting in Scrum.

is to define the portfolio and the roadmap of the project, which are fundamental for scaling agile [13]. The portfolio is obtained by defining the *feature pool* and the *feature tree*, which serve as the input to construct the roadmap through the *feature Olympic pool* (see Section 9.4.1) (see Figure 9.7).

The feature Olympic pool provides the basis for easily constructing a tailored product backlog based on releases and features and refined into user stories (see Section 9.4.1). The result is the *product backlog*, a list of user stories that describes the product features using scenarios written by customers, without techno-syntax, and includes the acceptance criteria that validate them. Then, user stories are prioritized and divided into *sprints*, which consist of 2-4-week periods of development time.

Each sprint has two preparation meetings—a *backlog grooming and sprint agile architecting meeting*, and a *sprint planning meeting*—in which the product owner and team plan what to do for the sprint (see Figure 9.7).

The traditional Scrum life cycle has been tailored in the past few years to include the backlog grooming sessions [4,16] due to the need to focus on what is coming up in the next sprint. Backlog grooming sessions give agile teams the opportunity to look further into the future of their product(s), alerting them to technical challenges. The purpose of these sessions is to make improvements in the product backlog through the following activities: breaking down epics, estimating backlog items, looking deeper into the backlog to do longer-range technical planning, and prioritizing the backlog [16]. Prioritization entails making decisions about the technologies, architecture, and design options to deliver requirements. These decisions may aim to (1) implement functionally complete features early, (2) implement the requirements exhibiting uncertainty or risk (fail as early as possible) early, or (3) delay decisions until the last responsible moment. Delaying decisions provides agile teams with more time to evaluate options and gather feedback from customers. In backlog grooming sessions, the role of software architecture is vital to understand a working product, to look further into the future, to engage in technical planning, and to prioritize the backlog items. It rationalizes the increments and changing features while trying to maintain the integrity of the architecture, taking into account the risks, dependencies, and tradeoffs with earlier architectural decisions. Grooming sessions are the perfect setting for analyzing *working architecture* (see Section 9.4.2.2) by using the presented CIA technique (see Section 9.4.3) to determine the impact of various decisions that can be made in the next sprints. The conclusions extracted from the analysis performed in the grooming session will be the pivotal criteria for the sprint planning meeting, where the features and user stories to be developed are selected to comprise the sprint backlog. The decision of which user stories are selected is also critical in the agile architecting performed in this backlog grooming and sprint agile architecting meeting. Agile architecting is addressed by identifying new components, PPCs, variants, and/or connections of the selected features/user stories, or updates of the existing working architecture.

The result of the sprint planning meeting is the *sprint backlog* (see Figure 9.7). The sprint backlog is the list of user stories and tasks that must be performed to achieve the sprint goal. During the sprint, *daily meetings* are conducted to track work progress in terms of the working product and its working architecture. At the end of each sprint, a *working product* is delivered together with its working architecture (see Figure 9.7). The construction of the architecture and its implementation take advantage of the flexibility of PPCs to easily adapt the working architecture, iteration after iteration (see Section 9.4.2.1). In the *sprint review meeting*, the product owner assesses the working product to either validate that user stories were met, or introduce changes into the user stories. A *retrospective meeting* is held to put continuous improvement into practice and to address what went well and what could be improved for the next sprint (see Figure 9.7).

9.6 AGILE ARCHITECTING IN PRACTICE

OPTIMETER has been developed in an i-smart software factory (iSSF) [20], which is deployed at the Technical University of Madrid (UPM[a]) and Indra Software Labs.[b] The iSSF is a software engineering research and education setting in close cooperation with the top industrial and research collaborators in Europe. The iSSF comprises laboratories in two different geographical locations in Madrid equipped with sophisticated computer and monitoring equipment.

---

[a]http://www.upm.es/internacional
[b]http://www.indracompany.com/en

The OPTIMETER I has been iteratively and incrementally developed in the iSSF in a tailored Scrum for agile architecting of eight sprints (one sprint $= 2$ weeks). In total, 10 people participated in the OPTIMETER I project: four developers, one product owner, one deputy product owner, one Scrum master (who performs the tasks of both the Scrum master and a part-time architect), one full-time architect, and two observers. The observers had access to all project information and collaborated directly with product owners and fellow team members to collect data and information for evaluating the results obtained from the application of the tailored Scrum for agile architecting.

Before starting the sprints, the project requirements were defined in terms of features using the feature pool and the feature tree (see Figures 9.3a and 9.4). From this analysis, 18 features were defined (see Figure 9.4) and prioritized in the feature Olympic pool (see Figure 9.3b). The product backlog was defined by breaking down the 18 features into 31 user stories (see Figure 9.5). At this point, the sprints started.

Sprint 1 focused on implementing feature *F2_MeterStoring*. The user stories planned for the sprint were US1, US2, and US3. The resulting working architecture was composed of the component *DBManager*, which implemented the configuration of the Berkeley DB; the component *Proof*, which implemented access to the database; and finally the design decision *DD001BigDataOracle/BerkeleyDB*, which contained the rationale for using Berkeley DB (see Section 9.4.3).

Sprint 2 focused on implementing feature *F1_MeterReading* and partially implementing *F3_MeterDataAccess*, specifically *F4_DataLoading* and *F5_DataQuering*. The user stories planned for this sprint were US2-US10. During the grooming session, the CIA was carried out by architects to analyze the impact of adding the new features or user stories to the working architecture of Sprint 1 (see Figure 9.8a). At this time, the working architecture was in too early a stage for the CIA algorithm to provide any impact that could be relevant for architects in the decision-making process of adding these features or user stories. Therefore, the resulting working architecture was designed following the guidelines presented in Section 9.4.2.2 (see Figure 9.8b). It was composed of the component *MeterCapturer*, which read the text files of metering data and processed the previously read data to form key/value pairs, and the PPCs *DataLoader* and *DataQuery*, which implement data loading and data querying, respectively. As the functionalities for data loading and data querying could not be fully implemented in this sprint, and increments in following sprints could refine these components, the architects decided to implement these functionalities using PPCs. Finally, the design decision *DD002* contained the rationale for reading metering data in key/value pairs. Finally, between *DD002* and *DD001*, there was a dependency relationship between the need to read data in key/value pairs and the use of the database manager BerkeleyDB.

Sprint 3 focused on completing feature *F3_MeterDataAccess*, specifically *F6_HighPerformanceDataAccessing*. The user stories planned for the sprint ranged from US11 to US17. The CIA retrieved the design decisions and components that could have been impacted as a consequence of adding these user stories in the working architecture of Sprint 2 (see Figure 9.8b). As explained in Section 1.4.3, the CIA

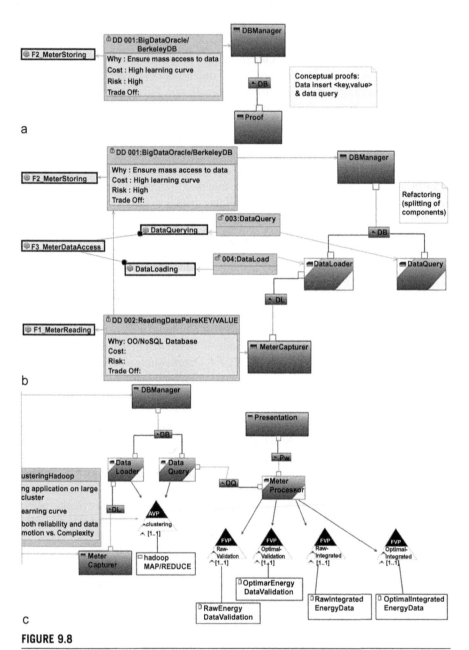

FIGURE 9.8

Working architecture of OPTIMETER in action: (a) Sprint 1, (b) Sprint 2, and (c) Sprints 4 and 5.

retrieved the PPCs *DataQuery* and *DataLoader* as the potential candidates to be impacted by the high-performance feature increment. Therefore, the resulting working architecture was refined by adding and modifying the following elements: First, the variant *HadoopMap/Reduce* implemented the operations for clustering and distributing work around a cluster to improve the data accessing performance (data loading and data querying). The PPCs *DataLoader* and *DataQuery* were extended with this functionality through the variability point *clustering* (see Figure 9.6). Design decision *DD005* maintained the rationale for clustering, as well as a dependency on the design decision *DD001* (see Figure 9.6).

Sprint 4 focused on implementing feature *F4_MeterDataProcess*. The user stories planned for the sprint were US18-US21. This feature had no prior dependencies on others, so the CIA algorithm did not retrieve any impact on the working architecture. In the working architecture of this sprint, the PPC *MeterProcessor* was created and extended by the algorithms to validate metering data and to calculate optimal vectors through the variability points *RawValidation, Optimal-Validation, RawIntegrated,* and *OptimalIntegrated*. These algorithms were implemented in the variants shown in Figure 9.8c, such as *RawEnergyDataValidation*.

Sprints 5-8 focused on implementing features *F13_GUI* and *F16_MeterProvider* and their user stories (see Figure 9.5). These features had no prior dependencies on others, so the CIA algorithm did not retrieve any impact on the working architecture and their components were added. For an example, see the component *Presentation* of Figure 9.8c representing *F13*.

The adoption of the new tailored Scrum for agile architecting for the OPTI-METER project was challenging because before starting, the agile team preferred to use conventional agile methods. Specifically, this initial refusal was due to the fact that its adoption implied learning new mechanisms and modifying the working methodology, which clearly highlight the need to invest time in training the team. The team was certain of the need to invest more time; in particular, the learning and usage of PPCs required extra effort. However, later, and particularly when the product became more complex, the team began to react positively. This shift happened once the architecting mechanisms and the architects helped the rest of the team to manage the project's complexity by prioritizing features and user stories, refactoring and restructuring the architecture, taking into account design decisions, rationale, constraints, and tradeoffs with other design decisions.

9.7 FINDINGS ABOUT AGILE ARCHITECTING

To scale ASD for the development of large and complex software in which several agile teams can be involved, software architecture is fundamental. However, it is critical to have an understanding of how architecting can be integrated into the agile process. Previous studies defined two important premises: (1) software architecture should be a value for agile projects' development, and (2) agile practitioners tend to avoid software architecture, because they conceive of architecture as a heavy and complicated task. From these two main premises and through our experience, we have defined a baseline to achieve a mutual understanding between software architecture and Agile, based on the following principles: (1) the design of the architecture should be adapted to the incremental and iterative life cycle; (2) software architecture must deliver value to the agile process; (3) the design of the architecture should be a guided task with the purpose of being lightweight and easy for agile practitioners, and (4) the design of the software architecture should be integrated with the rest of the agile processes and their results.

This baseline serves as the foundation for all of the mechanisms that have been presented in this chapter for agile architecting. The use of these mechanisms permits the smooth integration of software architecture and Agile. The mechanisms that constitute this *tailored Scrum for agile architecting* help to meet the agile values and perform some of the agile practices. In addition, they are aligned with the four agile values, namely [3]: (1) Individuals and interactions over processes and tools: The architecture team is part of the agile team and backlog grooming and sprint agile architecting meetings increase the interaction and the shared knowledge among team members; (2) Working software over comprehensive documentation: PPCs and their working architecture is software that is delivered in each working product; (3) Customer collaboration over contract negotiation: Feature pools, feature trees, and feature-user story product backlogs provide the vision of a product that customers desire without overloading the documentation of a project; and (4) Responding to change over following a plan: Changes are welcome for all mechanisms by adding, updating, or removing features, user stories, components, PPCs, variants, or design decisions guiding the change design decision using CIA.

Our experience of (1) constructing working architectures using PPCs in several products in the context of the i-smart software factory, (2) integrating working architectures with the Scrum process through user stories and features, and (3) exploiting this integration to store design decisions and to systematically support agile architecting decisions based on change impact, has been successful by dealing with most of the required needs in the software products that we have developed.

Acknowledgments

This work has been partially supported by: (1) The Spanish Ministry of Science and Innovation (MICINN) through the R&D+i projects INNOSEP (TIN2009-13849) and i-Smart Software Factory (IPT-430000-2010-038); (2) The Spanish Ministry of Industry (MITYC) through the R&D project IMPONET (ITEA2 09030—TSI-02400-2010-103); and (3) The Centre for Industrial Technological Development (CDTI) through R&D projects NEMO&CODED (ITEA2 08022 IDI-20110864) and Energos (CEN-20091048).

References

[1] Abrahamsson P, Babar M, Kruchten P. Agility and architecture: can they coexist? IEEE Softw 2010;27(2):16–22.

[2] Babar MA, Abrahamsson P. Architecture-centric methods and agile approaches. In: Agile processes in software engineering and extreme programming (XP); 2008.

[3] Beck K, Beedle M, Bennekum A, Cockburn A, Cunninham W, Fowler M, et al. Manifesto for agile software development; 2001. http://agilemanifesto.org.

[4] Leffingwell D. Agile software requirements lean requirements practices for teams, programs, and the enterprise. Upper Saddle River, NJ: Addison-Wesley; 2011.

[5] Rasmusson J. The agile samurai: how agile masters deliver great software, pragmatic bookshelf series. Raleigh, NC: Pragmatic Bookshelf; 2010.

[6] Dyba T, Dingsoyr T. Empirical studies of agile software development: a systematic review. Inform Softw Tech 2008;50(9–10):833–59.

[7] Bowers J, et al. Tailoring XP for large system mission critical software development. In: 2nd XP universe and first agile universe conference on extreme programming and agile methods XP/agile universe. Berlin: Springer-Verlag; 2002.

[8] Falessi D, et al. Peaceful coexistence: agile developer perspectives on software architecture. IEEE Softw 2010;27(2):23–5.

[9] Booch G. An architectural oxymoron. IEEE Softw 2010;27(5):95–6.

[10] Cockburn A. Agile software development: the cooperative game. 2nd ed. Boston, MA: Addison-Wesley Professional; 2006.

[11] Smits H. Levels of agile planning: from enterprise product vision to team stand-up, white paper. Rally Software Development Corporation; 2006.

[12] Larman C, Vodde B. Scaling lean & agile development: thinking and organizational tools for large-scale scrum. Boston, MA: Addison-Wesley; 2009.

[13] Leffingwell D. Scaling software agility: best practices for large enterprises, the agile software development series. Boston, MA: Addison-Wesley; 2007.

[14] Kruchten P. On software architecture, agile development, value & cost. Pittsburgh: Keynote SATURN; 2008.

[15] Bosch J. Architecture in the age of compositionality. In: European conference on software architecture (ECSA). LNCS, vol. 6285. Berlin: Springer-Verlag; 2010.

[16] Pichler R. Agile product management with scrum: creating products that customers love. Amsterdam: Addison-Wesley Professional; 2010.

[17] Pérez J, Díaz J, Garbajosa J, Alarcón PP. Flexible working architectures: agile architecting using PPCs. In: 4th European conference on software architecture (ECSA). LNCS, vol. 6285; 2010.

[18] Pérez J, Diaz J, Costa-Soria C, Garbajosa J. Plastic partial components: a solution to support variability in architectural components. In: The joint working IEEE/IFIP conference on software architecture & european conference on software architecture (WICSA/ECSA). Los Alamitos, CA: IEEE Computer Society; 2009.

[19] Díaz J, et al. Change impact analysis in product-line architectures. In: 5th European conference on software architecture (ECSA). LNCS, vol. 6903; 2011.

[20] Gonzalez Ortega E, Luis Martín Ruiz J, Garbajosa J, Yagüe A. Making software factory truly global: the smart software factory project. Software Factory Magazine 2010;1(1):19.

[21] Madison J. Agile architecture interactions. IEEE Softw 2010;27(2):41–8.

[22] Booch G. The defenestration of superfluous architectural accoutrements. Keynote software architecture challenges, the 21st century, USC; 2009.

[23] Ihme T, Abrahamsson P. Agile architecting: the use of architectural patterns in mobile java applications. IJAM 2005;8(2):97–112.

[24] Chivers H, Paige RF, Ge X. Agile security using an incremental security architecture. In: The 6th international conference on extreme programming and agile processes in software engineering; 2005, LNCS.

[25] Intelligent monitoring of power NETworks (IMPONET), ITEA 2 project, http://innovationenergy.org/imponet/.

[26] Massoud S, Wollenberg BF. Toward a smart grid: power delivery for the 21st century. IEEE P&E Magazine 2005;3(5):34–41.

[27] Lasseter R, et al. Integration of distributed energy resources. The CERTS microgrid concept. Berkeley, CA: Lawrence Berkeley National Laboratory; 2002, LBNL-50829.

[28] Leffingwell D, Widrig D. Managing software requirements: a use case approach. 3rd ed. Boston, MA: Pearson Education; 2003.

[29] Nord RL, et al. In search of a metric for managing architectural technical debt. In: Working IEEE/IFIP conference on software architecture (WICSA); 2012.

[30] Bachmann F, Nord RL, Ozkaya I. Architectural tactics to support rapid and agile stability. CrossTalk: J Defense Softw Eng pp. 20–25 May/June 2012.

[31] Pham A. Scrum in action agile software project management and development. Boston, MA: Course Technology PTR; 2011.

[32] Bode S, Riebisch M. Impact evaluation for quality-oriented architectural decisions regarding evolvability. In: 4th European conference on software architecture (ECSA); 2010.

[33] Highsmith J. Agile project management: creating innovative products. 2nd ed. Boston, MA: Addison-Wesley Professional, 2009.

[34] Pohl K, Bckle G, Linden F. Software product line engineering: foundations principles and techniques. Berlin, Heidelberg: Springer; 2005.

[35] Galster M, Avgeriou P. Handling variability in software architecture: problems and implications. In: 9th Working IEEE/IFIP conference on software architecture WICSA; 2011.

[36] Svahnberg M, van Gurp J, Bosch J. A taxonomy of variability realization techniques: research articles. Softw Pract Exper 2005;35(8):705–54.

[37] Reinertsen DG. The principles of product development flow: second generation lean product development. Redondo Beach, CA: Celeritas Publishing; 2009.

[38] Assmann U. Invasive software composition. Secaucus, NJ: Springer; 2003.

[39] Kruchten P. Software architecture and agile software development an oxymoron? Keynote software architecture challenges in the 21st century, workshop. Los Angeles, USA: University of Southern California (USC); June 8, 2009.

[40] Fowler M, et al. Refactoring: improving the design of existing code. Reading, MA: Addison-Wesley; 1999.

[41] McMahon P. Extending agile methods: a distributed project and organizational improvement perspective. CrossTalk: J Defense Softw Eng 2005;18(5):16–9.

[42] Arnold RS. Software change impact analysis. Los Alamitos, CA: IEEE Computer Society; 1996.

[43] Ramil J, Lehman M. Metrics of software evolution as effort predictors—a case study. In: International conference on software maintenance; 2000.

[44] Mens T, Demeyer S, Mens T. Introduction and roadmap: history and challenges of software evolution. In: Software evolution. Berlin: Springer; 2008.

[45] Pfleeger S, Bohner S. A framework for software maintenance metrics. In: Conference on software maintenance; 1990.

[46] Chen C-Y, Chen P-C. A holistic approach to managing software change impact. J Syst Softw 2009;82(12):2051–67.

[47] Cho H, et al. Model-driven domain analysis and software development: architectures and functions. In: Model-driven impact analysis of software product lines. Hershey, PA: IGI Global; 2011.

[48] Díaz J, et al. Change-impact driven agile architecting. In: HICSS '13: Hawaii international conference on system sciences. IEEE Computer Society; January 2013. p. 4780–9

[49] Bosch J. Software architecture: the next step. In: Software architecture. LNCS, vol. 3047. Berlin: Springer; 2004.

Agile Architecting in Specific Domains

Architecture-Centric Testing for Security: An Agile Perspective

10

Sarah Al-Azzani, Ahmad Al-Natour, and Rami Bahsoon

University of Birmingham, Birmingham, UK

CHAPTER CONTENTS

10.1 INTRODUCTION

The use of software system architecture in security testing can play a vital role in developing secure systems [1]. Its abstraction unnecessarily hides details about the implementation, allowing testers to focus their attention on design choices to reveal design vulnerabilities. As for compositional security, executable architectures allows developers to exercise the integration of system components before they are built to iteratively refine ambiguous requirements, search for hidden behavior caused by composing functional requirements, and generate test cases at early stages. Unfortunately, the importance of architecture-level testing for security to defend against design vulnerabilities that are believed to be the hardest type to find and correct and are the most critical to address has been recognized only recently [2]. On the same level, there is an increasing interest in recognizing the role of architecture in agile development [3,4] and the possibilities of merging both approaches to achieve adaptation and anticipation of requirements without losing the speed of delivery.

In this chapter, we discuss the importance of architecture in agile development systems and present the application of incremental architecture-level testing for securing systems developed using agile principles [5]. This approach uses the concept of implied scenarios [6] that arise from the composition of requirement scenarios to search for hidden vulnerabilities in the system. We show how the architecture can be test-driven, incremental, and adaptive to new and incomplete requirements. We stand by the argument that the architecture can be used to allow for co-processing of design and testing and that it does not require detailed design but merely relies on the functionality. Drawing on a nontrivial case study of identity management systems, we demonstrate how the integration of architecture and agile processes enables software developers to focus on security as a nonfunctional requirement while strongly calling for the participation of stakeholders to verify the correctness of requirements.

In the following sections, we discuss the motivation of the work by briefly reviewing existing security testing methods, their drawbacks, and the need for design-specific testing methods. We introduce the concept of the implied scenario and its role in our approach. We then discuss the agility of the approach and its application in a case study. Finally, we summarize the chapter by recalling the coexistence of architecture and agile development.

10.2 RESEARCH MOTIVATION

Security testing is fundamentally different from traditional testing because it emphasizes what an application should not do rather than what it should do. Therefore we distinguish between positive requirements, such as disabling user accounts after three unsuccessful login attempts, and negative requirements, such as the system prevents unauthorized users from accessing system resources [7]. Unlike functional testing, security testing focuses more on negative behavior (i.e., any undesirable behavior that affects the security of the system, such as breaching confidentiality of data). To apply the standard testing approach to negative requirements, one would need to create every possible set of negative conditions that tests the requirement, which is infeasible because one cannot reliably enumerate all the possible ways in which a negative requirement can be tested. It is also challenging because it is not always possible to map a requirement to a specific software artifact when the requirement is not implemented in a specific place. Since negative requirement testing creates a challenge for traditional testing, one needs to explore new testing methodologies that highlight the presence of negative behavior and how it manifests in the system to guard against its occurrence.

The challenge in achieving compositional security is that security is a global property, yet many big systems are built using smaller components; thus, most vulnerabilities arise from unexpected interactions between different system components [8]. When components are put together, predicting the consequences of their composition is difficult [9]. These compositional consequences are referred to as implied scenarios [10]; they occur when different functionalities are composed together. Implied scenarios can model positive consequences or a design vulnerability that combines several legitimate behaviors to produce emergent abusive behavior. In general, a vulnerability is a weakness in the security system that might be exploited to cause loss or harm [11]. Often, vulnerabilities are characterized by the result of their exploitation with respect to security properties [12], such as breach of confidentiality, loss of availability, and data tempering. Design vulnerabilities are a subtype of vulnerabilities that are associated with design defects causing security violations; avoiding *design-level vulnerabilities* is among the most important challenges faced today by software developers [13]. Their fundamental importance lies in the fact that even the most secure implementation cannot defend against defective design. In a recent case study, a design vulnerability allowed ciphered text to be accessible to the user to provide a sense of data security. This was identified as a major design vulnerability because it allowed the user to cryptanalyze the ciphered text to identify the cryptographic key used during encryption. These design vulnerabilities cannot be easily identified using implementation-level testing methods; they require a design-specific testing methodology to be detected. Thus, the role of architecture manifests itself such that as requirements are elicited, one can execute their composition to predict the consequences of the composition and search for incompatibilities between requirements. We define architecture as "the selection of the structural elements and their interfaces by which the system is composed together with their behavior as specified in the collaboration among those elements, and the composition of these elements into progressively larger subsystems" [14]. And since agile systems[a] are built incrementally, applying iterative testing based on these requirements can speed up deliveries by addressing compositional faults before the system is built. These requirements can be documented in the agile development lifecycle to enhance communication between team members and to verify the requirements with stakeholders [3].

In this chapter, we try to answer the following questions:

- Why can't current testing methodologies fulfill the role of security testing?
- Can we combine architecture with agile development such that both support each other to reduce conflicts?
- How can implied scenarios be aligned with agile practices to architect secure software systems?

---

[a]We refer to systems that are built using an agile methodology as "agile systems."

10.3 OVERVIEW OF LIMITATIONS IN CURRENT POST-IMPLEMENTATION METHODS

The overall goal of security testing is to reduce vulnerabilities within a software system [15]. A vulnerability allows an attacker to violate the integrity of the system. When an attack is successful, the security of a system is said to be compromised. In past years, there was much focus on implementation vulnerabilities, such as buffer-overflows, invalid inputs, and general code-level testing, while very little attention was paid to design vulnerabilities [9]. We summarize the current state of security testing to motivate the need for further research to address its limitations. Current security testing approaches can be summarized under three main headings.

10.3.1 Functional testing of security apparatuses

The most basic premise behind traditional functional testing is that it is meant to validate that the software fulfills its requirements and it functions as intended. Functional security testing tests the security mechanisms implemented in the system (such as authorization check-points) to verify that it behaves as expected. This is largely based on security software requirements. For example, testing for a requirement that states "a login page must only verify correct passwords" may be tested with an incorrect password to increase confidence that the authorization mechanism behaves as expected; however, this testing does not guarantee that an attacker cannot brute force the system and succeed at logging in. Verifying the correct behavior of the system does not guarantee the absence of undocumented behaviors; it only verifies that the system behaves according to the specification.

Requirements-based testing is an example of functional testing [16], where test cases are associated with requirements to ensure that all requirements are covered. In security testing, the requirements are associated with the security properties of the system, such as confidentiality and integrity of data. Functional testing is also done via specification-based testing [17,18] where test cases are derived automatically from specifications, such as interfaces. There is also code-based testing [19] that aims to uncover code-based vulnerabilities, such as buffer-overflows.

A general problem associated with functional testing is that it addresses what the program should do; in other words, it does not aim to investigate what the application may still do beyond the requirements or specifications. In security testing, it is important to test for situations that are not covered in the specifications. We believe that testing functionality is significantly different from testing for security. This is because security, unlike functionality, is not an externally observable property, and hence, one cannot easily predict its results or consequences.

10.3.2 Penetration testing

Penetration testing takes the form of black-box testing of the system using a predefined set of test cases that represent known exploits. It is performed using either existing tools [20,21] or by hiring security experts that try to attack the system and exploit any potential weaknesses in the system. Although this approach is attractive, its main problem with respect to agile development is that it is not design-specific testing; testers run the same set of test cases on different systems and rely on the fact that developers often make similar mistakes and repeat them. In addition, penetration testing—whether done by hiring a red-team or by using vulnerability-scanning tools—addresses known attacks, but determined attackers often look for novel ways of attacking a system. The system's response to such attacks is observed and any inappropriate behavior is noted. This process requires knowledge of both the desired behavior and certain implementation details that are the source of vulnerabilities [22]. Although redesigning a feature in agile development might not be expensive to perform, patching a system is cheaper and is likely to be considered before redesign. This step attempts to hide the symptoms of the problem as opposed to fixing it, which may bring many issues into the system such as writing a vulnerable patch or discovering new symptoms of the problem.

Security tools used in penetration testing, such ISS Scanner [23] and Cybercop [24], are generally limited in scope. They mainly address network security attacks, and are not flexible enough to allow testers to write custom attacks. Another problem with existing tools is that they can only be used after the system is built. In addition, most tools address IP networks; thus, a company wishing to test a different type of networks is required to purchase different tools as required. Although these "bad-ness-ometers" [25] are useful in displaying the negative state of the system, especially when the system configuration is well understood, they are not useful in nonstandard applications, and hence should not be the only way of testing an application. Other forms of security tools are static analysis tools that address code vulnerabilities, such as buffer-overflow. Both are very limited in scope since dynamic testing is also important, and both have high false-positive error rates.

10.3.3 Threat modeling

Threat modeling [26–29] is a methodical review of a system design or architecture to discover and correct design-level security problems. The review process determines an adversary's most likely courses of action in order to develop appropriate responses. It requires a clear understanding of the assets to be protected, the threat's objectives, and any factors in the environment that could influence the threat's capability or decisions. Such information might not be present during the initial design of the agile system. This process results in a threat model that describes the potential attacks on the system to be used to understand how attacks can manifest themselves, and to evaluate critical decisions that will affect the security posture of the system [28]. Its difficulty lies in the fact that a change made to the design requires reanalysis of the system's security status. Thus, in development cycles where requirements might not be fully stated initially, constant changes might leave the models redundant. Threat modeling addresses designing a secure system—not quite for the testing phase, although the list of potential vulnerabilities may still be used as test cases.

10.3.4 **Discussion**

To summarize the common problems with respect to agile development is agile development advocates testing first with a focus on implementation. Such tests are likely to only reveal implementation vulnerabilities, and overlook design vulnerabilities. Thus, one needs a testing methodology that tests the architecture design while adapting to changes in the requirements iteratively. In addition, testing for security cannot be fully automated; such attempts have failed, except in a few cases [30]. One cannot replace human expertise, because hacking is a creative process, and creativity cannot be easily automated. Moreover, each application has its own design, and each design has its own weaknesses and needs to be tested individually, while current methods use predetermined vulnerability databases to discover known vulnerabilities in the system. However, security testing is motivated by addressing undocumented assumptions and areas of particular complexity to determine how software can be compromised [31]. Existing techniques fail to address implicit assumptions, mainly because testers rely on the system specifications and code [15]. Developers build a certain mental view of the software, which is limited because the software is too complex for a human to carry a complete, detailed mental picture of it. It is then the tester's responsibility to violate these assumptions, and thereby try to uncover vulnerabilities. Security testers must consider actions that are outside the range of normal activity and might not even be regarded as legitimate tests under other circumstances. Furthermore, all existing approaches rely on the tester's expertise to craft security test cases. This is often problematic because testers are required to think like attackers, and because security test cases don't often cause direct security exploits, which presents an observability problem. Important test cases might be missed because the application appeared to behave as it should, with disregard to the additional behaviors that appears from the composition of the correct behavior.

Achieving security requires a tester to test like a detective, following clues to insecure behavior and then exploring potential vulnerabilities [32]. This is because attackers intentionally probe unspecified behaviors in the system. They attempt to make the application behave in an unanticipated manner, and then determine the attacks associated with that behavior. It is important to observe that detecting insecure behavior will speed up the process of detecting vulnerabilities in a systematic fashion. The remaining question to be addressed is, "How do we determine insecure behavior in the system, while still maintaining observability of the problems associated with the behavior, and also target implicit assumptions related to the design of the system?" In this chapter, we try to move toward this goal using architecture-level testing. We define vulnerability testing in our context as testing the system for harmful additional behavior not directly specified in the system model.

The inherent characteristics of agile software development serve testing for security well in that agility promotes flexibility through its support of decomposition and incremental requirements. This is believed to assist testing for security in two ways:

1. It allows security testers to focus on emergent compositional behavior; it is critical to gather understanding of all possible behaviors that can be triggered by attackers.

2. Testing partial design supports focusing on more problematic areas in the code, such as the meeting points of areas with high and low security status. Areas of high security often require higher privileges, where an authorization point or other security feature might be installed; a vulnerability might occur if confidential information flows into nonsecured areas. Thus, the process eases the detection of vulnerabilities through continuous inspection of partially-related code to reveal potential threats in critical areas.

10.4 INTRODUCING IMPLIED SCENARIOS

Since security testers are required to consider actions that are outside the range of normal activity and specification, we discuss our vision of how testers can use existing methods to look beyond the specifications. In this section, we introduce the concept of implied scenarios and their role in detecting compositional security flaws.

Scenarios define an ordered sequence of events; in software architecture, scenarios have been employed in modeling architectural properties [33,34] and in identifying component interactions [35]. Each scenario models a partial behavior between components, and thus, the composition of all scenarios is likely to exhibit more behaviors than described by the specified scenarios. These undocumented behaviors, known as "implied scenarios," may arise as a result of components having only local views of the execution [10]. An implied scenario may be an acceptable scenario that has been overlooked, indicating incomplete specifications. Alternatively, implied scenarios may represent an unacceptable behavior that may present attackers with the opportunity for a potential exploit. The notion of implied scenarios was first introduced in [10] for a restricted scenario language. The work is limited to a set of message sequence charts (MSCs) that specify a finite set of system behaviors. This work has been extended in Ref. [36] to provide a more expressive scenario language that allows for an infinite number of system behaviors. But then, how are implied scenarios detected?

10.4.1 Detecting implied scenarios

The extension provided in Ref. [36] introduced an algorithm that analyzes scenarios modeled on MSC specifications. These scenarios consist of message events sent and received between components, which are linked together according to a directed graph (high-level MSC (hMSC)) that defines possible continuations/loops between scenarios. With these two inputs, the algorithm performs the following steps:

1. Breaks down the continuation/loops of scenarios into several individual label transition systems (LTSs); one component model is synthesized at a time, representing its behavior across all scenarios. This is accomplished by (a) collecting the component behavior in all MSCs, and (b) linking all its behavior according to the hMSC.

2. Uses the collection of component LTS models, to compose an architecture LTS model in parallel by (a) mapping nodes to behavior and to their adjacent nodes, and (b) then connecting nodes according to the hMSC. This architecture model takes into account the behavior described by the MSC scenarios (thus preserving the components structures and interfaces) and the global behavior described by the hMSC. The joint behavior is the result of all LTSs executing asynchronously while synchronizing on all shared messages. Thus, any of the LTSs can perform a transition independently of the other LTSs, as long as the transition label is not shared with the other LTSs [36]. Because non-shared transitions can be performed independently across different LTSs, the notion of the architecture is weak such that it allows for additional unspecified behaviors to emerge that are valid paths in the hMSC along with exhibiting all traces specified by the MSCs.

3. Builds a new trace model that captures exactly the set of traces defined by the MSC semantics to compare how close the architecture model is to the global behavior required. Then, any trace that is not specified in the trace model would correspond to an implied scenario. This trace model is built using a coordinator component that is responsible for allowing/disallowing components to move from one MSC to another. This way, components can be guaranteed not to follow different sequences of MSCs.

4. Compares whether the architecture model exhibits more traces than the trace model, given the traces of both models. This is done by (a) defining the trace model as a safe property that accepts traces that behave correctly according to the MSCs and hMSC specifications, and (b) checking whether the architecture violates the property. Violations are then reported as implied scenario MSCs.

Implied scenarios arise because the scenario-based modeling of the system describes the desired global behavior, whereas in reality each component in concurrent state models acts locally based on local information. These counter-example traces may correspond directly to attack scenarios, where a security property is violated and which can be discovered using automated verification techniques to identify scenarios where security-related properties are violated. In contrast to previous approaches that mainly address well-known vulnerabilities, our approach benefits from existing model-based techniques to automatically seek out and identify vulnerabilities in the design itself. For formal definition of implied scenarios, please see Ref. [36].

We introduced the application of implied scenario detection to determine unspecified behavior in the architecture because implied scenarios can address the following issues:

1. Relying on the architecture of the system allows us to address implicit assumptions made by designers regarding the behavior of system components. In the real world, a designer might explicitly specify that an application performs scenarios X, Y, and Z. As these scenarios are composed together, a fourth scenario, W, might arise. Such unspecified scenarios, namely W, might result in a security failure if exploited by an attacker. Thus, it is important to discover all possible behaviors of the system and decide whether the behavior is legitimate or not.

2. Existing tools for detecting implied scenarios allow us to observe the side effects of the implied scenario on the system, and determine how these scenarios can be triggered by attackers (vulnerabilities), and more importantly how the execution of these scenarios can affect the security of the system before building the system.
3. The detected implied scenarios can then be used as test cases to aid security testers in determining important test cases. Since implied scenarios allow us to explore unspecified behaviors based on the assumptions made in the system architecture, we believe such application in security testing will improve the process of detecting threats and violations of security assumptions within the architecture.

10.5 APPROACH

It is essential to acquire full knowledge of possible behaviors of a system to ensure that the system behaves as securely as required, and that any additional behaviors do not violate the desired global security behavior. Briefly, our notion of architecture consists of the following:

- The *component structure*: which consists of a list of all components that appear in the modeled scenarios and their composed behavior
- The *component interface*: where, given a component c of some scenario, the interface of c is determined by the set of messages that are sent and received by this component

Our proposal for using implied scenarios consists of three main stages.

10.5.1 Stage 1: implied scenario detection

A prerequisite for detecting implied scenarios is modeling the high-level design of the system in MSC specification language. These scenarios reflect the high-level desired functionality/requirements. Once the requirement scenarios are determined, they are fed into the Labelled Transition System Analyser - Message Sequence Chart (LTSA-MSC) tool with a roadmap for continuation (hMSC). When the scenarios are composed together to create the architecture model, we start collecting all detected implied scenarios without regard to which of these scenarios are security threats. By using this information, which is generated based on the system design, we provide assurance on the security status of the system itself and the design choices, rather than the security mechanisms implemented. At this stage, new requirements can be added and removed, and only the hMSC needs to be changed; thus, adding and removing requirements is a straight-forward task. The system then builds incrementally as new requirements are added. In addition, models of new requirements and detected implied scenarios can be used to verify behavior with the stakeholders.

10.5.2 Stage 2: review of detected implied scenarios

The focus is on investigating the security breaches of the detected implied scenarios against all categories of attacks. This is because an implied scenario may fall into several categories of attacks, and hence, may be exploited in different ways. We do not impose restrictions on which classification scheme is used; however, we base our classification scheme on Howard and Longstaff's published scheme [37]. The aim of their taxonomy is to define a common language for computer security incidents. This taxonomy is also beneficial because it classifies a range of types of people who may launch an attack or invoke a particular malicious behavior. It should be noted that the purpose of categorizing vulnerabilities is to provide a checklist-based approach whereby the tester can have reasonable confidence that all potential attack methods/results have been considered. This in turn provides confidence in the completeness of the vulnerability analysis process. It also helps us identify the types of attacks detectable using implied scenarios, and which architectures are more prone to certain attacks. Ultimately, the result of the review is to ensure that all detected behaviors are studied for any potential malicious use. At this stage, detected vulnerabilities can be communicated across testers and developers in a readable scenario form as generated by the tool in step 1.

Human involvement is needed primarily to evaluate the security of the detected implied behaviors and to create test cases to exercise the system. Although it may be possible to define security properties to fully automate the approach, we believe that such a step is likely to neglect important implied scenarios that do not violate the defined security properties.

10.5.3 Stage 3: performing live security testing

Any malicious behaviors found in the review process are then used as test cases to exercise the system's resistance to these attacks. Because implied scenarios are in the form of scenarios, performing a security test is relatively straight forward, and is no different practically from common functional testing. Some calibration might be needed to perform some of the tests. For example, in order to test whether a race condition can take place on the system, we might need to perform an extra wait operation on one of components to allow an event to take place in a certain order; this does not affect how the system behaves/resists the attack, but is required because race conditions happen in extremely short time intervals. Testing can begin as soon as vulnerable implied scenarios are detected, and as the architecture is refined, more tested cases can be created.

10.6 THE AGILITY OF THE APPROACH

For an approach to be consistent with agile principles, it must meet certain criteria to be integrated in the agile development system. Contrary to what some believe, requirements do not need to be gathered all up front in one phase; our approach responds to changes by:

1. Supporting incremental elaboration of requirements by automatically searching for potential requirements; this supports customer collaboration to verify the validity of detected behavior, as well as prediction of behavior to avoid costly correction of integration problems.

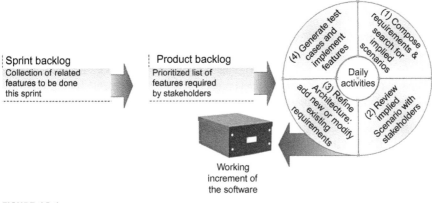

Sprint backlog
Collection of related features to be done this sprint

Product backlog
Prioritized list of features required by stakeholders

(1) Compose requirements & search for implied scenarios

(2) Review implied Scenario with stakeholders

(3) Refine Architecture: add new or modify existing requirements

(4) Generate test cases and implement features

Daily activities

Working increment of the software

FIGURE 10.1

Mapping between the implied scenario detection approach and Scrum.

2. Reconstruction of architecture as new information becomes available to address requirement ambiguities, and to allow stakeholders to periodically see the progress and make adjustments to the requirements as needed.

With respect to testing, our approach supports test-driven development where the focus is on reusing and testing the integration of components built iteratively and ensuring that when components are composed, a correct overall behavior can be maintained. Figure 10.1 illustrates how the iterative process of our approach maps to Scrum to produce a working increment of the developed software. The process starts by first collecting related requirements to be implemented, then prioritizing these requirements, then composing them incrementally while adding or removing requirements as the system evolves to produce a working increment of the software. Test cases can be derived from requirements regardless of the programming language or technology utilized, which allows it to be used to test existing systems. In addition, relying on requirement functionality and behavior helps in achieving tractability between the code and the architecture, as well as ensuring consistent understanding between team members.

Finally, the type of documentation required is lightweight, and is essential to enumerate the requirements in scaled projects.

10.7 IDENTITY MANAGEMENT CASE STUDY

In this section, we look at the practical application of implied-scenario-detection algorithms on two identity-management models designed by a project funded by Vodafone. The evaluation of the models was conducted as part of masters projects in security, involving two students over a period of 2 months. During the 2 months, the students were briefed for 1 h about the use of the LTSA-MSC tool used to detect implied scenarios, and how to create MSCs; they were not required to understand what implied scenarios are, or how they are detected. The students modeled the system in MSC using the LTSA-MSC tools and all generated implied scenarios were recorded and evaluated. The use of sequence charts is believed to be one of the most widely used models in the software industry [38], thus using such models does not introduce an overhead on the industry to adopt the approach. Another prerequisite for the approach is basic understanding about security properties, and how they are violated.

10.7.1 Case study background

The case study aimed at evaluating two identity management models (device-based and service-based) [39] implemented in an online bargain shop (OBS) for security vulnerabilities. Retailers and wholesalers can subscribe to the OBS system in order to advertise their online products, while buyers can sign up to OBS to browse offerings and search for and buy products. The architecture uses temporary sessions assigned for every user. The user will access the portal by providing a username and password, which in turn will provide access to a third party web service (e.g., Amazon). Once the user enters the credentials, the portal will forward the request for authentication to the session generator, which in turn will determine whether the username and password are valid by comparing them with the values stored in the user credential database. The desired communication is illustrated in Figure 10.2.

Device-based identity utilizes security credentials on the device to authenticate with services and uses the identity provider (IdP) to distribute the public key for the identity and maintains a list of attributes. It introduces a security token, which is sent to the users' device for authentication. Security credentials are stored in the device and are used to identify the service and authenticate the device requesting the service; thus, "each device maintains its own credentials for the user identity" [39]. The desired behavior is illustrated in Figure 10.3.

10.7.2 Approach and results

Each model contained four legitimate scenarios generated from the code with its hMSC. We have applied our approach to both models and compared our results with respect to the following security properties [12]: confidentiality, integrity, authentication, and availability. As new behaviors were detected using the LTSA-MSC tool, the developers were involved to decide whether the behavior was positive or not (i.e., "Is it a design defect with potential security implications, or is it an undesirable inference?"). In cases where additional behaviors were positive, they were added to the model supporting continuous refinement and addition of new requirements. Further investigation was performed incrementally and iteratively to ensure that additional behaviors do not cause integration errors.

The device-based model proved to be more vulnerable to security vulnerability exploitation, since it had a total of three negative implied scenarios and violated the confidentiality, integrity, and availability requirements. On the other hand, the

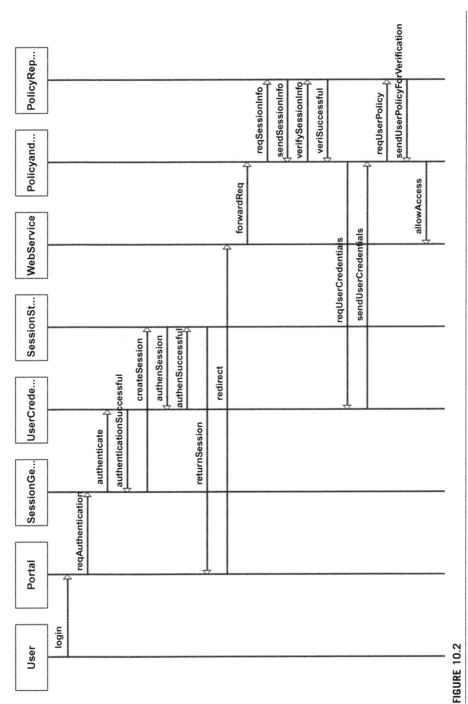

FIGURE 10.2

Service-based identity management model for an online shopping system.

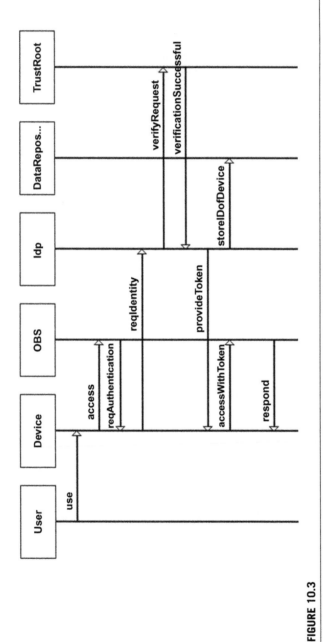

FIGURE 10.3

Device-based identity management model for a shopping system.

Table 10.1 Comparison of Implied Scenario Detection in Service- and Device-Based Models

	Total Implied Scenarios	Negative Implied Scenarios	Confidentiality Violation	Integrity Violation	Availability Violation	Authen- tication Violation
Device-based	4	3	Yes	Yes	Yes	No
Service-based	2	1	No	No	No	Yes

service-based model shows only one negative implied scenario which violated the authentication requirement as presented in Table 10.1.

The implied scenarios found are as follows:

- *Implied scenarios 1 and 2*: Ambiguous behavior is exhibited when multiple login attempts are carried out instantly. This happens in both models. It indicates possibilities of brute force attack on the server until a successful login attempt is made. The architecture does not guard against flooded requests of login attempts. This could disrupt the availability of the service leading to a denial of service attack, since no firewall is implemented to block such behavior. This can also raise an alarm for how the system disposes credentials when the server fails to respond. A common improper handling of exceptions can leave the credentials floating in the memory.
- *Implied scenario 3*: Another possibility is masquerading attack, in which a user attempts to login, and once a successful confirmation is returned, the confirmation is intercepted by an attacker that attempts to replay the confirmation to gain access to the user's account. This is modeled in Figure 10.3, where the first part of the diagram models the legitimate behavior and the second part models the attempt to access the server using replayed confirmation. Since the models do not present encryption mechanisms, modification of the credentials may occur, thus violating the integrity requirement of the model.
- *Implied scenario 4*: An application with an improper threading mechanism in concurrent applications may face problematic interleavings that return wrong sessions to the wrong person, granting the user more privileges than they own.
- *Implied scenarios 5 and 6*: These model positive behaviors; one models a valid request of service after authentication is successful, and one models a login attempt after authentication is successful (allowing for concurrent access from different features, and re-verification of authorization).

The amount of effort required to accomplish the study involved learning to use the tool and modeling the system, which the students reported no difficulty in learning; by the end of the 1 hour introduction to the tool, the students were able to use it on their own. The process of modeling the actual identity management models was also straightforward because the developer of the models was present to confirm that the students' models were correct before the evaluation took place. Finally, the number of acceptable implied scenarios were minimal ($\sim$2), so the effort required to evaluate their potential security implication paid off in comparison with the negative implied scenarios detected ($\sim$4) and acknowledged by the developer. It is also worth mentioning that implied scenarios are difficult to detect manually, and thus the time required to detect them is significantly reduced using automated tools.

Now that we have an overview of potential design vulnerabilities, one can either refine the code to reflect the architecture to make it more secure and to prevent problems from occurring (where possible), or one can create concrete test cases that test the possible consequences of the execution, or increase/decrease the number of requirements and reevaluate the outcome. This can take place concurrently with the implementation process. We have looked into refining the service-based model, for which we have proposed a hybrid model with two-factor authentication. In addition to securing the model, it aims to decentralize the task of identity management in general and to distribute the burden of identity management by using both the trust root (for device identity authentication), and the IdP (for user identity authentication). Moreover, the use of one-time password (OTP) will provide additional authentication, and its use as an authentication configuration enables our model to support single sign-on, which in itself reduces phishing attacks and password fatigue. As Figure 10.5 shows, the IdP will verify the identity of the user and send an acknowledgment back to the session generator. Once the OBS receives the redirect from the portal, it will forward the request to access the service to the policy and access control module, which will request the identity of the device from the IdP. The IdP then sends the identity to the trust root for verification, which in turn will request an OTP from the server. The server will compute the OTP (using either time-synchronized functions or mathematical hash functions) and will send it to the device so the user can log in using the OTP. When the user logs in to the service, the OTP will be verified by the server and access will be granted.

10.8 FURTHER DISCUSSION

We now report on the following criteria:

- *Agility of the approach*: The approach proved to be flexible in responding to changes involved in the requirements. Its benefits include (1) its support for continuous evolvement, (2) its ability to *improve productivity*, since it reduces staff effort and time required to perform integration checks as new requirements are added, (3) its ability to produce *better quality of product*, since it targets inspecting hidden, potentially dangerous behaviors, and (4) its support for systematic review of the system. However, once the scenarios are detected, human judgment is required to determine how the insecure behavior might affect the security of the system. This guided testing helps identify vulnerable areas for testers to examine.

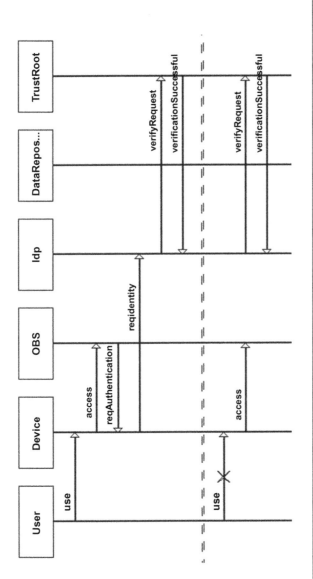

FIGURE 10.4

Potential masquerading attack on the service-based identity management model.

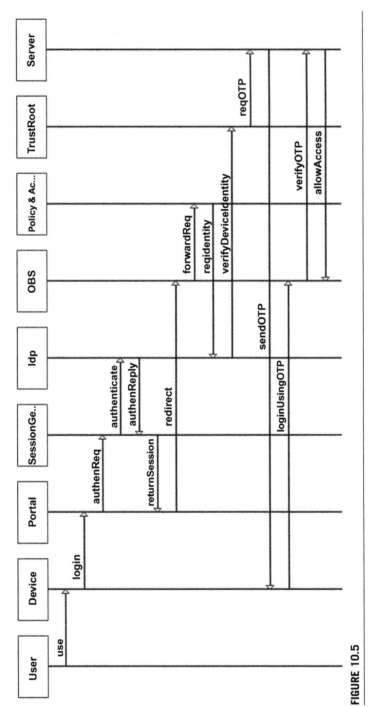

FIGURE 10.5

A hybrid model with two-factor authentication proposed to secure the service-based model.

We sped up this process by determining categories of attack results that might occur if insecure behaviors are executed.

- *Phases of application*: Because we are working at the architectural level to address security testing, our approach can be integrated into the analysis, design, implementation, or testing phase of the development cycle, as long as the global and individual behaviors of components are identified. Because agile development is test-driven, testing can begin as early as some of the requirements are available. Our approach to security testing supports a highly iterative process; for example, in cases of adaptation to new requirements, these requirements can be added to the LTSA-MSC in the form of new behavioral scenarios. As these new scenarios are added, the approach can be automatically reiterated to detect new implied scenarios. The testers will only need to review new sets of detected implied scenarios, which reduces the necessary time because reviews are not repeated for implied scenarios that have already been detected.

- *Generality and applicability of approach*: We have specifically chosen to work on the architecture of the system because it offers an adequate level of generality. Almost every system can be modeled in terms of components and interactions, and every system has an architecture, whether it is modeled or not. We have also chosen scenario-based specification because it is popular for modeling behaviors. Unified Modelling Language (UML) 2.0 and MSC are among the most commonly used scenario-based specifications, and many software engineers are familiar with these modeling languages. Thus, we are not requiring additional training for testers. Furthermore, the detection of implied scenarios has been applied to different types of applications, including component-based systems [40], Java systems [41], and in this example we have applied it successfully to an identity management system.

- *Scalability*: This approach supports breaking down the system into groups of requirements, either to perform detailed dynamic analysis for certain groups of requirements (e.g., problematic areas) or for evolving the requirements for specific functionality or subsystems. Once a group of functionalities is determined, our approach supports composing these functionalities incrementally to reach a larger subsystem.

10.9 AGILE DEVELOPMENT, ARCHITECTURE, AND SECURITY TESTING

Moving from implementation testing to architecture-level testing offers several advantages, which we summarize as follows:

1. Identifying developer's assumptions based on the code can be a difficult task for testers, since the assumptions are not abstracted from the code. Identifying assumptions as discussed in Section 10.3.2 is critical for security testing.
2. Supports high-level view the system to address scalability and complexity of systems. For example, the use of code to test an object-oriented system, is

complex and tedious task [42] especially for large applications. On an average sized system, architecture can help scale its size especially on situations where there is a large, distributed team.

3. Abstraction allows us to omit parts that are not necessarily important for security testing. This helps focus attention on components that are more vulnerable than others. Abstraction is also useful for capturing attack patterns in the system, without the need for an in-depth description of the attack.

4. Traditional software testing techniques consider only a static view of code, which is not sufficient for testing dynamic behavior of the system [43]. Testing the live system is very expensive. Thus, using an executable architecture is a cost-effective approach that allows us to experiment with the behavior of the system.

5. Applications often contain third-party components. Since it may not be viable to modify the source of such components (either because the code was shipped in binary form or because the license agreement is prohibitive), it is not obvious how security vulnerabilities could be detected at coding level. Our approach relies on the interfaces of components, and the safety of their integration.

6. Applications may be written in a variety of languages. In cases of code testing, there is no easy way to abstract security-related code behind a clean Application programming interface (API) [44]. As a consequence, security-related code will be scattered throughout the application, increasing the difficulty of detecting vulnerabilities.

7. Architecture-level testing facilitates better communication between testers, developers, and stakeholders, since abstracted models are easier to read and understand than large amounts of code.

8. The test process and test case generation can be planned at an early stage of the software development life cycle, allowing coding and testing to be carried out in parallel, which fulfills the requirement of test-driven development.

These points highlight a promising use of the architecture for agile development. Its use does not conflict with the principles of agile development as demonstrated by our case study; iteration can be achieved, adapting to changing requirements, continuous integration, and test-driven.

10.10 RELATED WORK

The closest work to ours is that produced by Ramakrishnan and Sekar [8]. In their work, they create a model for each system component and then compose them to show different interactions between these components. Then they verify this composite model by searching for a scenario where a formally defined security property is violated. The major difference in our approach is that we do not model each component independently; instead, we model all interaction scenarios between these components. We also do not formally define security properties, and instead study all unspecified behaviors for potentially dangerous behaviors. Defining a security property for automation might restrict the results of the approach because automation may lead to false positives and negatives, and thus overlook scenarios.

Another related work is that of Salas et al. [45]. In their work, they build three models: (1) a specification model that reflects the desired behavior, (2) an implementation model that reflects low-level details of the system, with a particular focus on security concerns, and (3) an attacker model that represents the intentions of an attacker. The purpose of the first two models is to show nonconformance between the specification and its implementation, and then the attacker's model is compared to the implementation model. The major difference between our work and theirs is that we only use a single model that reflects the implementation model. We also do not aim to verify the presence of previously identified threats (through other means of threat-detection), but instead, we aim to provide the detect mechanism itself to identify potential threats.

10.11 CONCLUSION

We aim in this research to continue to push against the limitations of the state of the art in securing our systems. We have presented the application of test-driven, architecture-level security testing for agile development. The application is motivated to complement limitations in existing security testing techniques. We hypothesized that the application of implied scenario detection [46] at the architecture level does not conflict with the principles of agile development. We have demonstrated that the architecture can be adaptive, iterative, and test-driven. We have also demonstrated that testing individual functionalities does not help to identify compositional security violations, and that the use of implied scenarios reveals inconsistencies in the composition of functional scenarios. Using a case study, our results validated our hypothesis, and the use of implied scenarios detected several threats that are likely to have been missed using implementation-testing methods. We conclude that the use of architecture for agile development is highly effective for guiding testers to evaluate security vulnerabilities. We have discussed the usefulness of incorporating the system architecture along with the code. We have presented a real-world example in which our approach detected four threats. In our future work, we intend to generate test cases and perform live testing on a distributed system.

References

[1] Shreyas D, Software Engineering and Security: Towards Architecting Secure Software. Term paper for ICS 221-Seminar in Software Engineering, Irvine: University of California; 2001. http://www.dsc.ufcg.edu.br/~jacques/cursos/map/recursos/SoftwareEngineeringandSecurity.pdf

[2] McGraw G, Potter B. Software security testing. IEEE Secur Priv 2004;2(5):81–5.

[3] Falessi D, Cantone G, Sarcia' SA, Calavaro G, Subiaco P, D'Amore C. Peaceful coexistence: agile developer perspectives on software architecture. IEEE Softw 2010;27(2):23–5.

[4] Abrahamsson P, Ali Babar M, Kruchten P. Agility and architecture: can they coexist? IEEE Softw 2010;27(2):16–22.

[5] Ambler S. Agile modeling: effective practices for extreme programming and the unified process. New York: Wiley; 2002.

[6] Uchitel S, Chatley R, Kramer J, Magee J. LTSA-MSC: tool support for behaviour model elaboration using implied scenarios. In: Joint European conference on theory and practice of software (ETAPS 2003), Warsaw, Poland; 2003.

[7] Fink G, Bishop M. Property-based testing: a new approach to testing for assurance. ACM SIGSOFT Softw Eng Notes 1997;22(4):74–80.

[8] Ramakrishnan C, Sekar R. Model-based vulnerability analysis of computer systems. In: Second international workshop on verification, model checking, and abstract interpretation (VMCAI), Pisa, Italy; 1998.

[9] Wing J. A call to action look beyond the horizon. IEEE Secur Priv 2003;1(6):62–7.

[10] Alur R, Etessami K, Yannakakis M. Inference of message sequence charts. In: ICSE '00: proceedings of the 22nd international conference on software engineering. New York, NY: ACM; 2000. p. 304–13.

[11] Pfleeger CP. Security in computing. Upper Saddle River, NJ: Prentice-Hall; 1997.

[12] Avizienis A, Randell B, Landwehr C. Basic concepts and taxonomy of dependable and secure computing. IEEE Trans Dependable Secure Comput 2004;1(1):11–33.

[13] Rehman S, Mustafa K. Research on software design level security vulnerabilities. ACM SIGSOFT Softw Eng Notes 2009;34(6):1–5.

[14] IBM. Rational unified process. URL: http://www-306.ibm.com/software/awdtools/rup/?S_TACT=105AGY59&S_CMP=WIKI&ca=dtl-08rupsite; 2007.

[15] Michael CC, Radosevich W. Risk-based and functional security testing. Technical report, Build security; 2005.

[16] Mogyorodi G. Requirements-based testing: an overview. In: TOOLS '01: Proceedings of the 39th international conference and exhibition on technology of object-oriented languages and systems (TOOLS39). Washington, DC: IEEE Computer Society; 2001.

[17] Stocks P, Carrington D. A framework for specification-based testing. IEEE Trans Softw Eng 1996;22(11):777–93.

[18] Wimmel G, Jürjens J. Specification-based test generation for security-critical systems using mutations. In: International conference on formal engineering methods (ICFEM); 2002.

[19] Antoniol G. Keynote paper: search based software testing for software security: breaking code to make it safer. In: ICSTW '09: proceedings of the IEEE international conference on software testing, verification, and validation workshops. Washington, DC: IEEE Computer Society; 2009.

[20] Lodderstedt T, Basin DA, Doser J. SecureUML: a UML-based modeling language for model-driven security. In: UML '02: proceedings of the 5th international conference on the unified modeling language. London: Springer; 2002.

[21] Ahn G-J, Shin ME. Role-based authorization constraints specification using object constraint language. In: WETICE '01: proceedings of the 10th IEEE international workshops on enabling technologies. Washington, DC: IEEE Computer Society; 2001.

[22] Jacobson I, Booch G, Rumbaugh J. The unified software development process. Boston, MA: Addison-Wesley Longman Publishing Co., Inc.; 1999.

[23] Internet security systems, internet scanner (ISS). Web. URL: http://www.iss.net/; 2003.

[24] Network associates, cybercop scanner. Web. URL: http://www.nss.co.uk/grouptests/va/edition2/nai_cybercop_scanner/nai_cybercop_scanner.htm.

[25] McGraw G. Software security: building security. Boston, MA: Addison-Wesley Professional; 2006.

[26] Whittle J, Wijesekera D, Hartong M. Executable misuse cases for modeling security concerns. In: ICSE '08: proceedings of the 30th international conference on software engineering. New York, NY: ACM; 2008.

[27] Hernan S, Lambert S, Ostwald T, Shostack A. Threat modeling: uncover security design flaws using the stride approach, MSDN Magazine 2006. http://msdn.microsoft.com/en-us/magazine/cc163519.aspx.

[28] Swiderski F, Snyder W. Threat modeling. Redmond, WA: Microsoft Press; 2004.

[29] Schneier B. Attack Trees. Dr. Dobb's Journal Dec 1999;24(12):21–9.

[30] Turpe S. Security testing: Turning practice into theory. In: IEEE international conference on software testing verification and validation workshop, ICSTW '08; 2008. p. 1–10.

[31] Howard M, LeBlanc DC. Writing secure code. Redmond, WA: Microsoft Press; 2002.

[32] Thompson HH. Why security testing is hard. IEEE Secur Priv 2003;1(4):83–6.

[33] Kazman R, Abowd G, Bass L, Clements P. Scenario-based analysis of software architecture. IEEE Softw 1996;13(6):47–55.

[34] Babar MA, Gorton I. Comparison of scenario-based software architecture evaluation methods. In: Asia-Pacific software engineering conference; 2004. p. 600–7.

[35] OMG Unified Modeling Language™ (OMG UML), Infrastructure. Version 2.4.1, formal/2011-08-05, August 2011. Object Management Group. http://www.omg.org/spec/UML/2.4.1/Infrastructure.

[36] Uchitel S, Kramer J, Magee J. Detecting implied scenarios in message sequence chart specifications. ACM SIGSOFT Softw Eng Notes 2001;26(5):74–82.

[37] Howard JD, Longstaff TA. A Common Language for Computer Security Incidents. Sandia National Laboratories; October 1998 [Sandia Report: SAND98-8667]. http://infoserve.sandia.gov/sand_doc/1998/988667.pdf.

[38] Samuel P, Joseph AT. Test sequence generation from UML sequence diagrams. In: Software engineering, artificial intelligence, networking, and parallel/distributed computing. SNPD '08. Ninth ACIS international conference; 2008.

[39] Staite C. Device based identity management. URL: http://www.cs.bham.ac.uk/cxs548/papers/device-based.pdf; 2010.

[40] Rodrigues GN, Rosenblum DS, Uchitel S. Using scenarios to predict the reliability of concurrent component-based software systems. In: FASE; 2005.

[41] de Sousa FC, Mendon N, Uchitel S, Kramer J. Detecting implied scenarios from execution traces. In: Reverse engineering, working conference; 2007.

[42] Kundu D, Samanta D. A novel approach to generate test cases from UML activity diagrams. JOT 2009;8(3):65–83.

[43] Binder RV. Testing object-oriented systems: models, patterns, and tools. Boston, MA: Addison-Wesley Longman Publishing Co., Inc.; 1999.

[44] Scott D, Sharp R. Abstracting application-level web security. In: WWW '02: proceedings of the 11th international conference on world wide web. New York, NY: ACM; 2002. p. 396–407.

[45] Salas PAP, Krishnan P, Ross KJ. Model-based security vulnerability testing. In: ASWEC '07: proceedings of the 2007 Australian software engineering conference. Washington, DC: IEEE Computer Society; 2007. p. 284–96.

[46] Al-Azzani S, Bahsoon R. Semi-automated detection of architectural threats for security testing. In: ESEC/FSE doctoral symposium '09: proceedings of the doctoral symposium for ESEC/FSE on doctoral symposium. New York, NY: ACM; 2009. p. 25–6.

Supporting Agile Software Development and Deployment in the Cloud: A Multitenant, Multitarget Architecture

11

Antonio Rico[*], Manuel Noguera[*], José Luis Garrido[*],
Kawtar Benghazi[*], Lawrence Chung[†]

[*]*Universidad de Granada, Granada, Spain*
[†]*University of Texas at Dallas, Richardson, TX, USA*

CHAPTER CONTENTS

11.1 INTRODUCTION

Cloud computing is enabling everyone to have access to high computational capabilities. Computation is served as a commodity by cloud providers [1], whereas cloud clients (Information Technology (IT) companies) are able to access these IT resources on demand. This new paradigm, also known as Software as a Service (SaaS), has changed the way in which software is distributed. In SaaS, applications are no longer purchased (unlike its predecessor, software on premises) but consumed; small- and medium-sized companies afford top-end applications, paying software vendors (SaaS providers) for the use.

In this context, another paradigm—multitenancy (MT)—has become a key technology for the success of SaaS [2–4]. In MT, clients reduce the cost of software use by sharing expenditures, whereas software vendors maximize sales profits by reaching larger markets. MT architectures (MTAs) allow multiple customers (i.e., tenants) to be aggregated into the same application. Tenants share not only the application, but also capital and operational expenses [5].

Agility has been widely advocated in the past few years as a development philosophy that improves efficiency in software construction [6]. Most agility methods and techniques focus on the organization of the members in software teams and the extensive adoption of demonstrated software engineering best practices, such as code refactoring. *Agilists* consider software architecture something "evil" from the past, a bad habit that only carries tons of documentation, big up-front design, and you ain't gonna need it (YAGNI) [7].

However, in the cloud multitenant situation, where easy scalability is key, architectures supporting agility and rapid provisioning become critical. In SaaS, MT applications demand has to be supported by architectural styles that allow rapid subscription configuration. MTAs need to provide an "administrative framework that improves management efficiency for administering the system" [5]. Cloud SaaS architectures should not be considered evil but as helpful tools and assets for agile teams.

According to Liu [8], "the adoption of SaaS is growing and evolving in the enterprise application markets." SaaS includes all kinds of software applications: customer relationship management (CRM), enterprise resource planning (ERP), content management systems (CMSs), and document management systems (DMSs), among others. In traditional SaaS MT systems, each MT application usually deploys a single functionality and is shared among tenants with similar functional needs. In this regard, we could call actual MT applications *monotarget* because they target a single area in the spectrum of potential clients.

We previously introduced a proposal for improving MTAs, called multitenancy multitarget (MT^2) [9]. This novel architecture adds new components to an underlying MT foundation to support multiple functionalities. In this chapter, we illustrate how MT^2 fosters deployment (since just one system is needed to support multiple services) and aim to support agility in development by avoiding unnecessary replications; customers in turn reduce learning effort because one application is needed to cover all services. The applicability and benefits of the proposal are illustrated through a real MT^2 system called Globalgest [10,11], which is currently in service.

This chapter is organized as follows. First, a definition of cloud computing and its services is provided. Second, we go deeper into MT and explain the general model of this architectural pattern. Third, we discuss agility in SaaS MT applications and the recent discussion to combine traditional agile software development with architecture. Fourth, the proposal is introduced and is followed by the presentation of a real MT^2 implementation (Globalgest). Finally, conclusions and future work are summarized.

11.2 **CLOUD COMPUTING**

The National Institute of Standards and Technology defines cloud computing as "a model for enabling ubiquitous, convenient, on-demand network access to a shared pool of configurable computing resources (e.g., networks, servers, storage, applications, and services) that can be rapidly provisioned and released with minimal management effort or service provider interaction" [12].

In other words, cloud computing means the use of computer resources at different levels over a *cloud*. A cloud is a datacenter providing computing infrastructure (hardware and software) and accessed over the Internet. This way, companies are able to migrate their IT infrastructure, reducing capital and operational expenses. Depending on the organizations operating on the infrastructure, clouds can be classified into private, community, public, or hybrid [12]. Services consumed by customers over a cloud are called *cloud services*, and can be organized in three levels [4,12,13]:

– *Software as a Service (SaaS)*: Consumption of software applications deployed in the cloud. Platform and infrastructure are transparent to users.
– *Platform as a Service (PaaS)*: Capacity to deploy applications into the cloud. Customers do not control lower-level computing resources, such as operating systems or network.
– *Infrastructure as a Service (IaaS)*: Provision of storage, computing, network, and other primary computing resources.

Though this classification of cloud services seems to be agreed in literature, there is still no common understanding on the definition of cloud computing. In Berkeley's definition [1,14], cloud computing is considered the sum of *utility computing* and SaaS, and does not include private clouds. Utility computing [15] refers to the use of computer resources on demand. This way, Berkeley considers IaaS a utility computing service, whereas PaaS is halfway between cloud computing and utility computing.

In SaaS, companies are no longer owners of the applications, but subscribers to them. According to Ref. [16], "The basic long-term vision of SaaS is centered around separating software possession and ownership from its use." Unlike its predecessor, *Software on Premises*, applications are now installed in a cloud and accessed over the Internet; users are not owners of the software any more, but consumers of web applications.

Previous attempts to migrate application provisioning to the cloud have failed. In ASP (application service provider), applications were also deployed over a network instead of being executed on local servers. However, in this model, clients would not benefit from cost reduction since servers where private and used only by their owner companies. SaaS, on the other hand, is focused on exploiting economies of scale by consolidating several customers onto the same operational system. Companies afford top-quality enterprise applications, while providers maximize sales profits targeting the market of small- and medium-sized companies. Among other reasons, ASP failed because it did not even contemplate the possibility of serving different companies using the same software instance [17] or the ability to provide customized applications [18].

11.3 MULTITENANCY ARCHITECTURES

MT is an architectural pattern for SaaS applications that permits several customers (tenants) to share the same instance of the software [19]. A tenant is an organizational unit that pays for the use of the SaaS application on a regular basis (according to the subscription contract). One tenant might consist of many end-users, therefore MT applications might also be multi-users; we will call *tenancy* the set of users of one tenant that run the same customized version of the application instance. The number of instances running in a multitenant environment might be more than one, resulting in a MT farm. This situation could occur not only because of performance issues (some tenants might get greedy on computer resources), but also because of country legislations stating the obligation to store data within country borders [20].

The multitenant model is considered an essential characteristic for cloud computing and its software delivery model [4,12]. Salesforce.com, one of the most popular cloud providers, states [3]: "hosting models that do not offer the leverage of MT do not belong in the same discussion as the value proposition implied by the term SaaS." Chong, in his article *Architecture Strategies for Catching the Long Tail* [2], believes three attributes are to be considered in a good SaaS application architecture: scalability, configurability, and multitenant efficiency.

The use of metadata in multitenant applications lets tenants customize the system within the tenancy in three different levels: database model, user interface, and business logic. This way, MT seems to be transparent for customers giving the impression that they are running a dedicated instance of the application. Customization and security rely on the model chosen to store data. Several authors have proposed different approaches [5,21–23]. Though using different terminology, they all agree that the distinction is given by the level of isolation on tenant's data.

Basically, MTA models have two tiers: administrative and instance. The administrative tier [5] provides the functionalities responsible for rapid account management, while the instance tier hosts the applications that tenants execute according to subscription contracts defined at the administrative level. In Figure 11.1, the multitenant master panel (MTMP) represents the administrative level to control a farm with four application instances.

In a MT farm, the MTMP must ensure system performance is balanced and have the capability to move or scale out tenants to (new) servers of the farm. This component stores data in the administrative database.

Figure 11.2 details the instance level of the architecture. The lower level tiers perform changes dictated by the business layer in both the multitenant database

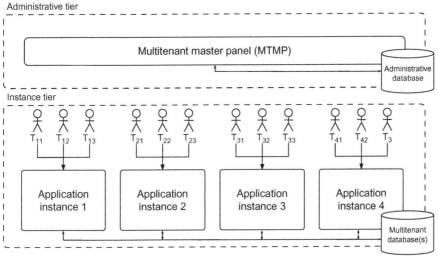

FIGURE 11.1

Administrative and instance tiers in an MT environment.

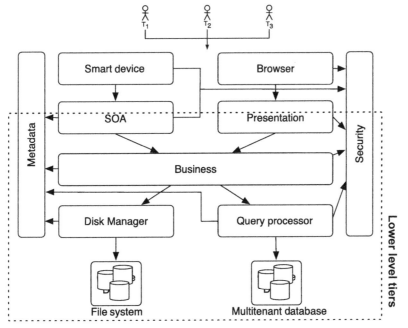

FIGURE 11.2

Multitenant architecture detailed: instance tier.

and file system. Intermediate layers, such as presentation or Service-Oriented Architecture (SOA) services, communicate with browsers and smart devices respectively to produce end-users' output. Metadata are responsible for system customization so that tenants can get a specific user experience. This customization includes data model extension, adaptation of the presentation layer to corporative image, and business workflow personalization. Security services must be present in all multiuser systems. In multitenant environments, the complexity of this component increases; systems must maintain privacy not only among end users, but also among different tenants.

11.4 AGILITY AND MULTITENANT ARCHITECTURES

The term *agile* has been long used in software development to refer to a set of methods following the guidelines established in *The Agile Manifesto* [24]. This manifesto states four basic values:

- Individuals and interactions over processes and tools
- Working software over comprehensive documentation
- Customer collaboration over contract negotiation
- Responding to change over following a plan

Agile software development is a philosophy that separates radically from traditional methods of development, like the waterfall model. Focused more on team organizations, agile methodologies like Scrum [25] or Xtreme Programming [26] have a reputation of paying little attention to software architecture [27]. Support of teams through certain validated software assets, from development frameworks to architectural designs that foster reuse and make development easier, seems to have been disregarded so far.

The concept of architecture, involving big up-front design and YAGNI, has terrorized agile teams that fear to end up sunken under a massive pile of documentation. Proponents of agility think that that architecture should emerge gradually in every sprint; they *embrace the change* and prefer adaptive systems instead of the use of predefined architectures that limit the system evolution. However, as well as these claims, agile methods strive to deliver working and valuable software early and often to clients. If so, it would be worthy to start from a proven and supportive architecture rather than starting from scratch. In cloud MT systems, other issues, such as rapid deployment, may be complementary to agile philosophy; there should be a fast change to the system so as to accommodate potential tenants in as short a period of time as possible. In this regard, architecture should not be doomed as a forbidden non-agile malpractice.

Recently, prominent authors from the system and software engineering communities have claimed and advocated in favor of coexistence between agile and architecture [28–30]. According to Ref. [7], "certain classes of system, ignoring architectural issues too long, 'hit a wall' and collapse by lack of an architectural focus." In Ref. [30], Madison talks about *agile architecture* as a combination of these two streams; this work gives the architect an essential role and indicates that this new architectural direction should include a wide range of options instead of a closed solution.

SaaS MTAs seek to leverage economies of scale due to software instance sharing among tenants, whatever the kind of application deployed. Literature has not yet covered how this architecture may support or even be Agile-compatible.

MTAs and other technologies, like software product line engineering (SPLE) [31], may support agility with complementary issues (e.g., rapid deployment, quality, and time-to-market). As seen in Figure 11.1, the MTMP component is responsible for accounts creation; clients can be registered in the system and ready to access the application within minutes. These two sides are not incompatible; they just are different, and can be combined together.

According to Ref. [32], "Agility is the ability to rapidly and cost-effectively adapt to market and environmental aspects." This affirmation, originally applied to SPLE, can be perfectly extended to SaaS MT applications. In SPLE, new modifications are made to artifacts to cope with new requirements of the market; these artifacts are used in the platform so that new versions of the products satisfy them. In MT, with just one application instance (except in cases of a MT farm), propagation of change is almost instantaneous. Moreover, changes are carried out over existing working development projects rather than from scratch.

To sum up, MT not only tries to provide cost reduction for clients and maximization of provider profits, but also aims to support agility claims in different ways by:

- Deployment because clients are rapidly registered into the system.
- Maintenance and scalability when new requirements are needed.
- Development since changes are not made from scratch.

Architectures that aim to support agility are key in this new SaaS paradigm; without the rapid and effective management or ease of upgrade that MTAs provide, SaaS would be doomed to failure like ASP.

11.5 MULTITENANCY MONOTARGET: AGILITY CHALLENGES

The market that SaaS applications serve on demand is vast. Companies willing to change their traditional on-premises software will find their corresponding application in the cloud. CRMs, ERPs, CMSs, DMSs or even *vertical specialized* [33] systems, like a real estate CRM [34], are served on demand by SaaS providers and can be subscribed to within minutes.

Traditionally, current multitenant applications deploy a single functionality or are aimed to serve a specific line-of-business (*LOB*). A company needing a CRM will compare among those providers in the market serving CRM applications and subscribe to the one that best fits its needs. If this same company would need a CMS or ERP, it would probably end up subscribing to another SaaS vendor offering those services on demand (see Figure 11.3a).

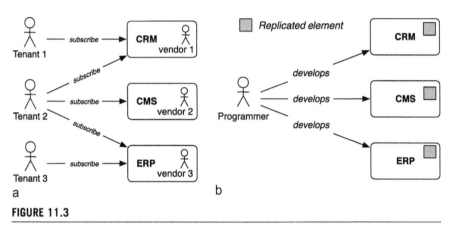

FIGURE 11.3

(a) Subscriptions depend on functional needs. (b) Replication of common development components.

With this model, where the market has different applications for different functionalities, companies have to subscribe to as many applications as the services they need. In traditional MT, tenants share not only application instances, but also the functionality deployed. We could say that actual multitenancy is *monotarget*; vendors will have to develop new software applications if they want to target potential clients from other LOBs or with different functional needs.

Many of these multitenant applications could share common lower development components in their architecture. Database connectors, user authentication, or general user interface components (graphics, style sheets, etc.) among others, might be the same in any SaaS application whether it is for a CRM, CMS, or ERP. However, as shown in Figure 11.3b, all these common components are to be replicated over all these different implementations.

In terms of agility, replication means losing valuable time. During the development process, programmers will have to duplicate and adapt/reconnect components over implementations; vendors serving different applications will have to manage different MTMPs with duplicated records of the same multisubscribed customers; moreover, customers in turn will have bigger learning effort required as different applications need to be learned and used.

11.6 SUPPORTING AGILITY: MULTITENANCY MULTITARGET

MT^2 is a proposal to extend MTAs that allows multiple functionalities to be offered in the same operational system. The main idea behind MT^2 is reusability of common MT components. Several MT applications are grouped into a single MT^2 system and used as assets to meta-generate customized service applications for clients. In MT^2, just one application instance is needed to manage different functionalities.

Subscription determines the service(s) and therefore the functionalities to be deployed during execution time.

MT^2 achieves reusability (and thus supports agility) by removing useless replication of common features. In multitenancy monotarget, functionalities are deployed in different applications; hence components are replicated. In multitarget, shared components are reutilized among all functionalities; cloud agile teams could boost deployment, since just one application is needed to host many functionalities.

This way, applications are distributed among tenants with different functional needs and vendors can host tenants from heterogeneous market sectors. This multifunctional situation seeks several benefits as follows:

– Companies are able to subscribe to only one SaaS MT^2 application, speeding up the learning process (Figure 11.4a, Tenant 2).
– Vendors have a multitarget market (Figure 11.4a, Vendor 1), broadening the spectrum of potential customers and making subscriber's management faster thanks to the *multitarget master panel* (MTMP).
– Developers in turn avoid unnecessary replications, and therefore reduce time-to-market (see Figure 11.4b).

To this end, new components are added to the traditional MTA (Figure 11.2). Figure 11.5 represents the model of MT^2A with those new components with a thicker edge. These components enhance traditional MTAs, giving the ability to execute different functionalities depending on a tenant's contract. Applications therefore could be completely different among tenants; this meta-application profile of MT^2 involves changes in both administrative and instance tiers.

In addition to traditional MT duties, this multiservice profile implies new commitments. These novel features try to support agility and are described in the next subsections.

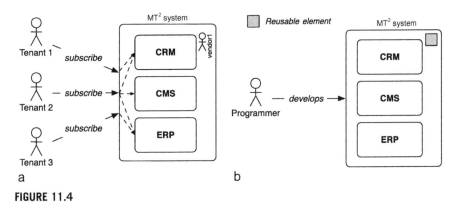

FIGURE 11.4

(a) MT^2 systems allow tenants to subscribe to multiple functionalities while providers manage one MT^2MP. (b) Reusability of common resources in MT^2.

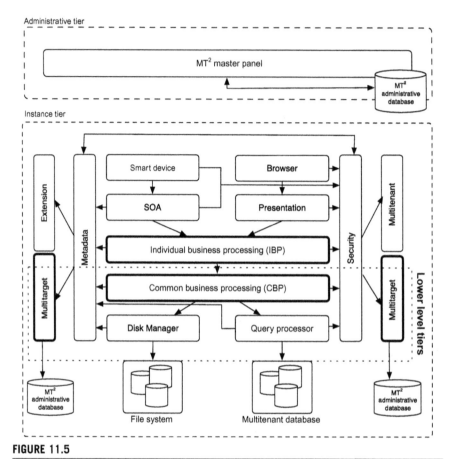

FIGURE 11.5

MT² architecture model.

11.6.1 Functional portfolio management

The set of functionalities deployed in an MT² system is called the *functional portfolio*. The number of functionalities in the portfolio may differ depending on vendor. MT² systems seek scalability not only at the tenant level, but also at the functional level. New MT² systems may deploy just a few features, but can increase the portfolio over time. Previous MT² systems are supposed to have larger functional portfolios, since new functionalities are added on customers' demands and remain on the portfolio, unless outdated. The MT²MP must support the creation, addition, or deletion of functionalities in the portfolio.

11.6.2 Multitarget metadata (MT² metadata)

Multitarget metadata links tenants' accounts not to only functionalities subscribed to by tenants, but also to contractual features of this relationship. For instance, if a tenant wants to subscribe to *SMS* functionality, we should at least set the number of text

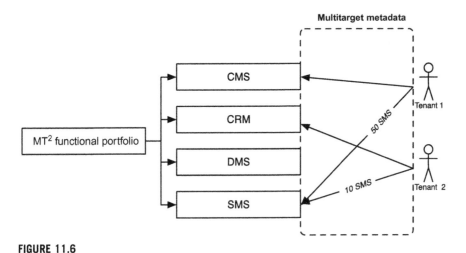

FIGURE 11.6

Multitarget metadata contains subscription details and contractual features for each tenant.

messages contracted; setting this parameter in other functionalities, such as *client management*, does not make sense. Every subscription to functionalities has its own conditions, and these are reflected in the multitarget metadata of each tenant.

Subscriptions to functionalities are defined by multitarget metadata. Figure 11.6 shows an example of an MT^2 system with four functionalities in the portfolio and two tenants. In this case, Tenant 1 is subscribed to CMS and SMS, whereas Tenant 2 has contracted CRM and SMS; as we see, relationship to SMS is present in both tenancies using MT^2 metadata, but the number of text messages to be sent differs.

With this extension, vendors can have all their SaaS applications unified. To this end, they need to configure an MT^2 system with a functional portfolio including all previously deployed functionalities. Clients from different applications are to be registered in the MT^2MP, setting up a subscription linking the functionality from the previous monotarget SaaS application. This centralization improves agility in deployment; just one multitarget master panel is needed to control all clients and applications (now as functionalities in the MT^2 system). MT^2 systems can be scaled with tenants with changing functional needs; resource optimization is easier to achieve with the consequent reduction of costs. Vendors and customers can leverage this unification not only for an even more attractive price, but also because the new set of functionalities offered could be deployed within minutes by means of the MT^2MP.

11.6.3 **Business process reutilization**

Reusability of common features along all functionalities is the main cause of this MT^2 extension. In a multitarget environment, business layers are divided into:

– *Common Business Processing (CBP)*: It includes those elements that are business-independent and reusable across all functionalities.

– *Individual Business Processing* (*IBP*): It includes those elements that are business-dependent and which are specifically designed to support one functionality.

During the execution timeline of their application instances, all tenants will import CBP elements statically; however, IBP elements will be imported dynamically depending on tenants' subscriptions. In Figure 11.7, a tenant has a subscription to functionalities F2 and F4. In this case, all CBP components are imported statically. However, in the dynamic IBP selection for importation, just F2 and F4 components will be included. Security services will check subscription and will confirm that only these two functionalities are to be deployed during execution.

As mentioned above, CBP represents all those components reused in different functionalities; agility in development is reached due to reusability. Features such as privacy or system authentication are no longer to be developed in future functionalities; they are already in the CBP layer. Furthermore, development effort is reduced not only because of reutilization of CBP elements, but also for their extension. For instance (see Figure 11.8), if a programmer needs to develop a specific feature and

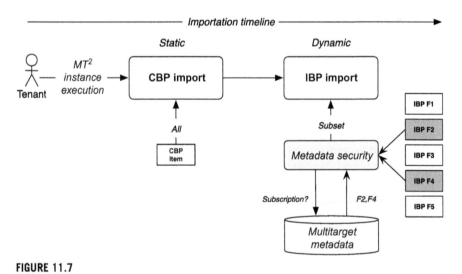

FIGURE 11.7

Static and dynamic import in MT².

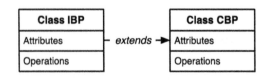

FIGURE 11.8

Agility in development for extension of CBP classes.

encapsulate it within a class; that class does not need to be developed from the beginning; it can be coded by extending one existing class from the CBP layer.

11.6.4 **Multitarget security**

MT^2 environments deploy different functionalities depending on tenants' subscriptions; tenants share applications, but functional deployment may differ. In this situation, security components become more complex in architecture, since end users are allowed to execute those functionalities present in the subscription and not others. Multitarget involves new guarantees for the security layer at two levels:

– *Tenant level*: Tenants should not deploy functionalities that are not included in subscription. Security must ensure that forbidden functionalities are not deployed.
– *End-user level*: MT applications are multiuser environments at instance level. Tenants end-users have different roles that determine their capabilities in the system. In MT^2, tenants may have a subscription to a certain functionality, but not all the tenancy should have access to it. Admin users of the tenancy must have the capability to decide for each user what functionalities to deploy from the tenant portfolio. For instance, a company could have a subscription to accounting and agenda functionalities; however, leaking of important financial data is not desirable, so accounting functionality could be hidden from certain users of the tenancy for security reasons.

11.7 **GLOBALGEST: A REAL MT^2 SYSTEM**

Globalgest [10,11] is an example of a business-oriented application based on MT^2 architecture. It has been implemented by 21 companies and deploys more than 100 functionalities. Combinations of this portfolio allow Globalgest to serve businesses from different industries, such as a medical clinic or an IT company, by choosing different functional subscriptions for them [35].

Globalgest is a single application that serves companies from different industries without duplicating development efforts. MT^2 architecture allows Globalgest to deploy and host several functionalities configuring a client's functional subscription on demand.

Rapid provisioning is key in Globalgest; customers require a fast response that is reached thanks to the administrative level of the architecture—the MT^2 master panel.

Setting up a new client account in Globalgest is easy and entails only a few steps. Once logged into the system as an MT^2 administrator, a user will be able to access the administrative level. As seen in Figures 11.9 and 11.10, this process is quite simple:

1. Open the MT^{2}MP
2. Click on *Insert new account*
3. Fill in tenant details: Contact, billing, shipping

FIGURE 11.9

MT²MP: inserting new account.

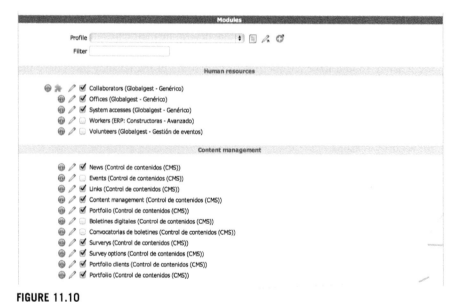

FIGURE 11.10

Functional selection in the MT²MP.

4. Set subscription details:

4.1 Expiration and method of payment

4.2 Create admin user for the tenancy

4.3 Set functionalities desired by the customer by just clicking on the check fields

The agility with which this operation can be performed is very noticeable; tenants can be registered within minutes. Steps 1-4.3 might be common to other monotarget applications, but the main difference and benefit that MT² provides to Globalgest is in Step 4.3. In this phase, clients are registered with a personalized service by choosing the functionalities desired (Figure 11.10). In traditional MT, this possibility is not present, because it is monofunctional; therefore, customers with different functional requirements might be registered in as many MT applications as functional needs.

The major advantage of Globalgest against their MT competitors is multiservice, and therefore the agility, in providing different services with just one software instance. Subscribing to an ERP or a CRM can be a difficult decision. However, that might not be the case for other, less important functionalities (CMS, for instance). Clients can be registered with a set of these simpler functionalities and once they get used to the interface and have passed the learning curve, they will more likely step forward and upgrade their subscription to more complex functionalities. In contrast, for the Globalgest vendor this upgrade operation is just a click away thanks to the MT^{2}MP.

Furthermore, Globalgest has a functional portfolio that can increase its number of functionalities with time. As these new features are incorporated into the system, tenants can upgrade their subscription—either because these new functionalities complement others already contracted, or because they are newly interested. In any case, the Globalgest vendor is one step ahead of its competitors again.

As explained before, in Globalgest, functionalities do not need to be developed from scratch. The MT^2 architecture allows developers to achieve agility in development because common components over functionalities are reused and not replicated. Programmed with PHP as its server language and MySQL as its database engine, the CBP layer includes these main classes:

- *SQLConnector.php*: Database processing and query management
- *HTMLCreator.php*: Creation of HTML data (tables, inputs, forms, dialogs, etc.)
- *Controller.php*: Security and the tenant's privacy
- *FileConnector.php*: File system access
- *WSConnector.php*: Responsible for SOA

During execution time in all functionalities, these classes are instantiated and developers can make use of them instead of reprogramming. If new specific programming is needed for the functionality, new IBP classes can be encoded; unlike MT applications, these new classes can be encoded extending existing CBP classes.

Figure 11.11 shows a real example of how a CPB class (*HTMLCreator*) is extended for specific purposes in SMS functionality. In this example, a new popup

```
1   <?
2
3   class h_sms extends HTMLCreator{
4
5
6       function sin_sms(){
7           global $t;
8           $html = $this->img("128.png",NULL,"",WWWBASE."modulos/sms/img/iconos/");
9           $html.="<br/>".$t->get("error_no_telefonos_sms");
10          return $this->popup($html);
11
12      }
13
14  }
15
16
17  ?>
```

FIGURE 11.11

CBP class extension.

FIGURE 11.12

Popup generated when trying to use SMS functionality in Globalgest.

(Figure 11.12) will appear to the user when trying to text a person with no numbers on its record.

Agility becomes especially critical when the company that owns the software lacks human resources. For very small IT companies, MT's support for agility is not enough. MT^2 provides not only rapid deployment, but also agility for development and eases the general management of the system. Multitarget applications like Globalgest can serve dozens of tenants with just one system administrator.

11.8 RELATED WORK

Some similarities can be seen to SPLE [31,36] due to reusability of common components. However, SPLE involves obtaining personalized software products from the platform, whereas MT^2 just uses the same components running in the same software instance. In MT^2, reusability takes place during execution time, whereas SPLE reuses the artifacts during development. Moreover, with MT^2, services deployed for a customer could change by just modifying the functional contract; in SPLE, a product cannot be changed once it has been released from the platform.

Salesforce.com [37] is another SaaS platform offering different functionalities that can be subscribed to piecewise. However, to the best of our knowledge, no underlying architectural models of this multifunctional architecture or evidence of their existence have been provided (i.e., it is not clear if Salesforce.com has a core architecture and, if so, how it evolves). The novelty of this approach is the extension from traditional MTA to MT^2A where the CBP elements are key for software reuse.

Fink and Markovich [33] explain three different verticalization strategies for IT development companies. Horizontal strategies are general solutions suitable for many sectors that potentially appeal to most or all market users. Vertical strategies are tailored products designed specifically for one sector. Small and medium business (SMB) companies choose this strategy due to its capacity limitations, whereas large, specialized companies may develop many vertical solutions to different markets, adopting a multivertical strategy. MT^2 breaks this limitation to SMB companies, since with just one application instance they are able to manage not only multiple customers, but also multiple targets. Contribution is for a cloud multitenant environment, where sharing is key. A vertical solution could be better for just one client and one project, but not for the SaaS model. MT^2 tries to go a step further and use the same application for clients with different needs.

Zaidman [20] proposes an architecture model for MT SaaS applications to avoid maintenance problems. It defines the key characteristics in MT and explains opportunities in SaaS MT applications, like zero-downtime or security, but does not consider coexistence of different business logics for the same system, which MT^2 does.

Kr et al. [38] presented a backend customization approach for MT SaaS applications. Extensibility and customization of database models is well understood, and there are many approaches. In contrast, personalization of user interfaces and especially business logic models is still a challenge. This approach is related to customization of the business logic, but within the same functionality for all tenants. It does not consider multifunctionality.

Banks et al. [39] introduced a conceptual prototype, called Fractal, which is an application for collaboration among tenants within an MT environment. It explores the key requirements for creating a collaborating platform. In subsequent versions of MT^2, we will try to study possible controlled collaborations among tenants.

In Ref. [40], a framework for reengineering applications to support MT is explained. It does not consider multiservice provisioning.

11.9 CONCLUSIONS AND FUTURE WORK

Cloud computing and its new software delivery model (SaaS) are increasingly being adopted for current software vendors. SaaS has become a common software distribution formula for users [41]; according to Ref. [42], SaaS revenue is expected to reach nearly 5 billion dollars. The adoption of SaaS is just a matter of time, if it has not been already done.

MT is a key feature and an essential characteristic in cloud computing. MT architectures allow SaaS applications to aggregate users into the system on demand, vendors leverage scalability to reduce the general cost of applications, and users afford top-quality implementations: everybody wins.

There is a recent debate on the coexistence between agility and architecture, claiming that these two cultures should not be considered opposite. In cloud environments, architectures supporting claims such as the quick delivery of working software to clients should not be left separate from the agile movement.

Traditionally, applications aim to serve one single purpose, and therefore different purposes involve different applications. MT applications are thereby monotarget, because they target one line of business.

In this chapter, we have presented multitarget as an extension to MTAs. Thanks to the reuse of common features, MT^2 allows traditional monotarget applications to support multiple functionalities and deploy them selectively depending on subscription contract. MT^{2}A is an example of the fruitful combination of agility and architecture, in the sense that it makes possible a rapid delivery of working, multifunctional software to clients by taking advantage of a consolidated and proven (working) software architecture. MT^2 aims to support agility not only for deployment due to unification, but also for development.

Although MT^2 is already implemented in Globalgest, the novelty of this approach opens a big field for further study of this architecture. New challenges are to be overcome and new benefits are to be found. The complexity of the architectural model needs further study and detail—especially in the administrative tier. There are many aspects to be considered when providing a multifunctional service; functionalities, for instance, may be dependent on each other (*appointments* and *agenda* may be dependent to the entities involved, like *clients* or *human resources*). This dependency control should be reflected in the MT^2 architecture.

Benefits in terms of agility should be demonstrated with some empirical/estimated data about development and deployment times and costs and more detailed examples of code and specific pictures are also needed. Besides the benefits, the shortcomings of MT^2, such as application centralization, need to be explained and solved.

The MT^{2}MP can be considered in the range of meta-applications; new tenants can be set up by means of this master panel giving out service-customized applications on demand. We will further study the relationship between MT^2 and the world of meta-applications.

The next step in MT^2 will be called MT$^{2.0}$. The multitarget profile of MT^2 involves providing service to clients from different sectors and lines of business. If these companies from different industries already cooperate daily in the real world, why not do it via networking using multitarget systems? We will deepen the study of networking among tenants; a collaboration that will be reflected by controlled data sharing and interaction among users from different tenancies.

References

[1] Ambrust M, Fox A, Griffith R, Joseph AD, Katz RH, Konwinski A, et al. Above the clouds: A Berkeley view of cloud computing. Berkeley: Dept. Electrical Eng. and Comput. Sciences, University of California; 2009, Rep. UCB/EECS. 28; 2009.

[2] Chong F, Carraro G. Architecture strategies for catching the long tail: what is software as a service? Most. 479069; 2006. p. 1–22.

[3] Coffee P. Busting Myths of On-Demand: Why Multi-Tenancy Matters; 2007. Salesforce. com White Paper, http://wiki.apexdevnet.com/images/0/04/MythbustMultiT.PDF.

[4] Qaisar EJ. Introduction to cloud computing for developers: key concepts, the players and their offerings. In: 2012 IEEE TCF information technology professional conference; 2012. p. 1–6.

[5] Jacobs D, Aulbach S. Ruminations on multi-tenant databases. Fachtagung fur Datenbanksysteme in Business, Technologie und Web (BTW), Aachen, Germany, March 5–9, 2007.

[6] Block M. Evolving to agile: a story of agile adoption at a small SaaS company. In: AGILE conference; 2011. p. 234–9.

[7] Kruchten P. Software architecture and agile software development: a clash of two cultures? In: 2010 ACM/IEEE 32nd international conference on software engineering, Cape Town, South Africa; 2010. p. 497–8.

[8] Liu S, Zhang Y, Meng X. Towards High Maturity in SaaS Applications Based on Virtualization. Int. J. Inform. Syst. Service Sector 2011;3:39–53.

[9] Rico A, Noguera M, Garrido JL, Benghazi K, Chung L. Multi-Tenancy Multi-Target (MT2): A SaaS Architecture for the Cloud. In: Advanced Information Systems Engineering Workshops; 2012. p. 214–27.

[10] Rico A. Desarrollo TIC. SEO, web, and software development, http://www.desarrollotic.com/.

[11] Rico, A. Software de Gestión ERP y CRM en la Nube - Globalgest ERP. (n.d.). Retrieved July 14, 2013, from http://globalgest-saas.com/.

[12] Mell P, Grance T. The NIST definition of cloud computing (draft). NIST special publication 2011;800(145):7.

[13] Vaquero L, Rodero-Merino L. A break in the clouds: towards a cloud definition. ACM SIGCOMM 2008;39(1):50–5.

[14] Armbrust M, Stoica I, Zaharia M, Fox A, Griffith R, Joseph AD, et al. A view of cloud computing. Communications of the ACM 2010;53(4):50. http://dx.doi.org/10.1145/1721654.1721672.

[15] Parkhill DF. Challenge of the computer utility. Reading, MA: Addison-Wesley Educational Publishers; 1966.

[16] Turner M, et al. Turning software into a service. Computer 2003;36(10):38–44.

[17] Liu G, et al. Software design on a SaaS platform. In: 2010 2nd International conference on computer engineering and technology; 2010. p. V4-355–8.

[18] Papazoglou M. Service-oriented computing: concepts, characteristics and directions. In Proceedings of the 7th International Conference on Properties and Applications of Dielectric Materials (Cat. No.03CH37417). IEEE Comput. Soc; p. 3–12. http://dx.doi.org/10.1109/WISE.2003.1254461

[19] Bezemer C, Zaidman A. Challenges of reengineering into multi-tenant SaaS applications: challenges; 2010.

[20] Zaidman A. Multi-tenant SaaS applications: maintenance dream or nightmare? Position paper.

[21] Aulbach S, et al. A comparison of flexible schemas for software as a service. ACME 2009;881–8.

[22] Aulbach S, Grust T, Jacobs D, Kemper A, Rittinger J. Multi-tenant databases for software as a service: In: Proceedings of the 2008 ACM SIGMOD international conference on Management of data - SIGMOD '08. New York, USA: ACM Press; 2008. p. 1195.

[23] Chong F, et al. Multi-tenant data architecture three approaches to managing multi-tenant data architecture. 479086; June 2006. p. 1–18.

[24] Beck K, et al. Manifesto for agile software development, http://agilemanifesto.org/.

[25] Schwaber K, Beedle M. Agile software development with scrum. Englewood Cliffs, NJ: Prentice Hall; 2001.

[26] Beck K. Embracing change with extreme programming. Computer 1999;32(10):70–7. http://dx.doi.org/10.1109/2.796139.

[27] Hanssen GK, Fægri TE. Process fusion: an industrial case study on agile software product line engineering. J Syst Softw 2008;81(6):843–54.

[28] Abrahamsson P, et al. Agility and architecture: can they coexist? IEEE Softw 2010;27 (2):16–22.

[29] Booch G. An architectural oxymoron. IEEE Softw 2010;27(5):96.

[30] Madison J. Agile architecture interactions. IEEE Softw 2010;27(2):41–8.

[31] Pohl K, et al. Software product line engineering: foundations, principles, and techniques. Secaucus, NJ: Springer-Verlag New York Inc; 2005.

[32] Clements P, McGregor J. Better, faster, cheaper: pick any three. Bus Horiz 2012;55 (2):201–8.

[33] Fink L, Markovich S. Generic verticalization strategies in enterprise system markets: an exploratory framework. J Inform Tech 2008;23(4):281–96.

[34] TIC D. NetPropertyAgent—SaaS real estate CRM, http://www.netpropertyagent.com/.

[35] Ortega AR, et al. Multi-tenancy multi-target (MT2): a SaaS architecture for the cloud. In: CAiSE workshops; 2012. p. 214–27.

[36] Clements P, Northrop L. Software product lines. Boston: Addison-Wesley; 2002.

[37] SalesForce.com, http://www.salesforce.com/.

[38] Kr J, et al. Customizing enterprise software as a service applications: back-end extension in a multi-tenancy environment. Work 2009;24(I):66–77.

[39] Banks D, Erickson J, Rhodes M. Multi-tenancy in cloud-based collaboration services. Hewlett-Packard Development Company, LP; 2009. Retrieved from http://www.hpl. hp.com/techreports/2009/HPL-2009-17.pdf.

[40] Almorsy M, Grundy J, Ibrahim AS. SMURF: Supporting Multi-tenancy Using Re-aspects Framework. In: 2012 17th International Conference on Engineering of Complex Computer Systems (ICECCS); 2012. p. 361–70.

[41] Benefield R. Agile deployment: lean service management and deployment strategies for the SaaS enterprise; 2009. p. 1–5.

[42] A worlwide review of SaaS growth, http://www.vi.net/blog/2012/01/a-worlwide-review-of-software-as-a-service-saas-growth/.

Industrial Viewpoints on Agile Architecting

Agile Architecting: Enabling the Delivery of Complex Agile Systems Development Projects

12

Richard Hopkins[*] **and Stephen Harcombe**[†]

[*]*IBM, Cleveland, UK*
[†]*Northwich, Cheshire, UK*

12.1 AGILE AND COMPLEX SYSTEMS DEVELOPMENT APPROACHES NEED TO MERGE AND ADAPT

Architecture is often seen as the antithesis of agile. It constrains choices; it enables a level of complexity and rigor. The designer and developer can't have a free reign to solve a problem in the way that might suit them at the time. It might even spoil their fun. Today's projects that have a strong architectural focus also tend to implement strong software engineering processes, such as Capability Maturity Model Integration (CMMI), and rely on detailed project plans [1].

We believe strongly that this conflict between agile and architecture is a fallacy that has arisen because of an unfortunate and unnecessary polarization of perception in the information technology (IT) industry between agile and plan-driven projects. Agile projects are characterized by a small bubble of fleet-of-foot, savant-led developers interacting directly with end users, whereas plan-driven projects are characterized as a waterfall, heavyweight plans burdened with over-complex architecture. Agile delivers early; plan-driven delivers late, if at all.

The authors have experienced both approaches on large-scale complex IT system development projects and they both have the capability to be unsuccessful.

- To accelerate their progress, the complex agile projects often develop an obstinate myopia to the real world they are deploying into. This can be a deliberate choice to keep things simple and avoid big requirements and design work up front, or it can result from a lack of expensive representative test environments early in the development life cycle. Either way, they then go expensively awry late in their life cycle when catastrophes involving integration or operational requirements manifest themselves (an anti-pattern we call the Agile Bubble).
- In contrast, plan-based projects with exhaustively documented architectures are often so hidebound by process that they take so much time and cash before benefits can be realized that real-world events often overtake them.

In either case, the end result is wasted time and money. This conflation of architecture with heavyweight process is an unnecessary one. So is the myopia of the Agile Bubble. Indeed, we will argue in this chapter that a strong architecture is a prerequisite for using agile on complex systems development projects for the following reasons:

- it reduces costs by providing a necessary guiding vision and structure that obviates the need for heavyweight processes and enables the use of low-cost resources and a lower total cost of ownership (TCO);
- it minimizes rework by solving difficult problems early; and
- it accelerates delivery by widening the full delivery pipeline (not just the development process).

Creating and conforming to architecture to enable these benefits does not necessitate heavyweight process or constraining project plans; a strong architecture will actually obviate the need for such things. This chapter provides guidance on successfully combining agile and architecture to result in the desired speed to market while at the same time ensuring that the broad considerations of any complex IT system delivery are successfully taken into account.

Achieving a necessary balance between process, architecture, and speed to market is critically important. At a time when budgets are squeezed and results are required immediately, it is no surprise that businesses are currently trying to simultaneously apply agile practices *and* low-cost resources to situations where previously only large-scale systems engineering approaches have been tried. Not all are succeeding. This chapter looks at a set of proven mechanisms that can be used to architect a complex agile project in a cost effective manner.

12.1.1 Why do complex system development best practices need to incorporate agile best practices?

The world has changed—we are now part of a global civilization—and the economics of IT projects have changed along with it; the combined accepted wisdom of agile development and complex systems development need to be reevaluated in light of these economically driven changes.

The bar chart in Figure 12.1 shows how the IT industry's almost universal adoption of low-cost, off-shore delivery locations for much of its design, coding, and unit testing needs has resulted in a significant reduction of IT project costs. In general, dramatic savings already have been realized without adapting project life cycles, but the eagle-eyed reader will note that the proportion of the project cost being spent on the coding and unit testing of the solution is a diminished proportion of the whole. To continue reducing the costs of complex system development projects, the focus will naturally switch to requirements, design, governance (including project management), late-stage testing, and deployment; there is little to be gained by further streamlining development itself.

Efficient projects should not assume a comprehensive requirement or design phase up front; this will be seen as prohibitively expensive, and such effort must be focused on and targeted to areas of risk. Nor is there the budget to fund large numbers of duration-based roles over an extended period to govern and apply complex governance or processes. Standard complex systems development approaches need to adapt to become more agile. Agile provides a way to achieve many of these cost reduction elements, but strong architecture is needed to provide the necessary control and direction that is otherwise sacrificed.

By focusing on a strong architecture and effective technical governance and exploiting the latest collaborative technologies (Rational Team Concert being one such example), we can make these expensive "overhead" elements as small as possible without jeopardizing delivery. As this chapter shows, this requires:

- a shift in emphasis to consider the whole delivery life cycle, not just agile development;
- new levels of cooperation between technicians at all stages of the delivery life cycle.

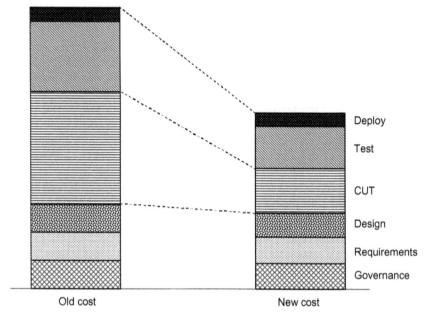

FIGURE 12.1

Comparison of overall costs between two complex agile development projects of the same size before and after the introduction of off-shore development capability; the code and unit testing elements (CUT) of the cost are significantly reduced.

In today's economic climate, delivering value as quickly as possible is far more valuable than delivering an optimal or gold-plated solution later than it is needed. The old adage of "Better 80% on time and budget than 100% late" has never been more relevant.

Agile delivery, where business-case–led increments can be delivered in stages, is therefore hugely important to meet the business need of faster delivery. However, to also meet the economic imperative of being low cost, this approach will also need to:

- maximize off-shoring;
- reduce the reliance on artisan developers;
- reduce project management costs;
- optimize for testing rather than build (testing is now by far the more expensive aspect of the complex project).

12.1.2 Why do complex system development projects need architecture?

Agile is all too often seen and portrayed as a mechanism for accelerating the delivery of a system, but clearly agile development practices only address part of that journey. For large-scale developments, however, it is difficult to maintain the acceleration that agile promises without introducing architecture as a necessary prerequisite to the project. This is because agile on its own is limited by the nature of its core processes. The client workshops and multi-skilled teams must be kept small, and adding more people into the teams simply slows them down; this means that it is nigh-on impossible to include all the perspectives and skills that need to be represented in a complex environment within a relatively self-contained team without causing stakeholder overload or a surfeit of people with specialist capabilities.

This chapter considers why architecture is a vital part of enabling large scale, complex, agile delivery and provides what practical steps need to be taken to ensure success without burdening a project with heavyweight deliverables or laborious procedures.

Establishing the right mindset is important; there needs to be just enough architecture, and no more.

12.2 IDENTIFYING THE RIGHT AMOUNT OF ARCHITECTURE

The authors are not great fans of the TOGAF/Visio/hand-waving school of IT architects who depart from projects long before fingers touch keyboards to write code. Such architects often create beautiful architectures with so many layers of abstraction that they make filo pastry look like suet. These are the fluffy, ivory tower brigade. Their desire to document every perspective and rigorously follow process is one of the reasons why architecture is often identified as anti-agile and suggests that any attempt to establish a useful architecture is bad practice. Architecture becomes condemned by the term "big design up front."

It is important to realize, however, that lead architects on a large agile project need to bring something vital to the system that a senior developer often cannot. That is the trained ability to look at the problem being addressed from a number of different perspectives.

Each business problem is different and will require multiple viewpoints to capture its unique aspects. It is the architect's job to work out which perspectives are architecturally significant for this particular problem and incrementally document them. The traditional eight perspectives are data, function, infrastructure, and integration with separate diagrammatic standards for the dynamic (behavior) and static (structural) aspects. But within each of these eight core areas, there are diagrams that deliberately span these viewpoints (e.g., the Unified Modelling Language (UML) deployment diagram) or document them at different levels of abstraction (e.g., UML class, component and composite structure diagrams). Selecting the right communications vehicle to incrementally describe the essential concepts of the problem and its solution to all of the relevant stakeholders is the key skill of the architect. Agilely inclined architects will ask hard (sometimes seemingly dumb) questions and only document those perspectives that are required for an essential understanding; they will steadfastly resist the non-Agile tradition of lengthily documenting all viewpoints because most will be uninteresting.

Taking inspiration from Barry Boehm's iterative spiral method [2] from the late 1980s, we would recommend that any large project starts with a risk-based analysis up front to identify and isolate areas of known complexity and perform some proactive engineering and coding to form a harness for an agile development to iterate on top of.

For each of the selected important perspectives, it is vital for the architect to decide how the most risky aspects of each important perspective will be *tested* as early as possible in the project life cycle. Initially, that is done by describing at a conceptual level (ideally diagrammatically) the problem and proposed solution for that area.

Sometimes a problem/solution pair will be arrived at via harvesting ideas or aspects from existing systems or even selecting commercial-off-the-shelf (COTS) software for particular areas. Sometimes it will be by identifying the architecturally significant stories or use cases and ensuring they are implemented early. In some cases, specific effort will need to be expended to create technical prototypes (see later in this chapter).

Once this is conceptually described, the architect can decide with the agile team leads how it will be tested. Testing does not necessarily need to be dynamic execution of final code; static testing or simulations are equally valid methods. However, the aim should be to reduce risk by testing as realistically as possible or affordable.

Once this process of early proving is mapped out (and a simple dependency picture will do nicely) the agile architect must stick around. The architect's vision must become a shared vision, so it will need to morph as unexpected problems arise or unforeseen changes become necessary.

We often see the view espoused that on agile projects the architect is part of the team rather than an isolated and remote figure, and with this we wholeheartedly agree [3]. Lead architects should walk the floors of the delivery and attend as many of the detailed design discussions as they plausibly can. Their job is to ask and answer awkward and difficult questions about their architecture.

Above all else, short stand-up "Hill Street Blues" meetings first thing every morning ("Let's be careful out there") are vital to ensure communication is flowing and priorities are set correctly.

However, an architect who wants to please everyone is no use to anyone (good architecture and design is always a successful example of usually unpopular but occasionally serendipitous tradeoffs). They must achieve a strong and benevolent dictatorship where they are prepared to delegate lower-level decisions with the faith that their overarching guidance will not be ignored. Without a strong lead architect and architecture, process will flow into the gaps formed by uncertainty, slowing progress and increasing the likelihood of either decision paralysis or the formation of islands of secession. The agile architect must also be prepared to change their mind in the light of overwhelming evidence (though not necessarily opinion) that they are wrong.

Having established this lightweight, agile architecture definition, the complex, agile, architected development project can now realize a number of benefits when compared to more conventional agile projects, including:

- Reduce costs by:
  - Enabling the use of off-shore design and development;
  - Considering TCO from the start.

- Minimize rework by:
  - Exercising reasonable foresight;
  - Commissioning prototypes.
- Widen the full delivery pipeline to accelerate delivery by:
  - Maximizing capacity;
  - Enabling early integration;
  - Enabling continuous "all phase" integration and testing;
  - Automating deployment.

12.3 COST REDUCTION THROUGH ARCHITECTURE

On our complex, agile, system development projects, we use the minimal architectural elements identified above to reduce the overall costs of the system; this includes the following:

- Enabling the use of off-shore development;
- Considering the TCO of the solution.

12.3.1 Reduce costs by enabling the use of off-shore development

We have found that the traditional "us and them" approach to off-shoring, where a specification is passed from one agile requirements and design team in one geographic location (usually colocated with the end users) to a different development team (usually in a low-cost development location), does not work for complex agile software developments. In such circumstances, organizational boundaries and different time zones often ensure that communication is too weak to deliver effectively.

For complex agile system development projects, we have identified that the most successful approach is a single team where the organizational structure for all stages of the life cycle is managed by one organization (whether on-shore or off-shore). This is a cultural and organizational change from most prior implementations of development off-shoring, but has proven to be hugely successful. It requires the following:

- A single organization whose structure is functionally driven and is entirely location independent;
- The same functional elements to be present in all locations (though different proportions may occur at each location);
- The same standards, processes and tools at each location;
- A single management team that is location independent with a single global leader (ideally someone from the off-shore location based on-shore, or vice versa);
- Willingness by senior executives to tour all locations equally and provide business context and vision to the work that is being performed;

- A single mechanism to break down, distribute, and track work across the organization that is also transparent to location (a set of collaborative application life cycle management tools, such as Rational Team Concert, Requirements Composer, or Quality Manager).

This approach can lead to some interesting anomalies—for example, security-based testing traditionally used for repatriation of code is applied equally to all code irrespective of who wrote it or in which location. The costs of such overheads, however, are minor compared to the overall benefit of a low-cost delivery organization that does not suffer from the many pitfalls of an "us and them" or "throw it over the wall" culture.

To make use of such an organization to exploit agile best practices, we have found that a strongly architected, coherent, loosely coupled solution is a necessary prerequisite. In the next section, we discuss the strengths that such architectures bring to a large-scale, complex, agile project.

12.3.2 Reduce costs by considering Total Cost of Ownership (TCO)

The lead architect on a major agile development does not have the luxury of architecting in a bubble; they must put themselves in place as the custodian of the system over its lifetime. The lifetimes of systems vary, but it is fair to say that the complexity of a system is generally proportionate to its ultimate longevity.

Even for systems that are designed to be tactical, if they are successful and sufficiently challenging to replace, it is quite typical for them to last longer than the technologies that underpin them are in widespread use.

> One "tactical" system I delivered was based on C++ and a thick Java client. It has lasted more than decade after that style of system was regarded as old hat, and the products used to create it have long since passed out of mainstream support. RH

It is therefore important from a cost-reduction perspective that architecture is established that is easy to understand and supports a low TCO.

As we have already seen, the total cost of acquisition of a project today as a function of the whole is constantly reducing. More and more design, application development and testing are being moved to lower-cost, often off-shore locations. It is not quite so straightforward to move application maintenance tasks off-shore, however. Application maintenance often needs to look at the context and data of a problem— and that data might just be personal or sensitive data that cannot, under law, be exported from the originating region or country. Therefore, when looking at software costs, the equation between total cost of acquisition and TCO means that TCO should be regarded as increasingly important. Architecture is a key way of keeping application maintenance costs down; it does so by the following means:

- reducing duplication between systems;
- promoting reuse of existing services;

- standardizing skill sets and tools;
- where possible, reducing the skills required to perform frequent application changes (e.g., enabling the end user to make changes).

The agile architect needs to carefully think through the implications of the development and run-time software that they select: Is it supportable in the longer term? Can I implement that component via an existing service? Am I unnecessarily introducing a specialist skill set?

12.4 MINIMIZE REWORK THROUGH ARCHITECTURE

Rework is a necessary and expected part of the agile life cycle, and the removal of detailed plans and reams of documentation means that such rework costs less. However the degree of rework experienced will tend to increase with the complexity and longevity of the project, so complex agile projects have been known to die under the weight of their own refactoring with each iteration becoming less productive than the previous one. Again, this is one area where the agile architect should focus, heading off problems before they arise.

12.4.1 Minimize rework through reasonable foresight

Agile methods are deliberately silent when it comes to predicting the future; it is generally regarded as a futile activity. The rule is to start simple in terms of both requirement and solution, and to engineer in the necessary levels of complexity as they are discovered. In general this is a good rule; it reduces the ability of the team to over-engineer the solution and make it unnecessarily flexible.

There is an assumption in this approach that software is relatively inexpensive to change, and therefore rework can be easily tolerated. Whilst software is indeed abstract in many senses of the word, fast and cheap change is not always the case. Refactoring a data model that is at the heart of a system can impact tens of thousands of lines of code if the data model is tightly linked to the components that use it. Even in systems where there is loose coupling between layers and components, radical change to a shared component can cause havoc.

One project I was involved in was performing major reengineering of a number of core business systems. The task was known to be difficult and complex and the existing systems had accumulated tens of thousands of function points worth of complexity over the years. Following a pure agile approach would mean that the new systems would be built from the ground up using only as much complexity as was strictly necessary to solve the problem. Occam's razor in action! The project started out well enough by following the simple, happy path scenarios that were relatively trivial in nature. These paths got gradually more complex in terms of the situation being modeled, but a whole dimension of the necessary problem space was held back. This was the need for the system to cope with complex change in the past and then process the forward

Continued

> **Cont'd**
>
> consequences of this change. This was known to be a difficult problem—which is precisely why it was kept to the end of the process.
>
> Unfortunately when the time came to address these new scenarios, right at the end of the development process, it was clear that a wholesale change would be needed to the data model and the way the system worked for it to be able to cope with these more difficult elements. Refactoring is a way of life in agile projects, but even today's deliberately layered architectures find it difficult to adapt to a necessary wholesale change to the underpinning data model of the solution. Huge amounts of rework is required to get the system to cope with its full requirement; unfortunately, by holding off the complex scenarios in this area to the end of the project, a huge amount of risk and unexpected expense was injected right at the end, undermining the good work that had been done to date.
>
> Should a good architecture and well-architected data model have been able to cope with such a problem? Absolutely, it would have done so; at least three good examples of existing data models that could do that were available to the project team right from the start; any of these would have been able to cope with all of the scenarios. In addition, it was not as if this complex requirement was not known from the start; all previous systems had to cope with this requirement and clearly the new one would have to. RH

Building in additional design and build effort for areas of known variability is deeply important; even if traditional agile techniques would suggest leaving the area until last.

As mentioned in the previous section; this decision to deliberately engineer in some variability is one of those viewpoint-based decisions that the architect must make for themselves. The requirement may not yet be defined by an end user story (or may not even be definable by an end user story), but should be based on the balance of probability of need and the cost of the potential over-engineering.

Nearly all aspects of a software development are cheap to change at the beginning of a large project. As code accumulates, some things remain inexpensive to change, whilst others become very expensive. Some examples are given in Table 12.1.

If the architect has identified that the areas that become increasingly expensive are poorly defined at the start of the project, then there is a clear need to extend the design activity to include one or more of:

- technology that will permit later variability;
- the design of an abstraction layer that can help insulate the system from late change;
- the commissioning of a prototype to help refine the requirement.

Making such preparations early in the life cycle avoids costly mistakes and more than justifies the additional time spent in design or development.

12.4.2 Minimize rework via prototypes

One of the key activities that good architects perform to move a project forward is to make reasoned, formal and documented decisions. The design authority of any project should be regarded as the place to make any far-reaching decision on the solution

System Type	**Ability to Change at Any Point in Development at Roughly the Same Cost**	**Increasingly Expensive to Change as Project Development Proceeds**
On-line transaction processing	User interface Reports	Data model Data access layer Underlying frameworks (e.g., J2EE to.NET) Auditing
Data warehouse	Reports Dashboards Data sources	Removing data Response time requirements Changing dimensions Security
Integration gateway	Message payload structures Data model Routing rules	Message header structures Message patterns

Table 12.1 Varying Development Costs by System Type

and should be the preferred route to any external escalation. Of course, on agile projects the lead architect is often asked to make critical decisions when requirements are poorly understood or the cost/benefits of a decision cannot easily be determined.

As already identified, these early decisions are often arranged around the key viewpoints relevant to the problem at hand. For those elements that are identified as the key areas of risk, early mitigations should involve identifying focused solutions and then exploring them via a testable hypothesis.

Some testing is quick and low-cost; static testing of architecture, for example, can be performed via walkthroughs or CRC sessions (recording "Class Name, Responsibilities, Collaborators" for each service defined; see later in this chapter for a very brief overview of the CRC technique), or through more formal evaluations of the architecture, such as the architecture tradeoff analysis method (ATAM) [4].

However, to investigate the most critical of these hypotheses, it is often wise to build prototypes to fully understand the requirement, its implications and, especially in the case of nonfunctional requirements, any necessary tradeoffs. All prototypes should be created with a set of tests and acceptance criteria in mind.

Prototypes do not necessarily involve executable code; CRC sessions can, for example, be used to create low-fidelity prototypes of service operations (and are genuinely disposable!).

Prototypes can be used in almost every situation (user interfaces, system interfaces, technical prototypes, code generators) and at varying levels of fidelity. Higher-fidelity prototypes should be designed in such a way that some reuse is plausible; low-fidelity prototypes should be discarded as the rework to bring them to production strength is likely to be significant.

12.5 ACCELERATE DELIVERY THROUGH ARCHITECTURE

12.5.1 Accelerate the delivery pipeline by incorporating multiple perspectives

One of the frequent issues seen in the implementation of standard agile practices is the Agile Bubble anti-pattern. An anti-pattern is a pattern of behavior that initially appears to be good or best practice, but later turns out to be flawed. The Agile Bubble anti-pattern trades off fast initial progress (that only succeeds by ignoring the real world) for later and much more expensive rework when the outside world impinges on the development project.

As is well known, the cost of fixing a defect rises by a factor of at least ten and sometimes one hundred times between requirements and deployment [5]. Defects discovered late due to the Agile Bubble myopia, usually in integration or operational testing, are therefore very expensive to correct.

As already discussed, one of the best ways to combat such myopia is to identify the key viewpoints that the architecture should be concerned with (for complex problems, a number of linked viewpoints are sometimes required, forming concentric onion rings at different levels of abstraction).

Closely aligned to this idea is the need to capture the context of the solution from varying perspectives and scales. The architect should draw up at least one business and system context for the system under consideration.

The business context should show all the stakeholders that the architect needs to consider. These are not just the run-time business people involved in using the system, but also the operators and its testers. Multiple business contexts may be required, but ensuring complete coverage is important. It is also important to note that the business context should necessarily extend beyond the boundaries of the system context.

For example, in providing a new banking system, it will be necessary to conduct testing of existing business processes where the endpoints are well outside the scope of the new system. Equating the testing scope with the scope of the system is a major mistake and could prevent a speedy go-live until after extensive business-wide regression testing has been completed.

Working on such a business context early will result in two critical enablers for such testing to be identified and commissioned. This is wise, as they are typically costly and time-consuming to produce or source:

- The test environments themselves may well have a wider context than originally envisaged and require access to legacy components and legacy knowledge. Legacy knowledge may be hard to acquire if it is held by people who perceive the introduction of a new solution as a threat to their established skill sets or employment prospects.
- A business process model against which the new regression tests may be prepared and conducted.

It is vitally important that as the project progresses the use case model or user stories also reflect and provide coverage of the key architecturally significant scenarios for these additional stakeholders.

The failure to adequately model testers and operators will lead to omissions in environment specifications and can present a risk to the ability to test or operate aspects of a system or solution at all. Our experience is that incompleteness of the actor model and incomplete architecture in regard to testing and operations have contributed to schedule delay and cost overrun in many agile projects. If, however, the test infrastructure, test system, operational procedures and programs (such as batch and housekeeping) are designed at the same time as the solution components, then the risk of such overruns can be considerably mitigated.

The focus of agile projects on their interface with the business often means that the perspective of the hosting organization is an afterthought. The requirements of the hosting company must be captured and tested as nonfunctional requirements. The Agile Bubble often means this is a blind spot. It is crucial before the start of any agile project that the key target characteristics and constraints of the target system are reasonably well described. Some nonfunctional characteristics need to be part of a design from the start, because retrofitting them to a project is immensely more expensive than having built them in from scratch.

12.5.2 Accelerate delivery by maximizing capacity

In more ways than one, architecture is all about avoiding bottlenecks. In architecture, the term *bottleneck* typically refers to a design problem that is preventing processing from occurring at full speed. In this section, we consider bottlenecks in the delivery life cycle rather than in operations. A good architecture will avoid bottlenecks in both.

Indeed, one of the quickest ways to diagnose the health of a complex agile IT project is to take a look at the architecture, the development team organization and the structure of its iterations. If you can't easily perceive a link between all three that is driven by the architecture, then delivery is unlikely to be smooth. It's not enough for the architect to design the system itself; the organizational structure of development and the development iterations also need to be clearly aligned via the architecture to maximize the chance of successful delivery.

Architecture is all too often seen as a set of documents to be produced for a target system or a way of documenting the desired "to be" state of a set of IT systems. Quite often, such architectures are "ivory tower" architectures that are somewhat removed from the task of building and maintaining a complex system. Those IT system perspectives are not wrong in themselves, but very good architectures are actually about organizing work.

In these days where design, code, and unit testing costs have significantly reduced due to the widespread use of packages, global delivery, powerful frameworks, and productive languages, it is rare to find a situation where a business case *cannot* be made for automation using IT. The only thing that keeps projects mercifully constrained in terms of size is the need for overall deliverability and a desire to reduce the time to market for IT-driven innovations. Projects that are too large take too long to deliver and are more likely to fail.

As a result, the environment in which we increasingly find ourselves is one where complex agile deliveries are constrained primarily by the *development capacity* that can be reliably applied to any given problem and the amount of time available for the delivery. For greater competitive advantage, increasing the development capacity of a system will generally be a good thing, because you can either choose to deliver function to the end user earlier; or provide more function in the same timescales.

That is where architecture steps nobly into the spotlight. Good architecture, especially in complex IT landscapes, allows you to get more heads around the problem—at the expense of additional integration, of course, but this is no bad thing if handled correctly.

Good architecture is all about splitting stuff reliably into self-contained parcels that allow work on them to continue relatively independently in parallel (often these days in different locations). Whilst we find it hard to believe there is an easy "optimal" balance between partitioning and complexity, Roger Sessions argues very convincingly in *Simple Architectures for Complex Enterprises* [6] that strong synergistic partitioning is a necessary mechanism for containing high levels of complexity. His formulas prove that simple iterative partitions that give rise to autonomous business components provide the right kind of partitioning. This suggests strongly that a holistic view of the business in its context (as previously indicated) is a necessary precursor to achieving a good solution.

For those more comfortable with a heuristic rather than mathematical way to increase capacity and reduce complexity, splitting systems into services is a good way of enabling successful partitioning via a few governing principles and the inherent technical standards. The three simple criteria we've deployed for services are that they should be comprehensible, composable, and characterizable:

- Comprehensible—services should make sense.
  - They must be understandable from a business perspective using clearly understood nouns to describe them and verbs for their actions.
  - They must have a reasonable number of operations (see the CRC technique below as one way of containing this).
  - The service must make sense in that it is functionally complete (e.g., supports a full set of create, read, update, and delete operations, or equivalent).
  - The service must have a sensible set of closely related responsibilities.
  - The service should be capable of independent unit testing and release.
- Composable—services should be reusable in a wide variety of contexts.
  - The services must fit together in an overall structure that has no gaps or overlaps.
  - The interfaces should be stateless and not rely on the service maintaining any memory of previous interactions between calls.

- To compensate for this, the service interface names should explicitly expose any life cycle or order that is inherent in the design of the service.
- The services must be reusable in a variety of contexts.
- Any internal complexity should be hidden behind a simple façade.
- Characterizable—just as the functional characteristics of a service should be coherent, the nonfunctional characteristics of the service should also be consistent.
  - If a service has time-critical and non–time-critical elements, it probably needs to be two separate services.
  - If a service is mostly stable, but has one frequently changing element it would probably make more sense for it to be split into two.

Creating the initial breakdown of a system into services is not something that the lead architect should do in isolation. On IT projects it often appears to us that all the really expensive mistakes are made at the start of the project, so on this occasion multiple heads are usually better than one (though design by committee needs to be avoided too, so the lead architects must not abdicate their judgment to the multitude!).

A really good technique that benefits from the involvement of multiple people is to dynamically create a service model using the CRC card technique. This technique uses index cards (you can even get Post-it versions of them these days to stick on the wall) to represent services. On the card is written the name, responsibilities, and collaboration partners of the service. Architecturally significant scenarios are played through interactively with participants role-playing their services. As a result, new responsibilities and collaborations are added as needed. If a service gets too complex, then the workshop participants attempt to break it down into smaller services. It is usually best for the lead architect to distribute ownership of the cards to the team leaders so that they can identify with the services.

Once the shape of the services is determined, architectural layering can be used to create additional capacity. Using proven architectural layering patterns like model-view-controller (usually implemented via a preexisting framework), or J2EE/.Net standards, and broader standards like SOA, will encourage the separation of different concerns into different areas of the architecture. Each of those layers is likely to a have a subtly different skill set associated with them and are designed to be largely independent of the other layers surrounding them. Such partitioning and layering therefore:

- Assists with scaling the team
- Provides convenient points for in driving tests and exercising the architecture
- Helps isolate the risk of change.

A strong architecture that provides a self-evident way of breaking down work into small, relatively independent chunks goes a long way to both increase development capacity and obviate the need for a detailed project plan, replacing it instead with sensible work items that can be allocated to iterations and ultimately to releases.

12.5.3 **Accelerate delivery through early integration**

We would hypothesize that small- and medium-scale agile deliveries are primarily concerned with the functionality and end user experience of the new system that is being built. There is, unfortunately, mounting evidence that the same is also true of many large-scale agile deliveries.

Traditional agile is helpfully tactile; it produces early tangible and visible results; it is therefore hugely attractive and seductive. Unfortunately the early intangibles tend to become highly observable later in the project (mismatched interfaces, hidden logic, poor data cleanliness, lack of a full business context, etc.) The Agile Bubble anti-pattern enshrines the idea that the new system is revolutionary and can effectively ignore the legacy business or IT landscape around it. It is a highly attractive idea that initially speeds up delivery and ensures that the agile workshops can think freely about the user paradigm they are going to use and relinquish the shackles of old-style thinking. Such optimism often comes at a price later in the project, however, when the constraints of the existing environment come into sharp focus during integration testing.

I was once asked to review an agile project that had been resolutely stuck at 80% complete for a few months; could I come in and unstick it? The project had been a paragon of agile virtue. The user was at the very center of the design and sophisticated end user experience had been demonstrated on a regular basis to all stakeholders. The user interface provided an entirely new conceptual model that was intuitive and was being found to be highly attractive to customers. As each feature had been completed, the project's dashboard had turned increasingly green; over 80% of the function had now been delivered and tested, well ahead of time and budget. Then progress began to slow and eventually stopped; the management called in an external review to find out what was going wrong. Was it a fault of the new technology, the project organization or the approach being followed?

The technology was indeed new, but didn't appear to be the problem—though the lack of progress was focused strongly around the integration of the new system with the existing IT that the new technology supported. The project itself was well organized and had sophisticated tooling and tracking mechanisms. The approach and method was exemplary and was regarded as best practice by agile industry luminaries.

The fundamental problem was that the constraints of the existing IT landscape had not been taken into account right from the start of the agile process. The new paradigm was powerful and intuitive, but simply could not be supported by the core systems of the organization.

The project ended up with a number of equally unpalatable options:

- Start again, this time injecting the key limitations of the legacy into the system as design constraints;
- Design and build an additional, reasonably complex system to act as middleman between the new and old systems (a cache, an operational data store, or a data replication solution);
- Undergo a massive reengineering of the core systems to accommodate the new paradigm.

Ultimately the decision had to be made to start again, balancing and tempering the more extreme aspects of the new paradigm with the known limitations of the existing systems. Considerable time and effort had been wasted. RH

The Agile Bubble anti-pattern is something we've come across time and time again where insufficient time and effort has been spent in harvesting the constraints that the system will be subject to and finding a way to play these into the agile sessions.

All designers find it hard to create an effective design when there are a myriad of constraints. Constraints impose a straightjacket, and in complex environments there are likely to be many forms of constraints. These include the following:

- the need to meet regulatory compliance;
- self-imposed constraints, such as enterprise architecture;
- external project constraints, such as budget or time pressures;
- internal constraints, such as a limited choice of platforms or development languages due to organizational or commercial constraints;
- existing systems and their interfaces.

With such a wide range, it is worth trying to characterize them along with some suggestions on how an agile project might handle them, as summarized in Table 12.2.

Certainly, where the constraints are immovable, numerous and detailed, we have found techniques that provide a fast, iterative development capability to be most

Table 12.2 Dealing with Different Types of Constraints on Large Agile Projects

	Low Ability to Influence Constraints	**High Ability to Influence Constraints**
Constraints with high impact to project	Constraint examples: • Regulatory • Existing systems • Project budget • Project timescales Suggested mitigations: Ensure compliance via initial planning and analysis phase. For complex constraints (such as existing systems), ensure that information is collated to allow it to be played into agile workshops as it is needed In highly complex situations, use brownfield development techniques (see below)	Constraint examples: • Project scope • Project nonfunctional requirements Suggested mitigations: Prioritize according to the business value; ensure that the nonfunctional requirements are considered holistically in an early architecture design stage Iteratively and incrementally engineer the supporting application framework and the application, refining the two in parallel, iteratively addition support for nonfunctional requirements
Constraints with low impact to project	Constraint example: • Enterprise architecture Suggested mitigations: Assure or demonstrate compliance at end of each phase	Constraint examples: • Conflicting requirements • Orphaned requirements without business goal or user justification Suggested mitigations: Engineer these constraints out of the project via negotiation

suitable. Once such technique, called brownfield development, has been described in detail in the book *Eating the IT Elephant* [7]. This approach is used to iteratively create and refine complex system components by harvesting information about the existing IT landscape and then using that information to generate the components. It is an extension of model-driven development and architecture where the models are at least partially derived from existing assets. We have used this technique highly successfully to create interfaces to poorly understood legacy systems and to accelerate the reengineering of complex system landscapes.

Such an approach is inherently agile, as often the only way to iteratively build up knowledge about whether a component will work in the environment is to deploy it into that environment and test it.

A good example of this approach is with respect to interface generation. If you have a semantically strong description of an interface (as described in the book *Eating the IT Elephant*), it is possible to do two complementary things: you can generate the code that implements the interface, but you can also generate a representative sample of test data that corresponds to the interface definition. You can guarantee your data will work through your use of the interface, minimizing downstream issues—unless, of course, you have an error in your interface or data generation libraries. However, when you test the interface (with all those possible combinations of generated data) against the system that you're trying to interface to, real lessons can be learned. If you get an error in your automated run of tests, then you simply need to refine your definition of the interface to allow for this unforeseen circumstance. The tighter interface definition (along with the automatically similarly improved generated test data) can then be run again and again until no errors are detected. At that point, it is highly likely you have iteratively "discovered" the true behavior of the interface, irrespective of how obscure its documentation or implementation is.

On one project, we automated this process such that the entire build and test cycle could be conducted for all the interfaces in the system twice a day. By doing so, rather than finding out in late stage testing that the interfaces would not work, we had them all fully tested and working before some more traditional elements of the system had finished development. This is an agile approach, but one that requires significant discipline to execute and some up-front investment. As with all code generation approaches, the business case for building the necessary code and data generation and test harnesses has to be justified based on the scale and complexity of the problem.

In the case of this particular integration, two systems integrators had previously failed to get similar interfaces to work with the same systems, so the investment was well worth it; indeed, those interfaces were one of the high-risk viewpoint elements that we identified early in the project.

12.5.4 **Accelerate delivery via early and continuous testing**

As we saw at the beginning of this chapter, the late-stage testing elements of a project (typically system, integration, and acceptance testing) are an increasingly large proportion of the cost for large-scale complex system development projects. While smaller agile projects can typically perform all stages of testing simultaneously, this is not always possible for large-scale agile projects.

This is primarily because they typically involve a large number of major components or services that need to be brought together, often involving multiple external stakeholders with non-agile practices. Security can also place limitations on where and how late stage testing can take place.

As a result, while the iteration and release cycle of the core agile elements may be fast, the heartbeat of external systems may be much slower. Consequently, on very large agile projects, some emergence of plan-driven, late-stage testing is likely. Clearly, what is required is a mechanism to minimize this impact.

Our recommended way to deal with this conundrum is to identify points of stability within or at the boundaries of the system—especially those that impose a high level of constraint—and then work in an ordered fashion outwards from those points of stability (as per the interface generation example above). The technique is akin to seeding a nucleus in a supersaturated salt solution. Those initial, small points of stability grow, coalesce, and meet and over time form a single, stable, orderly crystal.

This assembling of a complete solution from its component parts should commence as soon as two components that are connected by an interface are available following completion of their lower-level tests. It ends when the whole solution has been tested, in its appropriate business context. In the same way that architectures have several levels of design hierarchy, so the integration sequence of components may be complex and has to be supported by the test systems and data previously planned. The consequence of this for complex agile projects is clear: beyond "point to point" testing of paired components, integration testing activities should be planned in advance, deliberately creating islands of stability and allowing for the timely construction of test systems and data (see Figure 12.2).

A large complex agile systems-integration project has a structure similar to that of the Earth. At its heart are the fast-moving, agile projects that provide early demonstrable value. As you move further away from the agile core, however, the speed and energy slows; in the mantle are slower-moving projects, and at the surface are the slower-moving components that must be integrated with. These components might be legacy systems or the hardware elements of embedded systems. When a release is required for deployment, the outer layers cool and solidify first with each layer in turn freezing as paired testing of components fixes layers in place. Eventually this cooling process reaches the core and the release is ready for deployment.

To accelerate this "cooling," each component should have a test system constructed first, using fakes, mocks, stubs, harnesses, or simulators as appropriate. The completed component under test can then be subject to testing within its test harness. This means that before a developer commits their changes back to the library, it should be possible to build a release and perform a series of these automated tests. Each component is therefore not subject to a single pass through each phase of testing, but repeatedly (preferably streamlined and automated) retested in response to design change and defect correction. These should include all unit tests, component integration tests and a limited number of automated acceptance tests.

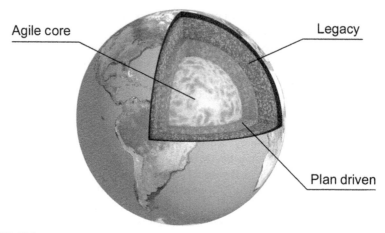

FIGURE 12.2

A complex agile systems integration project represented as a cross-section of the Earth.

These tests should be run in virtualized representative sandbox environments (inexpensive cloud or highly virtualized platforms are superb for this). It is vitally important to perform deep testing down to acceptance (including nonfunctional acceptance) levels as part of this development process; early feedback is highly useful, because it reduces overall development and testing risk.

The lead architect should also have determined a series of nonfunctional static tests for new code that can be checked via automated routines. This would include checks for the duplicated code, maximum levels of cyclomatic complexity and style checking. Code should not get checked back in until it meets all these tests.

Post commit of code, there should be a regular "smoke test" of the system as a whole to exercise its major areas of component integration and expected user behavior. This should be performed on a daily basis and ideally should also look at key areas of performance and capacity testing.

At each stage of design, the test system and test data approach should be designed at the same time as the component. In the same way that components may be assembled in several stages of decomposition from the overall solution to the lowest level of design (the "unit" level), the definition, and order, of test systems and components under test should be defined. For each test system (at whatever level), the test data approach should ensure that the data will support the proposed test cases, including referential integrity across the test system. At the highest levels of the hierarchy, the span of control is at its widest and consequently the supply of test data is more challenging.

Throughout this chapter, we have stressed that architectural documents should be kept to a very minimal, context-sensitive subset, and that models are vastly preferred to documents. However, central to the ability to define such a test solution in a complex environment is the availability of the logical and physical data models (LDM and PDM respectively) across the breadth of the solution. This aspect may not be popular with those brought up on objects and services, but to date we have identified no successful substitute. The creation of LDMs and PDMs should, therefore, be a specific area sponsored by the lead architect.

> I was asked to assist in the construction of a funds switch, and run it as a managed service. The task was to effectively create an ATM network hub and connect it to existing client systems and financial institutions for the generation of payments, balance requests, and other ATM-like services.
>
> I had to implement this on mainframe technology, architecting for resilience (Sysplexed Logical Partitions (LPARs)), security (Triple-Data Encryption Standard (DES) encrypted network) and very demanding performance and volumes, as well as for functional correctness and auditability. This was the largest government IT project in that year. The consequences of system failure were dire and could easily lead to hardship and civil unrest.
>
> I encouraged architecting for testing from the outset. The overall network architecture was a hub and spoke. Because we were building the hub and had to test it in isolation prior to overall System of Systems integration, we had to simulate every other party in the network. These simulators were designed and built iteratively as part of the project development.
>
> I always knew that we had a challenging timescale to meet. I therefore tested deeply (from unit to acceptance) at the earliest meaningful point; with multiple overlapping test phases. The hub had virtually no defects in integration, or in the subsequent live operation, which started precisely on time. After some years, the client passed the service over to a cheaper provider who was unwilling to invest in the required test-driven approach—with the consequence that system failures occurred, leading to dissatisfaction with the system and negative publicity. SH

The lead architect must take into account the mechanisms by which testing can be automated. Standard test-driven development (where a test is engineered first to ensure that the code that is then developed will meet it) is not enough. The architect also needs to ensure that there is clear, consistent abstraction around the key layers of the architecture (especially user interface, data access and database) to enable the cost-effective automation of a much wider range of tests.

12.5.5 Accelerate delivery via an automated deployment pipeline

Performing such automated testing requires that that deployment is also a repeatable and fast process. We need to ensure that, as far as possible, the same deployment tool that is used in production is used in all stages of non-development testing. This may require us to adopt operator's tools that may be different from our own (it is unusual for a complex client environment hosting not to be outsourced in some way, and cloud deployment tools will increasingly be the norm).

Adopting these tools is a very small price to pay to avoid having environments built by different teams in different ways using imprecise specifications or having to invest in overly elaborate and detailed environment specifications.

The *development* deployment scripts should be capable of deploying *production* environments including necessary resilience or scaling aspects; for the earlier, less-representative test environments, the scripts could be written in such a way that they missed out certain aspects of the deployment. This allows a single script to be maintained whilst still enabling multiple small, low-cost testing environments or sandboxes to be set up to speed up the continuous integration and testing cycle.

This technique is vital because if the deployment tools and scripts are exercised on an almost daily basis, then the final deployment into production is a process that has been performed many times before. It becomes as tested and reliable as the other elements of the development process. This technique is described in highly effective detail in the book *Continuous Deployment* [8].

Standardization and machine virtualization are our friends here. It is becoming ever easier and faster to create exact copies of machines that can then be minimally customized and configured using automated scripts. In addition, it is becoming easier and cheaper to create two-sided configurations for live environments for candidate deployments (e.g., one side of the system is deployed so the world can see it, with the other side deployed so only internal users can see it). In such circumstances, having common deployment scripts that are frequently exercised gives the business (and the hosting company) much greater freedom to perform frequent updates to highly visible systems.

However, this does mean that everything must be carefully version controlled, including server images, source files, configuration scripts, configuration information, and of course the tests themselves. This, again, is where today's sophisticated, collaborative application life cycle management tools are invaluable.

As we described earlier, the lead architects' job is not just to design the production system and its environments; early care should be taken around the tool chain and the mechanisms by which systems and the code they run is configured, deployed, and tested. This is just as important an area of scalability and project performance as the nonfunctional elements of the live system mentioned earlier.

However, in today's multi-supplier environments, where hosting is often performed by a different company from the one that is performing the application development, there can be a lack of trust or a need to prove the fitness (or otherwise) of a software release before it can be deployed. The technical and commercial effort of architecting a formal deployment process between two parties and then optimizing it should not be underestimated, but it is a necessary prerequisite to a successful agile strategy.

We have seen two highly successful strategies for this process. Interestingly, they are mutually exclusive. The first is the aggressive approach, where no release is ever backed out. Any new release is restrictively deployed, into an area where family and friends can use it, for example. This deployment is performed during the normal working week when the full strength development, delivery, and hosting teams are all on hand. If the deployment does not work, then it gets fixed—and it continues to get fixed until it works. Nothing is ever backed out; deployment is a one-way street. Once the release is stable, it is rolled out over the whole of the estate. Some packages are so complex, or data changes in a release are so significant, that this is often the only option.

This approach might seem a little radical for some organizations, and therefore the alternative approach is one where the ability to back out a release is given the same focus and level of automation as the mechanism to deploy it. The ability to reliably roll back a release means that the company (which is probably more risk averse than the other example above) can be reassured that it is not taking too much of a chance when rolling out a release rather quicker than it once might have done.

Whichever approach suits the business, the need for careful control over versioning and deployment technologies is imperative. In complex environments, such facilities will take longer to set up than a base agile capability and so should be an early focus of activity.

Following the testing and deployment strategies above means that testing ultimately becomes a process that is controlled by the testers themselves. This may sound a little strange and it may be hard to believe that this is not normally the case, but generally speaking testers have little such control. Traditionally testers have been hugely constrained by the availability of environments and working deployed code; to a degree, they must dance to the development team's tune. Especially in large complex projects, testing duration is always squeezed—even when it is highly efficient and risk focused. However, if the lead architect takes a test-driven, full life cycle perspective right from the start of the project, then this approach provides for accelerated delivery even in the most complex of environments.

12.6 CONCLUSION

Ensuring that agility is maintained throughout the life cycle of a large complex systems development program is not just a matter of following standard agile development patterns; it also requires a strong architecture and architectural approach. Placing the architecture at the heart of the program and focusing on key viewpoints and risks means that lightweight processes can be used even in the most complex of circumstances without jeopardizing delivery.

To achieve this, the lead architect must encourage the adoption of sophisticated life cycle management tooling and guide the incremental optimization of the entire delivery pipeline from user requirement to operator deployment and application maintenance.

The resulting approach:

- Reduces costs by providing a necessary guiding vision and a structure that obviates the need for heavyweight processes and enables the use of low-cost resources and reduced TCO;
- Minimizes rework by solving difficult problems early;
- Accelerates delivery by widening the full delivery pipeline (not just the development process).

In this chapter, we have addressed the myth that a strong architecture implies heavyweight process. Indeed, we hope that we have shown that our approach for the delivery of complex agile systems development projects is predicated on the combined application of strong architecture and agile practices, and that these practices are mutually reinforcing.

References

[1] Bohem B, Turner R. Balancing agility with discipline: a guide for the perplexed. London: Pearson Education; 2004.

[2] Boehm B. A spiral model of software development and enhancement. ACM SIGSOFT Software Engineering Notes. ACM 1986;11(4):14–24.

[3] Coplien JO, Harrison NB. Organisational patterns of agile software development. Upper Saddle River, NJ: Pearson Prentice Hall; 2005.

[4] Bass L, Clements P, Kazman R. 2nd ed. Software architecture in practice. Boston, MA: Addison Wesley Professional; 2003.

[5] McConnell S. Code complete. 2nd ed. Redmond, WA: Microsoft Press; 2004.

[6] Sessions R. Simple architectures for complex enterprises. Redmond, WA: Microsoft Press; 2008.

[7] Hopkins R, Jenkins K. Eating the IT elephant: moving from greenfield development to brownfield. Upper Saddle River, NJ: Pearson; 2008.

[8] Humble J, Farley D. Continuous deployment. Boston, MA: Pearson Education; 2011.

Building a Platform for Innovation: Architecture and Agile as Key Enablers

13

Peter Eeles

IBM, London, UK

CHAPTER CONTENTS

13.1 INTRODUCTION

As Charles Darwin taught us, the evolution of a species (and its ongoing survival) is driven by an ability to adapt to a changing environment [1]. Information technology (IT) organizations are no different; for example, a financial services or pharmaceutical organization may need to adapt to new regulations that represent a change to their environment (or face impending fines from their respective regulatory body). Similarly, an organization cannot simply stand still because its competition is continually changing the market environment with the introduction of new products. This latter case requires an organization to proactively consider change in the form of innovation.

In all cases, from the perspective of an IT department, the ability to adapt and innovate is driven by two key enablers. The first enabler is directly related to the makeup of their IT systems—their *architecture*. Systems that are architecturally elegant are, by definition, easier to change than those whose architectures are perceived as big balls of spaghetti containing many intertwined and hard-to-understand elements. The second enabler is the approach taken to create and change IT systems and, in particular, the adoption of *agile* practices.

In summary, building a platform for innovation is driven by the two key enablers of architecture and agile, and it should be noted that this chapter focuses largely on agile *with* architecture rather than agile *versus* architecture. In addition, after several years of introducing both architecture and agile practices into many organizations, both large and small, my view is that there are technology-independent factors that also need to be considered (especially those related to organizational change), and overlooking any one of these factors can be a real impediment to a successful outcome. In essence, bringing architecture and agile together is fundamentally difficult.

The purpose of this chapter is to consider both technical and nontechnical factors in building a platform for innovation and is organized accordingly. The chapter first examines the apparent conflicts between architecture-centric and agile-centric approaches. A summary of proven architecture practices follows before considering those practices introduced by iterative development, agile, and disciplined agile. The chapter concludes by introducing several practical lessons learned that go beyond the introduction of architecture and agile practices but are key considerations in building a platform for innovation.

On a side note, although widely used, the phrase *agile architecture* is ambiguous and I do not use it because it is not clear if it refers to the architecture itself (which exhibits *agility* or flexibility) or to the process that was used to create the solution. In this chapter, I focus on the latter. Grady Booch [2] provides a nice distinction between the two meanings.

13.2 WORLDS COLLIDE

If there is a single factor that makes the alignment of architecture and agile difficult, it is this: those with an architecture bent would prefer to lock down key decisions, those that are most difficult to change, as early as possible in a project, whereas agile purists, on the other hand, would prefer to leave such decisions to the last possible moment.

> The tension seems to lie on the axis of adaptation versus anticipation. Agile methods want to be resolutely adaptive: deciding at the "last responsible moment" for when changes occur. Agile methods perceive software architecture as pushing too hard on the anticipation side: planning too much in advance [3,4].

Such widely differing views are worrying and real, with agile purists being critical of big design up front (BDUF) and preferring to embrace principles such as "you ain't gonna need it" (YAGNI), and seasoned architects being critical of a lack of forethought and a tendency to increase technical debt as a result. The clash of cultures is nicely expressed by Kruchten:

I see two parties not really understanding the real issues at hand, stopping at a very shallow, caricatural view of the "other culture", not understanding enough of the surroundings, beliefs, values of the other one, and stopping very quickly at judging behaviors [4].

Known authorities in the agile space alerted us to the dangers of taking an extreme view, one way or the other, over a decade ago:

Current modeling approaches can often prove dysfunctional. In the one extreme, modeling is nonexistent, often resulting in significant rework when the software proves to be poorly thought through. The other extreme is when excessive models and documents are produced, which slows your development efforts down to a snail's pace [5].

And now, a decade later, the tensions seem to be alive and well:

Another fear is that an over-focus on early results in large systems can lead to major rework when the initial architecture does not scale up [6].

Although agile strategies appear to work better than traditional strategies, it has become clear to us that the pendulum has swung too far the other way. We have gone from overly bureaucratic and document-centric processes to almost nothing but code [7].

This chapter considers a balance between the two extremes and does so by focusing on the essential practices that are the foundation of both architecture and agile. The analysis of essential practices is expressed in terms of different software development lifecycles, because each has provided a valuable contribution to effective software development. The complementary nature of this heritage when applied to more recent thinking is expressed in Scrum:

Scrum is a management and control process that cuts through complexity to focus on building software to meet business needs. Scrum is superimposed on top of and wraps existing engineering practices, development methodologies, and standards [8].

13.3 AN ARCHITECTURE HERITAGE

One of the reasons that architecture gets bad press in the agile world is that it is often linked to *plan-centric methods*—methods that try to impose artificial (and often detailed) plans in situations where much is unknown. Such methods are often characterized as *traditional* or *waterfall*. Agile methods, on the other hand, acknowledge such situations by embracing one of the values expressed in the Agile Manifesto: "Responding to change over following a plan" [9].

There is also a perception that architecture-centric methods are overly focused on the production of detailed models and associated design documentation when one of the tenets of agile, also expressed in the agile manifesto, is "Working software over comprehensive documentation."

> *Software architecture has a history of excesses that in part spurred the reaction called Agile. Software architecture of the 1980s was famous for producing reams of documentation that no one read [10].*

But surely it can't all be bad? Of course not; the criticisms outlined above are the result of the poor application of either method or architecture practices. So what are those architecture practices that should be considered on *any* project? In 2008, I coauthored *The Process of Software Architecting* with my colleague Peter Cripps [11]. In it, we explored those practices embraced by successful architects by trawling through many different methods and interviewing many successful architects. The core architecture-centric practices that we repeatedly encountered were as follows:

- *Multiple Views*: When communicating the architecture, ensure that all relevant views of the architecture are considered. For example, you might have a view to show the key components of the system, and another to show the hardware on which those components are deployed. Kruchten's "4 + 1 view model of software architecture" is one example of an architecture description framework based on multiple views [12].
- *Quality Attribute-Driven Development*: The architecture of a system is not only focused on realizing the functional requirements, but also the nonfunctional requirements. Nonfunctional requirements include quality attributes, such as scalability and availability, and constraints, such as the mandatory use of particular technologies. A focus on quality attributes and the associated tactics that can help address them has been well documented [13].
- *Component-Based Development*: This practice defines a system's functional architecture by breaking the system up into a number of collaborating components. It focuses on identifying the major abstractions of the system and making decisions on how the system will be built.
- *Asset Reuse*: There is almost always an opportunity to reuse assets when developing a solution, but there is often an inconsistent understanding of the different types of assets at the disposal of the architect. Asset types include reference architectures, patterns, and component libraries.
- *Decision Capture*: When it comes to architecture, we often need to explore different options (based on appropriate rationale) before selecting a preference. Capturing decisions in an appropriate form can help the architects recall why they made a decision, and also help others who may need to evolve the architecture. Architecture decisions are a key input when communicating the architecture.
- *Architecture Proving*: Several approaches can be applied to prove that an architecture is fit-for-purpose. This includes the creation of an architecture proof-of-concept (which may be on paper, or in executable code), as well as appropriate verification, validation, and review activities.

These practices apply irrespective of method or lifecycle and apply equally to waterfall, iterative, and agile methods.

Software architecture is part of product quality and isn't tied to a particular process, technology, culture, or tool [14].

13.4 ITERATIVE DEVELOPMENT

An improvement on waterfall methods, and a precursor to agile methods, is *iterative development*. This practice is at the heart of many methods, including the Rational Unified Process (RUP), a representation of which is shown in Figure 13.1 [15].

This representation has two dimensions—content (the vertical axis, showing various *disciplines*) and time (the horizontal access, showing *iterations* and *phases*). Although an architecture discipline is shown, it is of course the time dimension that is of most interest when it comes to understanding the mechanics of iterative development and its influence on architecture. The key concepts of iterations and phases (explained below) underpin two key practices that result from this approach:

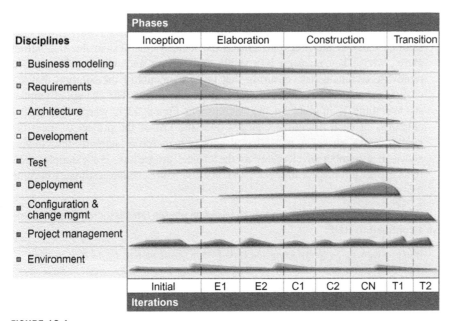

FIGURE 13.1

Rational Unified Process.

- *Iterative Development*: As the project progresses, releases provide incremental improvements in capability until the final system is complete. An iterative development process is similar to "growing" software, where the end product matures over time. Each iteration results in a better understanding of the requirements, a more robust architecture, a more experienced development organization, and a more complete implementation.

  Establish an iterative life-cycle process that confronts risk early. With today's sophisticated software systems, it is not possible to define the entire problem, design the entire solution, build the software, then test the end product in sequence. Instead, an iterative process that refines the problem understanding, an effective solution, and an effective plan over several iterations encourages a balanced treatment of all stakeholder objectives. Major risks must be addressed early to increase predictability and avoid expensive downstream scrap and rework [16].

- *Risk-Value Lifecycle*: There is more to an iterative development process than a stream of iterations; there must be an overall framework in which the iterations are performed, representing the strategic plan for the project and driving the goals and objectives of each of the iterations. Such a framework is provided in the RUP, whose phases are labeled *inception, elaboration, construction,* and *transition*. Each phase concludes with a major milestone and an assessment to determine whether the objectives of the phase have been met. A satisfactory assessment allows the project to move to the next phase.

  Phases also answer the question "what should an iteration focus on?" RUP phases support a risk-value approach that results in risk being removed from the solution early in the lifecycle. This is particularly manifest in the elaboration phase, whose key measure is a stable architecture and which is focused on removing technical risk, ensuring that those elements of the solution that are costly to change are considered sooner rather than later. The change of emphasis over time is implied by the "humps" in Figure 13.1, where the relative emphasis of each discipline changes over the life of the project to meet the goals of each phase. A phase-based approach therefore supports the convergence of a number of elements as the project progresses. For example, risks reduce over the project lifecycle, and any cost and schedule estimates become more accurate.

Of course, such an iterative approach based on phases (and associated milestones) isn't confined to RUP:

When reviewing projects using the risk-driven spiral model, I find that to keep from losing their way, such projects—particularly larger ones—need to have at least three major anchor-point milestones to serve as project progress indicators and stakeholder commitment points [17].

The RUP (and other iterative methods) introduce other practices that are also relevant to the work of the architect. Although these practices apply equally to plan-centric methods, they have been given a particular emphasis when applied in conjunction with an iterative approach and so are included here.

- *Shared Vision*: This practice ensures that all stakeholders, both consumers and producers of the solution, share a common view of the problems being solved and the key characteristics of the solution (albeit at a high level). In essence, this practice is focused on aligning expectations and ensuring market acceptance. This practice ensures that there is an alignment between product strategy and the output from the development team.
- *Use Case-Driven Development*: The practice of describing primarily functional requirements with use cases is well-documented. Aside from the technique itself, use cases (and flows through each use case) make natural units of implementation in an iterative development approach, because use cases influence planning, architecture, development, and testing.
- *Release Planning*: This practice is focused on the just-in-time project planning needed to scope the release of executable software within an iteration. This iteration-specific planning complements any high-level planning that considers the project as a whole.

13.5 ALONG CAME AGILE

Although the foundations of the agile movement are well known [9], my own reaction was somewhat mixed once mainstream agile methods appeared—especially since they seemed to reinvent the wheel (and terminology) in parts. Why did Scrum use the word "sprint" when "iteration" would do? I guess it was all part of the story. Let's face it, rugby players sprint when going for the line. I can't imagine for one minute a rugby player receiving the ball and then iterating as fast as they could.

> We now have the agile method wars – branded methods based on metaphors, unique terminology, and sometimes questionable certification programs [7].

Over time, of course, agile methods have proven to add incredible value. In particular, I believe they ground us in what matters most in building software in a timely, cost-efficient, and quality manner. Whether we're talking Extreme Programming (XP), Scrum, or some other agile method, they each live and breathe certain principles and each draw upon practices that have stood the test of time.

So what's so different about agile? Specifically, how does it differ from iterative development? The fact is, agile approaches introduce new practices—and for good reason. Schwaber tells us of his experiences in working with the process theory experts at the DuPont Experimental Station:

> They were amazed and appalled that my industry, systems development, was trying to do its work using a completely inappropriate process control model. They said systems development had so much complexity and unpredictability that it had to be managed by a process control model they referred to as 'empirical' . . . I

realized why the industry was in such trouble and had such a poor reputation. We were wasting our time trying to control our work by thinking we had an assembly line when the only proper control was frequent and first-hand inspection, followed by immediate adjustments [8].

Of course, we could say that iterative development addresses this finding. However, agile methods take the notions of *continuous delivery, team development*, and *stakeholder interaction* to a new level. In keeping with the previous sections of this chapter, I'd like to summarize what I see as the key practices that distinguish an agile method from other methods and, in particular, iterative development. Of course, there are other practices too, some that are method specific and others that are not, but they are not as core as those listed below.

- *Test-Driven Development (TDD)*: The test approach advocated by TDD is primarily targeted at programmers, but is a cornerstone of any agile method. Creating tests that, essentially, define the specification of what the code should do first, helps focus programmers on meeting this specification. "This develops into a natural and efficient rhythm—test, code, refactor, test, code, refactor" [18].
- *Continuous Integration*: This practice encourages frequent integration and testing of programming changes. "Team programming isn't a divide and conquer problem. It is a divide, conquer, and integrate problem" [18].
- *Refactoring*: This practice is focused on changing an existing body of code in order to improve its internal structure. In a sense, this practice is focused on addressing technical debt, albeit at a local level (because it is typically applied to isolated bodies of code, rather than the system as a whole). In practice, teams that also perform a level of design (and create models) also update these designs where relevant.
- *Whole Team*: Agile methods focus on the value of highly collaborative teams as exemplified by Scrum's daily standup meeting. It is also the team that decides how the project goals will be met and will *self-organize* accordingly. This means that team composition may change over time because the team, as a whole, should always have the right skills at any point in time to complete the tasks at hand. This practice also instills a sense of collective ownership and responsibility.
- *User Story-Driven Development*: This practice describes the capture of both functional and nonfunctional requirements in a lightweight manner (more lightweight than use cases) and encourages collaboration with the relevant stakeholders throughout a project. User stories influence planning, development, and testing.
- *Team Change Management*: This practice supports the logging of defects or new requirements, by any member of the team, that are within the scope of the current iteration. Such requests are captured as work items and placed on a product backlog (as exemplified by Scrum), which is ultimately reviewed by the team as part of their planning.

And what of architecture in an agile world? One of the great myths of agile is that the design somehow emerges from a soup of code. This is simply not true or sensible, as observed by Martin Fowler way back in 2000:

Essentially evolutionary design means that the design of the system grows as the system is implemented. Design is part of the programming processes and as the program evolves the design changes. In its common usage, evolutionary design is a disaster. The design ends up being the aggregation of a bunch of ad-hoc tactical decisions, each of which makes the code harder to alter [19].

Unsurprisingly, agile teams do embrace certain architecture practices in their work:

There seems to be a fear in the agile community that if we use terms such as "model" or "document" that suddenly the "evil bureaucrats" will dig their claws into our projects and force us to write detailed, big requirements specifications or to take a big-design-up-front approach... the strange thing is that agilists are, in fact, modeling on a regular basis, even though they're not directly talking about it [20].

And the case for architecture is well-understood:

Not all change is equal. There are a few basic architectural decisions that you need to get right at the beginning of development, because they fix the constraints of the system for its life. Examples of these may be choice of language, architectural layering decisions, or the choice to interact with an existing database also used by other applications [21].

    Look at a large successful software system and beneath it you'll find an architecture that's kept its evolution on track [22].

13.6 AGILE WITH DISCIPLINE

In an ideal world, processors would be infinitely fast and disk drives would have infinite capacity. Teams would also be colocated. The point is, there are real-world considerations that limit the art of the possible in an agile world. For example, when a high degree of complexity is involved in large-scale efforts, some have noted the need to introduce new techniques and, in particular, the importance of architecture:

When developing complex, large-scale applications, many have reported that agile methods must be adapted to include more kinds of architectural information. We see evidence of this in the zero-feature release, the architectural spike, and agile practices that recognize the architect role [14].

    Architecture is an important topic, especially when development is distributed over several sites, and/or when the development is based on legacy systems [6].

Scaling factors, such as team distribution and solution complexity, apply to both small and large organizations, and a consideration of these factors can be found in the disciplined agile delivery approach—a hybrid of agile and traditional methods as documented in [7]. This approach introduces an agile scaling model, which considers the factors summarized in Table 13.1.

Table 13.1 Disciplined Agile Scaling Factors

Scaling Factor	Agile	Disciplined Agile
Team Size	Under 10 developers	1000 s of developers
Geographic Distribution	Co-located teams	Distributed teams
Regulatory Compliance	Low-risk	Critical and audited
Domain Complexity	Straightforward	Complex
Organization Distribution	One group, same company	Many groups, many companies
Technical Complexity	Homogenous	Heterogeneous, legacy
Organizational Complexity	Flexible	Rigid
Enterprise Discipline	Project focus	Enterprise focus

These factors force adjustments in important areas to the practical realizations of agility at scale. They encourage a disciplined approach to the scaling of agile techniques. My experience with several large enterprise software delivery organizations suggests that agile approaches can be successful in almost every kind of development team and in almost all organizations. Each situation has its own specific needs and variations, yet the basic core agile principles can provide significant results when applied with care, and with realistic expectations [23].

A consideration of these scaling factors has resulted in the introduction of additional practices. In several cases, these are not new practices at all but recognition that large, complex, enterprise-wide distributed development and the like require us to embrace certain approaches even though they take us away from an idealized view of agile. Some examples are:

- *Measured Performance*: This practice allows project- and portfolio-level measurements to inform key business decisions. For example, knowing that the *burndown* of a project's product backlog is not on a downward trajectory may indicate that more (or better-skilled) resources are required on the project. Similarly, observing a lot of requirements churn (changes to already-defined requirements) may indicate that the project's business representative may not have the domain knowledge required. Measured performance is good for both the project team and the business.
- *Formal Change Management*: This practice provides a controlled approach for managing changes and is (as the name suggests) more formal than the team change management practice. This practice is often applied when approval is required from stakeholders outside of the project team, or when a deliverable has been baselined as part of a contract and the deliverable needs to be modified.
- *Concurrent Testing*: While a project team may embrace TDD, there is often an independent test team present (especially in larger organizations) that typically provides a level of user-acceptance testing before the solution is put into production. The purpose of this practice is to bring this "external" team in sync with the

project team and have them work in step with the project so that their work isn't compressed into a separate activity at the end of an iteration or release.

Concluding a whirlwind tour of the heritage of certain practices, a summary of waterfall, iterative, agile, and disciplined agile practices that have been mentioned is given in Table 13.2, which I use for two key purposes:

- *Enablement*: Considering this set of practices can help practitioners in their agile journey. Conveying the principles and practices of agile to a practitioner who has used an iterative approach, such as RUP, is a very different affair from someone who's only ever followed a waterfall approach. This then translates into a different focus of any enablement activities.
- *Practice selection*: It should have become clear by now that there is no one-size-fits-all method that caters to all situations. Furthermore, the set of practices discussed in this chapter can be seen as a list from which to choose for any given situation. In particular, we can see that, rather than viewing waterfall, iterative, agile, and disciplined agile as competing approaches, they are—at least from a practice perspective—highly complementary in that the practices they espouse can be combined as required.

In fact, standard configurations of the alignment of architecture practices and agile practices are emerging...Nord and Tomayko show an alignment of the Software Engineering Institute's approaches (such as attribute-driven design within XP [14]), and Madison discusses the application of architecture practices within a "hybrid of Scrum, XP, and sequential project management" [24].

Our experience is that "core" agile methods such as Scrum work wonderfully for small project teams addressing straightforward problems in which there is little risk or consequence of failure. However, "out of the box", these methods do not give adequate consideration to the risks associated with delivering solutions on larger enterprise projects, and as a result we're seeing organizations investing a lot of effort creating hybrid methodologies combining techniques from many sources [7].

Table 13.2 Practice Summary

Waterfall	Iterative	Agile	Disciplined Agile
Multiple views	Iterative development	Test-driven development	Measured performance
Quality attribute-driven development	Risk-value Lifecycle	Continuous integration	Formal change management
Component-based development	Shared vision	Refactoring	Concurrent testing
Asset reuse	Use case-driven Development	Whole team	
Decision capture	Release planning	User story-driven development	
Architecture proving		Team change management	

Although each approach has a home ground of project characteristics within which it performs very well, and much better than the other, outside each approach's home ground, a combined approach is feasible and preferable [17].

13.7 BEYOND ARCHITECTURE AND AGILE

The application of these practices isn't as straightforward as you might think. Despite all of the provisos outlined above, successfully integrating these practices into the day-to-day working of practitioners requires us to embrace lessons learned, as discussed in this section.

13.7.1 Define a project lifecycle selection framework

Should every project follow an agile approach? In short, an appropriate balance between many different factors needs to be achieved.

There are definite home grounds for pure agile and pure plan-driven methods, although there are very few methods at the extremes. There is a relationship with a method's position between the home grounds and the type of project and environment where it will most likely succeed [25].

A summary of relevant factors, which I've applied as part of a "project lifecycle selection framework," is given in Table 13.3 (all elements are phrased such that a positive response favors an agile approach).

Why wouldn't you always use agile methods? Well, shock-horror, maybe they are not always the best approach for the circumstances! So how do we decide? It is tempting to thinking that all projects should be handled in an agile way. Indeed, I am convinced that all projects would benefit from the improved collaboration and communications encouraged on agile projects. However, collaboration and communications are just two attributes of agile projects and we must consider wider parameters that influence project success or failure [26].

When applying the framework, each factor is also given a weighting, and after receiving appropriate input, a first-pass assessment can be made of any points of sensitivity if we were to take an agile approach. For example, if (as the first characteristic of business flexibility implies) management is *not* willing to accept that business parameters (e.g., cost, schedule, and intermediate milestones) are flexible, then we might have a problem implementing iterative development—one of the cornerstones of an agile approach.

I've learned from experience that in practice it is essential to limit the scaling of agile approaches to projects with properties that are well matched to the characteristics of agility, at least when establishing new practices in a complex organization undergoing significant change [23].

Table 13.3 Lifecycle Selection Criteria

Management Influences	
Business Flexibility	Management are willing to accept that business parameters, such as cost, schedule, and intermediate milestones, are flexible
Empowered Teams	Management is willing to allow the team (including the product owner) to make key project decisions
Stakeholder Influences	
Acceptance of Agile	Stakeholders understand and accept agile practices and the consequences of following these
Number of Stakeholders	The number and diversity of stakeholder relationships to be managed is limited
Stakeholder Responsiveness	The business representative, end users, and testers are committed to spending a good deal of time working with the team in an iterative fashion
Project Team Influences	
Team Skills	Individuals on the team are team players, good communicators, and are familiar with agile practices
Embracing Change	Team members expect and embrace frequent changes and iterative refinement of the solution
Colocated Teams	The project team will be co-located
Team Stability	Individuals will be assigned to the team for the duration of the project
Team Roles	Team members are able (and willing) to take on multiple roles during the project and to take on new roles if/when needed
Agile Disciplines	Team members have proven ability in performing disciplines that are critical for agile development with short iterations (design, testing and configuration management)
Technology Influences	
Development Environment	The development environment (method, tools, training) will support an agile way of working (such as automated regression test, continuous integration, and real-time dashboards) and is sufficiently mature
Execution Environment	The execution environment can support regular releases
Solution Influences	
Requirements Churn	There is a strong likelihood that there will be significant changes to requirements (and the solution) during the project
Solution Complexity	The required solution is relatively complex (e.g., requires the use of unfamiliar technologies) and/or there are many different solution options
Time-to-market	The deadline (time) is the most important factor for the solution, while the scope of the solution is flexible

Continued

Table 13.3 Lifecycle Selection Criteria—cont'd	
Management Influences	
Dependencies	There are no (or only a few) dependencies on internal or external suppliers
Release Frequency	The solution can be subdivided into viable and meaningful business releases that can be delivered within 3-4 months
Demonstrability	The solution can be easily demonstrated on an incremental basis (through a user interface, for example)

13.7.2 Tailor the method

Aside from the selection of an appropriate project lifecycle and the selection of appropriate practices, it is sometimes necessary to also look at additional method tailoring. In particular, the key elements of any method—roles, tasks, and work products—should be examined to ensure that they are minimal but sufficient for the job at hand. Differences between rather abstract *small* and *large* projects are given in Table 13.4.

One mistake that I've seen made in organizations adopting agile is to measure successful tailoring by the reduction in the number of work products defined. This is, in my opinion, a completely bogus measure. If I take the 20 work products I might create on a project and mandate that, to keep things simple, we're only going to have two work products, have I really improved anything? Given that the same information needs to be captured, surely this only makes things worse as different practitioners compete to work on the same work products.

Table 13.4 Method-Tailoring Considerations		
Element	**Small Project**	**Large Project**
Role	No specific architect role is required (architecture-related considerations will be handled by the team)	Different individuals are assigned to the following architecture-centric roles: Application Architect, Infrastructure Architect, Data Architect, and Security Architect
Task	An Architecture Overview is created as a sketch on a whiteboard and then photographed (it is not kept up to date)	An Architecture Overview is created as a UML model that is maintained
Work Product	Functional and Deployment viewpoints are used to communicate the architecture	Requirements, Functional, Deployment, Validation, Performance, and Security viewpoints are used to communicate the architecture

13.7.3 **Consider all elements of a development environment**

In adopting agile (or any other method, for that matter) in an organization of any reasonable size, it quickly becomes clear that a focus purely on method is insufficient. In addition to other technology-related elements, such as software development tools, we also need to focus on the people aspect since, as a colleague once told me, "Tools don't write software; people do."

In order to put some structure into the key items that must be considered in a successful "transformation," I defined a comprehensive definition of all elements of a development environment that should be considered, as shown in Figure 13.2 [27].

The key elements of this framework are as follows:

- *Method*: A key element of any development environment is the method that is followed, formally or informally, by practitioners. Key method-related elements are roles, work products, tasks, and processes. Supplementary method elements are standards, guidelines, checklists, templates, and examples.
- *Tools*: Development tooling automates aspects of the method being followed. For example, we may use a tool for storing and managing requirements on a development project, use a tool for visually modeling our architectures and designs, use tools for testing our software, and so on. Tool integrations are another important element. Tools are particularly relevant in an agile world,

FIGURE 13.2

Elements of a development environment.

since practices such as continuous integration are only effective if fit-for-purpose tools are used.

- *Infrastructure*: A development environment considers infrastructure in terms of both hardware and software. As well as the obvious infrastructure required to host any development tools, we may require supporting hardware and software, such as operating system software, a database management system, or board-level controls and test harnesses if developing for real-time or embedded devices.
- *Enablement*: Enablement (training and mentoring) of practitioners in the use of the development environment contributes to its successful adoption. An aspect of a development environment is therefore the definition and creation of training and mentoring materials that can be applied. Mature organizations also pay particular attention to the professionalization of their staff and any alignment with external standards, certifications, and professional bodies.
- *Organization*: Another consideration of a development environment is ensuring that an appropriate organization is in place to define, deploy, and manage it. This may include specialists in certain aspects of the development environment (such as method experts, tool specialists, trainers, and mentors), personnel to administer and support the environment, personnel with appropriate skills on the company helpdesk, and appropriate communities of practice.
- *Adoption*: In addition to the elements listed above, we should also be concerned with the adoption of the environment within an organization, a business unit, or a development project. Key adoption-related elements are an adoption plan, techniques for driving the organizational changes required to introduce and embed the development environment into the day-to-day working practices of the affected organizational areas, and a definition of environment metrics that are used to gauge the effectiveness of the environment.
- *Cross Cutting Concerns*: Also shown in Figure 13.2 are crosscutting concerns that represent the requirements on the development environment (and the development environment must realize that fact), and can be considered in terms of functionality, qualities, and constraints.

13.7.4 Adopt change incrementally

Knowing *what* needs to change is only half the picture; we also need to know *how* to go about making a change. There are several frameworks that focus on how to go about organizational change, an oft-cited work being *Leading Change* by John Kotter, which provides an eight-step approach [28]. One specific success pattern, when it comes to improving an IT organization's development capability, is to adopt change incrementally.

In essence, this practice suggests that we shouldn't change everything at once, for the simple reason that people (and departments and organizations) can only absorb so much change at once. When it comes to the adoption of agile, for example, we may choose to introduce certain practices before others so that practitioners become familiar with these before moving on to further practices. This is exactly the approach

I took with a large European bank, and it worked well. Of course, some practices are dependent on others—with certain core practices, such as iterative development, typically being tackled early on.

There are also different routes to the end goal of changing the way an entire organization works. Two dimensions to be considered are the organizational scope (the number of users impacted) and the technical scope (the number of practices to be introduced, along with other elements of a development environment, such as tools). This is shown in Figure 13.3, where we see two possible paths to a goal of introducing a set of practices across an entire organization. One path is to introduce a small number of practices to a team before they are extended further to several projects and eventually to the entire organization. Once this is successful (and an understanding of how change can be effectively achieved in the organization has been established), then additional practices can be applied across the organization. An alternative route is to introduce practices in a piecemeal fashion to a small group of individuals until they are completely up to speed. These individuals would then act as champions on different projects and enable others who would themselves become champions. Eventually, the entire organization is enabled. Other (hybrid) approaches are also possible, of course.

13.7.5 Implement a center of excellence

In many organizations, the various elements that comprise a development environment are considered the responsibility of different departments. Responsibility for process improvement lies in one department, the provisioning of infrastructure and tools in another, enablement within a training department, and so on. In practice,

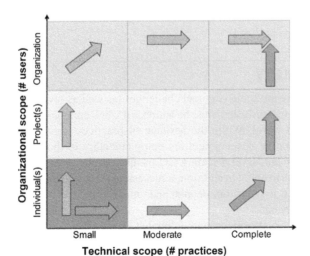

FIGURE 13.3

Incremental adoption patterns.

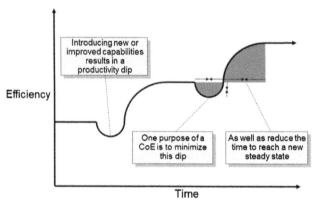

FIGURE 13.4

Minimizing the productivity dip.

it makes a lot of sense to coordinate all of these elements (even if it is a "virtual" organization with only one or two full-time staff) within a single body, referred to as a center of excellence (CoE). The CoE is responsible for provisioning a development environment as a service to projects, where consideration of the Information Technology Infrastructure Library (ITIL) in terms of service management is wholly appropriate, especially in very large organizations. Specifically, before (or as) a project starts, the project may request certain tools to be made available and infrastructure provisioned, team members to receive certain training, and mentors to be made available—and having a single "port of call" is an efficient means of making this happen.

One way of looking at a CoE is that its primary purpose is to reduce the inevitable productivity dip that arises when teams are introduced to new practices, as shown in Figure 13.4.

13.8 SUMMARY

In summary, there are some very real challenges (as well as several myths) concerning architecture and agile that must be addressed when embracing architecture practices in an agile world. While the heritage of practices from architecture-centric methods and iterative development are complementary to those that are the basis of agile development, several scaling factors also require us to consider a more disciplined approach to agile. In addition, a successful transition to agile within an organization requires a focus on people and appropriate techniques for managing organizational change.

In particular, a platform for innovation that embraces architecture and agile practices can benefit from several lessons learned. These include the implementation of a project lifecycle selection framework, an approach for tailoring any defined method, a consideration of all elements of a development environment, incremental adoption of change, and the implementation of a CoE.

References

[1] Darwin C. On the origin of species by means of natural selection. London: John Murray; 1859.

[2] Booch G. An architectural oxymoron. IEEE Softw 2010;27(5):95–6.

[3] Abrahamsson P, Babar MA, Kruchten P. Agility and architecture: can they coexist? IEEE Softw 2010;27(2):16–22.

[4] Kruchten P. Software architecture and agile software development: a clash of two cultures? In: 2010 ACM/IEEE 32nd international conference on software engineering. Cape Town: IEEE; 2010. p. 497–8.

[5] Ambler S. Agile modeling. New York: Wiley; 2002.

[6] Pei Breivold H, Sundmark D, Wallin P, Larsson S. What does research say about agile and architecture? In: 2010 Fifth international conference on software engineering advances (ICSEA). Los Alamitos, California: IEEE; 2010. p. 32–7.

[7] Ambler S, Lines M. Disciplined agile delivery. Boston: IBM Press; 2012.

[8] Schwaber K, Beedle M. Agile software development with scrum. Upper Saddle River, NJ: Prentice Hall; 2002.

[9] Manifesto for agile software development. Retrieved 2001, from agile manifesto: http://agilemanifesto.org/; 2001.

[10] Coplien JO, Bjørnvig G. Lean architecture. West Sussex: Wiley; 2010.

[11] Eeles P, Cripps P. The process of software architecting. Upper Saddle River, NJ: Addison-Wesley; 2009.

[12] Kruchten P. The "4+1" view model of architecture. IEEE Softw 1995;12(6):42–50.

[13] Bass L, Clements P, Kazman R. Software architecture in practice. Boston: Addison-Wesley; 2003.

[14] Nord RL, Tomayko JE. Software architecture-centric methods and agile development. IEEE Softw 2006;23(2):47–53.

[15] Rational Unified Process version 7.5.1. IBM; 2010.

[16] Royce W. Software project management—a unified framework. Boston, MA: Addison-Wesley; 1998.

[17] Boehm B. Get ready for agile methods, with care. IEEE Computer 2002;35(1):64–9.

[18] Beck K. Extreme programming explained. Boston: Addison-Wesley; 2005.

[19] Fowler M. Is design dead? Retrieved 2012, from martinfowler.com: http://martinfowler.com/articles/designDead.html; 2000.

[20] Ambler S, Gonzalez C. Agile model-driven development. Retrieved 2008, from sticky minds: www.stickyminds.com/BetterSoftware/magazine.asp?fn=cifea&ac=367.

[21] Poppendieck M, Poppendieck T. Lean software development. Boston: Addison-Wesley; 2003.

[22] Spinellis D. Software tracks. IEEE Softw 2010;27(2):10–1.

[23] Brown AW. Enterprise software delivery. Boston: Addison-Wesley; 2012.

[24] Madison J. Agile-architecture interactions. IEEE Softw 2010;27(2):41–8.

[25] Boehm B, Turner R. Balancing agility and discipline. Boston: Addison-Wesley; 2003.

[26] Griffiths M. Agile suitability filters. Retrieved 2009, from leading answers: http://leadinganswers.typepad.com/leading_answers/files/agile_suitability_filters.pdf; 2007.

[27] Eeles P. Define the scope of your development environment. Retrieved 2011, from IBM developer works: www.ibm.com/developerworks/rational/library/define-scope-development-environment/index.html; 2011.

[28] Kotter JP. Leading change. Boston, MA: Harvard Business Review Press; 1996.

Opportunities, Threats, and Limitations of Emergent Architecture

14

Uwe Friedrichsen

Codecentric AG, Solingen, Germany

CHAPTER CONTENTS

14.1 INTRODUCTION

One of the most discussed topics in the area of architecture in an agile context is *emergent architecture*. It is closely related to the discussion of whether an architect is still needed in agile projects or whether all of the architectural work can be done by the development team. Before analyzing this claim, it is necessary to clarify what the term *emergent architecture* exactly means. To do this, a definition of *emergence* is required.

14.1.1 A brief definition of emergence

Jerry Goldstein uses the following definition for emergence: "[Emergence is] the arising of novel and coherent structures, patterns, and properties during the process of self-organization in complex systems" [1]; Wikipedia[a] notes that "...emergence is the way complex systems and patterns arise out of a multiplicity of relatively simple interactions" [2].

Many more (similar) definitions exist, but those two are sufficient to identify the core characteristics that are relevant in the context of emergent architecture:

- *Complex systems*—Emergence happens within complex environments.
- *Structures, patterns, and properties*—Emergence creates new structures, patterns, and properties (usually to solve a complex task).
- *Arise*—This is the most important characteristic of emergence. The creation of novel structures and patterns is not an explicit act but happens as a side effect of executing a seemingly unrelated task over and over again.
- *Relatively simple interactions*—The seemingly unrelated tasks are at least an order of magnitude simpler than the emerging result.
- *Self-organization*—Coming from systems theory, self-organization always has a goal (a task to be solved or a desired end state to be reached) and is limited by a set of constraints.

In a less formal way, people often refer to emergence if they say something like, "The result is more than the sum of its parts" or "One plus one is more than two."

14.1.2 The idea of emergent architecture

After clarifying the term *emergence* and its characteristics, it can be used to define emergent architecture. The goal of emergent architecture is to create the architecture for a (nontrivial) system—its fundamental structures, patterns, and properties. The interactions used to achieve this goal are activities developers usually execute all the time:

- (Business) features are implemented in a continuous cycle of implementation and refactoring. Often, this cycle is extended to a full test-driven development cycle: Write a test that fails; write some code so the test succeeds; refactor the code without breaking the test; continue with the next test.

In addition, a few guiding principles are used to provide the direction of the refactoring:

- Often, the SOLID principles [3] are used—a few principles that help you create better object-oriented designs. These principles often are complemented by some

---

[a]The use of Wikipedia as a reference is heavily discussed, especially in the academic community. It is used in this situation because it is sufficient with respect to the intention.

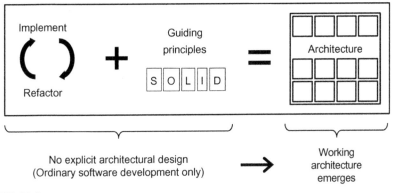

FIGURE 14.1

The claim of emergent architecture.

more principles (see also Ref. [3]). It is important to note that the SOLID principles are not architectural principles but design principles. They address a much more detailed level of software than architecture usually does.

The claim of emergent architecture is that executing the implement-and-refactor cycle over and over again, using some design principles like the SOLID principles for guiding the refactoring, will result in a complete architecture—without doing any explicit architectural work (see Figure 14.1).

Advocates of emergent architecture also claim that the resulting architecture is not only sufficient, but optimal, using the following reasoning: A refactoring always aims to create the simplest and smallest solution that works and fulfills the guiding principles. Because the simplest and smallest solution is also the solution that can be maintained and changed best, an emergent architecture is also an optimal architecture. Many agile advocates derive from this idea that architects are not needed anymore because the development team alone can create the architecture by doing their normal development work.

However, the author's observations in concrete commercial projects did not prove the claim described before. After a while, projects working with a purely emergent architecture approach suffered from problems that are usually addressed by architectural work. Often, good high-level abstractions were missing, which resulted in decreased understandability of the overall system and in reduced changeability. Also, distinct responsibilities were not separated properly, also resulting in reduced changeability. In one project, this became so extreme that the development team did not dare implement a change to the business logic in a system they had just started implementing from scratch 5 months earlier.

The remainder of this chapter will examine if and to what extent the claim of emergent architecture holds true. Therefore, first the purpose, activities, and objectives of architectural work will be examined. Afterwards it will be analyzed if emergent architecture is suitable to replace the different activities and objectives of architectural work with respect to its purpose. In the discussion, the strengths and weaknesses of explicit and emergent architectural work will be contrasted with each other, and a joint approach will be recommended.

14.2 PURPOSE, ACTIVITIES, AND OBJECTIVES OF ARCHITECTURE

To analyze whether emergent architecture can replace explicit architectural work, it is first necessary to have a solid understanding of the purpose, activities, and objectives of architectural work. The problem with most existing definitions is that they are either incomplete—usually only focusing on the objectives—or blurry. This makes it impossible to challenge emergent architecture if it suits the definition.

Therefore, this chapter uses a different approach. It tries to answer the following questions (see also Figure 14.2):

- *Why?*—Why is architectural work done at all? What is its purpose? What is it good for?
- *How?*—How is architectural work done? What are the activities of solid architectural work?
- *What?*—What are the objectives of architecture? What are the important pieces?

The answers to these questions are based on the experience of the author of this chapter. They are the result of years of observations in commercial projects, discussions

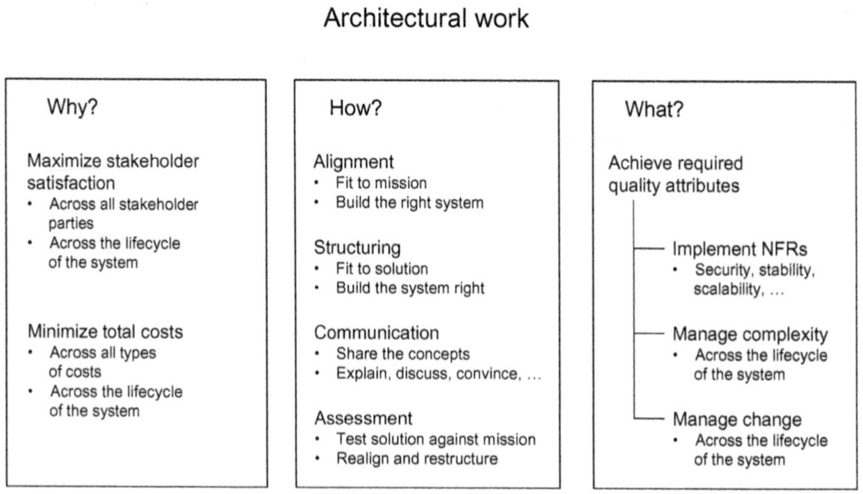

Architectural work

Why?	How?	What?
Maximize stakeholder satisfaction • Across all stakeholder parties • Across the lifecycle of the system	Alignment • Fit to mission • Build the right system Structuring • Fit to solution • Build the system right	Achieve required quality attributes ├─ Implement NFRs • Security, stability, scalability, ...

Minimize total costs
• Across all types of costs
• Across the lifecycle of the system
	Communication
	• Share the concepts
	• Explain, discuss, convince, ...
	
	Assessment
	• Test solution against mission
	• Realign and restructure
		├─ Manage complexity
		  • Across the lifecycle of the system
		
		└─ Manage change
		  • Across the lifecycle of the system

FIGURE 14.2

Architecture—Purpose, activities, and objectives.

with many other IT people—especially architects—and testing the answers against various descriptions in the literature.[b]

14.2.1 Purpose—the Why of architecture

Almost all definitions of architecture only address the *What* question. Therefore, an empirical approach is used to answer the *Why* of architecture: If the "Why?" question is asked often enough in a commercial software project, it will boil down to the following two motivations, almost regardless of the concrete activity the question is asked about:

- Maximize the satisfaction of someone
- Minimize of the cost of something

For architecture, both motivations need to be considered. What makes architecture special with respect to many other activities is the fact that the two purposes described before have more than one dimension:

- Architecture aims to maximize the satisfaction of *all involved stakeholder parties*. It is not enough to satisfy a single party—for example, the developers. The operations department also needs to be considered, as well as the project managers, the support team, and so on. Typical stakeholder parties are developers, users, customers, management, project managers, deployment managers, operations, infrastructure management, security officers, support, hotline staff, and more. Of course, it is not possible to maximize the satisfaction of each party individually, but a balanced compromise needs to be found that maximizes the overall satisfaction of all involved parties.
- Architecture aims to minimize the *overall costs*. As with the satisfaction of the stakeholder parties, it is necessary to look at all types of costs and not to focus on only one type of cost. Typical cost types are development, hardware, license, deployment, operations, power, support, maintenance, usage, and more. Again, it is not possible to minimize each cost type individually, but the overall costs (i.e., the sum of the different cost types) have to be optimized.
- Time is the second dimension architecture has to take into account: It is not sufficient to maximize satisfaction and minimize costs for a limited time frame (usually a project). Instead, *the whole (remaining) lifecycle* of the affected system needs to be considered. For example: It is relatively easy to minimize development costs for a project, but usually the upcoming projects and the maintenance team will have to pay a high interest if they are not taken into account beforehand. On the other hand, it does not make sense to create a highly adaptable solution for a system that is close to the end of its lifecycle.

---

[b]This way, the definition of architecture given in this chapter is not a formal, academic one. It is an empirical one based on experience. It is up to the reader to decide if he or she is willing to accept a definition of this kind.

In summary, the purpose of architecture is to maximize the satisfaction of the involved stakeholders and to minimize the overall costs across the lifecycle of the affected system(s).[c]

14.2.2 Activities—the How of architecture

Since most definitions of architecture only revolve around the *What* of architecture, a mixed approach is used to answer the *How* question: First, the author observed the activities of several experienced architects over time and categorized them into distinct activity types. To test the completeness of the activities identified this way, existing architecture process models like the one for arc42 [4] were used to check if any of the activities were not covered by the activity types discovered before. Using this approach, the following four types of activities were identified:

- *Alignment*—all activities are related to making sure the solution will fit its mission. This consists of talking to the stakeholders, figuring out their needs, drivers, and requirements, negotiating compromises, resolving contradictions in requirements, and more. In a less formal way, alignment is about doing the right thing. Based on the author's observations, activities of this type are often neglected by less experienced architects.
- *Structuring*—all activities are related to creating a solution design. This consists of taking the information gathered in alignment and turning it into a solution design. The solution design should reflect the requirements and be as easy to understand as possible. In a less formal way, structuring is about doing the thing right. Based on the author's observations, less experienced architects only focus on activities of this type.
- *Communication*—"Selling" a solution design is an important—yet often underestimated—part of architectural work. This consists of explaining the concepts and ideas in the design, which decisions were made and why they were made, convincing people to ensure the design is implemented, and more.
- *Assessment*—Architectural designs need to be validated to see if they still fit their mission. Requirements change over time, new drivers and needs emerge, and the existing architecture might not support them properly anymore. Also, solution designs often degenerate over time as a result of varying teams working on the software while not having the original concepts and ideas in their minds. Thus, it is necessary to assess the architecture of a system for its fittingness on a regular base and to derive necessary actions to refit the solution with its missions.

It is possible to split up the activity types further, but this granularity is sufficient with respect to the question of whether emergent architecture can replace explicit architectural work. Two additional observations allow us to ignore two out of the four activity types for the rest of the chapter:

---

[c]This is an important reason why architecture is so hard to understand for many people and many definitions are so vague: The rationale of an architectural decision often remains unclear if one looks at only one stakeholder party or one cost type, and the fact that cause and effect are often separated by months or years makes it even harder.

- *Communication* is always required: A structure that seems to be evident for one person can be perceived very differently by a second person, and often design decisions are not obvious. Therefore, architecture always needs to be communicated—no matter if it was designed explicitly or was emergent.
- *Assessment* can be treated as a subset of alignment in the given context: The activities related to assessments are similar to the ones related to alignment, but an assessment usually has a much more limited scope. Therefore, it is sufficient to challenge emergent architecture with the alignment activities.

14.2.3 Objectives—the What of architecture

Dozens—if not hundreds—of definitions exist that describe the *What* of architecture (see Ref. [5] for a collection of definitions the Software Engineering Institute of the Carnegie Mellon University gathered over the years). The perfect definition does not exist; creating unification or intersection of all definitions is not possible.[d] In this chapter, the following definition is used:

The objective of architecture is to achieve the required software quality attributes.

This definition is used because it is better actionable than many other definitions. It is possible to list the software quality attributes and to check if they can be achieved using emergent architecture. To list the software quality attributes, the ISO/IEC 9126 standard [6] is used. It defines the following software quality attributes:

- *Functionality*—A set of attributes that bear on the existence of a set of functions and their specified properties. The functions satisfy stated or implied needs.
  - Suitability
  - Accuracy
  - Interoperability
  - Security
  - Functionality Compliance
- *Reliability*—A set of attributes that bear on the capability of software to maintain its level of performance under stated conditions for a stated period of time.
  - Maturity
  - Fault Tolerance
  - Recoverability
  - Reliability Compliance
- *Usability*—A set of attributes that bear on the effort needed for use, and on the individual assessment of such use, by a stated or implied set of users.
  - Understandability
  - Learnability
  - Operability

---

[d]All definitions are more or less correct, but each one has a different focus. Therefore, most people usually pick an arbitrary definition depending on the key aspect they want to stress in their current context.

- Attractiveness
- Usability Compliance
- *Efficiency*—A set of attributes that bear on the relationship between the level of performance of the software and the amount of resources used under stated conditions.
  - Time Behavior
  - Resource Utilization
  - Efficiency Compliance
- *Maintainability*—A set of attributes that bear on the effort needed to make specified modifications.
  - Analyzability
  - Changeability
  - Stability
  - Testability
  - Maintainability Compliance
- *Portability*—A set of attributes that bear on the ability of software to be transferred from one environment to another.
  - Adaptability
  - Installability
  - Coexistence
  - Replaceability
  - Portability Compliance

The quality attributes in the areas of *functionality, reliability, usability, efficiency,* and *portability* address system properties that can be implemented like normal functional requirements: The requirement needs to be understood: a solution is designed, implemented (or configured), and delivered—with or without feedback and refinement cycles. In an agile approach, the requirements can even be written down as user stories. The only difference from functional requirements is that expertise in a different domain (for example, the security domain) is required.

The attributes in the area of *maintainability*, on the other hand, need a fundamentally different approach. They address the management of complexity and change, which matches the definition of architecture that John Zachman came up with: "The reasons you need architecture: complexity and change" [7]. Mapping these quality attributes to design actions leads to *design for understandability* (manages complexity) and *design for change* (manages change). Figure 14.3 summarizes the different objectives that can be derived from the software quality attributes.

14.3 ANALYSIS OF EMERGENT ARCHITECTURE

Having examined the purpose, activities, and objectives of architecture, the next step is to analyze whether the described activities can be replaced by emergent architecture with respect to the purpose of architecture.

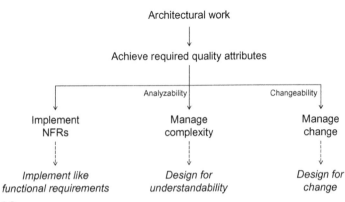

FIGURE 14.3

Objectives of architectural work.

14.3.1 **Alignment**

Alignment is the part of architectural work where an architect makes sure that the solution fits its mission (does the right thing). This basically consists of many discussions with stakeholders, trying to understand their needs and drivers to make sure that the requirements are understood correctly, that no important requirements are missing, that conflicts and contradicting requirements are resolved, and that the knowledge is spread in the implementation team. This kind of work requires at least the following skill set (see Refs. [8,9] for more details):

- Interacting with the involved parties through (pro-)active communication, negotiation, mediation, teamwork, conflict resolution, finding compromises, listening, talking, convincing, and more.
- Understanding the stakeholders' 'languages' to be able to understand their drivers, needs, and requirements.
- Speaking in the stakeholders' 'languages' to become accepted as professional peers. Stakeholders often do not accept people who do not "talk their language."—making communication a lot harder and reducing the willingness of the stakeholders to discuss their problems and requirements.
- Understanding the surrounding organization and politics, so as to not get caught in the crossfire.

Alignment is a crucial success factor with regard to the purposes of architectural work.[e] Two observations can be made with respect to emergent architecture:

- Alignment is not emergent, but explicit work. It does not emerge from the repeating cycle of implementation and refactorings.

---

[e]Yet, surprisingly often it is neglected in discussions and articles about architecture.

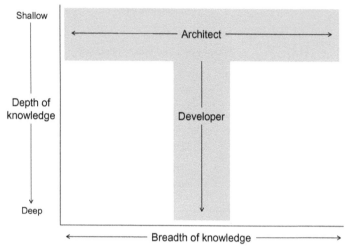

FIGURE 14.4

Different skill sets for architects and developers.

Source: Stefan Zörner.

- The skill set required for alignment is not a developer skill set. The alignment skill set is very different from a skill set required to implement software, and it takes a lot of time and experience to build it up. Also, this skill set cannot be acquired only by implementing software.

Figure 14.4 explains the latter observation in more detail. It shows a simplified knowledge distribution for different roles. On the X-axis the breadth of knowledge is shown, and on the Y-axis the depth of knowledge is shown. As a software developer, a very deep understanding in a quite limited domain is needed: programming language, frameworks, libraries, design patterns, coding techniques, and so on.

On the other hand, architectural work (and especially alignment) requires a very broad knowledge: knowing the domains of the involved stakeholders well enough to understand their needs and requirements and to be able to communicate on a peer level. A lot of soft skills are also required.

This observation leads to the following conclusion: the concept that an agile developer team can replace an architect completely is questionable because it cannot be assumed in general that a developer team has the required skill set to do the alignment work.

This still leaves the alternative to not do alignment work at all and to rely on pure emergent architecture to produce the required results without explicit alignment work. Two observations can be made with regard to this approach:

- Without talking to stakeholders intensely and resolving conflicts actively, the risk is very high that architectural requirements are not correctly understood and implemented. Even if this might become visible in a later feedback cycle, it would violate the purpose of architectural work: to maximize stakeholder satisfaction and to minimize overall costs. Additionally, the consequences of wrong architectural decisions might not become visible for a long time—especially if they affect understandability or changeability (i.e., the immediate feedback cycles of agile approaches might not help).

- Without alignment, there is a high risk that the needs of developers are overemphasized while the requirements of all other stakeholder parties are neglected. This would also violate the purpose of architecture.

In summary: Alignment is a crucial part of architectural work; *it needs to be done explicitly and cannot be omitted or replaced by an emergent approach* without violating the purpose of architectural work.

14.3.2 **Structuring**

Structuring as an architectural activity is needed for *orientation* and *communication*. The *orientation* aspect refers to the fact that human brains are not capable of dealing with lots of information on the same level. To overcome this limitation, information is put into structures that help people to find a specific piece of information easily and to communicate efficiently about information pieces and relations amongst them. Typical software systems consist of thousands or millions of information details which make an organizing structure indispensable.

As a means of orientation, a structure always supports a specific use case. It is important to note that a structure that supports one use case very well might not support a second use case at all. As an example, structuring a lot of e-mails by date helps to efficiently find e-mails that were received in a specific timeframe. But this structure does not help at all if all e-mails related to a specific topic should be found. In general, it is not possible to create a structure that supports all possible use cases equally well.

The use cases that architectural structure needs to support are the objectives of architecture: implementation of nonfunctional requirements, design for understandability, and design for change. The next sections will analyze whether emergent architecture helps to support these use cases.

One additional observation can be made with respect to emergent architecture: the architectural structure needs to be communicated and is used as a means of *communication*. For all stakeholder groups who are not developers, this means that some architectural documentation that is not a code, must be created because a code is only understood by developers. The creation of this documentation is always explicit work. It is not a result of the emergent coding and refactoring cycle. Therefore, structuring *always involves some documentation that is not emergent*.

14.3.3 Implementation of nonfunctional requirements

This activity consists of the implementation of the requirements derived from the quality attributes in the sections *functionality, reliability, usability, efficiency,* and *portability* as described in the section about architecture objectives.

The implementation of these requirements does not necessarily require an architect, but does require a domain expert with respect to the particular nonfunctional domain (e.g., security). In non-agile project settings, it is the responsibility of an architect to make sure these requirements are taken into account, but it is also possible to impose this responsibility on the whole team.

These nonfunctional requirements are implemented as functional requirements. This also consists of the architectural activities of alignment, structuring, design for understandability, and design for change. The rest of the implementation requires a domain expert with respect to the requirements, not an architect. Therefore, this activity does not need to be analyzed in more detail. It is sufficient to analyze the architectural parts of it, which is done in the other four sections.

14.3.4 Design for understandability

Design for understandability is closely correlated to the structuring of the solution domain. Structure is required to keep track of the vast quantity of information, but there are also limitations to structure. Too much structure is also confusing because in this case the human brain is not capable of keeping track of the details of the structure. Therefore, it is important to keep the architectural structure as simple as possible to meet the design for understandability objective.

To meet this objective, two concepts need to be combined:

* The initial architectural structure needs to be as small as possible. Only the structure that is necessary to start the implementation should be designed up front.
* The architectural structure needs to be simplified whenever possible throughout the whole lifecycle of the system. It takes effort to keep the structure of a system simple. Without explicit counteraction, the structure will become more complicated with every change of the system.

Jim Coplien and Gertrud Bjørnvig provide an approach to decide what belongs in the initial architectural structure [10]: they suggest separating what they call the "form" and the "structure"[f] of the system. The "form" is basically the essence of the system— the mind model behind it, the invariants of the participating domains. The "structure" is everything else. The "structure" is subject to change across the lifecycle of the system; therefore, it does not add value to include it in the initial architectural design.

Explicitly modeling the essence of the system helps to create an initial structure that has very stable interfaces. Since the initial structure reflects core concepts of the involved domains, the system becomes easier to understand. The stability of the

---

[f]Please note that Coplien and Bjørnvig use the term "structure" with a different meaning than this chapter does. Therefore, for better distinction the term is quoted whenever used in the way Coplien and Bjørnvig are using it.

interfaces also improves the changeability, because changes are kept local without compromising interfaces.

Distilling such an *initial structure* is explicit work. *It does not emerge from a repeating cycle of implementation and refactorings.* Also, finding adequate abstractions requires a specific skill set and a lot of experience because even if it is well understood what separation of concerns means, it is still not well explored how to design separations best. A few heuristics—like separation by responsibility, by different change rate, by organizational structure, or by skill distribution—are known (see Ref. [10] for a collection), but yet creating an initial structure is a challenging task that requires a lot of experience.

Basically, it is possible to use the emergent architecture cycle to let the domain essence evolve, but this usually takes more time and resources than an explicit approach. It usually takes several attempts and redrawn designs before an emergently developed architecture converges towards the domain essence, and there is a risk that the essence will never be reached. This would violate the purpose of architectural work: to minimize overall costs and to maximize overall satisfaction.

The second concept required for design for understandability is the continuous simplification of the architectural structure. This is the core objective of refactorings, which are part of the emergent architecture cycle. This primarily affects the "structure" of the system, not the "form." The latter comprises the invariants of the system and therefore normally should not change much after initial design. The "structure" on the other hand is subject to frequent changes and therefore *should be designed using the emergent architecture approach* instead of doing it explicitly.

Based on the experience of the author of this chapter, this approach still bears the risk of a lack of coordination. Development teams who are new to emergent architecture often forget to share their design decisions with each other. As a result, the same requirement is solved in several different ways and usually it requires a large effort to unify the solutions later to enhance understandability.

A common technique to address this risk is to communicate and discuss design decisions in the development team to share the knowledge. Alternatively, architectural constraints can be used. To avoid later unification work, the required architectural constraints are defined and discussed up front and the whole team adheres to them. Architectural constraints help to avoid duplicate solutions without specifying the architecture in detail, thus leaving enough room for the solution to evolve.

14.3.5 Design for change

Design for change is about future change request. Formally a system only needs to be open for the change requests that affect the system throughout its lifecycle to provide a perfect design for change.

The obvious problem is that future change requests cannot be anticipated. This often leads to the following types of reaction:

- Analysis paralysis—architects do not dare to make decisions because they are afraid to miss a design decision that might become important in the future

- Extremely generic and flexible architectures—decisions are delayed by keeping the structure unspecific and open to as many kinds of future change requests as possible
- Ignorance—potential future change requests are ignored. Instead, the system is designed only to reflect the known requirements.

All reactions are suboptimal and violate the purpose of architecture. The first one prevents implementation because decisions are required to start coding effectively. The standard reaction is that the developers start coding without any base architectural structure, which usually is suboptimal, too (see the previous subsection about design for understandability for details).

The second reaction compromises understandability. Every flexibility point in a system increases its complexity, which makes it harder to understand, but understandability is the prerequisite for changeability. It is not possible to change a system dependably without understanding it. Thus, too much flexibility compromises understandability and in turn changeability. It is a crucial part of architectural work to find a reasonable balance between understandability and flexibility.

The third reaction ignores information that is usually available at design time, which could help to make better decisions, violating the purpose of architectural work. Even though it is not possible to predict upcoming change requests exactly, it is possible to identify likelihoods for certain types of change requests. These can be used to make better decisions about where to put a flexibility point.

To identify the likelihoods of upcoming change requests, the following tools can be used:

- The *business domain* needs to be understood well. Most of the future change requests are rooted in the business domain. Understanding the concept of this domain makes it easier to create changeable designs.
- The *business strategy* should be examined. By gaining an understanding of where the company is heading and what their top objectives are, a lot of upcoming change requests can be anticipated.
- The *needs and drivers of the stakeholders* should be understood as well as possible. Both create a desire for change, which results in change requests.
- The *business and IT market trends* need to be analyzed (including competitor analysis). Understanding where the market is going to move to helps in understanding upcoming external pressure on the company, which usually results in change requests.
- *Scenario-based architecture assessment* workshop formats like the Architecture Tradeoff Analysis Method (ATAM) [11] or the Cost Benefit Analysis Method (CBAM) [12] can be used to identify and prioritize potential change requests in a very efficient manner.[g]

---

[g]Identifying and prioritizing future change requests that are going to affect the architecture are not actually the core objectives of those workshop formats, but they also deliver this information effectively.

Using these tools helps to distill the *direction of change*—the most likely types of upcoming change requests. Flexibility points should be provided for the most likely change requests. This does not necessarily mean to provide for something configurable. Often, it is sufficient to separate responsibilities by introducing an adequate interface to keep upcoming changes local. Since increased flexibility compromises understandability, it is important to not introduce too many flexibility points.

This approach does not help predict future change requests across the whole lifecycle of a system. Depending on the business and IT environment of the system, this approach usually helps predict future change requests for several months or up to a year, sometimes a bit longer than a year. Still, the architectural decisions made on this basis age because the drivers of change requests change over time, and eventually some decisions will become invalid.

Therefore, architecture and architectural decisions need to be reevaluated on a regular basis. This means the new direction of change needs to be distilled to figure out which flexibility points might have become obsolete and which new ones are needed. Using this approach, architecture can be kept lean and changeable across the whole lifecycle of the system.

Distilling the *direction of change* is explicit work. *It does not emerge from a repeating cycle of implementation and refactorings.* It is also possible to use the emergent architecture cycle to adapt the architecture to changing requirements, but this would usually take a lot more time and resources than the explicit approach. This in turn would violate the purpose of architectural work: to minimize overall costs and to maximize overall satisfaction.

14.4 DISCUSSION

In this discussion, the strength and weaknesses of explicit and emergent architectural work will be contrasted with each other and a joint approach will be recommended.

14.4.1 Comparison of explicit and emergent architecture

The previous section shows the following results for the question of whether architectural activities can be replaced by emergent architecture:

- *Alignment* cannot be replaced by emergent architecture.
- *Structuring* must support the objectives of architectural work: implementation of nonfunctional requirements, design for understandability, and design for change. Therefore, emergent architecture is challenged against the objectives, not against the structuring. If a structure is documented for communication with stakeholders who are not developers, this documentation must not be a code, which means it does not result from the emergent implement and refactor cycle.
- The *implementation of nonfunctional requirements* does not require an architect, but an expert for the particular domain. Therefore, this activity is

not treated as core architectural activity. It *can* be done by an architect, but it *does not need to* be done by an architect.

- *Design for understandability* can be done purely emergently, but that would usually violate the purpose of architectural work (maximizing overall stakeholder satisfaction, minimizing overall costs across the lifecycle of the system). A better approach is to design the essence of the system explicitly and let the rest evolve using emergent architecture—potentially guided by some architectural constraints to avoid duplicate solution designs.
- *Design for change* can be neglected using a purely emergent approach, but this would violate the purpose of architectural work. A better approach is to distill the direction of change from time to time (depending on the change rate of the system environment) to optimize the design decisions.

This summary leads to the comparison of explicit and emergent architectural work shown in Figure 14.5. In addition to the comparison itself, the figure also shows the relative effort of the distinct architectural activities if compared to each other (based on the experience of the author of the chapter):

- *Alignment* is a relatively big effort—especially in early system implementation phases. Lots of missing information needs to be gathered, vague requirements need to be clarified to make them implementable, conflicting requirements need to be resolved, and much more. At a given point in time, only the amount of alignment work necessary for the next iteration to be started safely should be done. This is comparable to the work a Scrum product owner needs to do to make sure the product backlog is ready for the next sprint.
- Creating *design for changeability* is a relatively small effort. Most of the required information can be gathered while doing alignment work, and any missing information usually can be gathered quite quickly. Distilling the direction of change and deciding about additional flexibility points is a straightforward activity if the required information is available.

Architectural activity	Alignment	Design for changeability	Design for understandability	
			Domain essence ("Form")	Detailled structure ("Structure")
Relative effort	Big	Small	Small	Huge
Explicit approach	(++)	(+)	(+)	(--)
Emergent approach	(--)	(-)	(o)	(++)

FIGURE 14.5

Comparison of explicit and emergent architectural work.

- Designing the *essence of the system* ("form") is usually a relatively small effort. Most of the required knowledge is gathered in alignment. The challenge is to find adequate abstractions. This requires a specific skill set and a lot of experience.
- Creating the *detailed structure* ("structure") is by far the biggest effort. All other activities require a lot less effort than this activity.

When looking at explicit and emergent architectural work, it can be observed that the two approaches complement one another. While explicit architectural work can cover all activities, it provides the highest value in alignment and design for change. It is also suitable to distill the essence of the system, with the limitation that it is not very well understood how to best create separations. Doing the whole detailed design explicitly is usually a waste of time and has little value. The architect becomes a bottleneck, doing work that often can be delegated to developers, and does not have sufficient time to do the activities of higher value. Often, a few architectural constraints are enough explicit work in this area.

On the other hand, emergent architecture is a good approach to create an understandable, detailed structure. The amount of work can be distributed well across the whole development team. A few architectural constraints can help to avoid unnecessary duplicate solutions. The domain essence can also be distilled over time using emergent architecture, but this usually costs extra time and effort, violating the purpose of architectural work. Emergent architecture does not provide support for design for change or alignment (i.e., there is a high risk that the purpose of architectural work is violated by dissatisfying stakeholders or increasing overall costs if the emergent approach is not supported by additional activities to provide for alignment and design for change).

One question often raised in this context is, "Why cannot a product owner in Scrum (or the customer on site in Extreme Programming) take care of alignment and distilling the direction of change?" This way, there would not be the need for an architect and the development team could use a pure emergent approach. The little penalty for creating the domain essence in an emergent fashion is accepted.

In principle there is nothing wrong with a product owner taking care of some aspects of architectural work, but based on the experience of the author of this chapter, there are some issues associated with this approach:

- Most product owners only take care of functional requirements. Their reasoning is that they are responsible for the product backlog, which only consists of entries bearing business value. Since nonfunctional requirements of any kind do not bear business value, they do not feel responsible for nonfunctional requirements. Even if this reasoning is wrong (security, availability or performance definitively have business value), it is common practice that product owners do not take care of architectural needs.
- Product owners adopt some responsibilities of the traditional project manager role. They are especially responsible for achieving the goals of the associated project. If they were not only responsible for the success of the project, but also

for the success of the systems, they might suffer from contradictory goals. There-fore, it makes sense to separate the responsibilities for a project and a system.[h]

- Architectural work requires software development knowledge, which many prod-uct owners do not have. Product owners are often employees of a business depart-ment or a different non-IT department. If a person does not have the required skills for a specific task, the person tends to neglect it and focus on different tasks which she is more capable of executing.
- Architectural work should come from the team—either the whole team, or at least some specifically skilled team members—to share the knowledge across the team. Product owners, driving the projects, are often not considered part of the team; product owners request, teams deliver. This often imposes a boundary on the knowledge flow.

In summary, it is sometimes possible to let a product owner take care of align-ment and distilling the direction of change, but for the reasons described above in most projects it does not work well.

14.4.2 A joint approach

Given the knowledge of the last section, a joint approach for agile architectural work can be framed using the particular strengths of the explicit and the emergent approaches.

This leads to the overall joint approach for agile architectural work shown in Figure 14.6. From a development process point of view, the following architectural activities are needed to transform the stakeholder's requirements and needs into a solution and working code:

- *Alignment* needs to be done to align the solution to its mission. Stakeholders need to be understood, requirements need to be clarified, and conflicts need to be resolved. This also means learning the stakeholders' "languages," and requires a lot of soft skills.
- *Design for change* consists of distilling the direction of change once in a while (the required frequency depends on the speed of change of the problem and the solution domain). The design of the domain essence also supports the changeabil-ity of the associated system.
- *Design for understandability* consists partially of designing the domain essence. Carving out the long-term stable parts of a system usually makes it a lot more understandable. But by far the largest chunk of the work is creating the detailed structure—the structure details needed to keep the solution understandable.
- *Structuring* is split into three pieces: The long-term stable parts, the mid-term sta-ble parts, and the volatile parts. The long-term stable parts are the essence

---

[h]Unfortunately, it is often forgotten to adapt the rights to the obligations. If someone is responsible for the success of a system and does not have any means to enforce required actions to be executed, the separation of responsibilities approach will not work.

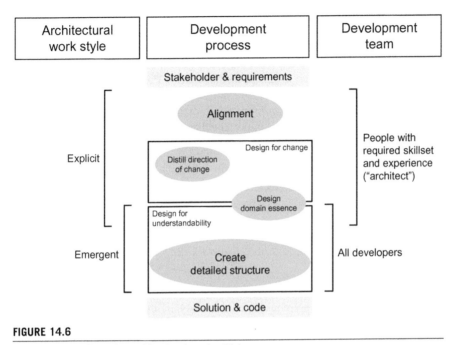

FIGURE 14.6

Joint approach for agile architectural work utilizing emergence.

("form") of the system, which needs to be distilled explicitly. To identify the mid-term stable parts and identify the proper additional flexibility points, design for change is used—which is also an explicit activity. The volatile parts evolve using emergent architecture, possibly guided by some architectural constraints to avoid duplicate solutions. As described before, the volatile part is by far the biggest part of the structuring effort. By using an emergent approach for this part, work is spread better and potentially scarce skills that are required for the other architectural activities are not wasted.

From an architectural work style perspective, the following observation can be made:

- Alignment, distilling the direction of change, and designing the domain essence are usually explicit architectural activities. They do not emerge from the emergent cycle of coding and refactoring. Even though it is possible to let the domain essence evolve from an emergent cycle, designing it explicitly usually conforms better to the goals of architectural work.
- Creating the detailed structure, and sometimes also designing the domain essence (with the limitations described before), can be done in an emergent way, leaving it to the emergent cycle of implementation and refactoring—accompanied by some guiding principles and some additional architectural constraints, if required.

From a team point of view, the following observations can be made:

- The emergent parts should be done by the whole development team.
- The explicit parts require a specific skill set and a lot of experience. Usually, only a few team members can take care of those tasks. For best knowledge sharing, these team members should also do normal software development. Based on the experience of the author, knowledge sharing works best if people work together on a task. Also, it is important that those specifically skilled people do not lose connection to the rest of the development team.[i]

This approach drastically reduces the amount of explicit architectural work, leveraging the power of emerging architecture. This way, the value of the overall architectural work is maximized and the skills of the persons involved are used best.

14.5 CONCLUSION

This chapter examined the claim that emergent architecture can replace explicit architectural work. As a prerequisite to the analysis, the purpose, activities, and objectives of architectural work were identified. After a careful examination, alignment, design for change, and design for understandability (which consists of distilling the essence of the system and detailed design) were identified as architectural activities that need to be analyzed with respect to the question of whether emergent architecture can replace explicit architectural work.

The analysis of the activities showed that alignment and design for change are not covered by the emergent architecture cycle consisting of coding and refactoring. Neglecting these activities would violate the purpose of architecture (i.e., overall stakeholder satisfaction would not be maximized and overall costs would not be minimized across the lifecycle of the corresponding system).

Distilling the essence ("form") of the system is also not covered by emergent architecture. It is possible to let the essence of the system evolve using emergent architecture, but this would also sacrifice the purpose of architecture by costing extra time and effort.

Creating an understandable, detailed design is very well covered by emergent architecture. Since this is by far the biggest activity of architectural work, it makes a lot of sense to use emergent architecture for it. This approach better spreads the majority of the architectural work and makes sure that potentially scarce skills are available for the other architectural activities that are not covered by emergent architecture.

---

[i]This is often a challenge, especially at the beginning of projects. Alignment uses up a lot of time, often leaving little opportunity for the people involved in it to perform other tasks. The author of this chapter does not know an easy solution for this problem, but it is important that the whole team deals with it actively.

A joint approach for agile architectural work was derived from the findings summarized before. It utilizes emergent architecture for the detailed design, while the other activities are done explicitly. The approach distributes the architectural work well across the team, and the potentially scarce people having the required skill set and experience can focus on the activities that are not covered by the emergent architecture cycle. This way, agile values are adopted best by maximizing the value created with the skills and experience available.

References

[1] Goldstein J. Emergence as a construct: history and issues. Emergence: complexity and organization (1.1) 49–72. Retrieved from http://www.anecdote.com.au/papers/EmergenceAsAConsutructIssue1_1_3.pdf; 1999.

[2] Wikipedia. Emergence. Retrieved from http://en.wikipedia.org/wiki/Emergence; 2012.

[3] Martin RC. The principles of OOD. Retrieved from http://butunclebob.com/ArticleS.UncleBob.PrinciplesOfOod; 2005.

[4] Starke G, Hruschka P. arc42 process model (available in German only). Retrieved from http://www.arc42.de/process/process/processdetails.html; 2012.

[5] Software Engineering Institute, Carnegie Mellon University. Community software architecture definitions. Retrieved from http://www.sei.cmu.edu/architecture/start/glossary/community.cfm; 2012.

[6] International Organization for Standardization. ISO/IEC 9126–1:2001 Software engineering—product quality—part 1: quality model. Retrieved from http://www.iso.org/iso/iso_catalogue/catalogue_tc/catalogue_detail.htm?csnumber=22749; 2011.

[7] Zachman JA. Introduction to the Zachman framework. [Presentation]. Presented at the enterprise architecture conference London 2008; 2007.

[8] Bredemeyer D, Malan R. The role of the architect. Retrieved from http://www.bredemeyer.com/pdf_files/role.pdf; 2006.

[9] Bredemeyer D, Malan R. Architect competence framework. Retrieved from http://www.bredemeyer.com/pdf_files/ArchitectCompetencyFramework.PDF; 2002.

[10] Coplien JO, Bjørnvig G. Lean architecture. Hoboken, NJ: John Wiley & Sons; 2010.

[11] Clements P, Kazman R, Klein M. Evaluating software architectures. Boston, MA: Addison-Wesley; 2002.

[12] Software Engineering Institute, Carnegie Mellon University. Cost benefit analysis method. Retrieved from http://www.sei.cmu.edu/architecture/tools/evaluate/cbam.cfm; 2012.

Architecture as a Key Driver for Agile Success: Experiences at Aviva UK

15

Ben Isotta-Riches and Janet Randell

Aviva, Norwich, UK

CHAPTER CONTENTS

15.1 INTRODUCTION

Aviva UK is part of a global organization that provides insurance, savings, and investment products to 43 million customers worldwide. Aviva is the UK's largest insurer, with more than 14 million customers, and is one of Europe's leading providers of life and general insurance. The UK business operates via a number of distribution channels including Internet, call center, broker, and corporate partners. The range of product offerings covers personal and commercial insurance, savings, investments, and pensions, and the company is frequently at the forefront of innovative new customer offerings, such as the provision of personal claims handlers.

In common with other large corporate organizations, Aviva has recognized the benefits of an agile approach to information technology (IT) change and has embarked on an agile transformation journey to give the business the agility and flexibility it needs in today's fast-changing business and financial environment. This chapter focuses on the experiences of Aviva UK during this transformation.

The waterfall approach has served us well historically. However, it has become increasingly clear that this approach alone no longer adequately supports the changing needs of the business. The pace of change in insurance markets is increasing rapidly, led by legislative changes, an increasing number and variety of competitor offerings, and the rapidly expanding range of opportunities offered by new technology and the use of social media. Financial markets change substantially in a period of days or even hours, reducing the validity, and therefore value, of change deliveries that are based on requirements documented and agreed to months, if not years, before deployment.

The key driver for transformation from the business side could be summarized as the need for business agility, interpreted as a shorter time from idea to delivery and increased flexibility in rebalancing investments as market demands evolve. To meet these needs requires IT to be able to respond to business requirements faster than ever before and, once engaged in the change delivery, to be responsive to changing requirements and priorities without increasing the risk and costs of the project.

Simultaneously, the IT department is increasingly focused on the need to drive further reductions in longer-term maintenance costs by increasing the quality and flexibility of delivered code. Although there is a strong focus on testing within the waterfall software delivery lifecycle, it is recognized that, in line with shifts in the industry, action must be taken to embed quality much earlier in the delivery life cycle.

The adoption of agile principles and practices is seen as a key enabler to achieve both business and IT aims. Transformation activity started in 2009, with the initiation of a small number of pilot projects.

Agile transformation is not, however, a trivial task for large and complex organizations such as Aviva UK. Many of the early adopters of agile approaches were small organizations, or at least had small, discrete IT development teams. These organizations have enjoyed considerable success; hence the increasing adoption of agile practices by larger, enterprise-scale organizations. Unfortunately, those that have applied an identical approach to the small, early adopters have frequently found themselves hitting significant issues and failing to achieve the expected benefits. The experience that our agile consultants brought to us was that a "pure" Scrum approach is unlikely to be successful in this type of organization: enhanced approaches and techniques are usually needed. These enhanced approaches must remain true to the agile manifesto and principles but must also acknowledge and allow for the size and complexity that is the reality both of our organization itself and the IT estate we manage (i.e., the complex portfolio of deployed IT applications and services). There are a range of changes to the "pure" Scrum approach that may be needed in a large corporate organization. However, we believe that the key driver for success in adopting agile practices within our organization is a focus on the impacts and requirements of the IT architecture, and we concentrate on these aspects for the purposes of this chapter.

In the early days of agile adoption, there was little mention of the word *architecture* in the available literature. Similarly, references to design activity tended to focus only on "in-sprint" design that would emerge during team collaboration and via refactoring. For example, *The Scrum Guide*, by Ken Schwaber and Jeff Sutherland

[1], makes no reference to architecture, and the only reference in Xprogramming. com [2] is the reference to build activity that may be undertaken as an "architectural spike." However, for large, complex organizations, the impacts of architectural complexity cannot be ignored, and a successful solution architecture and design is unlikely to emerge entirely as a result of in-sprint development.

Our own experiences of agile adoption, together with the external experience we have drawn on, have led us to the conclusion that there are three key architectural strategies that are necessary to drive agile success in a large, corporate organization such as Aviva UK. Before we describe these strategies in detail, we first provide some background to Aviva UK and the challenges inherent in a large-scale agile adoption for an organization of this size and complexity. We conclude by discussing how agile transformation and implementation of the architecture strategies must be pursued in parallel to drive early business benefit.

15.2 CHALLENGES TO AGILE ADOPTION AT AVIVA UK

Large financial services organizations like Aviva typically face a range of challenges to agile adoption. The complexity of these organizations will tend to be reflected in the IT systems that they have developed and delivered over time. As stated in Conway's law [3], *organizations which design systems ... are constrained to produce designs which are copies of the communication structures of these organizations.* This tendency, and the sheer size of the organizations themselves, will typically result in a number of characteristics that represent challenges to agile adoption:

- A mix of legacy and modern IT applications across the IT estate, using a range of technologies from legacy Cobol/CICS through to modern C# MVC frameworks and responsive design.
- A range of suppliers and external partners, including offshore development, fully outsourced IT services and delivery via external software houses.
- Some legacy, tightly coupled architecture components.
- Organizational separation of IT delivery participants, with some IT teams aligned to optimize business proximity and engagement and other teams aligned by application or technology to optimize application integrity, technical skill deployment and cost reduction.

These underlying architectural and organizational characteristics also drive a number of practices that can, in turn, represent further challenges to agile adoption. For example:

- Scheduled (e.g., quarterly) release processes, usually introduced to simplify the complexity of the configuration management involved in deploying multiple interdependent changes across multiple applications, but reducing the deployment flexibility that can be offered to the business as a result of using an agile approach.

- Restricted availability of integration testing environments due to the alignment of environments to waterfall lifecycles and the complexity of the environment requirements.
- "Silo" mentality, with the majority of resources familiar with a small number of IT components rather than the full end-to-end architecture.
- Project, rather than product, focus, with teams assembled for a particular project delivery and then disbanded.
- Milestone-based governance, based on waterfall phase completion.

In common with most large organizations, Aviva UK faced many of these challenges when embarking on our agile transformation. It would appear tempting, in the face of such challenges, to abandon agile principles and revert to traditional waterfall approaches. However, even working within these constraints, our early experiences in agile development convinced us that the short feedback loop inherent in the agile approach offered clear benefits in terms of the quality of the delivered solutions and their alignment to business requirements. We recognized, therefore, that a more flexible approach to agile adoption was necessary, and that failure to apply any agile principles and techniques at all—simply because it is not possible to implement them all—would be counter to agile incremental principles. The approach in Aviva UK has therefore been to work within these constraints while taking the necessary actions to address and/or remove them.

15.3 THE KEY ROLE OF ARCHITECTURE IN DRIVING AGILE SUCCESS

It can be seen from the analysis of the challenges described above that the complexity of the IT architecture is a significant underlying factor. Although there are a number of other factors that need to be addressed to scale agile adoption in large enterprise organizations, this chapter focuses on architecture strategies as the key driver for success.

Our experience in the early stages of agile transformation has led us to the conclusion that there are three key architectural strategies that are needed to drive agile success in large, corporate organizations—particularly those with complex legacy IT estates. These architectural strategies are described in detail in the following sections, but can be summarized as:

- Sufficient architecture and design activity must be completed during project initiation to set the context for, and ensure the success of, emergent design activity throughout the remainder of the project.
- The IT architecture strategy must drive a high level of independence between architecture layers by establishing effective abstraction and separation of concerns. The aim is to reduce the impact of integration complexity on speed and agility by allowing the impact of business changes to be either contained within one or two architectural layers, or for those changes to be decoupled and deployed separately in each layer.

- There must be a clear focus on the importance of the "change-time" attributes of architecture components, such as automated testing frameworks. These must be seen as fundamental requirements of the future strategic architecture, alongside the usual "run-time" attributes, such as performance.

15.3.1 Sufficient up-front architecture and design

In the previous section, we referred to the fact that much of the early agile literature makes no reference to the need for any architecture or design activity prior to starting development in sprints. Once the backlog is created, for example, Scrum practitioners are encouraged to make a start on development, completing any necessary design activity in-sprint. Although this approach works well on discrete, well-architected applications, it can be an extremely high-risk strategy when the IT landscape incorporates many different applications and technologies and where a variety of development skills are needed to create an integrated end-to-end solution. An organization such as Aviva UK has multiple teams, widely distributed knowledge and multiple possible impacts of architectural decisions. In this type of environment, there is a clear need to have a sufficient understanding and agreement of the overall architecture and context for the design to inform the build.

The challenge of up-front design was clearly demonstrated to us in one of our early agile projects. Although the need for up-front architecture was recognized, the team was keen to get started as soon as possible and development was initiated as soon as the backlog was prepared. The project in question involved the redevelopment of online policy administration functionality—improving the level of functionality, quality and stability of the application, as well as improving the customer experience. One aspect of this redevelopment involved refactoring some existing services that provided a range of read and update capabilities against our legacy policy administration system. Some of the early stories included both front-end screen and transactional changes, and new services. These therefore included developers from three separate teams, working in different technologies and on different underlying applications, representing different architectural layers. Unfortunately, development of these stories hit two significant issues:

- Insufficient time had been devoted to the overall service design and in particular how the transition from old, complex services to the new, more specific and fine-grained services would be managed. This made incremental delivery of working end-to-end software quite challenging.
- There was a disconnect between the speed of front-end development compared to the speed of service development. This caused the overall project to fall behind expected timescales to the extent that the project reverted to use of the old services to ensure that the delivery met business benefit expectations.

Both of these issues could have been successfully addressed if a little more time had been spent prior to the start of development in sprints in agreeing on the overall architecture and design approach—particularly increasing the level of understanding between the developers working on different aspects of the application and the dependencies between them.

There will be readers who say that the solution to the problems described above is to have multi-skilled teams who both understand, and are able to work on, the end-to-end solution. This may well be the case, but will take some time due to the cross-skilling required in a large organization with a varied IT estate. In such situations, there is a need to ensure that sufficient architecture and design activity is completed during initiation to mitigate the risk of starting development with too much uncertainty still unresolved. In this environment, attempting to develop the design purely incrementally during the sprints, without sufficient context setting up front, will almost certainly lead to significant problems: excessive rework, poor overall design, and project delays while impact analysis, architecture and design activity "catch up" with the build.

15.3.1.1 Determining what is "sufficient" up-front architecture and design activity

It is important to stress that this is not advocating "big design up front" as an effective design and architecture approach for agile projects. Neither is it removing the need for ongoing emergent architecture and design activity throughout the remainder of the project lifecycle. The aim is to complete *sufficient* architecture and design analysis to the point that there is an acceptable level of risk involved in starting development with some architectural and significant design questions still outstanding. Determining what it "sufficient" and completing the right level of up-front architecture and design activity are vital to enable setup of a successful agile project, but will vary from project to project. Fundamentally, it is a risk-based decision, and will always rely on the skill and experience of the project team members.

The ongoing management of uncertainty is fundamental to the agile approach. Where waterfall development approaches attempt to remove uncertainty at the start of the project, by completing all requirements gathering and design activity prior to commencing build, an agile project will start development with a significant level of uncertainty outstanding and will manage and reduce this uncertainty gradually throughout the project via incremental development and feedback. Successful management of this uncertainty is core to the successful delivery of the project, and the completion of sufficient architecture and design activity prior to starting build is a fundamental part of that uncertainty management. In our experience, the key factors that need to be taken into account when determining how much uncertainty to resolve prior to sprint one—and therefore how much architecture and design work is "sufficient"—are these:

- The potential impacts of the uncertainties on the architecture

Whilst there may be significant uncertainty in the requirements at the start of the project, these may not in themselves be significant to the design or architecture of the solution. The key is to determine which uncertainties need some form of resolution to ensure that the architecture you set out with is going to be fit for purpose and not require major and fundamental surgery in later sprints. There may well be no uncertainties that fall into this category, in which case little up-front architecture and design will be needed. However, there may be significant questions that would be overlooked in a purely emergent architecture and design approach, requiring significant rework—or worse—later in the process.

An illustration of the kinds of up-front architectural decisions needed arose in one of our recent agile projects that was aimed at increasing the resilience of our call center applications by enabling them to continue to function in the event of a failure in the back-end policy administration systems. There were a number of possible architectural solutions for this functionality, involving different choices in architecture components. It was necessary for the underlying approach to be agreed and validated against the overall architecture strategy prior to starting build. Failure to do so would almost certainly have resulted in very significant rework.

In contrast, in another of our early agile projects to enhance the Aviva UK Travel Insurance web application, a minimal approach to up-front architectural design was possible. The project included the creation of an online documentation facility that was defined at a very high level at the start of the project, and without clear guidance on the IT solution architecture. However, it was known from the architecture options available that none of the possible solutions would impact other, higher-priority, deliverables. Sprints therefore were initiated after a minimal period of architecture and design activity, and this activity continued in parallel to the build.

- The number of significant uncertainties

Although the individual impact of each identified uncertainty may be manageable, where there are a high number of significant uncertainties, the overall risk to the project will be high and it is likely that some additional time should be taken during project initiation to understand the impacts and mitigate the risks.

For example, in delivering complex web applications, two recent Aviva UK projects had very different experiences. One project took a "pure" Scrum approach and went straight into development of the screens. Some way through the project, as the more complex user journeys were created, it became clear that the overall journey structure was flawed, and significant rework was needed. In contrast, in the second project, a high-level view of the major customer journeys was generated prior to the start of the first sprint. This not only significantly reduced the level of rework later required, but also produced a higher-quality end product.

- The level of effort required to resolve the uncertainties

The complexity of the uncertainties is another key factor in establishing how much design to do up front. The effort required to resolve some of the key uncertainties, with potential material impacts on the suitability of the design, could drive a number of outcomes at this point. The decision will be based on an assessment of the relative costs of delaying the project to resolve the uncertainties against the possible cost of rework. If the costs of delay are high, then the decision may well be taken to progress against an assumption and accept the level of possible rework as a significant risk to the project.

During the early stages of our agile adoption, our experience has been that it has taken several projects for us to begin to get a feel for the right level of up-front design. Some projects slipped back towards waterfall as too many uncertainties were resolved in the up-front design stage during initiation, whilst others had difficult execution phases with delays and rework as a result of insufficient up-front impact analysis and design. There will always be variation in the level required, based on the nature of the project, the complexity of the impacted systems and the existing level of understanding of the solution architecture. However, in our experience in a large financial services environment, an element of up-front architecture and design activity is always required.

15.3.1.2 Continuing architecture and design activity during sprints

Once sufficient up-front analysis and design has been completed, there are a number of other key points that should be considered regarding the approach needed to continue with an emergent architecture and design approach throughout the remainder of the project. These include:

- Inclusion of solution architects in project teams

As we have previously discussed, the complexity of the Aviva UK IT estate means that developers will often have insufficient understanding of the end-to-end solution for a particular business change project. We have a team of solution architects who provide this integration knowledge and expertise and develop the high-level, end-to-end solution architecture and design. These solution architects are involved in the initial architecture and design activity on agile projects, and will usually be required to remain involved with the project team to assist in the ongoing development of the emergent architecture.

- "Just in time" approach to emergent architecture and design

Architecture and design uncertainties that remain unresolved during the project initiation cannot necessarily be left to be resolved within a sprint. In fact, this is rarely appropriate. At this point, the estimated effort required to resolve each uncertainty becomes a key factor in planning the approach to resolution. Resolving too early is likely to waste time and resources, since there may well be insufficient information available, and requirements are likely to change, impacting the validity of the agreed resolution. Leaving resolution too late, however, will impact project progress. Uncertainties therefore need to be closely tracked by both analysts and solution architects to ensure their timely resolution just prior to development within sprints.

Two aspects of our agile framework ensure that design activity to resolve uncertainties is completed at the "last responsible moment" prior to development: a design plan, and a "look ahead" meeting.

With respect to the design plan, we found that when an uncertainty is identified that will require some significant impact analysis, architecture and design activity to be completed, the estimated time needed to resolve that uncertainty should be annotated to the relevant story. As with relative estimation, this is not intended to be accurate or fully researched, but gives a view of the optimum timescales for architecture and design activity to start for that story. For example, in the Travel application example described earlier, the architecture and design activity needed to agree that the end-to-end solution for online documentation required 4 weeks (2 sprints). This information was attached to the online documentation story, clearly visible in the product backlog.

With respect to a "look ahead" meeting, we found that holding an additional meeting midway between the sprint kickoff and sprint review provides an opportunity for team members—particularly those focusing on design activity—to "look ahead" to future stories in the prioritized backlog and identify any actions that are needed, such as the following:

- To resolve any remaining significant uncertainties for the stories likely to be included in the next sprint. The definition of "significant" in this context is anything that would cause unacceptable delay to sprint progress if it were resolved in-sprint.
- To resolve any significant uncertainties for future stories as indicated by the lead times previously assigned to stories. For example, if the project is currently working on sprint 4, and a story that is likely to be included in sprint 6 has some architecture and design activity that is believed to need 2 sprints elapse time to complete, then that activity must be started immediately.

In this way, architecture and design activity continues throughout the life of the project delivery, both in-sprint and ahead of sprints, allowing the flow of valuable software delivery to continue smoothly without interruption or unnecessary delay.

Our agile framework, depicted in Figure 15.1, illustrates the aspects that are fundamental to architecture and design activity:

- Initiation, which includes sufficient up-front architecture and design;
- Uncertainty management (design plan), which ensures that ongoing emergent architecture and design activity is completed at the "last responsible moment";
- The "look ahead," which ensures sufficient focus on emergent architecture and design activity beyond the current sprint.

- Emergent architecture and design skills

Solution architects who are familiar with using a waterfall approach, and are therefore used to creating the complete high-level design up front, need to develop a different skill set. They need to both understand how much architecture and design activity to complete during initiation, and also develop the skills needed to evolve the architecture and design in response to changing requirements during the sprints. The cultural change here should not be underestimated, as this is a very different technique and requires a different approach to risk, complexity and ambiguity, as

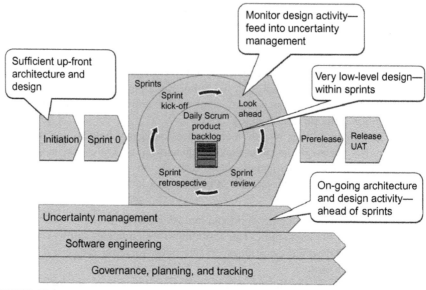

FIGURE 15.1

Aviva UK agile framework, highlighting the architecture and design activity.

well as to the principles of architecture and design. It also requires a significantly more collaborative approach, working with the business analysts, developers and testers throughout the project lifecycle. Supporting the solution architecture community through this change with training and awareness exercises is required to ensure success. In Aviva UK, we have used a number of methods to provide this support, including training, the use of skilled external resources, and the creation of role-specific peer-support groups.

• Architecture and design documentation

Not least amongst the challenges facing solution architects and designers who are accustomed to working in a waterfall delivery lifecycle is the question of architecture and design documentation. Using the waterfall approach, the documentation need is quite clear: to document the high level solution architecture and design of the end-to-end solution and provide sufficient information to allow the creation of detailed application designs, and subsequently, the build process for the applications. In an agile project, however, there is far greater use of verbal communication and collaboration to align application designers and developers, so that architecture and design documentation can, and should, be kept to a minimum. We have not yet finalized our guidelines in this area, but broadly recommend that architecture and design documentation should be sufficient to ensure a common understanding of the agreed scope, context and high-level component architecture of the solution. It must also be sufficient to enable future application changes to be effective. The documentation must be concise and easy to change, so diagrams are ideal, and indeed will frequently be sufficient.

• Designing for change

The ability to design in such a way as to facilitate future change is another core skill that is essential for success. Taking an agile approach by allowing requirements to emerge will in itself help to drive this behavior and develop the appropriate skills.

For example, experienced software designers at Aviva UK often state that "...in order to develop a good service, I need to know all the requirements up front." Taken to its logical conclusion, this means that any future change to the service is expected to be difficult. With such a high expectation for change and adaptability in today's environment, this is not a good mindset, and leads to inefficient behaviors. Instead, by forcing change during the development of the service through emergent requirements, the chances of easily incorporating future change are significantly increased.

15.3.2 Layered architecture enabling independent change agility

The need for a layered architecture, with a high level of independence between the layers, is the second key architectural strategy needed to drive success,

At Aviva UK, we are adapting the Gartner pace layering approach to corporate applications strategy to develop governance, development and management practices in our agile projects [4]. Pace layering can be seen as an architectural pattern taken from physical building architecture and then applied to the software arena. As Gartner states:

> The concept of pace layering (Brand 1994) [5] sees a building as a series of layers that have differing life spans. The site itself has an eternal life, whereas the building structure might last 50 to 100 years. Other layers such as the external cladding of the building or the interior walls might have a life of 20 years with internal design, decoration and furniture lasting for 5 to 10 years. In a rapidly moving world it makes sense to locate the capacity for change in those items with the potential shortest life span and avoid, if possible, creating some layers, such as internal dividing walls, that have a medium term life span and are a potential barrier to accommodating changing activities.

Gartner describes the application of this approach to software as allowing "different rates of change, depending on the type of application, providing slow change and high control for some, while a more agile and experimental approach for others." Designing the IT architecture to support this distinction is essential, and we later discuss the challenge of applying this pace layering approach to an IT estate not architected with this in mind. The most important part of this type of architectural layering is defining clear service boundaries and appropriately grained service interfaces between the layers to allow for change on either side of the service interface to be carried out transparently to the layers on either side of it. Integration complexity and a lack of effective service boundaries between architectural layers impact agility—particularly where one layer of the architecture can be developed at a significantly different pace to others.

The challenge to agility here is not the changes themselves in isolation, but the ability to test the impact of these with certainty and to coordinate releasing the changes into the production environment. Traditionally, a stack of interconnected applications in a large corporate environment would be tested together end-to-end, and then changes to those systems would be released on the same day as a single software release, with a limited number of these releases each year constrained by the cost of maintaining multiple environments.

The solution is to establish a layered architecture, decoupling those layers as far as possible. Creating effective service boundaries with well-defined interfaces should enable a scenario that makes it possible for changes to be implemented without the need to do extensive integration or regression testing above or below these service boundaries. Where such testing is required, a risk-based testing approach can be adopted to minimize the extent and focus of the testing required. This model in turn opens up the possibility of operating different release schedules for each of the layers in the architecture, maximizing the benefits by utilizing the inherent agility of each layer. This approach also enables the move to a more "product"-focused, continuous delivery philosophy, rather than a more inflexible "project"-focused approach.

To illustrate the advantages of this layered architectural approach, consider a typical quote system that is part of every General Insurance portfolio—an online web quotation interface connected to a policy administration system, which is in turn connected to a finance system, with a number of other downstream systems attached to it. In this scenario, it is highly likely that there will be different stakeholders driving change at different paces across this architecture stack:

- Marketing will push for rapid change to the user interface, driven by specific campaigns.
- There may be frequent product changes or iterative and experimental change, driven by multi-variant testing or insight from web analytics.
- Product launches will have longer timeframes, but will still be required to meet fixed marketing deadlines.
- Regulatory changes to finance systems may be introduced over an extended period of time, based on external factors.

In a scenario where the systems have not been designed with clear service interfaces between each layer, the pace of change across these systems is defined by the lowest common denominator due to the need to test and release these systems together. It is, however, unacceptable to everyone to have to make changes to web applications (particularly experimental user experience change) at the same pace as regulatory changes to the finance system. Many large complex organizations find themselves facing this dilemma as their legacy systems continue to undergo transformation activity.

The approach to this dilemma at Aviva UK has been to pursue a strategy to modernize its UK application stack: rearchitecting key applications to establish clear service interfaces to enable the benefits outlined above. The organization is only partway through this journey, but has already been able to realize some of the benefits discussed. This has included the introduction of new release windows (known as "delta releases") enabling some significant project deliveries outside their normal release cycle. These delta releases are targeted at changes where the impact is restricted (broadly) to one or two layers of the architecture, and where there is therefore little or no need for full integration testing. This strategy has enabled delivery of agile change independent of a full test and release cycle involving the wider system estate. Usage has predominantly been in the web application layer to date, as would be in line with the expectations of Gartner's pace layering approach. However, the approach will be expanded into deeper layers of the architecture as we gain further experience.

As previously outlined, other impacts and implications of our large, complex IT estates are:

- Changes requiring work across a number of different technologies increase the number of different skilled resources in the team, increasing the effort required for collaboration and communication.
- Testing environments required to support development across a complex integrated environment can be expensive and time-consuming to maintain.

These factors also drive the need to provide greater independence between tiers of the IT architecture, so that each tier can be changed and released independently to drive business benefit. The ultimate goal here would be for end-to-end stories that create business value to only require simultaneous changes in one or two tiers of the architecture; however, in practice this is unrealistic due to the nature of business changes required in typical corporate situations.

The layered architectural approach in use at Aviva UK is illustrated in Figure 15.2. Effective abstraction and separation of concerns between architecture layers will reduce the impact of integration complexity on speed and agility, by allowing the impact of business changes to either be contained within one or two architectural layers, or for those changes to be decoupled and deployed separately in each layer.

In line with Brand's pace layering approach, Gartner suggests that "to get the whole benefit, you need to differentiate governance and change processes by layer." The concept of pace layering in relation to the application of different delivery approaches has at times been divisive (including between the authors of this chapter) and has driven strong debates about both strategy and architecture in agile systems. There are several key areas of agreement, particularly around the need to have a strongly layered architecture to enable potentially different rates of change across the tiers. However, the concept of agile approaches being more appropriate in different layers of the architecture is a more contentious area.

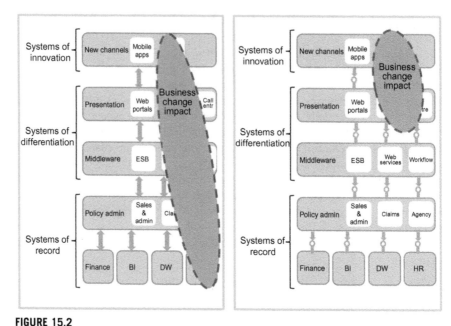

FIGURE 15.2

Aviva UK layered architectural approach (simplified).

In terms of the experiences at Aviva UK, we believe it is important not to lose sight of all the benefits to be derived from the use of agile practices. Many of those benefits are just as important for slower-paced regulatory change as for fast-paced user interface change. These slower-paced changes benefit from close collaboration with business stakeholders and a regular feedback loop; incremental build and test will drive higher quality than the traditional full build/test waterfall approach, and clear prioritization by business benefit drive efficiencies and maximize return on investment. Hence, agile is a clear benefit driver across all layers.

It is also imperative when following a layered architecture approach to not lose sight of the need to maintain the agile discipline of delivering incremental change that provides end-to-end business functionality and value. It will not always be possible for a change project to avoid making changes across multiple layers of the architecture, from web systems through to systems of record, to deliver the end-to-end solution. Adopting a truly layered architecture with sufficient loose coupling and clear separations of concerns between the layers of the architecture will increase the possibility of business functionality requiring changes in only one or two layers, and will provide a platform for agile change at varying speeds for each layer. However, there is still great value in using an agile approach across multiple layers when necessitated by the business requirement and incumbent architecture.

In summary, from the Aviva UK experiences we believe that in the longer term the debate will not center on the choice of "waterfall or agile" approaches, but will instead be focused on the speed of change, frequency of iterations and the level of quality-focused engineering and architecture practices being applied to enable these practices.

15.3.3 "Change-time" architecture and "run-time" architecture

It is well understood that to achieve the level of flexibility and quality required for successful agile delivery, the use of modern software engineering practices is essential. The tools, frameworks and processes needed to apply these practices must therefore be considered to be an integral part of the overall solution architecture. Architecture that does not include this framework cannot succeed, as the ability to change at low cost and low risk over time is a fundamental requirement underpinning the system's requirements.

Traditionally, architecture strategies and decision-making has been based on "run-time" attributes of the architecture components, such as scalability, resilience and performance. For an organization to develop greater agility, the architecture must, however, focus equally strongly on change attributes. The software engineering tools and practices must be seen as a part of the architecture, rather than an add-on to it.

An architecture that meets these "change-time" requirements must have a number of characteristics and components, including the following:

- The inclusion of automated testing frameworks as part of the core system (rather than being considered as "process elements"). Architecting the system alongside frameworks to enable effective testing and ease of development at a later date ensures that the system can be picked up and changed with lower overheads in the future.
- Componentization at a sufficient level of granularity to enable and support the use of test driven development, with appropriate stubs and/or mock-ups to enable testing at that level. For example, some legacy package software requires full compilation and deployment to implement minor changes, which does not easily align with agile development practices.
- Configuration management models that support rapid development and deployment of parallel streams of activity, enabling flexible support to the business.
- Infrastructure tools and practices that enable environments to be created dynamically, on demand, to support multiple project change demands.
- Environment configuration that enables automated, continuous integration (regular end-to-end build and deployment) and supports both stand-alone and integrated testing using virtualization and simulation techniques.

At Aviva UK, we experienced such challenges early in our agile transformation when we were evaluating software packages to replace a number of legacy applications supporting our commercial insurance business. Initial evaluations had focused on the traditional "run-time" capabilities of the candidate packages: functional scope, scalability, performance, resilience, and so on. However, it soon became clear that to protect and support future business agility, there were other features that were of equal importance. These were the "change-time" attributes: the ability to write automated tests to validate functionality at a low granular level, the ability to apply modern configuration management approaches to enable parallel development and "release on demand," and so on. Including these factors in the decision-making process provided a great deal of clarity and enabled a clear replacement winner to be chosen.

15.4 INCREMENTAL AGILE AND ARCHITECTURE TRANSFORMATION

In this chapter, we have put forward three key architectural strategies that we believe are critical to successful agile adoption in large, complex corporate environments. It must be remembered, however, that significant architectural change takes time to complete and must be integrated into the ongoing business change objectives of the organization. Hence, it is important that these architectural constraints do not unnecessarily impede the move to an agile culture and use of an agile framework. Taking an agile approach to the agile transformation journey itself will ensure early delivery of benefit for both business and IT.

This has certainly been our experience in Aviva UK. Despite the constraints and challenges discussed above, we have demonstrated significant benefit through our early agile transformation journey, such as increased levels of collaboration with the business, delivery prioritization based on business value, and the drive to embed quality throughout the life-cycle through early and repeated testing. These have all made very successful contributions to driving business benefit and agility.

We are aware, however, that a step-change increase in these benefits would be possible with an aligned architecture strategy focused on enabling agility in system delivery. Architectural transformation is therefore an essential element of our overall agile transformation activity. Each step we take towards establishing the loosely coupled, layered and service-based architecture described above will drive a corresponding, and even more significant, increase in the business and IT benefit that governs our use of an agile approach .

In practical terms, the focus on architectural transformation at Aviva UK will be achieved via our existing change book of work, and by implementing the necessary changes incrementally. New services will be written to support the requirements of a specific project, and will subsequently be enhanced to support further changes, enabling a gradual transition away from existing, tightly coupled applications. Where cost effective, however, aspects of the IT estate will be refactored explicitly to improve the architecture to enhance agility. We are also increasing our focus on the "change-time" attributes of our architectural components, allowing modern software engineering practices to be embedded across the IT estate.

Alongside the application architecture changes required, a move towards the use of agile practices also places new and different demands on the underlying infrastructure. The need for early and repeated end-to-end integration testing is driving investment in virtualization and mock-up techniques. Although techniques like test-driven development and business-driven development are relatively new introductions to Aviva UK, other aspects, such as configuration management, are not new. Use of agile techniques, based on loosely coupled and service-based architecture, does, however, bring new demands to configuration management techniques and disciplines. Recognizing this, we are increasing our focus here, with the development of new guidelines and processes together with the introduction of improved modern tools where appropriate.

Our education and training program will continue for at least the next few years. Alongside this program, however, we recognize the need for a particular focus on the cultural change required. Both of these activities are fundamental to success, particularly with respect to architecture and design. As discussed previously, understanding what constitutes "sufficient" architecture and design up front is a skill that requires not only practice and experience, but also a very different mindset and approach. Our architects and designers have worked for many years with a fundamental belief that they must "get it right" prior to handing anything over to the developers. It will take time to develop acceptance that it is permissible to change things later, together with the skill to design in such a way to facilitate these changes.

15.5 CONCLUSIONS

In this chapter, we have discussed the challenges facing large corporate organizations adopting an agile approach to change, based on our own experiences at Aviva UK. Agile transformation is essential to allow these organizations to respond to the speed of change in financial markets, rapidly changing technology capability, and increasingly high customer expectations. However, large organizations frequently find that the size, complexity and legacy attributes of their IT estates present significant challenges to the use of agile practices and application of agile principles, and therefore constrain the resulting benefits. In our experience, it has been essential for Aviva UK to understand and focus on the core objectives and principles underlying agile approaches, rather than on the mechanical application of simple agile methodologies, such as Scrum. This has ensured that we adopt an agile framework that acknowledges the reality of our organization and drives the maximum possible benefit for the business. This is not to say that the constraints should not be addressed and removed where possible; as we have described in this chapter, architecture strategies may need to be established to drive ongoing increases in the return on investment achievable.

Despite the challenges, the benefits of agile practices are clear—and at Aviva UK, our transformation journey is well underway. We understand the architectural strategies that are key drivers for success, and these are now embedded both in our agile framework and our architecture governance and strategic planning. We are seeing clear business benefits from the use of our agile framework today, and expect to see an increasing return on investment as we drive Architecture transformation to establish a layered architecture that supports fully effective modern software engineering approaches across the IT estate. It will take some time to fully realize that goal, but in true agile style, we are making a start and making the most of the incremental benefits to be gained along the way.

References

[1] Schwaber K, Sutherland J. The Scrum guide. Retrieved from: http://www.scrum.org/Scrum-Guides; 1991.
[2] Jeffries R. An agile software development resource. Retrieved from: http://xprogramming.com; 1999.
[3] Wikipedia. Conway's law. Retrieved from: http://en.wikipedia.org/wiki/Conway's_law; 2012.
[4] Gaughan D, Genovese Y, Shepherd J, Sribar V. How to use Pace Layering to develop a modern application strategy. ID G00208964, Gartner; 2010.
[5] Brand S. How buildings learn: what happens after they're built. New York: Viking Press; 1994.

Author Index

Note: Page numbers followed by *f* indicate figures, *t* indicate tables, and *np* indicate footnote.

Subject Index

Note: Page numbers followed by *f* indicate figures and *t* indicate tables.

Printed and bound by CPI Group (UK) Ltd, Croydon, CR0 4YY

03/10/2024

01040324-0015